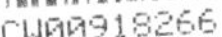

THE WORLD
STORMRIDER GUIDE
VOLUME THREE

LOW PRESSURE

THE WORLD
STORMRIDER GUIDE
VOLUME THREE

First published in 2009 by LOW PRESSURE LTD©
www.stormriderguides.com

General Enquiries
Tel/Fax +33 (0)5 58 77 76 85 enquiries@lowpressure.co.uk

Worldwide Surfspots 2.0 database, YEP©
Compilation of all weather and swell data YEP 2008©
using Visual Passage Planner software©

Creation of all zone maps YEP/Low Pressure Ltd 2008©

Creation of all other maps, graphic arrangement, pictograms, text and index Low Pressure Ltd 2008©

The representation in this guide of a road is no proof of the existence of a right of way, likewise the frontiers shown do not imply any recognition or official acceptance on the part of the publishers. Surfing is a dangerous and addictive activity. The authors and publishers take no responsibility for accident or injury as a result of using information contained within this guide.

A catalogue reference for this book can be obtained from the British Library. ISBN Softback: 978-0-9539840-6-0

Reproduction and Printing by Hong Kong Graphics and Printing on 100% chlorine-free paper stock from managed forests.

THE WORLD STORMRIDER GUIDE

VOLUME THREE

AL MACKINNON

Foreword

"The best surfer is the one that has the most fun"

If you happen to be a pro surfer, focusing on your own performance, you will be forced to look for the best waves offering the most power, shape, length and tube time to match your high skills. Searching for these world-class waves narrows your scope to a very selective number of locations and seasons that just may produce perfect surf. So the best surfers are increasingly competing for the best waves in an ever growing crowd at the world's quality line-ups. If you're an average surfer, like I am, you'll have realized that surfing can be many things, from a means of exercise to stay fit, to an excuse to travel around the world to meet different people, but most of all, we surf for enjoyment.

"Waves are everywhere, it's just a matter of frequency and quality."

After 25 years travelling for waves in about 50 countries, I've been looking not only at oceans, but open seas, closed seas, lakes, rivers (stationary waves and tidal bores), artificial reefs, wave-pools, Flowriders and artificial boat wake rides. Thanks to the almighty internet, dozens of swell forecast websites make it more likely we'll score those unusual swells from far off cyclones or strong local winds. Remember it only takes 250km (155mi) of open water to generate 2.5m (8ft) ocean waves if a 40km/h (25mp/h) wind blows steadily for 18 hours. Plus, waves that size are much more fun if you don't have to bite your neighbour's ankle to catch them.

Addu Atoll, Maldives

"It's very simple, I'm devoted to surfing and when I'm travelling, I like to evaluate human life, especially in its primitive form" Peter Troy

This 3rd volume is arguably the most valuable book of the trilogy because it gets you to the most unknown, crowd-free zones. It took us more years to produce because the only way to write reliable text and get the shots was to travel to quite a few of the remote zones. We went to the giant countries without surf culture like China, India or Colombia and the highly requested touristy zones like Phuket, Malta, Lazio or Antigua. We scoured for experts in the empty surf-rich countries like Namibia, South Africa, Peru and Chile. We got the low down on bizarre waves like Amazon's Pororoca or the US Great Lakes. Then we sailed to the far-fetched islands like Pohnpei, Kiribati, Maluku and the Maldivian central and southernmost atolls. Thanks go out to our other relentless trippers like Dustin Humphrey, Sam Bleakley, Randy Rarick, Stuart Butler, John Callahan and Erwan Simon who made professional contributions along with an army of dialled in locals.

We can always find a reason not to share a surf spot with others, but I prefer to keep thinking that the surf world will only get better making more spots known to the mainstream, so they can be officially recognized as a valuable recreational resource worth being protected.

Antony '*Yep*' Colas

1% of sales of this book will be donated to surfing related environmental organisations.

This page – Zambezi River Wave

Cover – Dylan Longbottom, P-Pass SIMON WILLIAMS

THE 80 ZONES

Conception and compilation
Antony 'YEP' Colas

Writers and Photo Collection
Antony 'YEP' Colas and Bruno Morand

Map Origination Jérôme Laigneau

Statistics Camille 'Soana' Enjalbert

THE WORLD STORMRIDER GUIDE VOLUME THREE

Publishing Directors
Dan Haylock Ollie Fitzjones Bruce Sutherland

Editor Bruce Sutherland

Design and Production Dan Haylock

Advertising and Distribution Ollie Fitzjones

Colour Correction Nick Farrow

Accounts Andrea Fitzjones

Photographic Contributors
Toby Adamson Airviewonline.com.au Wesley Allison
Gonzalo Barandiaran Thomas Bernardin Bluetrailz.com
Boozetentacle James Bott João Brilhante Chris Burkard Barry Church
Stuart Butler John Callahan Gilles Calvet Guillaume Capette
Emi Cataldi Bernard Choquet Antony "Yep" Colas
Ivan Martinez Cortez Sean Davey Dean Dampney Andrew Deming
Jeff Divine Miguel Dolce Mauricio Drunn Javier Fernandez
Steve Fitzpatrick Ludovic Franco Lara Gallini Rob Gilley
Ronan Gladu Gongaolas Kage Gozun Chuck Graham
Kevin Griffin Warren Hawke Dan Haylock Georg Hilmarsson
Dustin Humphrey Drew Kampion Bob Kemp Paul Kennedy
Michael Kew Gary Knights Jeremy Koreski Guillaume Larre
Ingrid Lindfors Mark Lumsden Al Mackinnon Baby Marmotte
Thiago Marques Marroke.com Greg Martin Laurent Masurel
Emi Mazzoni Simon McComb Jorgen Michaelsen Stephane Mira
Magnus Murray Nasser Brian Nejedley Tim Nunn Pete Ottery
Damien Poullenot Red Bull Stephane Robin Garth Robinson
Olivier Servaire Tom Shand Jack Shick Papito Sierra Smuggler
Stoner/Surfer surf-report.com Bruce Sutherland Tsuchiya Takahiro
Yannick Le Touquin Seth Tyler Willy Uribe Alan Van Gysen
Stefano Viola Scott Walls Colm Walsh Simon Williams Louis Wulff

Editorial Contributors
Teymour Adham Karl Azzopardi Jerome Blanco Stuart Butler
John Callahan Guillaume Capette Jay Chapelle Chuck Corbett
Dan Crockett Dale Dagger Joe Dunn Hussein Fayaz Govardhan
Georg Hilmarsson Michael Kew Serginho Laus Nicholai Lidow
Matt Lindsay Mike Loomis Mark Lumsden Lisa Makiiti
Allois Malfitani David Malherbe Arthur Moreno Magnus Murray
Yiorgos Papandreou Nahu Rifu Stéphane Robin Pete Robinson
Bob Samin Dave Scard Olivier Servaire Erwan Simon Justin Starow
Bruce Sutherland Fanny Terrer Wim Van Cleynenbreugel
Hiroshi Yonekawa

Special Thanks
Mireille Lahillole-Saubade Tiki Yates Camilo Gallardo
Patagonia Alex Dick-Read Drew Kampion Pete Feehan Tom Hautzel
Andrea Dillon Ty Ryder Sheila Jake Shani and Marla Fitzjones
Louise Aedan Anna Ella and Jamie Millais
Jo Finn Maisie & Sandy Finn Haylock Sue and John Hilary and Paul

ALAN VAN GYSEN

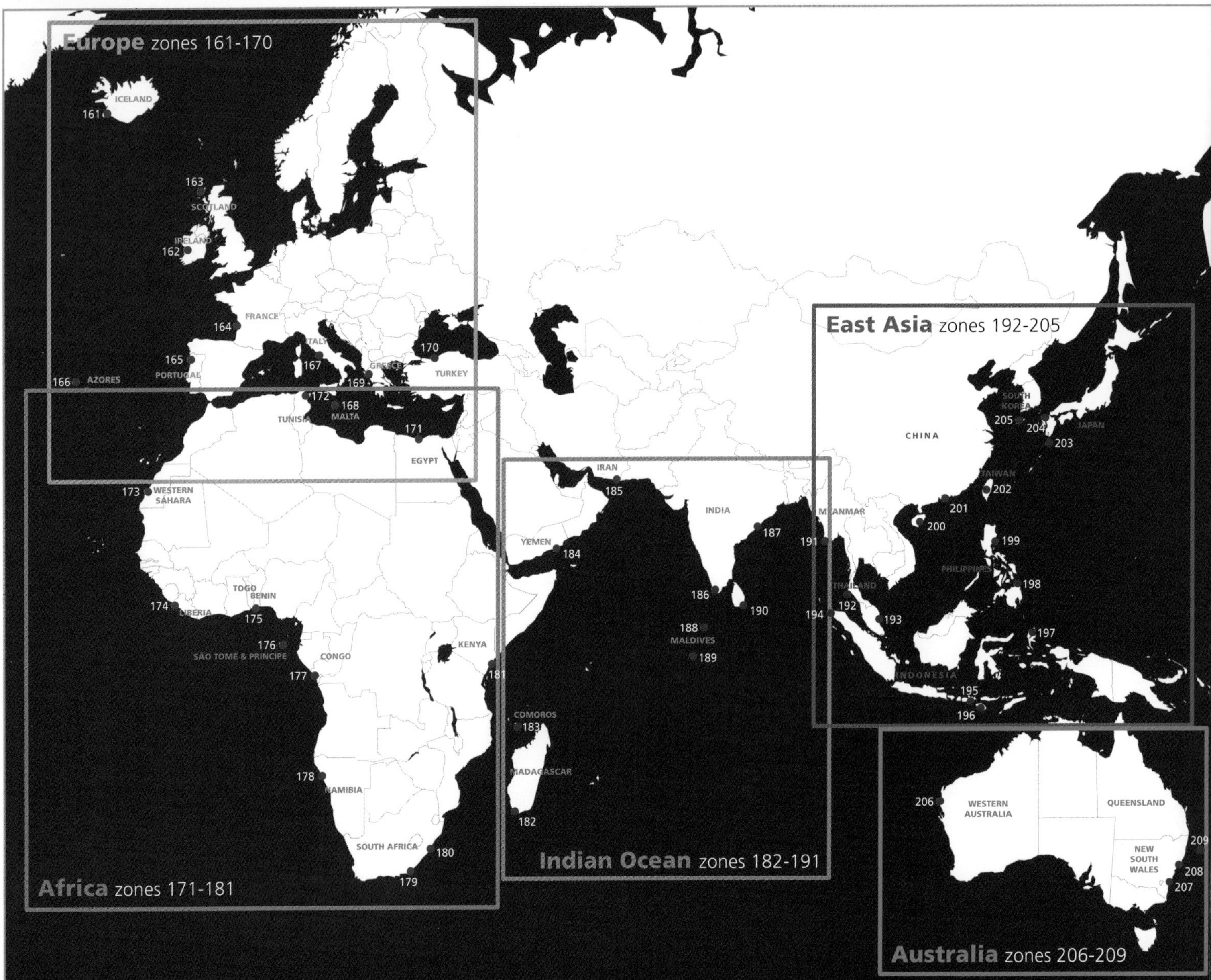

Contents Volume Three

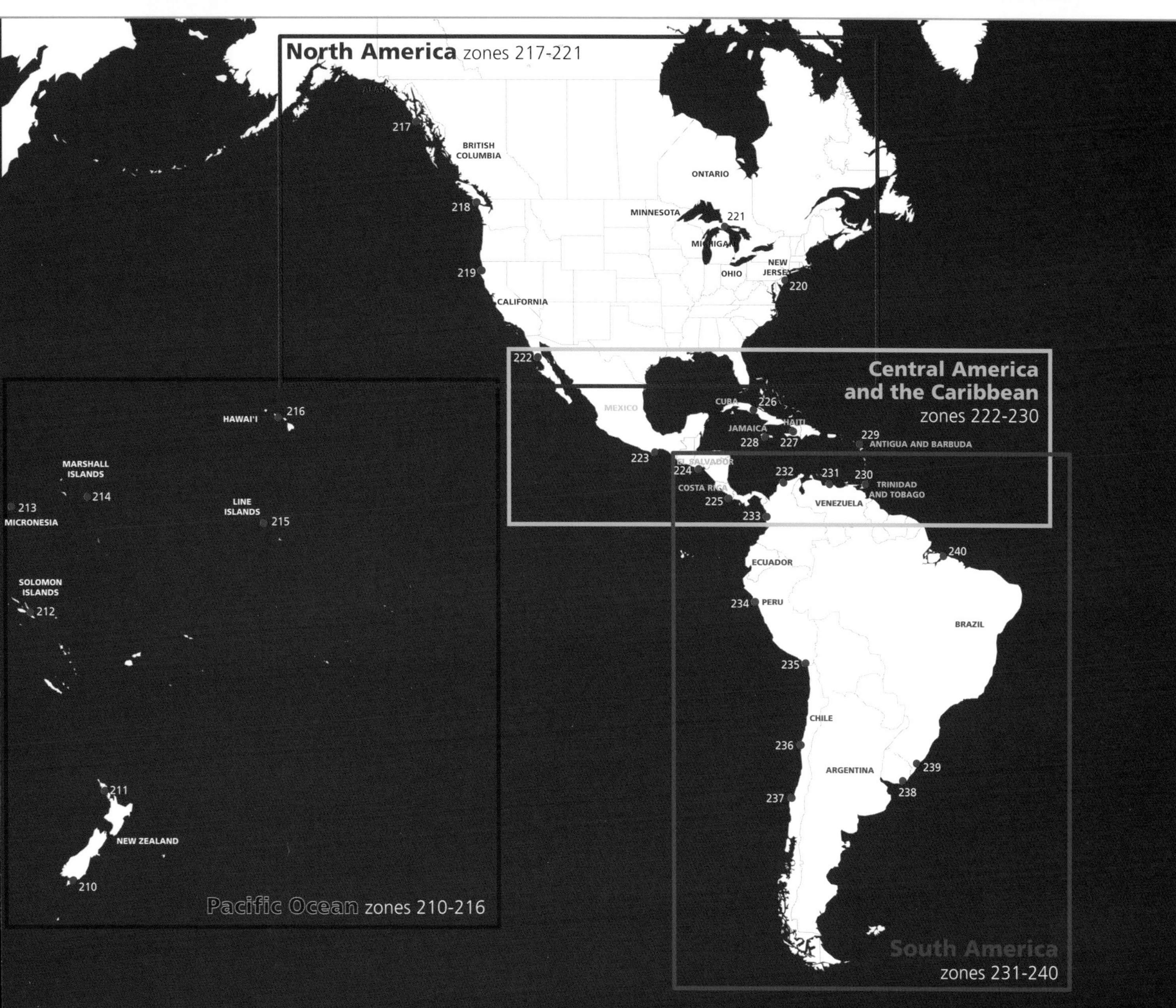

North America zones 217-221
Central America and the Caribbean zones 222-230
South America zones 231-240
Pacific Ocean zones 210-216
BRITISH COLUMBIA
ONTARIO
MINNESOTA
MICHIGAN
OHIO
NEW JERSEY
CALIFORNIA
MEXICO
CUBA
HAITI
JAMAICA
ANTIGUA AND BARBUDA
EL SALVADOR
COSTA RICA
TRINIDAD AND TOBAGO
VENEZUELA
ECUADOR
PERU
BRAZIL
CHILE
ARGENTINA
HAWAI'I
MARSHALL ISLANDS
LINE ISLANDS
MICRONESIA
SOLOMON ISLANDS
NEW ZEALAND

Top Left – **Duke Kahanamoku** BISHOP MUSEUM ARCHIVE
Bottom Left – **Malibu Beach scene, 1969** DREW KAMPION
Top Right – **Kelly Slater, La Graviere grab** AL MACKINNON
Bottom Right – **'Surf Riders, Honolulu' c1920**
PRINT BY ARTIST CHARLES BARTLETT FROM THE COLLECTION OF THE SURFING MUSEUM, ENGLAND
Other images – **Rapid advances in satellite mapping and GPS technology have exposed the world's coastline for all to see.** GOOGLE EARTH YEP ID 5114955

RINCON, Domes
Tamarin Bay
Google
Google
NEWPORT BEACH, River Jetties
SAN DIEGO, Windansea
Surf Culture
The World Stormrider Guide Volume Three

Today

Bø, Telemark
Borkum
München
Alpamare, Bad Tölz
Aileens, Co. Clare
Severn
Radetzky
Boscombe, Bournemouth
Mascaret, St Pardon
Belharra, Hendaye
Bremgarten
Nazare, Portugal
Turnagain Arm
Jozankei View Hotel, Hokkaido
Caribbean Bay, Kyongei-Do
Dino's Beach, Shanghai
Water Park Orange, Nishiwaki
Qiantang Dragon
NKK Wild Blue, Yokohama
Wild Wadi, Dubai
Karakami-Kanko, Osaka
Honey Lake, Shenzhen
Seagaia, Miyazaki
Jeddah Waterpark
Outer Log Cabins, Oahu
Jaws, Maui
Kovallam Reef
Sunway Lagoon, Kuala Lumpur
Zambezi
Lost City Pool, Sun City
Narrowneck, Gold Coast
Wave House, Durban
Cables, Cottesloe
Dungeons Capetown
Mount Reef Mt Maunganui
Xbox
Cyclops
Opunake
Shipstern Bluff
Papatowai, Owaka

Plotted on the map are some, (but by no means all) of the locations where variations on "normal" ocean waves can be found. Natural freaks include tow-in reefs, bores and river waves while the man-made pools, Flowriders and artificial reefs utilise contemporary engineering solutions to create more places for surfers to ride.

SEAN DAVEY

Innovations often draw on the past and stand-up paddle surfing has roots in both the Polynesian outrigger canoes and the totora reed surf craft of the ancient Peruvians.

Today

This text attempts to distill the current scene around the world, looking at each region's surf media, surf industry and competitive surfing agenda, identifying key people, places and products within each relevant nation.

Finally, there's a brief acknowledgment of that most ignoble of cultural phenomenon, simply known as localism. Described by some as 'a toxic spill' and mentioned in the 'Hazards' environment section (Vol Two), the territorial act of harassing visiting surfers has been around as long as surfing itself. Even the Hawai'ian kings segregated the population and kept the best waves for themselves. Modern day surfers will be all too aware that localism sentiment exists at many a famous break, but in fact it is the quiet, semi-secret spots that often suffer the worst injustices, dealt out by "we were here first – not in my back yard" hypocrites, selfishly and desperately trying to preserve a natural resource for their exclusive enjoyment. As publishers of guide books, we are complicit in the spread of surfing across the globe and some may argue that we are partly responsible for the overcrowding of some popular spots, creaking under the weight of swelling numbers of beginners taking up wave-riding. Whether this is down to a natural increase in surfing's popularity or whether it is a media-driven boom, we will never know, but these books are designed to open people's minds to the possibilities out there and spread the crowd across this incredible Planet Surf.

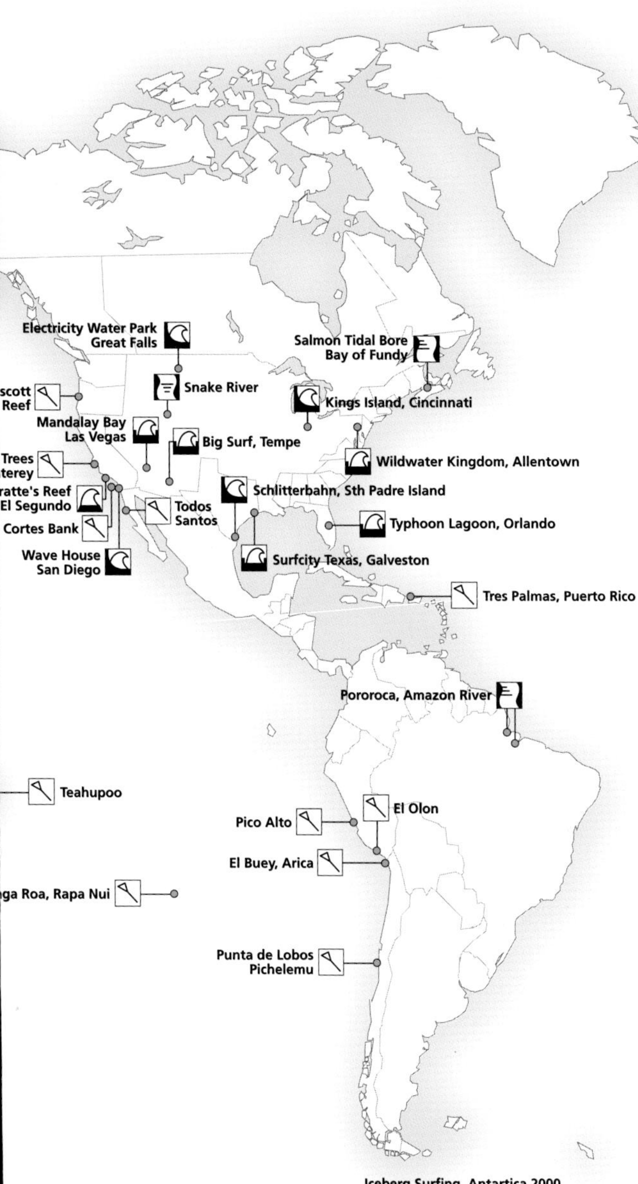

Sail power still offers a sustainable exploration alternative to plane travel. With enough time and a decent wetsuit there are plenty of empty waves left to discover on Planet Surf. Cruising Svalbard, Norway, inside the Arctic Circle, 2007.

DAN HAYLOCK

Alternative Wave Resources

Artificial surfing

Dungeons

AL MACKINNON

Mount Reef

ASR LTD

Tow-in Surfing

Method of using an auxiliary source of propulsion in order to catch waves and usually requires the rider to be strapped to the board. Personal water craft are the most commonly used vehicle, allowing riders to be "whipped" into increasingly large, fast-moving waves that would be impossible to paddle into. The genre began behind a zodiac inflatable boat in Hawaii and has also been successfully attempted using environmentally friendly kite power.

Artificial Reefs

A concept designed to utilise existing ocean swell resources, whereby a sub-surface structure is installed on the seafloor to create well-shaped surfing waves. Built from a variety of materials from old car tyres to sandbags, some artificial reefs even have adjustable height technology that allows the ideal depth of water to be maintained throughout tidal fluctuations. Heavy engineering and expense involved, but they also provide new habitat for marine species.

River waves

Le Mascaret

YEP

Zambezi

ALAN VAN GYSEN

Tidal Bore

Certain rivers that are open to an ocean with large tidal activity experience a wave phenomenon known as a tidal bore. The wave is created when river flow runs in the opposite direction to a surging tide, creating a wave that usually breaks on each riverbank, but can form wherever the water is shallow enough to break. Due to the river's linear geography, bore waves offer the longest distance rides on the planet.

Static River Waves

These waves are created by a fierce river current flowing over a rock or similar object that causes the surface waters to distort into a shape that is suitable for surfing. The speed and water depth of the river flow is critical and shallow rocks combined with downstream turbulence are major hazards. The most common result is a small, open face that's perfect for new school manoeuvres, but the rider must adjust to the idea of remaining virtually stationary.

Man made waves

Bø, Norway

JORGEN MICHAELSEN

Mt Olympus Water Park, Wisconsin

RUSTY MALKEMES

FlowRider

Sharing many of the same physical characteristics of a static river wave, the FlowRider was designed by Karl Ekstrom in California to provide a compact, mobile, artificial wave resource. A specific volume and velocity of water flows over a contoured fibreglass structure, allowing riders to drop and climb on the structure, utilising highly specialised boards with very short fins. FlowRiders can now be found in countries far from the coast, often appearing in water and amusement parks and have even been installed on cruise ships.

Wave Pools

Based on the principle of building a very large swimming pool then quickly introducing a large volume of water to the pool in an attempt to recreate ocean swell. The man-made swell then breaks over a bottom contour designed to maximise the surfing potential. Often using a giant cistern type system where tanks of water are literally flushed into the pool, both wave height and direction can be controlled, depending on the engineering.

SAVE THE WAVES COALITION IS AN ENVIRONMENTAL NONPROFIT ORGANIZATION DEDICATED TO PROTECTING AND PRESERVING COMMUNITY SURFING AREAS AND THEIR SURROUNDING ENVIRONMENTS WORLDWIDE, AND EDUCATING THE PUBLIC ABOUT THEIR VALUE. WE ARE A DEDICATED GROUP OF SURFERS, SCIENTISTS, AND ACTIVISTS, AND PUT EVERY DOLLAR WE RAISE TOWARDS PROTECTING THE SURF ZONE THROUGHOUT THE WORLD FROM HARMFUL COASTAL DEVELOPMENT.

CURRENT PROGRAMS

WORLD SURFING RESERVES
PROACTIVE DESIGNATION & PRESERVATION OF OUTSTANDING WAVES.

SURFONOMICS
ECONOMIC IMPACT STUDIES ON THE VALUE OF WAVES.

CHILE PROGRAM
CAMPAIGNS & REGIONAL EDUCATION TO APPLY PRESSURE FOR STRICTER COASTAL ENVIRONMENTAL LAWS.

DOCUMENTARY FILMS
LOST JEWEL OF THE ATLANTIC (2006) PULP, POO & PERFECTION (2007) ALL POINTS SOUTH (2008)

Save the Waves is a true grass-roots, member-supported organization. We operate with extremely low overhead, so that virtually all of the money we receive goes directly into our campaigns. Please donate and support our ongoing efforts to protect threatened surfing environments.

The "Old World" has more to offer than just the Atlantic. Seasonal Mediterranean procession at Banzai, Italy.

Europe

EMILIANO MAZZONI

Surf Culture

In 1779, while Captain Cook's ships returned to England from the South Pacific, minus the Captain, his First Lieutenant completed the great explorer's journal, which contained the first detailed description of surfing. Polynesians riding "the greatest swell...with a most astonishing velocity" painted a picture for the rest of the world to marvel at. Some of Cook's sailors tried to surf in Hawaii, reporting that the boards were 'so finely tuned' that even their best swimmers couldn't stay on them for more than 30 seconds. English swimming champion Charles Steedman's *How to Swim* book (1867), encouraged people to use a 5ft wooden surfboard in the waves. Hawaiian Princess Victoria Ka'iluani "loved being on the water again" whilst studying in Brighton in 1892, but evidence of her actually going surfing is lacking. Surfing had long been referred to as "The Sport of Kings" and many Europeans, including The Prince of Wales got their first taste of surfing direct from Duke Kahanamoku and the beach boys of Waikiki in the post WW1 years. Activity on European beaches was restricted to small groups of Hawaiian returnees like Nigel Oxenden who formed the Island Surf Club in Jersey in 1923. The following decade saw plenty of people taking the therapeutic Atlantic waters, but short paipo belly boards were the only surf craft readily available. Lewis Rosenberg made a longboard at his home in London and shot a film of their train journey to Cornwall to ride it in 1929. Isolated individuals like Jan Nederveen in the Netherlands were standing up on crude home-made equipment during the '30s. The "Fab Fifties" saw an increase of activity across Europe, fuelled by the Surf Lifesaving movement and surf skis, hollow paddleboards and solid wooden logs became essential lifeguarding equipment from Germany, through England and the surf clubs of France, to the US Army Bases in Morocco, and the Azores. Even Israel had a flowering scene courtesy of Dorian Paskowitz who imported balsa Hobies and gave lessons on Hilton Beach. Gidget, malibus and the advent of the light, fibreglass surfboards lit the touch-paper for growth and the sixties oversaw the pioneering of many a country's line-up including Ireland, Wales, Scotland, Spain and Portugal. Equipment manufacturers sprang up and names like Bilbo in Newquay and Barland in Biarritz led the way for boards and these labels often ended up in countries that had no domestic shapers. Many US servicemen and Aussie lifeguards helped spread the new equipment to the corners of Europe, along with surf travel pioneers like Peter Troy who introduced surfing to Italy and the Canary Islands. As wetsuits improved and Jack O'Neill wondered why he was selling so many wetsuits to Germany, the next wave of Euro countries entered the scene at the end of the seventies shortboard revolution and the beginning of the day-glo '80s. Sweden, Norway, Iceland, Belgium and Mediterranean coasts were late starters but many of the established windsurfing crew started crossing over on calm days and many of these colder climate coastlines are proving to be wave-rich. Recent additions to the surf EU include Greece, Malta, Turkey's Black Sea coast, and even some Baltic Sea nations.

WWW.THESURFINGMUSEUM.CO.UK

Several confirmed instances of stand-up surfing in England include Lewis Rosenberg, who made a longboard in London in 1929. Screen grab from the film of his train journey to Newquay to ride it.

Peerless, globe-trotting surf evangelist Peter Troy studies hard at La Barre, 1966. He introduced surfing to many countries including Italy and the Canary Islands and died in 2008, aged 69.

YEP/JOEL DE ROSNAY

Today

Europe is super-diverse, culturally speaking, but the surf community seems to show a unity unheard of in Brussels. France has emerged as the centre of the scene, with all the big multi-national brands taking up residence in the SW corner and distributing their goods into an ever-growing chain of mainstream fashion and surf stores around the continent. A stand full of surf magazines vie for their target market with established names like *Wavelength*, *Carve*, *The Surfers Path*, *Surf Session*, *Surf Europe*, *Tres60* and *Surfers* to name a few. Europe now hosts 2 WCT rounds at Hossegor and Mundaka, along with plenty of WQS and National competitions. The UK represents the largest population of surfers currently estimated at 250,000 and Plymouth University offer a Surf Science and Technology degree course. Spain has Europe's biggest surfboard factory (Pukas), who invite the world's best shapers to drop by and shape

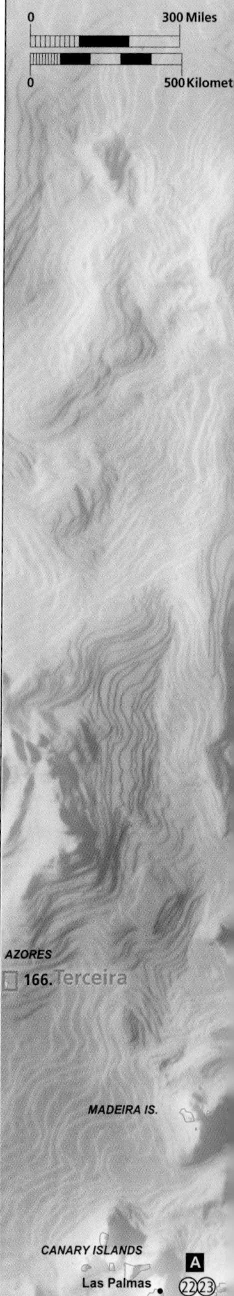

as many boards as possible as well as out-putting huge numbers of their own brand boards and accessories. There are hundreds of surf shops strung right across the continent, both on the coast and inland, servicing many land-locked surfers from countries like Switzerland and Austria. Surf schools have exploded across Europe and large numbers of colourful bibs on foamies and pop-outs are a common sight. Age and sex are no barrier as the number of females taking up surfing has increased markedly. National Surf Associations are doing their best to implement structure and regulate this fast-growing facet of the surf industry and naturally, numbers in the surf are increasing year on year. Overcrowding can lead to outbreaks of localism and violence, a problem currently being experienced on Lanzarote in the Canary Islands. At some breaks it is simply not possible for a visitor to surf as they are bullied and threatened with violence if they do not leave the water. Other hotspots exist, but as crowds grow it becomes more difficult for locals to impose their fascistic outlook, so ultra-crowded line-ups like Mundaka, Coxos and Hossegor now operate under a meritocracy where the best surfers and clued-up locals will generally catch the best waves, but there are still scraps to be found by the patient tourist. Europe still offers huge tracts of lightly surfed coastlines, especially in the northern climes and the possibility to cruise the coast in a van is still out there, despite increasingly expensive fuel and a general clamp-down on free-camping. Surf camps are prevalent in Southern Europe where the Algarve in Portugal has become the favoured spot to learn, while the Canaries remain the intermediate to expert's winter getaway.

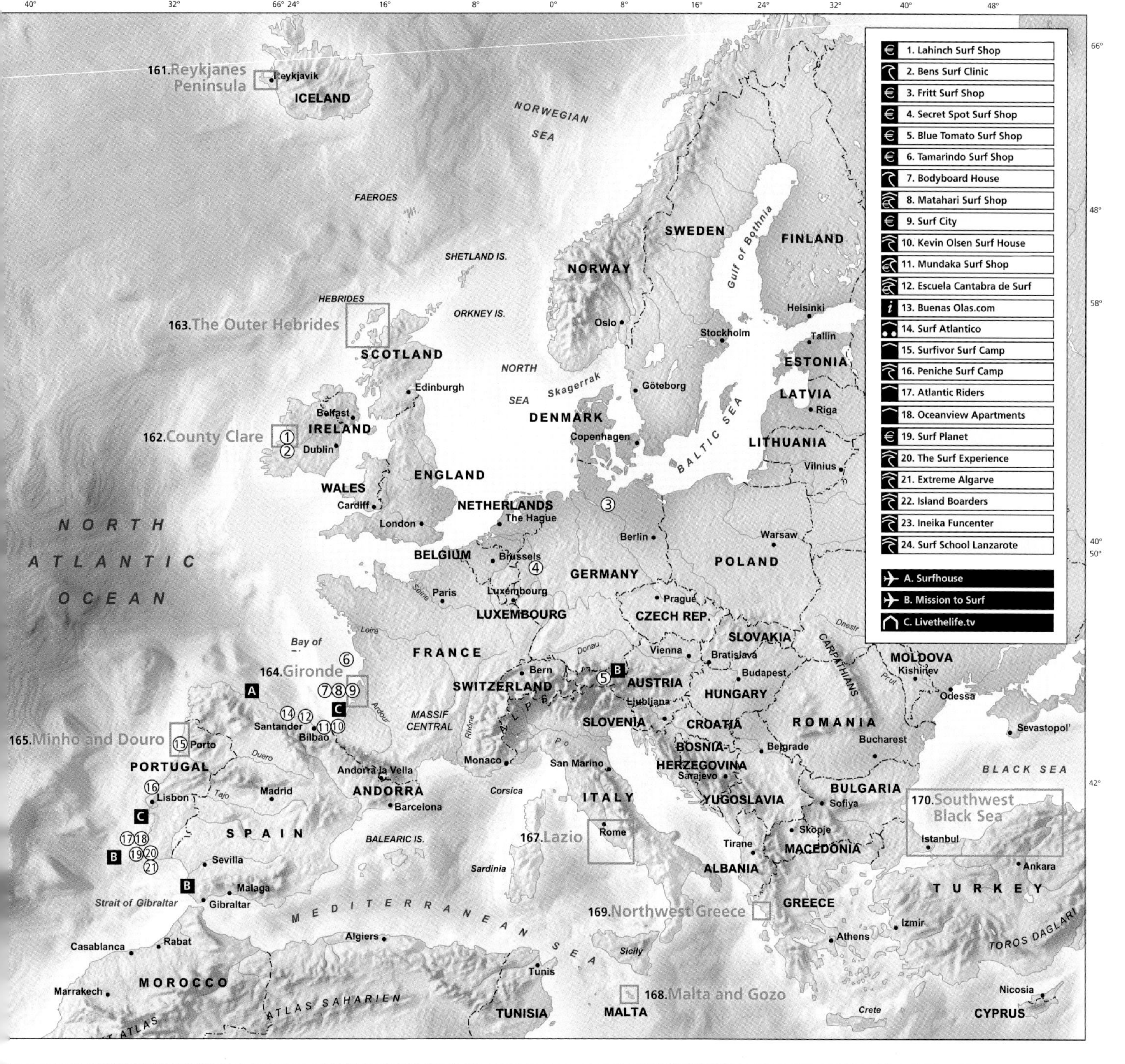

161. Reykjanes Peninsula

Thorli

GEORG HILMARSSON

Summary
+ Plenty of swell
+ Lava righthand points
+ Empty line-ups
+ Discovery potential
+ Unique, volcanic environment

– Inconsistent summers
– Lack of winter daylight
– Zero equipment available
– Expensive destination

With 4970km (3088mi) of coastline to explore, Iceland presents a rare opportunity to surf virgin territory, yet most Icelandic surfers only ride around the Reykjanes peninsula, close to Reykjavik in the southwest. The Reykjanes peninsula is covered in old lava flows, so most of the waves break over volcanic reef or basalt rocks, sharp substances that take their toll on booties. One exception is the black sand beach at Sandvik, providing a rare beginners spot, but it can often equal the ferocity of the reefbreaks when it's overhead. Thorli is another popular choice with a defined paddling channel and attracts the Reykjavik regulars to the south coast in N winds. The Snaefellness peninsula to the NW of Reykjavik also picks

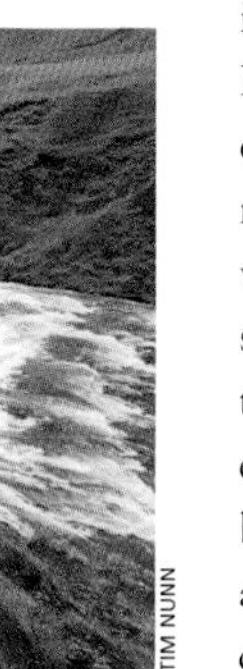
TIM NUNN

Sandvik

TIM NUNN

TRAVEL INFORMATION

Population: 309,699 (180,000 Reykjevik)
Coastline: 4,988km (3,100mi)
Time Zone: GMT
Contests: Local – The Much Colder Water Classic
Video: Seasons

Getting There – No Visa. Keflavík Airport (RKV) is 48kms (30mi) from Reykjavik. Iceland Express, Iceland Air, BA and SAS maintain regular scheduled and some seasonal flights. Air Iceland is the domestic airline. The Faroe Smyril Line operates a weekly service from Bergen in Norway and Hanstholm in Denmark to Lerwick in the Shetland Islands, the Faroe Islands, and Seydisfjördur in Iceland.

Getting Around – A rental car is essential (Atak: $600/wk), even though Reykjanes spots are within 1h drive. Most of the breaks are accessible by 2WD, but the Snaefellness is more difficult to access than the beachbreaks on the south-facing coast. Sharp rocks, undulating lava flows and soft alluvial sand and mud can trap all but the most adept of 4WD's.

Lodging and Food – Accommodation is expensive although 68 campgrounds are open from June to mid-September. Northern Light Inn in Grindavik is $220/dble room while Heimagisting Borg is $95/dble. Keflavik is another choice with more options. Expect to pay $20 for a simple meal. 500ml beer at the pub costs $10, so buy some booze at the Duty Free.

Weather – Iceland is located in one of the stormiest region of the North Atlantic between Greenland and Norway. It's also in the path of the warm Gulf Stream oceanic current, so the weather is very changeable throughout the year, but the water temps are surprisingly mild during winter considering the latitude. The north of Iceland lies inside the Arctic Circle (66°) and freezing cold air occasionally affects the island in winter and spring. Summers are often cool and cloudy with short spells of sunny, pleasant weather. Much of the precipitation is actually snow during winter and fall, which are the wettest months. Water temps bottom out around 3-4°C (37-39°F) requiring seriously thick 6mm rubber and 7mm boots and gloves. Late summer water can hit 12°C (54°F) so a 4/3 and no gloves is doable, but remember the windchill factor can have a big effect and the constant winds can often gust up to 100km/h (62mi/h).

Nature and Culture – Natural hot springs and snowboard fields are flat day options for those with extra cash. Midnight sun and northern lights are part of the experience. Travel the 1339km (832mi) long Ring Road around Iceland and gaze at glaciers, hot springs, geysers, active volcanoes and vast lava deserts.

Hazards and Hassles – Sharp volcanic rocks are unforgiving. Inclement weather can move in swiftly and bring thick fogs and sea mists. Lack of daylight and big tides can prevent sessions in winter and rip currents can be extra strong. Anywhere off the beaten track is a long way from help so solo missions are a bad idea. Take extra precautions.

Handy Hints – Equipment is hard to come by as there are no real surf shops selling hardware and if there were, prices would be very expensive. Take a gun and thicker board to float all the rubber. 2 wetsuits can help! Nikita is the only street clothing brand to come out of Reykjavik. ATMs can be found outside most banks and in shopping centres.

WEATHER STATISTICS	J/F	M/A	M/J	J/A	S/O	N/D
total rainfall (mm)	78	59	42	53	80	78
consistency (days/mth)	18	18	15	15	20	19
min temp (°C)	-2	0	5	8	4	-1
max temp (°C)	3	5	11	14	11	3

up plenty of swell from the S - W with more beachbreak than the Reykjanes but mainly 4WD access trails and few documented, bona fide surf spots. Vik is the most southern point on the island and draws in any hint of swell down a submarine canyon onto quality black sandbanks. American army troops started surfing on the Reykjanes peninsula in the '80s followed by local Icelanders in the early '90s. The small crew of active locals is only growing slowly, because it is difficult to learn in the heavy conditions. Many have learned to surf at lower latitudes and higher temperatures, then brought back boards and wetsuits for Iceland's conditions. Media coverage has increased in the last 2 years with international surfing magazines and independent surf film-makers taking numerous trips to showcase the incredible landscape and hopefully the surf. The non-surfing Icelandic public is a bit more aware of surfing now and the classic comment "you are gonna die" is fading away. These fears probably owe much to Iceland's long seafaring traditions and strong fishing capabilities, which have shaped the country into what it is today. Iceland´s maritime history is littered with stories of fishing boats foundering while trying to get back into harbours in giant swells, cultivating a huge respect for the ocean throughout the population.

At **Gardur**, the north side of the lighthouse holds big outside lefts that remain unridden but smaller waves form up in front of the little harbour, better at higher tides. It needs a big swell to get the north-facing reefs working in SW winds. Kelp and currents can be a problem. **The Rock** at Hafnir has a jacking take-off into a square barrel. It's short, critical and occasionally sucks dry as the tide increases and the break shifts closer to the beach but it requires an overhead swell to start breaking, plus a 9-10 second period. Remember that **Sandvik** is an exposed black sand beach providing one of the only beginner-friendly options in smaller swells, but this beachbreak can quickly change into huge barrels shaped by strong rips, challenging even the most experienced surfers. **Grindavik** may be considered as surf central with 3 quality breaks but hanging out at the beach after a surf and chilling with the crew while downing a cold one doesn't happen here. The main wave west of town is an exposed, swell-magnet reefbreak with racy right walls at all sizes and some lefts. Steep take-offs, bumpy faces, swirling rips and barely submerged urchin covered rocks are some of the hazards. On the other side of the main harbour is **Rolling Stones**, where fat rights and lefts break over a triangular boulder reef provided swell is from the SW and period is over 10 seconds. Further south out towards the end of the promontory, **Ollie's Shipwreck** is a long, leg-burning left reefbreak, but it often shoulders off between rocky sections and is rarely ridden by anyone. **Thorli** is the most surfed place in Iceland, thanks to its deep paddling channel (no duckdiving!) and the ability to handle all swells above chest high. Long rides with workable sections that continually wall up down the line and it is offshore in the prevailing westerlies. Strong currents and some pollution from the fish factory are the only downers. **Thorlakshofn Beach** will hold consistent peaks on any swell

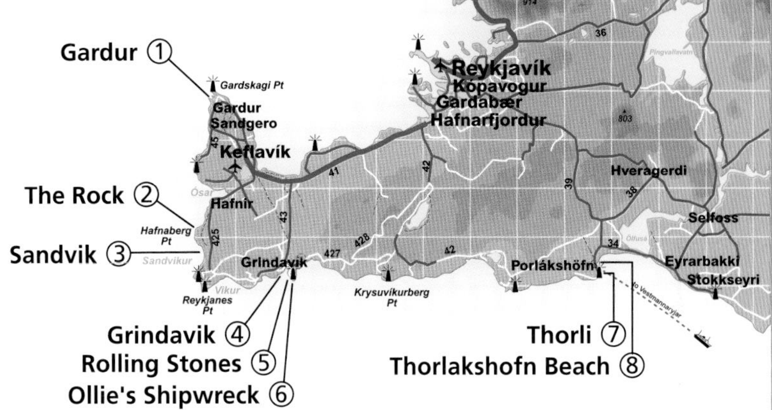

with S in it, but it is rarely ridden thanks to longshore drift and gruelling paddle-outs when over shoulder-high. Not worth the ice-cream headaches! All the Reykjanes spots are manageable with a normal car but a 4WD will prove to be very helpful if travelling north to the Snaefellsness peninsula or down south to Vik and beyond.

SURF STATISTICS			
Spot	Size	Btm	Type
①	20/5		
②	12/6		
③	15/2		
④	25/1		
⑤	20/3		
⑥	20/4		
⑦	18/5		
⑧	15/3		

Low pressure systems spawned in Baffin Bay, wind up south of Greenland, before sending groundswells slamming into the Reykjanes peninsula, the first stop on the transatlantic swell highway. These swells can be giant and very powerful, building suddenly and they are often accompanied by raw winds and stormy conditions. Winter is the most consistent swell season with excellent waves regularly hitting all sides of the Reykjanes. The problem in mid-winter is getting the right conditions to conspire in the very short span of daylight. Strong winds, chilling temperatures, snow storms and large tidal fluctuations are just some of the variables. September to November can be good months, with manageable air and water temperatures, and frequent low pressures. May-August sees plenty of summer flat spells in the southwest and could be a good time to explore the east and the north coasts for arctic wind swells. Tides exceed 5m (15ft) and there are only a few spots that can handle all tide heights. Even the main beachbreak at Sandvik struggles to break at high tide.

SURF STATISTICS	J F	M A	M J	J A	S O	N D
dominant swell	SE-W	SE-W	S-NW	S-NW	SE-W	SE-W
swell size (ft)	8	6-7	5	4	6	7
consistency (%)	10	70	60	50	70	60
dominant wind	NE-SE	NE-SE	NE-SE	W-N	NE-SE	NE-SE
average force	F5-F6	F5	F4	F3-F4	F4-F5	F5
consistency (%)	45	46	42	41	44	45
water temp.(°C)	5	7	8	11	9	8
wetsuit						

GEORG HIMARSSON
The Rock

162. County Clare

Eileens

AL MACKINNON

Summary
- \+ Very consistent swells
- \+ Challenging waves
- \+ Diversity of breaks
- \+ Good summer spot
- \+ Awesome landscapes

- – Often onshore
- – Winter storms
- – Cold water
- – Summer crowds
- – Few options for beginners

Despite the cold water, Ireland is often referred to as a surfer's paradise, thanks to it's perfect positioning in the middle of the tracks of the Atlantic swell train. Every possible swell direction will hit the Emerald Isle somewhere and the twisted littoral outline offers protection from malevolent winds and waves. Sandwiched between the more touristy counties of Galway and Kerry, County Clare is exposed to any ripple from the west, focusing both ankle-snappers and tow-in giants onto a bunch of reefs, points and beaches. A rare sandy beach and a handful of left reefs make the surf town and bustling seaside resort of Lahinch the county's focal point. It's the perfect base to explore the area, thanks to ample accommodation and abundant facilities, and the growing community of committed locals are usually friendly and tolerant of respectful visitors.

Secret spot

AL MACKINNON

Doolin Point

ROB GILLEY

Crab Island challenges the best surfers to make the long paddle from the pier to this heavy, barrelling, righthand

TRAVEL INFORMATION

Local Population: Co. Clare - 110,000
Coastline: Co. Clare - 366km (227mi)
Time Zone: GMT
Contests: Lahinch Surf School Ireland World Record
Video: The Elusive (2005), The Silver Surfari
Other Resources:
lahinchsurfshop.com
oceanscene.ie
lahinchsurfschool.com
irishsurfer.com
benssurfclinic.com

WEATHER STATISTICS	J/F	M/A	M/J	J/A	S/O	N/D
total rainfall (mm)	85	63	61	70	87	97
consistency (days/mth)	17	13	12	16	17	18
min temp (°C)	3	4	8	12	8	4
max temp (°C)	8	12	17	19	16	10

Getting Around – Rental cars cost $300/wk (Avis, Budget, Carhire), petrol is expensive and while new roads are improving, it takes time to cover seemingly short distances. Numerous campsites for campervans. Buses are cheap and take boards and are useful for intercity travel. Driving to Bundoran takes 3-4 hours.

Lodging and Food – Lahinch Hotel has double rooms and 8 bed dormitories from $22/night, only 50m from beach with cooking facilities. Many B&B's, but price range is higher ($45-90). "Bord de Mer" is French run and faces Cregg Beach. Camping is popular, free-camping still possible. Lots of great pubs, pay $15-20 for a meal or $6 for a meal in a glass – Guinness!

Weather – County Clare is bordered by the Atlantic Ocean and has a varied landscape from the rich pastureland to the rugged lunar-like stone pavements of The Burren. It has a mild but changeable climate all year-round and is not noted for any extreme weather conditions. Average temps range from 4°C to 9°C (39-48°F) during winter and between 15°C to 20°C (59-68°F) in summer. January and February are the coldest months while July and August are the hottest. In winter time, temps occasionally drop below freezing but snow rarely lingers. Annual average rainfall is 1000mm (40in), equally distributed throughout the year. Clare is prone to the full force of Atlantic storms, especially during autumn and winter. These storms can bring destructive winds and high rainfalls. Use a 5/4 or 4/3mm fullsuit most of the year, discarding the boots/gloves/hood and a mm of rubber from June to Sept.

Nature and Culture – County Clare is known for its beautiful natural scenery. The Cliffs of Moher are amongst the tallest in Europe (203m). Burren is a geological site with awesome lunar landscapes. Heaps of sacred sites (stone circles, dolmens, churches, castles). The county holds many traditional music festivals. Visit Lahinch Seaworld complex on a flat day.

Hazards and Hassles – Huge waves over shallow reefs, brain-numbingly cold water, and long hold-downs are some of the dangers on offer. Aggressive localism is rare, especially if you act and surf respectfully. Best to surf with a friend in remote spots as coastal rescue is not too developed. Ask permission when break access is through private land.

Handy Hints – Lahinch surf school has boards for rent, lessons with ex Irish champ John McCarthy ($40/2h). Specialist lessons with Ben's Surf Clinic or Lahinch Surf School has boards. Couple of surf shops in town (Ocean Scene, Lahinch, Green Room), but gear is expensive. Lahinch tends to become the Irish surfing capital during summer, when it gets very busy. Bring warm clothes for any season. Lahinch only has 650 inhabitants in winter.

reef, complete with vertical take-offs and thick-lipped slab sections to negotiate. Needs a W swell and E wind so it's inconsistent. Neighbouring **Doolin Point** is fickle too, but can deliver at its best a long, fast wall with barrelling sections. The tricky entrance and exit over sharp rocks keep crowds low. At the base of the massive Cliffs of Moher is the equally massive tow-in triangle, Aileens, for voyeurs only. The deep bay of Lahinch can offer some wind and size protection, producing great waves for beginners and shredders alike. Multiple A-frame peaks are on offer at the main **Lahinch Beach**, with smaller, mellower waves at the north end, but pay attention to the rocks at high tide. It also gets busy, and every spring, Lahinch surfers attempt to break the world record for the highest number of people surfing the same wave. **Lahinch Left** is an extremely long (300m+), fun reef at the south end of the beach, popular with locals and intermediate surfers. It's surfable on all tides when big, but better towards low when small. Further south lies **Cornish Left**, where a similar set-up delivers quieter, faster, hollower and shallower lefts. If it gets too big, check the less consistent lefts and occasional right at **Shit Creek**, a heavy reef in front of the discoloured, yet unpolluted rivermouth. Another sheltered, rocky cove can be found at **Cregg/Moy Beach**. Ask the land-owner for permission to reach **Green Point**, a rarely surfed, Mavericks-style peak that rears out of deep water to unload a chunky righthand barrel and suicidal slab of a left. The road south to Loop Head passes the booming rights at **Spanish Point**, so named because survivors of the wrecked Armada fleet came ashore here. The place is home to three quality reefs and a mellow beachbreak. **Outside Point** is a heavy, hazardous reef that hoovers up any swell going and handles serious size, but only experts can handle the thick barrels. Most surfers will prefer **Middle Point** at mid tide for its long, fast walls and tube sections. The outside reef filters the swell so only the larger ones will fuel **Inside Point**, a popular, short, 'funpark' peak that handles the wind better. When it's flat everywhere, drive further south on the N67 to **Doughmore** where a highly consistent beachbreak and right bank benefit from full exposure to W swells. Punishing paddle-outs, huge close-outs and dangerous rips are common when overhead. Only use the access paths provided by the golf course and don't stray across private property. In heavy NW swells, **Doonbeg** hides a sweet, hollow, lefthand reef in a sublime setting under the shadow of a ruined castle. Shallow and river-like rips, so leave it for the strong surfers only. In similar conditions, drive the 2km north to **Killard**, where average beachbreak peaks are offshore in the prevailing SW winds. Easy parking behind the beach, but it gets rippy too, when overhead.

As the most north-westerly outpost of Europe, Ireland is exposed to every raw groundswell the Atlantic can throw at it. Lahinch is battered by an average of 5 swells per week in winter, the main swell direction being from the W. Proximity to the storms can mean swells are disorganised and accompanied by strong winds, especially during winter. August to October should maximise the likelihood of good waves, because although the craggy west-facing coast receives ample swell, it also suffers from onshore winds most of the year and it's only when the wind swings to the elusive E direction that Clare reveals itself as Ireland's other world-class wave destination. Prevailing winds blow from the SW almost year-round, but hopefully the contorted coastline can offer some shelter. The tidal range is crucial and can reach 12ft (4m), so most spots will be stable for 2hrs at low tide and high tide.

GARY KNIGHTS

Spanish Point

SURF STATISTICS	J F	M A	M J	J A	S O	N D
dominant swell	SW-N	SW-N	W-N	W-N	SW-N	SW-N
swell size (ft)	6	5-6	3-4	2-3	4-5	5-6
consistency (%)	40	50	70	70	60	50
dominant wind	S-W	S-W	SW-NW	SW-NW	SW-NW	SW-NW
average force	F5	F4-F5	F4	F4	F4-F5	F5
consistency (%)	54	44	47	59	51	54
water temp.(°C)	8	9	12	16	13	10
wetsuit						

SURF STATISTICS

Spot	Size	Btm	Type
1	18/6		
2	15/4		
3	10/2		
4	12/3		
5	12/3		
6	12/3		
7	8/2		
8	20/6		
9	25/6		
10	12/3		
11	8/3		
12	6/2		
13	12/3		
14	8/2		

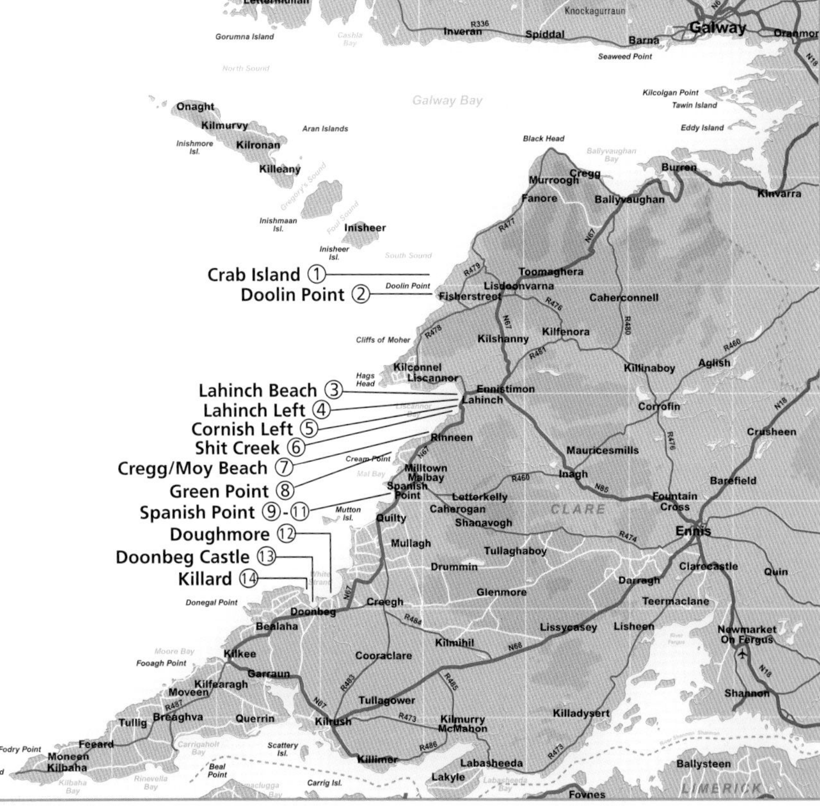

163. The Outer Hebrides

Barvas, Bus Stop and Bragar

MARK LUMSDEN

Summary
+ Powerful and consistent
+ Beach and pointbreaks
+ Clean water, no crowds
+ Long summer daylight hours
+ Northern Lights

– High latitude wind exposure
– Cold water
– Large tides
– Changeable, wet weather
– Remote, difficult access

Stretching for almost 125mi (200km) in length, the Hebrides archipelago lies off the northwest coast of Scotland between 57° and 58° North. The Inner Hebrides nestle surprisingly close to the mainland while the Outer Hebrides, which are often referred to as the Western Isles, sit a further 28mi (45km) out to sea. The area has so many islands, islets and coastline that the potential for finding virgin waves is still high. The Outer Hebrides receive the brunt of the Atlantic's force and have a helpful 180° swell window from the SW to NE. A good range of beaches, points and reefs exist and the small, committed group of local surfers are welcoming to visitors that play by the rules. Strong currents and powerful waves are the norm so seeking some local knowledge can prevent the unwary getting into trouble. The continental shelf is less extensive

Stones of Callanish

MARK LUMSDEN

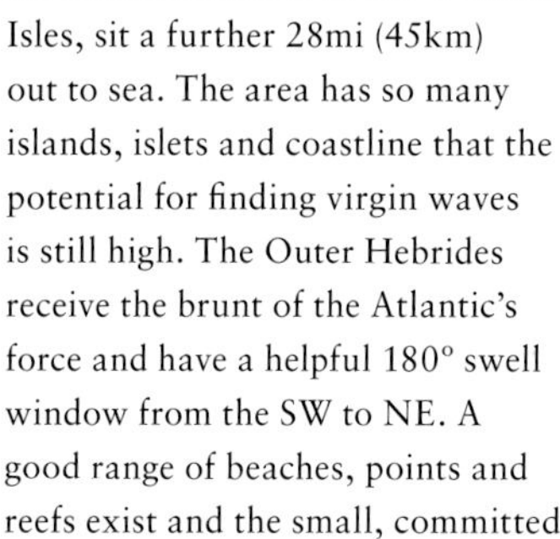

Europie

EMI MAZZONI

TRAVEL INFORMATION

Local Population: 26,370
Coastline:
Lewis - 546km (340mi)
Time Zone: GMT
Contests: Hebridean Surfing Festival
Other Resources:
hebrideansurf.co.uk
lewissurftrek.com
Video –
Cold Rush (2004)
The Elusive (2005)

Getting There – No visa required. Daily flights with BA (from $300 r/t from London) to Glasgow (GLA) or Inverness (INV) to Stornoway (SYY). BA no longer carry surfboards. CalMac run car ferries from Ullapool to Stornoway (2h40 o/w, $30/pax; $250/car r/t). Long vehicles and vans cost more. Book in advance if driving. Bus from Inverness-Ullapool is $22 r/t.

Getting Around – Lewis Car Rental charges $320/wk for group A. Lots of car ferry options to get there and travel between islands, adding to the driving costs. Stornoway is 45min from Tarbert. Driving is very relaxing and enjoyable with a good road network and little traffic out of Stornoway. All place names and direction signs are in Gaelic.

Lodging and Food – Fair Haven in Stornoway with Derek Macleod is $30/pax or jump in the Lewis Surf Trek van with Mark Lumsden. Stay in Stornoway for convenience or near west coast spots (Port Nis, Barabhas, Siabost). Galson Farm Bunkhouse is $18/pax or stay in the Guest House for a private room. Expect $20 for a good meal in a pub.

Weather – The climate of the Outer Hebrides is dominated by the Gulf Stream ocean current. Despite the northerly latitude, winters are rarely cold on the coast and summers rarely warm. Wind and rain are the dominant features with 45% of the rainfall between October and January. May is the driest month with about 16 days of rain and December the wettest with about 25. Total rainfall is 1200mm (47in) so it rarely pours and rains don't usually last all day as the famous Scottish "4 seasons in a day" weather is very changeable. January is generally the windiest month. In midsummer, there are barely 2 hours of darkness. Despite being 1300km (810mi) north of London, the mean minimum temps are about the same. Summer sea temps average out at 13°C (55°F) and in winter it gets no lower than 9°C (48°F). The Californians from San Francisco at the Hebridean International Surfing competition said the water was just like home!

Nature and Culture – Watch whales, orcas and Risso dolphins, which are most sociable from Aug-Oct. Numerous lochs to fish salmon or trout. Also great for diving, canoeing, sailing, mountain biking, climbing. Don't miss the 5,000 yr old standing Stones of Callanish or The Broch at Carloway, a mere 2000 years old. Autumn Aurora Borealis can be seen.

Hazards and Hassles – Waves can get powerful, even out of control, be ready to face an angry ocean with longer boards. Rips, rocks and isolation can increase the fear factor. No dangerous animals: even resident basking sharks are friendly and have no teeth. Stay warm and dry - bring appropriate clothing. Booties needed most of the time.

Handy Hints – Rent everything on Lewis if you're not staying long. Wetsuit: $20/day, board (beginner) $20/day, shortboard $40/day. Half day trip $60/pax. 2-day trip $180/pax. 5-day trip $500/pax (2-4 pax) on deluxe camper truck tour. In North Uist, ask for Niall at the Uist Outdoor Centre. Sunday is rest day, no transport.

WEATHER STATISTICS	J/F	M/A	M/J	J/A	S/O	N/D
total rainfall (mm)	105	91	66	88	134	117
consistency (days/mth)	18	17	16	17	22	23
min temp (°C)	1	2	7	10	7	2
max temp (°C)	7	9	13	16	13	8

than elsewhere in Britain and at these far northern latitudes, surfing until midnight is possible on midsummer days. The Inner Hebrides and mainland west coast also get waves, but the dominant winds are onshore. There are some sheltered gems that come to life in big W/NW swells. The Isle of Lewis came under the spotlight after veteran pro Derek Hynd and local surfer Derek Macleod organised the Hebridean Surfing Festival in Oct 2001, which used a novel scoring system based on a handicap criteria.

With numerous surf breaks on different sides of the islands, offshore winds can usually be found most days, grooming a variety of locations from beginner beachbreaks to world-class reefs. Stornoway was originally a Viking settlement and developed around it's sheltered natural harbour, where most visitors arrive by ferry. The closest beach is **Tolsta** that picks up any N swell onto some nice hollow banks. **Port of Ness** is a protected pocket of sand and scattered rocks facing the mainland and is a quick check from Europie if the wind is W. **Europie** is a consistent, fast, hollow beachbreak that sucks in swells of all sizes, but is extremely rippy when overhead. **Barvas** holds a long, reeling, righthander visible from the main road and capable of holding waves of consequence. Across the bay is **Bus Stop** aka Bru, a superb, ultra-long left point, breaking on boulders, which handles the prevailing SW winds. Remote **Bragar** is a fast outside ledge peeling into a bay offering some shelter from SW winds. **Dalbeg** is protected by a long jutting headland to the north and is best in peaky, summer swells as size will send it quickly out of control. Ultra-consistent **Dalmore** is one of the most popular breaks year-round, thanks to the changeable sandbars that range from fun walls to frightening tubes. Bhaltos or **Cliff** is another safe bet for challenging beachbreak with good tubes at low tide and long rides at other stages. Cliff probably handles the most size of any UK beachbreak with rips to match. Last on Lewis is **Mangersta**, a small sandy beach exposed to any W swell and wind, with a couple of peaks that are best around mid tide, providing the swell is around headhigh. On Harris, check **Scarasta**, a NW-facing crescent beach that can handle some SW wind in the lee of the southern corner. It may be smaller than the northern spots, but still breaks with power on a beautiful, isolated beach for solo surfing. The southern islands are a mission, but guarantee completely empty line-ups. The main North Uist break is **Hosta**, which faces northwest and is usually small and soft, but on the right swell, it can fire. A lot of other bays nearby are worth a check for small but consistent surf. Benbecula has **Culla Bay** a small bay on the west coast, which should have waves on a decent NW swell. Across the dunes from **Barra** island's famous beach airport is a long stretch of west-facing beachbreak plus there's a few more west coast beaches to check further south around Borgh. Far flung Vatersay island has one deeply indented, west-facing beach called **Bagh Siar**, which is often pounded by Atlantic swells from a westerly direction.

The Outer Hebrides are exposed to Atlantic swells from the S, W and N, including NE swells coming from the direction of Scandinavia. Lewis lies on the edge of a cauldron of ocean activity with most of the Western Isles consistently capturing vast chunks of North Atlantic swell. When west-facing spots become out of control, the normally flat north or even east-facing spots start breaking and provide good shelter from the dominant and blustery SW winds. The "Hebs" are a year-round destination, but it can get real big and nasty in the winter. Massive storms batter Scotland but even with such strong wave action the Scottish coast is remarkably resilient, thanks mainly to the NW shield being made of ultra-tough, ancient, metamorphic rocks, which take millennia to erode. The beaches of the Hebrides have the highest shell content in Scotland (90% on some beaches) so they look tropical when the sun is shining on the turquoise waters. Check the NOAA Buoy 64045, 300km NW of the Outer Hebrides. Tides are very significant with as much as 5m (15ft) of tidal range affecting the points and the beaches in smaller swells.

SURF STATISTICS			
Spot	Size	Btm	Type
1	10/1		
2	10/1		
3	15/1		
4	18/3		
5	15/4		
6	15/4		
7	10/2		
8	12/2		
9	18/2		
10	8/2		
11	10/2		
12	8/2		
13	8/2		
14	8/2		
15	8/1		

SURF STATISTICS	J F	M A	M J	J A	S O	N D
dominant swell	SW-N	SW-N	SW-N	SW-N	SW-N	SW-N
swell size (ft)	6-7	5-6	4-5	4	5-6	6-7
consistency (%)	50	60	70	80	70	50
dominant wind	S-W	SW-NW	S-W	SW-NW	S-W	S-W
average force	F5	F4-F5	F4	F4	F4-F5	F5-F6
consistency (%)	53	46	43	48	54	51
water temp.(°C)	7	8	11	14	12	9
wetsuit						

Dalmore

GREG MARTIN

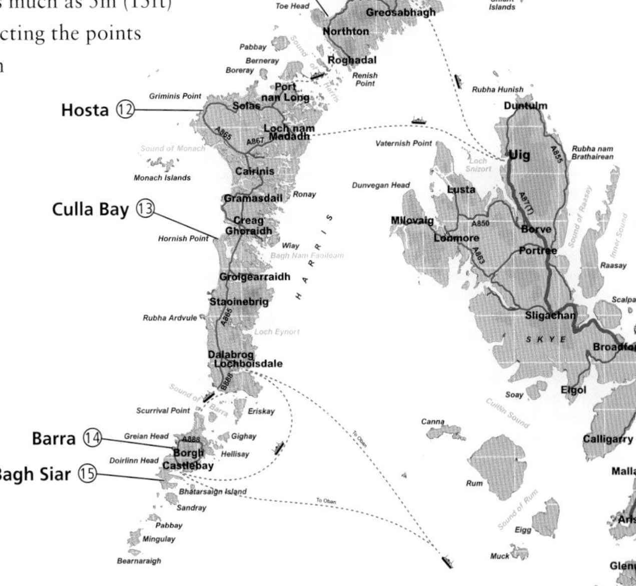

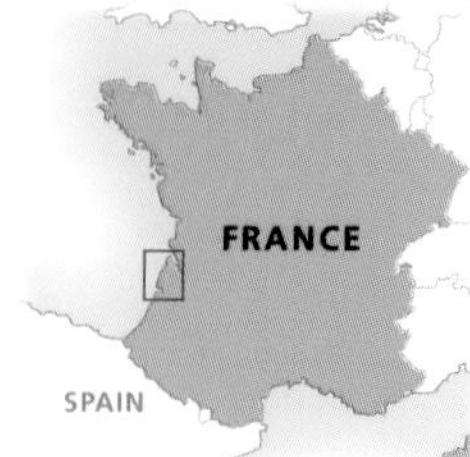

164. Gironde

Cap Ferret

DAMIEN POULLENOT

Summary
+ Empty peaks to find
+ Uncrowded off-season
+ Mascaret novelty
+ Excellent wines and oysters
+ Summer Party Scene

– Beachbreaks only
– Lack of epic spots
– Summer crowds
– Frequent onshores
– Often Maxed-out

Surfing in France centres around the Basque country and Les Landes, attracting many to the banner breaks of the Biarritz area or Hossegor. What many surfers don't realise is that the linear shores of Gironde can also offer very attractive and challenging beachbreaks, particularly in the smaller swells of summer. Furthermore, long stretches of beach remain unridden as crowds stay close to the towns and car parks even in summer, when a 20min walk could be rewarded. Each coastal town has its own wave variation and the quality of surf is always linked to the shape of the sand banks, the biggest one being the Dune du Pyla! Its 117m (384ft) high, making it the main tourist attraction around, along with the Bassin d'Arcachon and its famous oyster industry. Bordeaux sits just behind the coast, tempting wine lovers to taste the fruit of it's famous vines and the weather is even more stable than down south.

Le Mascaret

YEP

Le Verdon

BERNARD CHOQUET

TRAVEL INFORMATION

Local Population: Gironde - 1,376,000; Lacanau - 3,200
Coastline: 126km (78mi)
Time Zone: GMT +1
Contests: Lacanau Pro WQS 6* (August)
Other Resources:
lacanau-pro.com
surflacanau.com
bodyboardhouse.com
ssf.fr

Getting There – France is a Shengen state. Visas are required for Brazilians, Sth Africans and Japanese. Paris airports connect to Bordeaux (BOD) or take the TGV train (3h, potential $50 fee for boards). BOD is served from Italy (MyAir), Germany (Lufthansa), Canada (Air Transat), Sweden and Norway. Low cost flights from UK (Easyjet, bmibaby, FlyBe).

Getting Around – Rent cars in train stations and airports, from $300/wk. French road network is good but Bordeaux "Rocade" circular road gets busy. There are many parking lots close to the spots behind the dunes. Be aware driving the forest trails is prohibited and the fine is expensive. Bike trails are everywhere and offer good transit in the summer.

WEATHER STATISTICS	J/F	M/A	M/J	J/A	S/O	N/D
total rainfall (mm)	83	55	62	63	84	100
consistency (days/mth)	14	13	12	10	13	16
min temp (°C)	2	5	10	14	10	4
max temp (°C)	12	13	15	20	18	14

Lodging and Food – Always book in advance during summer, since Lacanau gets full. Surf Sans Frontières has rooms for $35/night (full board possible), Wave Trotter's Guest House is good too (ask at Mata Hari surf shop). Campgrounds are numerous. Try the excellent Arcachon oysters with a glass of Bordeaux white wine!

Weather – With its fine sandy beaches, large pine forests and big lakes, the coast of Gironde has a unique microclimate characterized by mild winters and relatively cool summers. Rain is frequent and gets stronger in autumn and winter, but the coast is less concerned due to strong influence of the ocean. Average annual rainfall is 935mm (37in). Summers are relatively hot with around 10 days per year above 30°C (86°F). Winters are usually cool, but freezing may occur. Occasionally, a strong, cold, dry N to NW wind known as Noroit blows. Use a 4/3mm fullsuit with boots and optional gloves/hood between December and April. A 3/2mm fullsuit is fine for spring and late autumn, while a shorty will be the best bet in July, August and maybe even September.

Nature and Culture – There are endless beaches skirted by sand dunes and thick forests, enjoy the relative wilderness. Dune du Pyla is worth the walk for the view over the Bassin d'Arcachon. Bordeaux vineyards are a perfect flat day idea. Lively bars and nightclubs during peak season. Winter is mellow.

Hazards and Hassles – Beware when the surf gets big and stormy, treacherous rips are common. Getting to the right spot before its optimum tide phase is the main worry, peaks are either crowded or empty. In the winter, beaches get plenty of trash from the ocean. Driving and parking are tricky from mid-July to mid-August.

Handy Hints – Gear is expensive and only a few surf shops are open year-round (especially in coastal towns). Try Mata Hari in Lacanau, Escape or Surfers in Bordeaux. Summer is always very busy, always book in advance. Don't be shocked by (semi)-naked people on the beach!

The Gironde estuary divides the rocky coastline of northern France from the endless sands to the south, and splits into the Dordogne and Garonne rivers which both host an occasional wave to ride! During the biggest spring and autumn tides, a slow tidal bore known as **Le Mascaret** can offer over 20 minutes of mellow and crowded surf, 5.5 hours after dead low at the ocean. St-Pardon is the local hub and delivers the best waves post summer when river levels are low. Inside the Gironde rivermouth, **Le Verdon** is the ultimate shelter when the Atlantic coast is onshore and out of control. Expect fast tubes on big high tides only, but gnarly rips and water pollution too. The offshore sandbanks at **Soulac** rivermouth create waves that are always smaller but hollower than surrounding spots. In larger swell you should head to **Le Gurp** where long tubing lefts can be on offer, despite the crowds and some attitude when on. More consistent waves can be found near the nudist hub of **Montalivet**, where the local surf club sometimes organise night surfing sessions. Beginners might prefer **Le Pin Sec**, an uncrowded stretch with endless choice of peaks and a nearby campsite across the forest of Flamand. **Hourtin** is a more open beachbreak that can line-up nicely on it's day, with bowly waves from low to mid tide. Crowds can be a problem in summer, so use the bike tracks to find your own peak. Ride to the opposite side of the lake for **Carcans**, a good beachbreak, often more walled-up than hollow, but plenty of power. **Lacanau** is an ASP contest venue since 1979 and it's also surf central for the Bordeaux area, because it is consistent and easily checked from the boardwalk at Plage Centrale. Check the banks at La Nord, La Sud or Super Sud, among 14km of beaches that are ideal with a medium size W-NW swell. It gets extremely lively in summer with all surf facilities and good campsites. Bordeaux surfers often head to the shifting sandbanks of **Le Porge** since it is the closest spot to town. That can mean crowds in season, but several parking lots lead to different peaks. For quieter waves, try **La Jenny**, where consistent and often hollow peaks can be found in small W swells. Access is N of the nudist camp entrance, but the long walk in means it is never crowded. In peaky summer swells the sandbars of **Le Grand Crohot** are often a good bet. It has plenty of "baïnes" and can be nice on the outside bars before it closes out at 2m+ (6ft+). If it gets too busy, walk to the quieter nudist beach of Petit Crohot. **Le Truc Vert** is the most popular spot on the Cap-Ferret peninsula thanks to the large campground and the good shape of the jetty influenced sandbanks. Expect summer crowds, strong currents and drift. There's more semi-secret spots further down the peninsula like **L'Horizon**, with banks that turn on in W windswells. The southernmost option on the peninsula is **La Pointe**. In very large swells, waves can wrap around Cap Ferret and break inside the Bassin d'Arcachon, throwing up tubey little rights. W winds are offshore but the hellish currents can make for bumpy rides. Great view of the massive Dune du Pyla in the background.

Because the coast faces west, it receives most of the very consistent high latitude W-NW swells, but also meets the dominant NW winds head-on. The lows track further north across the Atlantic in the summer, so swells tend to be from a more northerly direction, whereas the winter sees more W and SW swell. There is no immediate shelter so massive swells will hit the coast, but most spots won't handle more than 8ft (2.5m), so summer swells are usually the best. Winds come from the SW-NW quadrant with more NW winds in the summer. With high pressure over Biscay, winds will generally be offshore E in the morning before a moderate seabreeze picks up from around 10-11am. Tide ranges can reach 5m in the full moon and any sandbank can turn from ugly mush into a perfect peak, so get a tide chart!

SURF STATISTICS			
Spot	Size	Btm	Type
1	4 / 1		
2	6 / 2		
3	6 / 1		
4	8 / 1		
5	8 / 1		
6	8 / 1		
7	8 / 1		
8	8 / 1		
9	10 / 1		
10	8 / 1		
11	8 / 1		
12	8 / 1		
13	10 / 1		
14	8 / 1		
15	4 / 1		

SURF STATISTICS	J F	M A	M J	J A	S O	N D
dominant swell	W-NW	W-NW	W-NW	W-NW	W-NW	W-NW
swell size (ft)	7	5-6	4-5	2-3	4-5	6-7
consistency (%)	60	70	70	60	80	70
dominant wind	W-NW	W-NW	W-NW	W-NW	NE-E	W-NW
average force	F5	F4-F5	F3-F4	F3-F4	F3-F4	F5-F6
consistency (%)	37	37	37	40	47	40
water temp.(°C)	12	13	15	20	18	14
wetsuit						

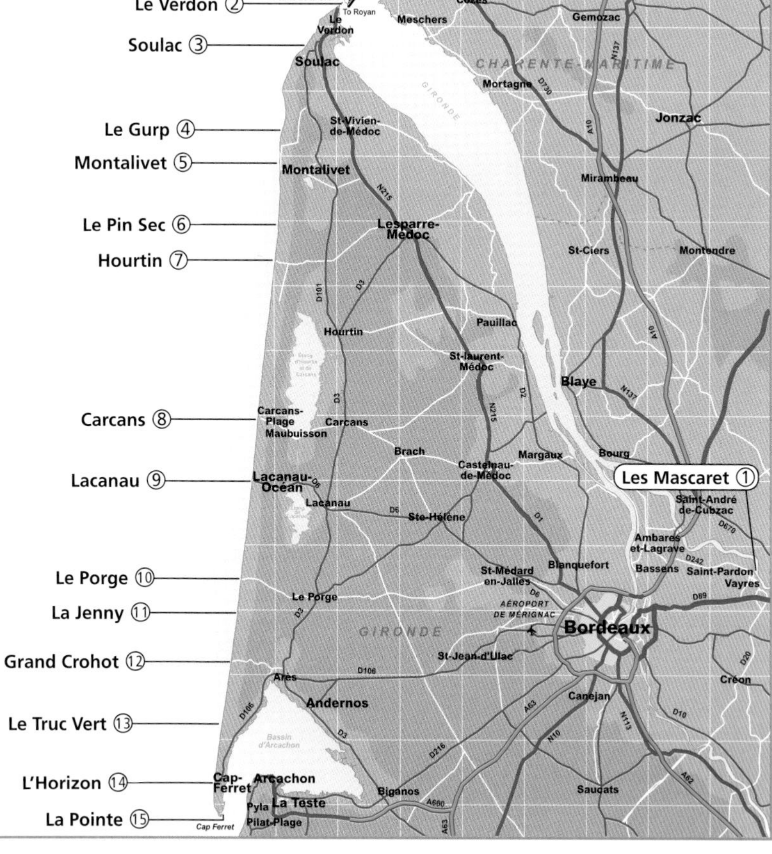

WWW.SURF-REPORT.COM

Lacanau

165. Minho and Douro

Espinho

MIGUEL DOLCE

Summary
- + High summer consistency
- + Not really crowded
- + Lots of open beachbreaks
- + Cultural attractions of Porto

- – Cool water in summer
- – Summer Nortada season
- – Lack of epic pointbreaks
- – Wettest region in Portugal
- – Seriously polluted around Porto

Sitting on the western edge of Europe, Portugal has always been a little bit different. The northern provinces of Minho and Douro have largely skipped the attention of visiting surfers, despite having a trove of surf and cultural resources. This super-consistent stretch of coast grabs the maximum from any swell direction and provides a wide range of wave breaking surfaces from gentle beaches and rivermouths to sheer slab reefs. Minho province shares many characteristics with its northern Spanish neighbour, Galicia, meaning lots of hills, lots of greenery and lots and lots of rain. Porto is the capital of Douro province, where it isn't quite as wet, but the bleak industrial landscape combines with the weather to help deter visiting surfers. However it's the pollution around Porto that might be the biggest turn off in north Portugal. It gets so dirty that the local authorities sometimes put a ban on people entering the sea at all! The mouth of the Douro River and the beaches a good way to the north and south are classed as one of the most polluted places in Europe and surfing should be avoided anywhere between Espinho and Vila do Conde. Situation is getting better thanks to EU grants helping to fund water treatment facilities. Crowds and localism are an issue at some of the banner breaks, but there is plenty of room to move and options for all levels of ability.

Viana do Castelo

MIGUEL DOLCE

TRAVEL INFORMATION

Local Population: 3,687,212
1.6M - Porto
Coastline: Portugal - 1,793km (1114mi)
Time Zone: GMT
Contests:
No major contest
Other Resources:
surfivorcamp.com
oportosurfcamp.com
atlanticriders.com
surfs-cool.com

Getting There – Non-EU get 90 days without a visa. Porto (OPO) is linked to European cities through 15 airlines, check Transavia, Ryanair & EasyJet. Nat'l airline TAP flies from NYC & Brasil, but far more international flights arrive in Lisbon (3h drive or local flight from US$200 rtn). Porto is 8h drive from Biarritz. Galicia to Porto is 2h drive and 5h to Algarve.

Getting Around – Rental cars start from $200/ week (Auto Jardim). Main roads are N13 and IC1. Portugal has a very high accident rate, fuel is more expensive than Spain, fast motorways are all toll roads. Traffic jams can occur in Porto. Efficient train service links the big cities. Atlantic Riders offers 6 day surfaris down south for $650.

Lodging and Food – Surfivor Camp in Cortegaça has packages around $500/wk. Oporto Surfcamp offers a wide variety of activities. Many pousadas, great camping in summer; Orbitür campsite in Viana do Castelo. Large variety of seafood, expect around $10 for a decent meal; try the caldo verde.

WEATHER STATISTICS	J/F	M/A	M/J	J/A	S/O	N/D
total rainfall (mm)	137	120	63	23	77	158
consistency (days/mth)	17	15	10	5	13	18
min temp (°C)	5	8	12	14	13	7
max temp (°C)	13	17	21	25	22	16

Weather – Viana do Castelo has a typical maritime temperate climate. Summers are sunny and gentle with temps between 12-24°C (54-75°F), but can rise to as high as 35°C (95°F) during occasional heat waves, which can last 5-10 days. In summer, oceanic fronts can bring rainy periods for a few days and are characterised by frequent showers, wind, and cool temperatures. Winter temps generally range between 7°C (45°F) and 16°C (61°F), but can occasionally drop below 0°C (32°F) at night. The weather is often rainy and windy for long stretches, although prolonged sunny periods do occur. Annual average rainfall is 1330mm (53in) and rain increases in frequency between September and late October, becoming less common in mid April or early May. Water temp is cool year-round. Use a 4/3 mm fullsuit with boots and optional gloves and hood between December and April.

Nature and Culture –Visit Porto and its 1000yr old historic centre, classified by Unesco. Also taste the typical wine called porto. The region is home to many wineries, try the Vinho Verde Route. Don't miss cities like Viana do Castelo or Braga, capital of the Minho region offering great nightlife. Serra da Estrela mountains are 3h from Porto.

Hazards and Hassles – Pollution is a major problem around Porto where the Douro river flows large amounts of industrial and residential effluent into the bordering line-ups, forcing beach closures that ban swimming and surfing. Locals can be protective of some spots – be cool and wait your turn. Erratic driving is commonplace, especially on Sundays. Watch your belongings, especially if you're camping.

Handy Hints – Main surf schools are Os Perafinas in Vila do Conde, Flower Power and Surf's Cool in Porto and Surfivor in Cortegaça. Surf supplies are available in the main surf hubs, try the Big Wave Surf Shop in Vila do Conde. Ear plugs can be useful to avoid diseases due to high pollution levels.

Barra do Porto

MIGUEL DOLCE

The Minho river demarcates the border with Spain and sometimes provides hollow rights at its mouth. The average quality and consistency beachbreak peaks of **Moledo do Minho** are adjacent to sand-covered reefs that can turn perfect at lower tides, but get crowded. The southern end of **Vila Praia de Âncora** offers a much more consistent beachbreak in NW swells and is usually quieter. The serious surf starts in **Afife** with a high quality beachbreak often likened to Supertubos, but without the crowds. It's consistent, very fast, hollow and prefers a SW swell with a low to mid tide. Viana do Castelo, home of the Portuguese branch of Surfrider Foundation, hides a beautiful beach S of town called **Cabedelo**. Take a ferry or drive around to access the quite inconsistent but large righthander breaking off the river jetty that offers some N wind protection. If it's too small, drive 30km (19mi) south to the very consistent west-facing beachbreak just north of **Esposende**. It won't handle much size, the water is very cold but crowds are minimal. Check **Aguçadoura** for an endless beach with numerous quality peaks, the water here is super clean but it gets out of control when big. 5km (3mi) offshore float the Pelamis "sea snakes" that use the energy of waves to generate electricity. Experts should try the quality reefbreak left at **Pòvoa do Varzim**; it's short, sharp, shallow and full of open barrels in a SW swell. The neighbouring town of **Vila do Conde** is a popular place for the people of Porto. Near a bunch of rocks on the town centre beach, breaks a short, hollow punchy lefthander that can get busy due to its reliability. On the other side of the river, **Azurara** delivers mediocre but consistent beach peaks with better wind protection and a good shorebreak for bodyboarding. It's the first spot north of Porto with genuinely clean water. Similar waves can be found in **Perafita**, but the background is much more industrial and the rocks surrounding the beach are even hot to the touch! There are plenty of barrels in **Leça** over highly consistent sandbars but few takers thanks to ridiculous pollution levels. In case of a massive swell, head to **Matosinhos** on the south side of the port and north of the rivermouth. The breakwater is a real swell filter here, but lifeguards red flag the beach when pollution levels are high (all the time), though many locals ignore the ban. The same extreme pollution affects all the breaks to the south including **Luz**, where the sandbars deliver semi-sheltered waves and the rare but epic rivermouth waves of Barra do Porto. **Miramar** can be excellent in summer, breaking right over the reef near the offshore island. It's fickle, but fast and hollow with potential barrels in a solid NW swell. **Espinho** is the best spot in north Portugal despite the pollution, localism and heavy crowds. The jetty of this dilapidated city holds a long, consistent tubey right with good protection from the "nortada" winds. Watch out for the inside section that closes-out over shallow rocks.

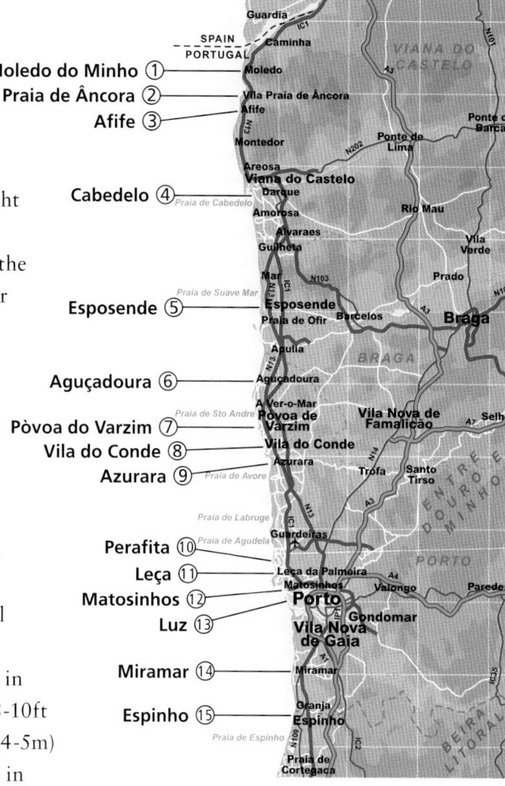

North Portugal has an Atlantic climate influenced by the Gulf Stream. The best time for a surf trip around here is late spring through to autumn. Because of its open exposure to the frequent NW swells, Portugal is hyper-consistent year-round and often receives massive swells in winter. Average swell is around 8-10ft (2.5-3m) in winter with 12-15ft (4-5m) peaks, and a solid 4-6ft (1.2-2m) in summer. Dominant winds are moderate N-NW, named "la Nortada", which often blows from April to September. Summer sea breezes often mess up the waves. Erosion has led to the construction of several jetties, offering good shelter from the big winter swells and pesky summer winds. Semi-diurnal tides reach up to 12ft (3.6m); avoid the highest tides as a vast majority of beachbreaks won't deliver their best.

Matosinhos

JOAO BRILHANTE

SURF STATISTICS	J F	M A	M J	J A	S O	N D
dominant swell	SW-NW	SW-N	NW-NE	NW-NE	SW-NW	SW-NW
swell size (ft)	6-7	5-6	4	3	5	6
consistency (%)	70	70	60	50	80	70
dominant wind	SW-NW	SW-NW	NW-NE	NW-NE	NW-NE	SW-NW
average force	F4-F5	F4-F5	F4	F3-F4	F4	F4-F5
consistency (%)	69	76	58	62	46	72
water temp.(°C)	12	13	15	18	17	14
wetsuit						

SURF STATISTICS

Spot	Size	Btm	Type
①	8/2		
②	8/1		
③	10/2		
④	8/2		
⑤	6/1		
⑥	8/2		
⑦	6/3		
⑧	8/2		
⑨	8/2		
⑩	8/2		
⑪	8/1		
⑫	8/2		
⑬	8/2		
⑭	12/2		
⑮	12/2		

Corvo
Graciosa
Flores
Faial
Terceira
Pico São Jorge
AZORES
São Miguel
Santa Maria

166. Terceira

Vietnam, Praia da Vitoria

ALL PHOTOS DAN HAYLOCK

Summary
+ 360° swell window
+ Epic Santa Catarina
+ Empty big wave spots
+ Beautiful landscapes
+ Pristine ocean environment

– Short-lived, disorganised swells
– E-facing spots need big swells
– Rapidly changing conditions
– Heavy waves, rocks and boulders
– Relatively expensive

Only the very tallest undersea mountains manage to break the surface of the empty Atlantic Ocean. The nine volcanic peaks of the Azores are all alone, almost equidistant from North America and Europe, with a full 360° swell window, right in the centre lane of the trans-Atlantic swell highway. Terceira simply means "3rd island", is fairly circular in shape and has the greatest concentration of east coast surf spots. The US has had a large military presence in the Azores for years and the ever expanding man-made harbour at Praia da Vitoria provided some protection for naval servicemen to surf Terceira as early as 1957. Some waves have been destroyed by jetty construction and a lot of the coast is inhospitable cliffs plunging into deep water, but when the big winter swells wrap down the east coast reefs, world-class waves appear for a small, dedicated and undoubtedly brave surfing community.

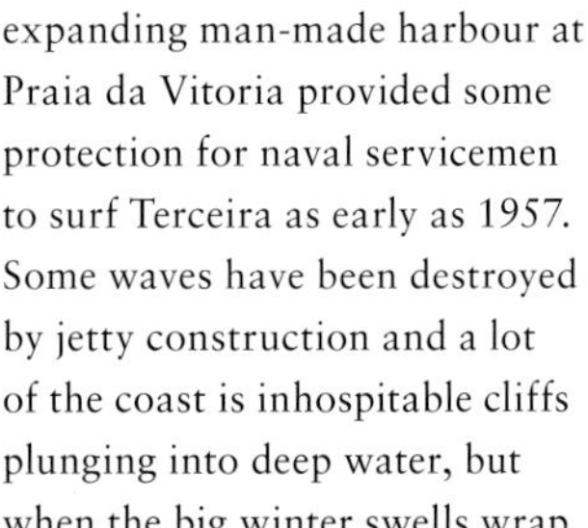

Santa Catarina

The gnarly offshore bombora reef at **Vila Nova** magnifies and bends W-N swells into super-heavy, thick, fast, barreling rights. Handles huge swells, is always bigger than it looks and is a high tide, experts only spot. **Quatro Ribeiras** has a powerful, challenging left off deepwater

TRAVEL INFORMATION

Local Population: 55,000
Coastline: 88km (55mi)
Time Zone: GMT -1
Contests: Local
Other Resources:
surfazores.com
titushapes.com

Getting There – EC/Portugal rules for visa. Daily 2h30 flights from Lisbon (LIS) to Praia da Vitoria (TER) with TAP or SATA (board charge). Charter flights from Boston, NYC, Canada and some European countries. SATA flies daily to other islands. Boardbags cost as much as a seat! From June to Sept, Atlantico Line ferries cruise between islands; Sao Miguel - Terceira = 5h30.

Getting Around – Expect to pay $420/wk at Ilha Verde for a group A car. Plenty of driving on slow and winding roads, except for link between Praia da Vitoria (airport) and Angra do Heroismo. Beware of cattle on roads at night.

WEATHER STATISTICS	J/F	M/A	M/J	J/A	S/O	N/D
total rainfall (mm)	137	114	60	43	112	128
consistency (days/mth)	20	17	12	10	16	19
min temp (°C)	12	12	14	18	16	13
max temp (°C)	16	16	20	24	23	18

Lodging and Food – Best is to stay in Praia. Good views from the 3star Hotel Varandas do Atlantico in Praia ($120/rm). Pousadas normally $80-100 and any cheaper options have to be searched out. Azores has good dairy products, fish, wines and Europe's only tea plantation. A good restaurant meal will be $30-40.

Weather – Terceira is dominated by mountains, covered with subtropical vegetation of all kinds and entirely bordered by high cliffs. The Gulf Stream brings a temperate climate, so summer days are sunny, evenings are cool, and there is occasional rainfall. The warm period extends from April through October, with temps from 13-24°C (56-75°F). Winter can be unpleasant, with high winds, heavy rains, overcast skies and temps between 8-21°C (47-70°). From November to March, violent winds can lash the islands for days. Annual rainfall is about 1000mm (40in). Winter days require a light fullsuit with occasional springsuit sessions in windless period.

Nature and Culture – Check the many natural swimming-pools like Biscoitos, set in volcanic rocks. May-October is Portuguese bullfighting season and whale watching time. Central area is marked by many craters, small lakes, and spectacular grottoes. Great views from Monte Brasil.

Hazards and Hassles – In 1981, an earthquake caused significant damage to Terceira. Volcanic eruptions are a threat although landslides are the main problem. Locals surfers are strongly determined and deserve respect especially at tight-knit take-off areas like Sta Catarina. Basalt rocks can be ultra sharp, some shark sightings at Quatro Ribeiras.

Handy Hints – Take a solid gun. If you break your board, there are 2 shapers in Porto Martins: Lucas makes SL surfboards and Tito does Titushapes. A new board would be $600-750. Spots like Santa Catarina might be destroyed by Tetrapods in new harbour projects. Visit neighbouring islands, especially Sao Jorge.

cliffs, that walls up and speeds across the bay before closing out on huge boulders that make it very difficult to get out of the water, especially after mid-tide. Righthander to the east is a bit mellower, but still very powerful. **Ponta do Queimado** has a sketchy, exposed, rocky left at the south end and more usable right at the north end below cliffs. The only reliable south coast spot is **Terreiro**, a high performance, steep, sectiony right that picks up all S swells but wraps in best on a W. Often crowded, some localism vibes plus man-o-war, urchins, broken bottles, rusty nails, steel bars, construction rubbish, and some residential pollution. **Salga** needs SW-W swell to line up properly. Changes with the tide from slopey shoulders to peeling walls. Inside section will stand up in front of pool. Dangerous when big. The short, sucky left at **Contendas** works on a big SW, SE or E swell, halving in size as it refracts and reforms into the bay. Shapes up perfectly with S groundswell, 12sec plus wave period and SW to NW wind. Closes out easily. **São Fernando** is a small wave

Contendas

spot that works best on N swells and is sheltered from NW winds. Easy, workable walls that back-off at higher tides. **Pescadore** holds full-on sucky barrels breaking next to a big rock on the inside of Ponta Negra. Seriously shallow, dangerous wave for experts only, who can hold their own with the tight local crew. A huge, long period, wrapping NW swell should light it up. **Ponta Negra** is an excellent, long, lefthand pointbreak on big NW swells and winds from W-NE. Breaks hard and fast, especially the mid-wave tube and the close-out end section, that has sent a dozen guys to the hospital. Often crowded and localised. There's a mushy right point in front of the swimming pool around the corner in Porto Martins. **Santa Catarina** explodes on a shallow reef close to shore, just south of the harbour jetty. Jacking air drop take-offs into a cavernous pit that peels both ways for a short but intense barrel ride. Perfect for bodyboarders and pro's, there's no room for error as dry reef is barely meters from the peak. Needs a medium to big NW swell to wrap in and any W in the wind. Ultra polluted by 3 outfalls, but government promising new treatment plants by 2010. Fairly consistent and sometimes crowded on weekends when localism is more likely. Respect required. Inside the harbour at **Praia da Vitória**, assorted reef waves like Dereitas and Esquerda do Chines (Chinese's Left) break off either side of an exposed rock and the left is a perfect hotdog wave in

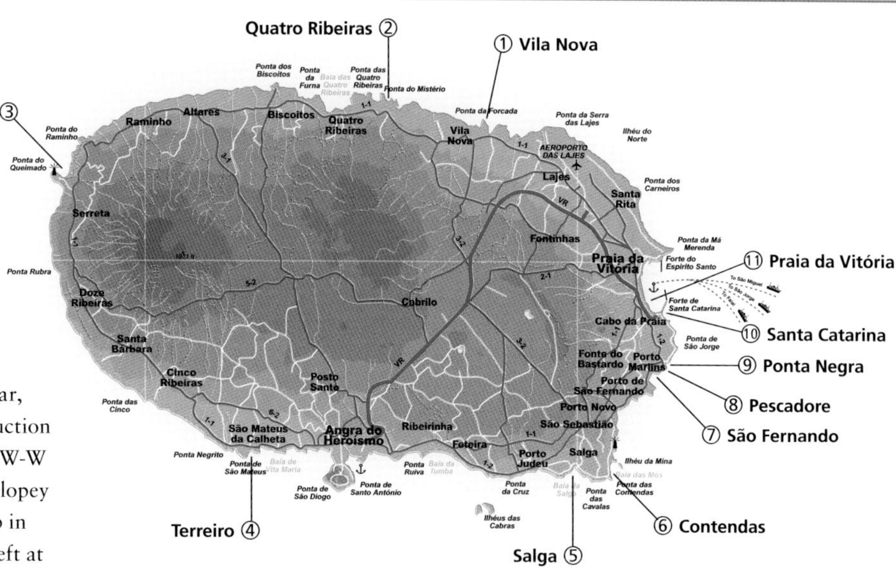

smaller N swells at high tide. Vietnam is the main left breaking wider than Chines. Fun, ripable walls plus the odd cover-up section and good length of ride on the lefts. Mid tide, big NW, N and NE swells and any W winds will be the best conditions. The reef is not too shallow or sharp, currents are minimal and the shifting take-off zone spreads the crowd of learners.

SURF STATISTICS			
Spot	Size	Btm	Type
①	25/6		
②	15/6		
③	10/4		
④	10/3		
⑤	15/4		
⑥	8/2		
⑦	6/2		
⑧	10/4		
⑨	18/4		
⑩	12/2		
⑪	10/2		

The Azores High is the major meteorological factor and if strongly established will hold off any storms from swinging straight over the top of the islands. This means 4-15ft (1.2-5m) winter swells usually arrive from the W-NW and slowly shift to N and then NE, before the next system moves through. Summer can see freak long-distance S swells all the way from the southern hemisphere or lined-up hurricane swell from the SW, along with localised wind swells from just about any direction. Being so close to the systems means winds can be strong and variable, veering S-SW in winter and N-NW in summer. Swells are a bit raw and disorganised, jumping in size with little warning. Tides only move a bit over 6ft (1.9m), but will affect many of the shallow reefs, while the beaches and points are generally unfazed.

SURF STATISTICS	J F	M A	M J	J A	S O	N D
dominant swell	NW-N	NW-N	NW-N	NW-N	NW-N	NW-N
swell size (ft)	6	5-6	4-5	3	5	6
consistency (%)	70	60	60	50	70	60
dominant wind	S-NW	S-NW	SW-N	W-NE	SW-N	S-NW
average force	F5	F5	F4	F3	F4	F4
consistency (%)	65	63	61	59	56	53
water temp.(°C)	16	17	18	22	22	19
wetsuit						

Salga

167. Lazio

Banzai

EMI MAZZONI

Summary
+ Sta. Marinella quality reefs
+ Unusual surf destination
+ Mediterranean climate
+ Great food and wines
+ Breathtaking cultural attractions

– Mostly inconsistent spots
– Potential crowds when good
– Often onshore or very windy
– Pollution
– Urchins

Few surfers would have guessed it, but Italy actually receives regular waves, sometimes as high as double overhead. Most Italians would say there are no waves in the tranquil Mediterranean because their beach experience is mainly associated with summer when wave height is usually tiny and crowd size is huge. But once all the tourists have gone home, winter approaches on the heels of low pressure weather systems, which have crossed the Iberian Peninsula from the Atlantic or formed up in the western Med. Tuned-in surfers then track the storm, hoping for strong onshore winds to blow hard and long enough to bring swell to the Italian coastline. The Lazio coast receives these swells from a full 180° window, anytime from autumn through winter to spring, with the closest spots sitting a mere 30min from Rome.

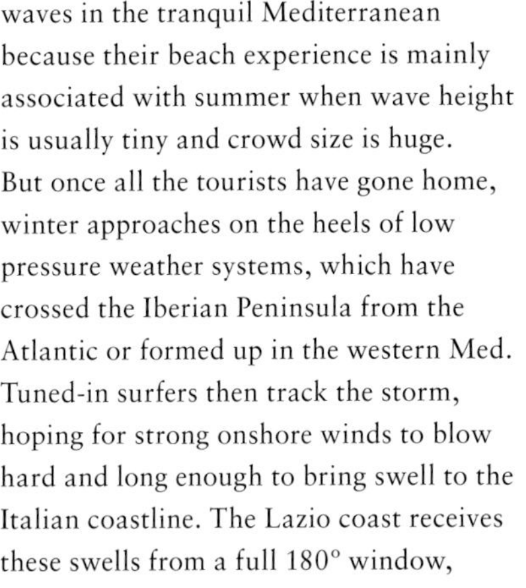
Santa Marinella

EMI CATALDI

Gaeta

STEFANO VIOLA

Civitavecchia is home to a playful A-frame peak in front of the restaurant **L'Ideale**. It's mainly a lefthander breaking over rock and sand in strong SE or after a SW swell. Quality reefbreaks dot the neighbouring city of Santa

TRAVEL INFORMATION

Local Population: 5.1M
Rome - 2.7M
Coastline:
Italy 7611km (4729mi)
Time Zone: GMT +1
Contests: Italia Surf Expo (Santa Marinella)
Video: Localize It
In Peninsula We Trust
Other Resources:
surfnews.it
surfreport.it
surf.it
smsurfclub.com
killersurf.it (Gaeta)
surfcorner.it

Getting There – Shengen state, non-EU get 90 days without visa except South Africans. Fiumicino (FCO) is Rome's main airport, with flights from just about anywhere in the world. Finding a flight during peak holiday times can be a nightmare. Alitalia is the national airline. Look for low cost flights within Europe. 7h drive from French border.

Getting Around – Check for rental car at airport, economy car from $280/wk (over 21, non EU need International license). Fuel and tolls are quite expensive. SS1 (Statale Aurelia) and SS148 (Pontina) are the main roads. Heavy traffic during beach season. Ferry to Sardinia sails from Civitavecchia.

Lodging and Food – Accommodation is not cheap. Try Rifugio dei Cardinali in Santa Marinella (double from $70/night + apartments for rent), or Residenza Isola (double $120/night). T-Village in Anzio has studios from $400 per week. Italy is renowned for excellent pastas, pizzas, wines and coffees. Expect $30 for a decent meal.

WEATHER STATISTICS	J/F	M/A	M/J	J/A	S/O	N/D
total rainfall (mm)	67	54	42	18	81	111
consistency (days/mth)	9	7	5	2	7	11
min temp (°C)	5	8	15	20	15	7
max temp (°C)	12	17	25	30	24	15

Weather – Rome offers a Mediterranean climate with hot summers and mild winters. In summer, temps rarely go under 28°C (82°F) but evenings are cooled by the ponentino, a W wind from the Tyrrhenian Sea. The winter climate sees warm, sunny weather punctuated by frosts and occasional light snowfalls. Winter temps stay around 13°C (56°F). Autumns feature more rain with average temps of 20°C (68°F). November is the rainiest month with heavy, persistent rain during the frequent SW and SE weather fronts. Average annual rainfall is 820mm (33in). The best time to go is in spring or early autumn, when the weather is pretty warm and the waves consistent. Use a 3/2mm fullsuit from December to April, a shorty or boardshorts for the rest of the year.

Nature and Culture – With 28 centuries of history, Italy is a huge cultural draw card. Visit Roman ruins archaeological sites, museums, churches, learn more about Renaissance art, or simply enjoy the pleasures of la dolce vita. Home of the Vatican, the world's smallest country!

Hazards and Hassles – The number of wave riders has shot up and crowds may occur every time it gets good. Watch out for rocks and urchins getting in/out of the water, some reefs are very shallow. Polluted breaks near the Tevere river. Shark attack against a surfer occurred in 1989 in Tuscany.

Handy Hints – A shortboard/fish combo covers all spots and conditions. Surf shops at the most popular breaks (Banzai Surf Shop in Santa Marinella) or in Rome (Waterworks, Salt Store). Booties are useful for protection from sharp rocks and the dreaded sea urchins! There is no heavy localism in Lazio, but the crew in Banzai is famous for being straight and vocal if you show disrespect or waste waves.

Marinella, without doubt the best surf around. Don't be discouraged by onshore winds, poor water quality and tricky access over rocks and urchins, because **Il Porto** is a powerful peak, south of the harbour with peeling rights and lefts in W and SW swells. If it's too crowded, just walk 200m down the beach to **La Roccetta**. This A-frame peak has a long but slow right plus a shorter but intense left with barrelling sections over a very shallow rock ledge. Accessible from the pier, **Il Bunker** is another powerful righthander breaking on a shallow reef in front of a WWII vestige. It needs a big swell to activate, preferably from the NW, it's not crowded but locals say water is dirty. **Ristorante** is inconsistent but the short, fast rights off the jetty, just north of Banzai offer potentially good rides in less crowded conditions. Rome's premier surf spot is **Banzai**, a name cribbed from the world-class Hawaiian spot. While the Italian version is less of a threat to life and limb, it nevertheless requires respect as it breaks over shallow, sharp, urchin infested reef and attracts loads of the best surfers to its hollow left and right waves. Home to 3 generations of Italian surfers, the reef miraculously breaks under SE to NW swells and is the 1st place to check on any conditions. Rome's longboarders often head to **Il Castello**, an average beachbreak just next to the castle in Santa Severa. Its peaks are best in SE windswell up to 5ft (1.5m). The long sandy beach of **Ostia** (the closest to Rome) offers several average, busy breaks in small, windless SW to NW swells and remains surfable with moderate onshores. Most of the beach is private so ask for access at the bars, and being close to the city means this break suffers from poor water quality as the Tevere River empties into the sea. On similar conditions, another consistent but polluted (it's a bit better than Ostia) beachbreak can be found at **Lido Garda**, just north of Anzio. **Marinaretti** next to Anzio harbour might offer better quality waves and a little shelter from onshore winds, but it suffers from an evident lack of consistency. The beachbreak of **La Chiesa** offers short rides in the seaside town of Nettuno and is a good alternative when Lido Garda & Marinaretti are too messy or overcrowded. **Artiglieria** in Sabaudia is a highly consistent beachbreak with plenty of fun peaks offering fast peeling waves with potential barrelling sections. Further down the picturesque coastal route 213, the south side of **Santa Agostino's** long beach holds surprisingly fast and powerful lefts. Check on a glassy SE swell, when the water will be clean and it never gets crowded. Under W and SW swells, the spots around Santa Agostino remain surfable for one extra precious day after the northern breaks have all gone flat. **Serapo** is a 2km stretch of beachbreaks in the heart of Gaeta offering several easy peaks under many conditions. The north side of the beach is surfable with big NW or small windless SW swells, while the south side works in SE swells.

Flexibility is the key as it is necessary to follow the swell and wind patterns as they swing from SE round to NW. Only long periods of strong winds are able to generate sufficient windswells. Finding a clean line-up is tricky in the short fetch and period conditions of the Med. The warm Sirocco wind originates over North Africa and acquires its humidity over the Mediterranean, where it can generate great SE swells but consistency is low (50 days per year). A spell of Sirocco weather in autumn often ends with very heavy rain accompanied by thunder. Mistral (NW) is the main source of wind in summer, it will generate good waves if it blows strong enough. The Libeccio (SW to W) is the third wind option. Long summer flat spells of weeks are not uncommon. Med tidal range is very small at 10-20cm (4-8in) on the Lazio shores, so it can only slightly influence the shallow reefs of Santa Marinella.

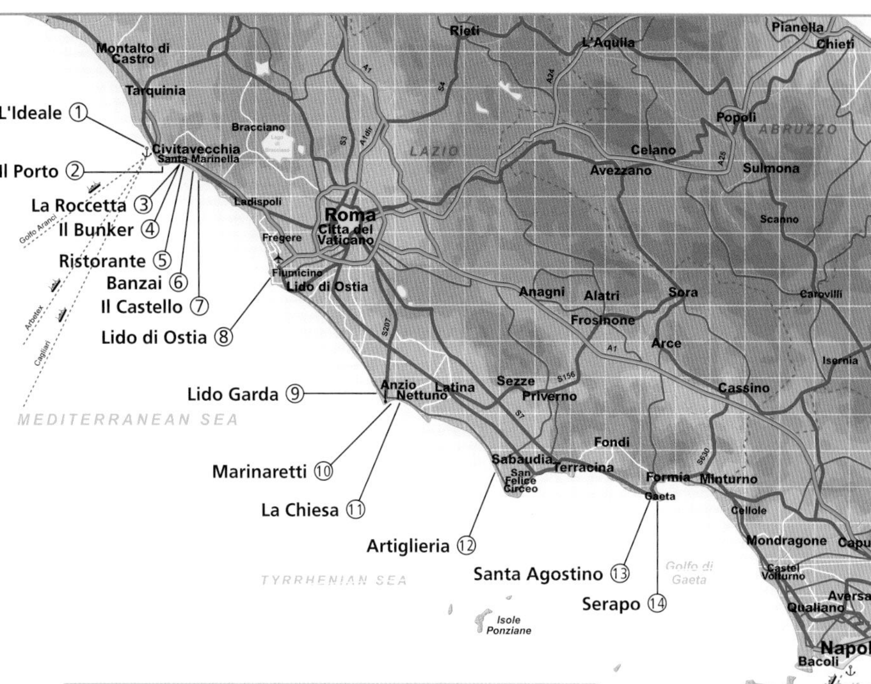

SURF STATISTICS	J F	M A	M J	J A	S O	N D
dominant swell	W-NW	SE-SW	SE-SW	W	SE-SW	W-NW
swell size (ft)	4	4-6	4-6	2	5-6	4-6
consistency (%)	25	40	40	20	45	40
dominant wind	W-NW	SE-SW	SE-SW	W	SE-SW	SE-SW
average force	F5	F4	F4	F2	F5	F5
consistency (%)	29	39	32	33	25	27
water temp.(°C)	13	14	19	24	22	17
wetsuit						

SURF STATISTICS			
Spot	Size	Btm	Type
①	8/2		
②	10/2		
③	6/2		
④	12/2		
⑤	8/2		
⑥	10/2		
⑦	5/1		
⑧	6/2		
⑨	6/1		
⑩	6/2		
⑪	6/3		
⑫	8/2		
⑬	8/2		
⑭	8/2		

LEONARDO D'ANGELO

Santa Agostino

168. Malta and Gozo

Riviera

ALL PHOTOS YEP

Summary
+ NW and NE swells
+ Quality reefs and beaches
+ No crowds
+ No tides
+ Architecture, history, scuba

– Winter only
– Lack of consistent spots
– Coastline cliffs
– Jellyfish & shallow rocks
– Urban sprawl & mad traffic

The southernmost limit of the European Community sits in the middle of the Mediterranean Sea, where it has withstood a pounding from millennia of Mistral or Grecale wind-driven waves. These 2 small dots in the Med suffer from poor water resources, sparse vegetation and no fauna apart from rabbits, but the Mediterraneans have always tried to settle down in Malta. The many rocky inlets make perfect natural harbours to tap the bountiful maritime resources and the soft, golden rock, known as "tuff", has been shaped into many caves, making easy homes for both cave dwellers and skilled builders. Malta & Gozo have an incredible history, with megalithic evidence as old as 5000 BC, about 1000 years before Stonehenge and a constant trail of invasions including the middle-age crusaders, British colonial rule and finally independence in 1964. British influence is still very strong with red pillar mailboxes, red telephone booths, pubs filled

Salt Pans

with snooker tables and dartboards as well as driving on the left, which gives Malta it's unique "Mediterenglish" feel. Unfortunately, it's got the 2nd highest density of cars after the USA, so expect some traffic and dangerous, erratic driving from the locals. Winter is the ideal time to go, not only to avoid the mad crowds of summer, but because this

TRAVEL INFORMATION

Local Population: 390,000
Coastline: Malta 246km (152mi) Gozo 67km (42mi)
Time Zone: GMT +2h
Contests: none
Other Resources: gozoweather.com/marine.shtml

Getting There – No visa for EEC residents. Malta (MLA) attracts many tourists through cheap package deals with flights included, often from UK and Northern Europe. Air Malta does not charge for boards, usually $200-350 from Europe. Ferry crossing to Gozo is easy with departures every 45min and 25min cruising time ($25 with car/2pax, cheaper after noon).

Getting Around – Driving on the left does not make it easy for continental drivers. Local drivers are pretty aggressive in the narrow streets of the villages and traffic can be heavy. Take the bus if going to La Valette! Rental cars are fairly cheap (130 euros/wk). The longest distance is 38km (24mi) from Cirkewwa in the north (ferry to Gozo) to southern Bubuggia.

WEATHER STATISTICS	J/F	M/A	M/J	J/A	S/O	N/D
total rainfall (mm)	75	27	7	4	46	101
consistency (days/mth)	10	4	1	1	5	11
min temp (°C)	10	12	17	22	20	14
max temp (°C)	15	17	24	29	26	18

Lodging and Food – Package deal hotels are usually huge with lots of tourists. Cheap guest-houses start from $30 for a double room in winter with breakfast. In winter, stay in Mellielah, St-Paul's Bay, Paceville, St-Julian's or Sliema. Not much local food (rabbits) but Italian restaurants are good; $20 for a meal.

Weather – The climate is typically Mediterranean, with hot, dry summers, warm and sporadically wet autumns, and short, cool winters with adequate rainfall. 75% of the total annual rainfall (600mm, 24in) falls between October and March; June, July, and August are normally quite dry. The temperature is very stable, the annual mean being 18°C (64°F) and the monthly averages ranging from 12°C (54°F) to 31°C (88°F). Winds are strong and frequent; the most common are the cool NW (Majjistral), the dry NE (Grigal, or Gregale), and the hot humid SE (Xlokk, or Sirocco). The relative humidity is consistently high and rarely falls below 40%. The sun shines for an average of 6.46 hrs each day in winter and 10.11 hrs in summer. The hottest period is from mid July to mid September. Water temps require light fullsuit in winter; use some neoprene for jellyfish in warmer months.

Nature and Culture – Scuba diving is big with countless diving centres around. Malta is an ideal place to visit with a non-surfer because of the abundance of architecture and sightseeing as well as lively pubs and discos in Paceville near La Valette.

Hazards and Hassles – There are locals in Malta, with a few expats like Jamie, Jay or Manuel along with locals like Karl and Matthews, but no crowds at all. Beware with pelagica noctiluca jellyfish in SW winds and some reefs can be nasty. Locals love horse racing on Sunday on main roads. Now, lots of guys do it with motor cycles too! Traffic and driving can be mad.

Handy Hints – A fish and a longboard will do. One shop sells a couple of boards but no choice and no rentals. Malta can be a stop-over for other Med trips. Good kitesurfing. A 23ft great white shark was caught here back in 1987.

is the best timing for the NW-NE swells. There is only a handful of occasional locals and most of the tourists are senior citizens, so getting the exposed north coast breaks to yourself is almost guaranteed. There is also the novelty factor of possibly riding the waves of the smallest enclosed sea in the world!

Gozo feels way more relaxed than Malta with less people, less cars, but also less surf below the breathtaking plunging cliff formations like the Azure Window or Fungus Rock. The phenomenon known as the **Inland Sea** is a 100m-radius semi-circular pond which looks like a quiet lake most of the year. The 60m cliff overlooking the pond is pierced with a small hole, allowing fishing boats to get out to sea. When NW storms hit, the Inland Sea becomes the smallest natural wave pool in the world! Sets pound into the rocky tunnel and radiate out in a perfect example of convex refraction, creating knee-high peaks over the rocky fingers of reef in the bay. A longboard and a large slice of swell and luck are needed. **Salt Pans** is the best wave around, starting fat and lumpy on the outside of the point before cleaning up and tubing through the inside near the cave. Handles as big as it gets (8ft/2.5m) but needs NE direction to get into the bay. **Marsalforn** has some scattered reefs to the east of the harbour in NW swells. Gozo's main beach is **Calypso's** at Ramla Bay where a decent NW swell will get lefts running down the beach or rights in a NE swell. A steep concrete road leads to **San Blas** a secluded beachbreak with generally ugly waves in a beautiful setting on NW–NE swells. At first sight, the natural fortress style of Malta's topography is not that great for surf, but there are a selection of reefs on the NE coast and an obvious cluster of 3 beaches to the west. **West Armier** faces the channel and surprisingly prefers big NW swells to create some shorebreak lefts over the sand and rock bottom. More anchorage than surf spot, the deep bay at **Mellieha** is a popular kite surf spot and will only have a weak wave in stormy NE swells. There's a backwashy wedge at the south end and more exposed beachbreak at Maiebah. Spinning down the side of St Paul's Island is **Apostle's Right**, a decent righthand reef during strong NE swells and is offshore in any S wind. Paddle from the salt pans on the beach and beware the nasty inside section. Popular with windsurfers, **Ghallis Rock** is an exposed outer reef that throws up shallow lefts that get bouncy on the inside. **Cementa** is a swell magnet reef, but the treacherous rights are only rideable on the outside section before the gnarly inside death section. The lefts are suicide. **Palm Beach** is a slab reef and the closest break to Valetta. Bumpy rights with shallow sections on a narrow beach, with a friendly bar and resident dolphin, next to a marine park. On rare SE swells, Marsaskala holds below average rights at **Mignuna Point** as well as the aquaculture centre and St Thomas Bay, but the rock shelves are usually too steep. The 3 west-facing beaches at Golden Bay, Ghajn Tuffieha Bay and Gnejna Bay were protected by concrete Tetrapods to resist German attacks during WW2 and they still present a potential hazard to water-users. **Boat Sheds** at Gnejna is sloppy, inconsistent and usually onshore in the NW wind. Malta's most consistent surf is found at **Riviera** in Ghajn Tuffieha Bay where hollow rights break next to the Riviera Bar and longer lefts wind into the inside with some great whackable and launchable sections. Unfortunately, in summer, it is packed with swimmers, but empty in the winter surf season. Finally, **Radisson's** is worth a check in bigger swells, when it is usually better than Riviera, producing some wedging lefts and strong currents.

SURF STATISTICS			
Spot	Size	Btm	Type
①	4/1		
②	8/2		
③	6/3		
④	6/1		
⑤	4/1		
⑥	4/2		
⑦	4/1		
⑧	5/2		
⑨	6/3		
⑩	8/4		
⑪	6/2		
⑫	5/3		
⑬	5/3		
⑭	6/1		
⑮	6/2		

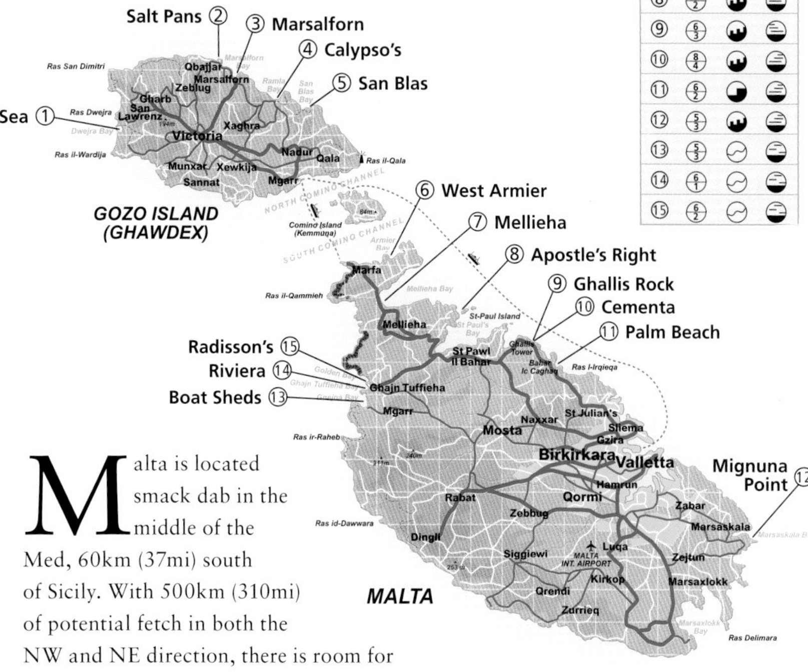

Malta is located smack dab in the middle of the Med, 60km (37mi) south of Sicily. With 500km (310mi) of potential fetch in both the NW and NE direction, there is room for good-size swells to build in the Ionian Sea and the Sicily Channel. There could be potential southern swells from Tunisia or Libya, but those wind trends are rare and southern spots are almost non-existent. The NW Mistral flux often regenerates after Tunisia in the Sicily Channel and produces the highest frequency of waves. The NE Grecale from Greece is less frequent but the NE swells from the Ionian Sea can be good and chunky, if a little short-lived. Obviously, swells rarely hang around for more than 24 hours and only short and mid-term (3 days) forecasts can be reliable. In Riviera, waves can be ridden from 1-6ft (0.3-2m) while Salt Pans on Gozo needs 3ft (1m) minimum to start breaking, but will be rideable up to 8ft (2.5m), which is as big as it gets and not big enough for a gun. No tide in the Med.

Ghallis Rock

SURF STATISTICS	J F	M A	M J	J A	S O	N D
dominant swell	NW-NE	NW-NE	NW-NE	NW-NE	NW-NE	NW-NE
swell size (ft)	2-3	2	1	0-1	1-2	2-3
consistency (%)	40	30	20	10	30	40
dominant wind	W-NW	W-NW	W-NW	W-NW	W-NW	W-NW
average force	F4-F5	F4	F3-F4	F3	F3-F4	F4-F5
consistency (%)	43	41	44	45	33	41
water temp.(°C)	15	16	20	25	23	18
wetsuit						

169. Northwest Greece

Kastro Point

ALL PHOTOS YANNICK LE TOUQUIN

Summary
+ Various winter swells
+ Quality waves for the Med
+ Best spot density in Greece
+ Beautiful mountainous region
+ Temples, mythology, sightseeing

– Inconsistent
– Short-lived swells
– Winter conditions
– Long drive from Athens

Everyone knows that the Greek civilisation dates back to ancient times but hardly anyone knows that the Minoan civilization on Crete island was utterly destroyed by a tsunami around 1450BC when the volcanic island of Santorini erupted with a force 10 times the strength of Krakatoa. The height of the wave at source was a staggering 690ft (210m), and by the time it hit Crete, nearly 120km (75mi) away, it was still around 200ft (61m) high, wiping the Minoan's coastal towns from the map and sinking their large fleet without trace. These days, the Greek-owned fleet is the largest in the world and their affinity with the sea is now extending to surfing. With slightly more than 1000 islands, the Greek coastline is split between 4,000km (2,485mi) of mainland and 10,000km (6213mi) of islands. The large, southern island of Crete, would seem to have the best swell exposure,

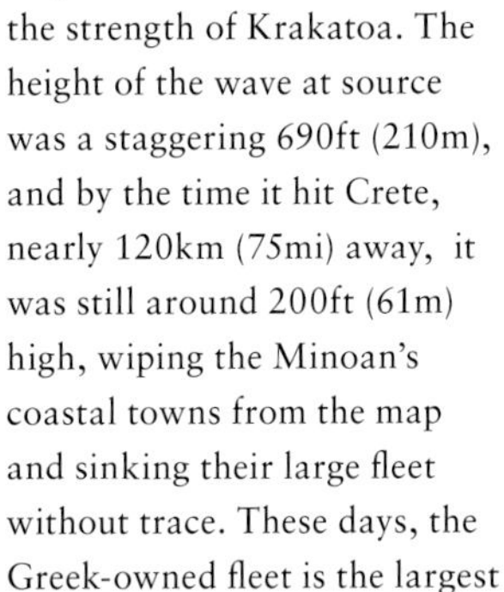

Parga

Little Bay

TRAVEL INFORMATION

Local Population: Epirus 373,420
Coastline: Epirus 70km (43mi)
Time Zone: GMT+2
Contests: Nationals (Lagouvardos, Crete)
Other Resources:
surfingreece.piczo.com
surfingparga.piczo.com

Getting There – No visa. Athens (ATH) is easily reached worldwide. Daily flights from/to Aktion Airport in Preveza (PVK) or direct charters from a few European cities. It's 5h drive from Athens. Many companies link Italy and Greece year round. Best is Bari or Brindisi to Corfù, Igoumenitsa (8h from Brindisi) and Patrasso. Parga is 47km (29mi) from Igoumenitsa.

Getting Around – It's only 62km (39mi) from Parga to Preveza, a mere 45min drive along the E55. Inland roads are slow. The Greek public transport system (KTEL) has daily buses which link Athens, Patra, Thessaloniki as well as nearby towns like Preveza, Arta, Ioannina and Igoumenitsa to Parga. Rental cars cost about $50/day. Driving and parking in winter is easy.

Lodging and Food – During July/August, accommodation is tight but domatios can be found on the hill near Kastro, ranging from $45-65/pax. Domatio owners usually meet the buses and offer their lodgings. In winter, it's cheaper and super easy. There are also three camp sites nearby. Greek food is delicious, expect $8-20 for a meal in a small restaurant.

WEATHER STATISTICS	J/F	M/A	M/J	J/A	S/O	N/D
total rainfall (mm)	133	81	24	15	114	179
consistency (days/mth)	12	8	4	3	9	14
min temp (°C)	6	9	18	23	17	10
max temp (°C)	14	18	28	33	27	17

Weather – The climate in Greece is typically Mediterranean, but each area has its own unique micro-climate and weather forecast. The weather in Western Greece, particularly in the coastal regions of Epirus (Ipeiros) and the Ionian Islands is mild and characterized by relative humidity. Summers are hot, while winters are temperate and enjoyable. Rainfall in this area of Greece is frequent (average rainfall 1094mm, among the highest in Greece), which accounts for its lush and wild vegetation. Due to its alpine nature, it gets colder away from the coast. The Mistro wind in summer is not as strong as Meltemi in the Aegean Sea, but is responsible for cooling down summer temps when the hopes of good surf is almost nil. In winter, the water can get down to 14°C (58°F) with the potential for high wind-chill factor.

Nature and Culture – In Preveza, savour genuine local delicacies at the dozens of small tavernas that line the narrow streets. Ioanina is built on the shores of lake Pamvotida and is the largest and prettiest city in Epirus, with old buildings, narrow streets and natural charms. Don't miss Perama's famous cave and the Mouzakei wax museum. Visit famous Greek temples. Drink some ouzo.

Hazards and Hassles – The beaches in summer are packed with thousands of sun-worshipping tourists. Even if waves break, you will have trouble not injuring swimmers. In winter, weather can be a bit chilly and wet. Waves and locals are mellow but beware with main storms. Driving in Athens can be intense.

Handy Hints – Frozen Wave Surfshop only in Athens at Neratziotissa Mall. Bring a longboard or a wider, thicker board to compensate for lack of power. Sell boards to the locals when leaving. Greek has a different alphabet – it's hard to read the road signs when driving.

but underwater topography is not that great and spots are far from each other. The countless Greek islands of the Aegean Sea experience a strong N wind known as the "Meltemi" in summer, whipping up many rideable waves on islands like Chis, Kos, Naxos, Rhodos or Thinos. From Athens, it's a straight shot to Peloponisos, which is exposed on both sides. However, it's the coast of Epirus, right below Albania, that gets both S swells from the Ionian Sea as well as NW swells from the southern Adriatic Sea, which combined with the highest density of quality surf spots, make this region Greek surf central. In 2005, *Surfing Magazine* published Poseidon Adventure: A Greek Surf Odyssey with Joe Curren, Mike Todd and Ben Bourgeois showcasing the surf potential. Italian and French surfers are starting to make the trip there when winter storms coincide with cheap air tickets, joining the growing number of locals riding some decent quality lefts.

The Greek name Epirus signifies mainland, to distinguish it from the Ionian islands like Kephalonia. Parga is a cosy little town with a beach, small harbour and narrow alleys that climb steeply up the hillside. In summer, it's packed with tourists but SW storms produce one of the most scenic lefts in the Med, **Kastro**. Waves wrap around the cliffs and jack up a bit to give extra power, making it a regular contest site. It can get crowded but wave sharing and a really friendly vibe is the norm in Greece. **Krioneri Beach** has a rocky left and **Panagis Island** is a 200m paddle for softer lefts in the waist to chest high range. On the north side of a deep, scalloped bay, **Amoudia Rights** break off the headland over sand, on SW swells and E winds. When short fetch, short duration NW swells hit, **Amoudia Left** is the place to check. A really long sandbank forms a fun pointbreak style left off the rivermouth jetty and it works in onshore NW winds. **Kerentza** is well protected from most winds and is usually uncrowded when a decent swell gets the rights working. Long and wide, **Loutsa Beach** is a sandy residential area and probably the most consistent beachbreak in Epirus. Picks up S-NW swells and it has easy parking and beach access in winter. Lygia could be the other town to hang out since there are 4 spots nearby. **Teris Point** shelters some average beachbreaks that usually line-up into rights during S-W swells. **Lygia** main beach and **Little Bay** are both ideal for longboards or beginners, hosting small mushy waves in any onshore windchop from the S or N. **The Reef** is the best wave in the area, often uncrowded with hollow sections over an urchin infested reef during SW-W swells and an E wind. Check the rivermouth rights at **Kattouristra**, but be aware the

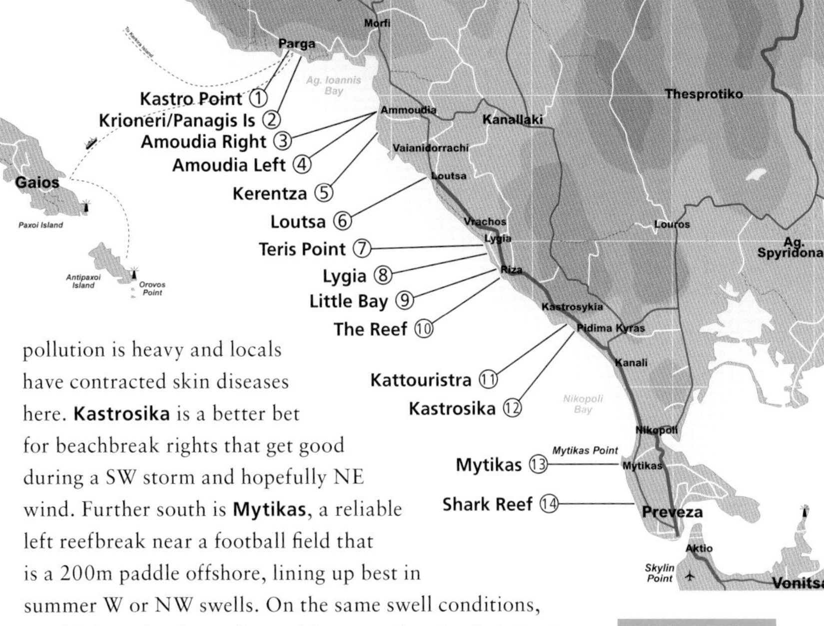

pollution is heavy and locals have contracted skin diseases here. **Kastrosika** is a better bet for beachbreak rights that get good during a SW storm and hopefully NE wind. Further south is **Mytikas**, a reliable left reefbreak near a football field that is a 200m paddle offshore, lining up best in summer W or NW swells. On the same swell conditions, good lefts unload on a flat urchin covered reef called **Shark Reef**, because the Preveza fishermen have caught some "men in grey suits" here.

SURF STATISTICS			
Spot	Size	Btm	Type
①			
②			
③			
④			
⑤			
⑥			
⑦			
⑧			
⑨			
⑩			
⑪			
⑫			
⑬			
⑭			

Amoudia Left

In Greece, generally speaking, S swells happen in winter and N swells happen in summer. Crete would be the only island to score both swell directions, making the best of the Libyan basin swells coming from the south. For the Greek islands, Meltemi N winds blow the strongest between June and September peaking July-August and creating excellent windsurf & kite conditions as well as 2-5ft (0.6-1.5m) onshore waves, although winter can also produce strong northern fetches. SW winds produce the longer period swells with 12-20ft (4-6m) seas in winter, being able to wrap into sheltered spots like Kastro at around headhigh. Swells can last 2-3 days when the situation is perfect but short-lived, 1 day swells are the norm, so stay alert. Epirus gets more offshore N-NE winds than any other region, blowing down from the alpine mountains, especially in winter. That's when the beachbreaks like Loutsa or Amoudia or the reefs like Lygia or Mytikas get clean and totally rideable. No tides in the Med!

SURF STATISTICS	J F	M A	M J	J A	S O	N D
dominant swell	SW-NW	SW-NW	W-NW	W-NW	SW-NW	SW-NW
swell size (ft)	2	1-2	0-1	0-1	1	2
consistency (%)	40	20	5	5	20	40
dominant wind	W-N	W-N	W-N	NW-N	NW-NE	W-N
average force	F4	F4	F3	F3-F4	F3-F4	F4
consistency (%)	46	50	60	62	55	43
water temp.(°C)	15	16	20	24	23	19
wetsuit						

Loutsa

170. Southwest Black Sea

Kalesi Reef

ALL PHOTOS YEP

Summary
+ 2 different swell directions
+ No tides
+ Totally virgin
+ Scenic coastal road
+ Istanbul, culture and snow resorts

– Inconsistent, short-lived swells
– Gutless small waves
– Cold and wet winter climate
– Long drives
– Lack of tourist infrastructure

The Black Sea is encircled by Bulgaria, Ukraine, Russia, Georgia and Turkey, with Istanbul straddling the narrow Bosphorus strait and therefore both the continents of Europe and Asia. There's a huge contrast between this bustling capital city and the rural Turkish coastline, where along the 'Kara Deniz' coastline, most families own just a tractor, and the roads are almost entirely clear. Turkey is one of the few surfing destinations where you actually surf in semi-fresh water, which greatly reduces buoyancy. Saltwater comes from the Mediterranean via the Bosphorus and the Sea of Marmara, whilst freshwater pours in from the bordering countries. Like bore-riders and lake surfers the world over, adjust your board accordingly. The winding coastal road from Erikli to Sinop reveals vast potential for untouched, empty waves.

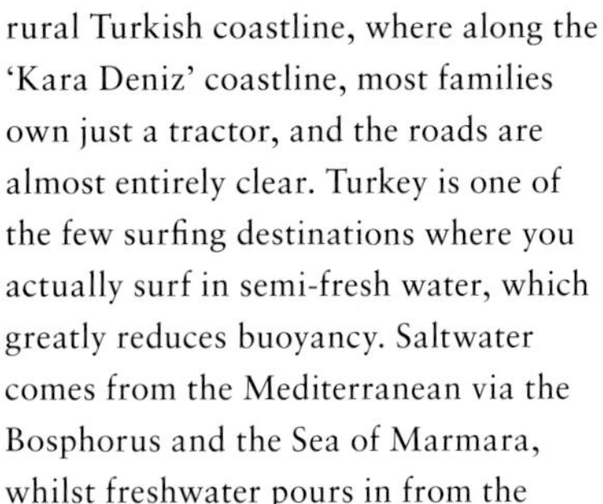

Boat Shed

Yalova Ferry Rights, Sea of Marmara

TRAVEL INFORMATION

Population: 70.5M
Coastline: Black Sea 1,595km (990mi)
Contests: None
Other Resources:
sinopetours.com
surfturkiye.com
guidetoturkey.com

Getting There – No visa needed. As a busy tourist hub, Istanbul (IST) is easy and fairly cheap to reach from Europe and Asia. It's 700kms (430mi) to Sinop, about an 8h drive or fly to Samsun (SSX), 1h east of Sinop but car rentals will be more expensive. Istanbul-Sinop ferry leaves 3 times weekly but not in winter. Igneada is a 4h drive from Istanbul, Kylios 45min.

Getting Around – Driving from one spot to another can take several hours and hopping from the NE to the exposed NW coast can take a day. Winding coastal roads, despite being slow, are super scenic and not busy. The main highway from Istanbul to Kastamonu is efficient. Beware of icy roads in the mountains. Driving in Istanbul itself is a bit mad. Petrol is also not cheap.

Lodging and Food – The best hotels in coastal towns won't cost more than $30 for a double, like Kasim in Sinop. Staying in minor seaside resorts off-season will be a problem, with only cheap basic rooms to rent. Food is rich and varied, and everyone drinks tea. Expect to pay $8 for a meal. Beer is for sale in Tekel shops. Avoid Ramadan time.

WEATHER STATISTICS	J/F	M/A	M/J	J/A	S/O	N/D
total rainfall (mm)	70	65	42	35	71	87
consistency (days/mth)	10	10	7	4	7	9
min temp (°C)	3	5	14	18	14	7
max temp (°C)	10	14	21	26	23	15

Weather – Being located halfway between the Mediterranean and the Russian continental mass, Turkey gets extreme variations of temperature. A central mountain range running parallel to the coast enhances this phenomenon. The Black Sea coast receives the greatest amount of rainfall, around 1,300mm (52in) a year, and is wetter in winter than summer and more severe the further east you go. Because of a steep mountainous coastline, sun exposure can be very different from one spot to another. Temps get chilly in winter down to 5-15°C (41-59°F), whilst the weather can be pleasantly warm from 15-25°C (59-77°F) in summer. Transition months (Oct-Nov, April-May) are probably the best months to visit. There is snow on interior roads from Nov to April. Water gets down to 6-7°C (43-45°F), especially close to rivermouths.

Nature and Culture – In autumn, the coastline is splendid with beautiful forests and virgin coast, especially between Amasra and Sinop. During flat spells, go snowboarding in nearby Kartalkaya, Uludag or Ilgaz. Towns like Safranbolu or Amasra have a great feel to them, and Istanbul is a trip of its own. Try ferryboat rides in Yalova or Bandirma, and visit the Prince's islands.

Hazards and Hassles – Driving can be sketchy on icy and snowy roads, and Istanbul traffic is a bit mad. Turkey is a tourist-friendly destination. Beware of hypothermia if you surf on windy, cold days. Some pollution problems are a possibility in major coastal towns. Swells are short-lived and require a degree of forecasting skill.

Handy Hints – The Aegean and Mediterranean Sea both have coastal resorts with wind/kite surfing centres like Bodrum or Alacati, but no surfing equipment is available. Could be a good trip for a couple. Don't miss the big Bazar markets and the Mosque in Istanbul. Learn some Turkish, it's not too difficult. You cannot access Bulgaria in a rental car. Take a 5mm fullsuit, boots, hood and gloves.

Near the town of Igneada, **Erikli** is one of the better waves in the Thrace region, a shallow rivermouth bar with short, thick rights and longer lefts. Heading west are a number of large beaches and rivermouths. These include **Kastro**, an exposed beachbreak, with a rivermouth and rocky headland. Many of the beaches in this region are inaccessible without a 4WD, although some are protected by jetties and have good access. Heading east beyond Bartin, **Bockoi Plaji** is large beach with multiple set-ups. The next surf spot is one of the gems of the region, located near an ancient **Zeus Temple** and the village of Kapisutu. A right point faces a rivermouth sheltered by a grey granite cliff, with a punchy beachbreak in the middle of the bay and good lefts on the west side of the cove. The drive from here to Sinop along the winding coast road makes an awesome road trip with a good swell running. The next stretch of coast offers potential for pointbreaks such as those at Ayancik, Turkeli, Hardi and Cayustlu to collect N swells. **Rivermouth Jetties** offer black sand beachbreak as you approach Cide, with **Yali Restaurant** offering beachbreak and potential for a right pointbreak. The next spot, **Hardi**, is a long lefthand pointbreak with several sections that needs a NNW swell to fire. **Hotel Touristik**, is another pointbreak, this time a righthander with three distinctive sections. After the exposed cobblestone lefts of **Crane Beach**, a excellent left pointbreak known as **Oluza River** can be seen from the main 57-53 road. **Boat Shed**, located further towards Sinop, is a swell-puller that closes out easily in a scenic cove with a single boat shed. Nearby **Farmland**, a fast, ledgy right most suited to bodyboarding, is accessible via a dirt track. There's also a long beach with a quality peak in the corner sheltered from N winds. The coast then extends to Ince Burun, which is too steep and rocky to create any good waves. This whole coastline can become hard to access after heavy rain. Sinop, located about 700km (430mi) from Istanbul, is a double-sided peninsula and one of the best areas to look for waves. The north side of the city is home to several reefs that can fire occasionally when decent NW swells hit. The beachbreak at **Kalesi Plaji** can be hollow and fast but the left boulder reef is even better with a clear paddling channel and a 4,000 year-old castle in sight. The lefts of **Kalesi Reef** are quite consistent but need a bigger swell to break clear of the rocks. **Gerze** holds short rights on a pebble headland that needs rare NE swell to break alongside 1km of pebble beachbreak. South and east from Sinop, the north-facing coastline collects the most swell in the Black Sea.

Kalesi Plaji

SURF STATISTICS			
Spot	Size	Btm	Type
1	4/1		
2	4/1		
3	4/1		
4	6/1		
5	4/1		
6	4/2		
7	4/2		
8	4/2		
9	6/2		
10	6/2		
11	4/1		
12	6/1		
13	6/1		
14	6/2		
15	4/2		

The Black Sea is hit by strong winter storms with a number of different fetches, due to the thermal differences between the Turkish mountains and the flat plains of the Northern Ukraine. The Black Sea is 600km (370mi) from east to west and 300km (180mi) north to south, with a prevailing NE wind blowing in its western part. This fetch is the most reliable swell-producer for western Turkey, as well as for Bulgaria. This stretch of coast receives 3-6ft (1-2m) waves during the storms, with 1-3ft (0.3-1m) clean surf in their aftermath. The rocky coastline around Sinop has better setups that make more of the swell, and more potential for offshore winds. The 800km (500mi) fetch extending east to Georgia has better potential for long-range swell, but storm activity is less likely and the weather is wetter. October through to March is the best season, but early winter has the mildest water temperatures. Tides in the region are not significant.

SURF STATISTICS	J F	M A	M J	J A	S O	N D
dominant swell	NW-NE	NW-NE	NW-NE	NW-NE	NW-NE	NW-NE
swell size (ft)	3	1-2	1	1-2	2	2-3
consistency (%)	30	20	10	15	20	30
dominant wind	E-NE	E-NE	E-NE	NE-E	NE-E	E-NE
average force	F4	F3-F4	F3	F3	F4	F4
consistency (%)	51	59	62	38	46	55
water temp.(°C)	7	9	17	24	20	13
wetsuit						

Kapisuyu Rights

Stricken by war and upheaval, many West African countries have been off the surf map for decades. In Liberia, there's a new government, new hope and new waves like Cotton Trees to embrace.

Africa

JOHN CALLAHAN/TROPICALPIX

Surf Culture

Africa presents a gargantuan coastline for surfing, but for the first half of the 20th century, only a handful of South Africans had paddled out, following Aussie surf champion Charles "Snow" MacAlister's 1928 demo. Durban lifeguards started catching waves on triple overhead, impossibly heavy, solid wood rescue boards just before WW2. By 1947, a core of watermen adept at swimming, diving and spearfishing were riding Blake-esque hollow paddleboards, covered in canvas instead of ply. Over in Cape Town, crayfish diver and "father of South African surfing" John Whitmore built the first lightweight board in 1954 from polystyrene, PVA glue, muslin and polyester resin. Subsequent liaisons with Dick Metz and Grubby Clark saw Whitmore import Clark Foam urethane blanks and launch SA's first large scale surfboard manufacturing. He pioneered many of the famous breaks including Elands, Mossel and Buffalo Bays, Port Elizabeth and East London, plus he told some Cape Town buddies there were killer waves at Jeffries Bay. Whitmore was instrumental in helping the Endless Summer crew discover Cape St Francis, which put the country on the world surf map. Surfriders Associations and National Championships were formed in '65 and in 1967, touring Aussies previewed the McTavish vee bottomed boards, heralding the beginning of the performance era. Meanwhile, in Morocco, US servicemen were getting to grips with the waves around Mehdiya from as early as 1954, but it wasn't until 1964 that French ex-pats encouraged locals like Mamoune to join them. The discovery of Anchor Point created a so called hippy trail, attracting surfers beyond Hendrix's drug crazed commune at Essaouira, and providing the ultimate winter hang-out for chilled-out Europeans. 1963 saw *Endless Summer* surfers Mike Hynson and Robert August credited with first surfer status in Senegal, Ghana and Nigeria, but it wasn't until Kevin Naughton and Craig Peterson explored the wilds of West Africa 11 years later that countries like Cote de Ivoire and Liberia were added. During a two month stint of gorging themselves on Robertsport's "best lefts in Africa", the government accused them of spying for the CIA and sending coded signals to a submarine through the movement of their turns on a wave! Randy Rarick was the first to ride the long lefts of Angola in 1974 and he continues to blaze trails across the African continent, visiting Sao Tome, Ghana, Liberia, and Kenya to name just a few. The seventies catapulted South Africa into becoming a surfing superpower as Shaun Tomson wowed the world with his barrel riding prowess, contests were held all over the country and the surf industry emerged to service a burgeoning local market. The '80s saw mainly French ex-pats realise the surf potential in various war-torn, ex-colonial states like Congo or the voodoo beachbreaks of Togo and Benin. Namibia was kept off limits by the diamond mining cartels, afraid that surfers would find rocks on the beach and hide them in their boards. Mozambique's disastrous civil war, landmines, floods and famine kept the curious at bay until the early nineties when Tom Curren and Shane Beschen discovered some fine right points. Only since the turn of the century have surfers been bothered to explore the Mediterranean coasts of Tunisia and Egypt and even today, large unexplored tracts of coast remain in Libya, Algeria, Western Sahara, Mauritania, Cape Verde, Guinea Bissau, Guinea, Sierra Leone, Nigeria, Cameroon, Gabon, Angola, Mozambique, Tanzania and just about all of Somalia.

JOHN CALLAHAN/TROPICALPIX

São Tomé is one of the few African countries with a history of wave-riding on wooden bellyboards. Local lad explores his roots, modern style.

Today

South Africa was the cradle and is still the powerhouse of surfing on the African continent. John Whitmore's early experiments with foam and then setting up foam blank blowing laid the foundations for a healthy board-building fraternity, with names like Spider Murphy building a solid reputation world-wide. Billabong and Quicksilver set up shop in the '80s, vying for the fashion souls and rubber sales of the 3rd largest surfing community in the world, sponsoring part of the surf contest boom that took place right around the country. 30 years of the Gunston 500 made it the world's longest running professional event, before Mr Price took over sponsorship and it is now one of the three Durban WQS events and the only African women's event. J-Bay is usually at the top of the WCT competitors favourite stops shortlist, allowing the world's best to surf the world's greatest right point with only one other person out. The surf media have also managed a long 32 year unbroken history with SA's flagship mag, *Zigzag*. The global trend of flourishing surf schools rings true, especially in summer, despite the low water temps around most of the coastline. Banner breaks are often dominated by un-sharing locals and J-Bay in particular has had a local enforcer attitude installed in the face of dangerously escalating crowd pressure. Emerging surf nations like Morocco have seen a rise in localism as indigenous and ex-pat crews try to lay claim to a resource that has long been plundered by visitors alone. Confrontation can be easily avoided considering how many quality waves this vast continent harbours. Just keep an eye out for the true locals cruising these waters and always surf with a friend.....

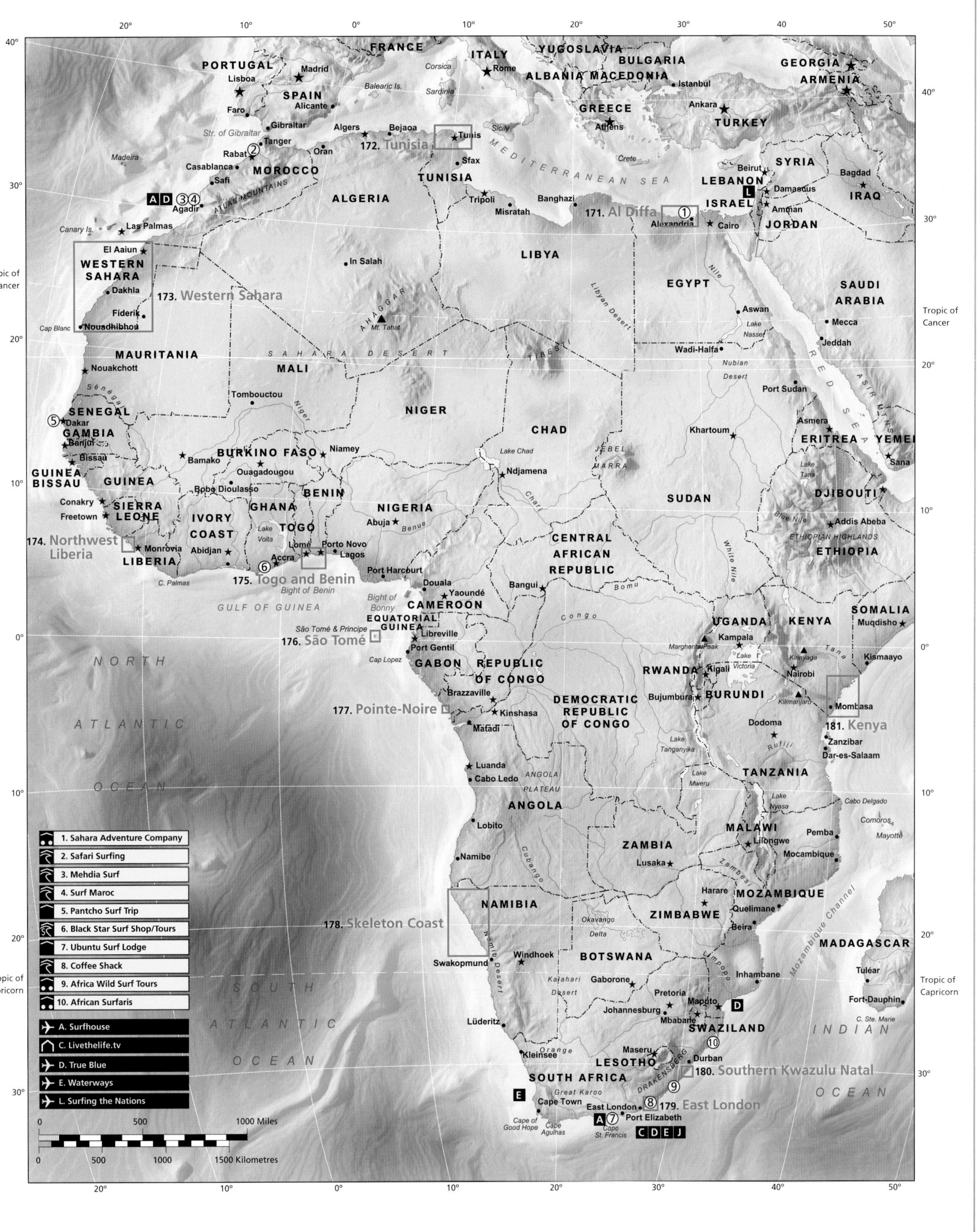

171. Al Diffa
172. Tunisia
173. Western Sahara
174. Northwest Liberia
175. Togo and Benin
176. São Tomé
177. Pointe-Noire
178. Skeleton Coast
179. East London
180. Southern Kwazulu Natal
181. Kenya
1. Sahara Adventure Company
2. Safari Surfing
3. Mehdia Surf
4. Surf Maroc
5. Pantcho Surf Trip
6. Black Star Surf Shop/Tours
7. Ubuntu Surf Lodge
8. Coffee Shack
9. Africa Wild Surf Tours
10. African Surfaris
A. Surfhouse
C. Livethelife.tv
D. True Blue
E. Waterways
L. Surfing the Nations
0 500 1000 Miles
0 500 1000 1500 Kilometres

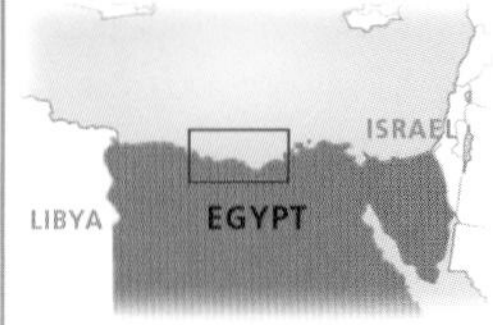

171. Al Diffa

Alexandria

Summary
+ Long fetch for Med
+ Ideal NW exposure
+ Quality Agibe left
+ Great tourist attractions
+ Ancient history

– Inconsistent swells
– Often windy and mushy
– Overdeveloped coastline in Alex
– Hassles with coastguard
– Heavy urban traffic

In 332 BC, Alexander the Great gave his name to what would become a prominent cultural, intellectual and political metropolis referred to as 'the shining pearl of the Mediterranean'. Alexandria is the second largest city and the chief port of Egypt, located on the northwest fringe of the Nile Delta and stands on the frontier between the lush, irrigated lands and the outskirts of the Sahara. The evolution of surfing in and around the city has been slow, and there remains only a tiny population of local surfers who have bought their boards off travelling Aussies and expats over the last decade or so. With a much larger surfing population in neighbouring Israel, just over the Gaza Strip, there may only be 60 rideable days a year but Alexandria boasts 30km of corniche up to 10 lanes wide, curving along a coast ideally exposed to the NW, providing a perfect view of the small, empty waves hitting numerous beaches and reefs.

YEP

YEP

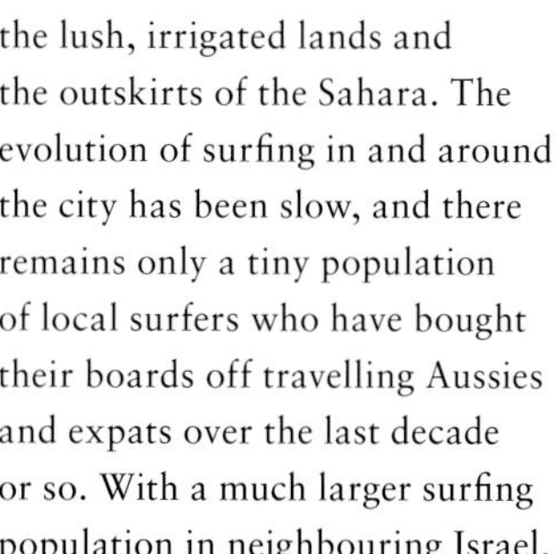

TRAVEL INFORMATION

Population: 79m
Alexandria 4m
Coastline:
500km (310mi)
Time Zone: GMT +2
Contests: None
Other Resources:
egypt-board-riding.com
saharaadventure company.com
Video:
Sipping Jetstreams

Getting There – Although there are flights to Alexandria (ALY), most flights will go to Cairo (CAI). Cheap package deals to the Red Sea and Nile River generally land too far away. Most visitors won't need a visa but will pay a small fee upon arrival ($20 for USA visitors). It's a 3h drive from Cairo to Alex. Driving through Cairo can be hectic during rush hours.

Getting Around – Car rental is fairly expensive ($60/day) and traffic can be intense, so trust Adham Coumpound Hotel services. They will pick up you at the airport and arrange your trips to Alexandria because they're surfers! It's 20min from Alex Corniche but you won't be missing the swell because of Internet. Large jeeps help to cruise the sandy areas.

Weather – Egypt receives fewer than 80mm (3.2in) of rain annually in most areas. Most rain falls along the coast, but even the wettest area around Alexandria does not exceed 200mm (8in). Alexandria itself has relatively high humidity, but sea breezes help keep the moisture down to a comfortable level. A phenomenon of the Egyptian climate is the hot spring E wind, known as the khamsin. It usually arrives in April but occasionally blows in March and May. The winds form into small but vigorous low-pressure areas in the Isthmus of Suez and sweep across the northern coast of Africa. Unobstructed by geographical features, the winds reach high velocities and carry great amounts of sand and dust from the desert. These sandstorms, often accompanied by winds of up to 140km/h (87mi/h), can cause temps to rise as much as 20°C in two hours. Take a light fullsuit in winter, mainly because of the wind chill.

WEATHER STATISTICS	J/F	M/A	M/J	J/A	S/O	N/D
total rainfall (mm)	35	65	0	0	3	44
consistency (days/mth)	6	2	0	0	1	5
min temp (°C)	11	14	19	23	21	15
max temp (°C)	19	22	27	30	29	23

Lodging and Food – Adham Compound hotel has nice rooms with sports facilities. You could stay on the Corniche hotels, but it is expensive and getting out of Alex can be tricky. Food is cheap and varied, with seafood and Mediterranean cooking.

Nature and Culture – It is quite possible that you won't surf every day, so make the most of the different activities. Don't miss the Great Sea of Sands at Siwa oasis, about 6h from Alex. Snowboard or buggy on the dunes! Visit the Library or Montazah castle in Alex or check out underwater temples scuba diving. The Gizeh pyramids near Cairo are only 3h away.

Hazards and Hassles – Egypt is a tourist friendly country and safety is fine but walking the streets is inadvisable in Alex or Cairo. The sea in summer can be really polluted by the Nile, but the surf happens in winter and the water is cleaner. Some beach access can be private and coastguards in winter may try to arrest surfers.

Handy Hints – There are very few local surfers, so everyone will enjoy sharing waves. Take all gear with you and plan to leave things behind or sell them when you leave. The Teymour brothers are surfers at Sahara Adventure Company and they will make sure you make the most of your stay in Alexandria.

Furthest west past Marsa Matruh is **Agiba Cove**, a perfect left that breaks over shallow and sharp reef. Unfortunately, this fjord-like bay needs a big swell to break up to shoulder high. **Agiba Beach** is a beautiful, turquoise-blue beachbreak that picks up all available swell and holds some of the biggest waves in the country. Nearby **Cleopatra Beach** can also offer up various rocky beachbreaks and a left point near the famous rock formation called Cleopatra's Bath. The coastal roads from here to Alexandria are often controlled by soldiers and can prove difficult to access. There are a variety of fast, sand and sandstone bottom breaks along the **Mersa Baghush** stretch of coast in NW swells, but there is no access to the exposed promontory of Ras El Hekma where there is a presidential residence. **Ghazala Bay** has deep water just offshore, so can pack some punch, but needs a large swell due to its easterly aspect. **Ras Gibeisa** is a real swell-puller, with a great left pointbreak possible and perfect longboard waves when small, however the coastguard can deny access. **Marakha** is another sand and sandstone break, with clean waves breaking opposite the Hilton. Between Marakha and **Sidi Krier**, over 30 access

Agiba Cove

STUART BUTLER

roads lead to large hotel complexes with Mediterranean blue beachbreaks, many of which are closeouts. Around **El Agamy** are a number of beach towns with unlimited beachbreak options; one good tip is the old WW2 jetty by the Bianky coastguard station. **Library**, so called because of its proximity to the oldest library in the world, is one of the best beachbreaks around Alexandria, consistent and capable of holding some of the largest surfable waves in Egypt. Watch out for a current that flows east; getting trapped on a rocky shoreline with no exit is the danger. Library is one of the only beaches where you are likely to encounter other surfers. Alexandria itself has a coastal road that provides good access to a number of different waves. The actual access to the beaches is

Agiba Cove

STUART BUTLER

harder to find, and some charge a small fee. **Stanley Bridge**, a tourist highlight, has a decent set up with both rights and lefts. However, concrete in the water and a police presence make actually surfing here unlikely. **Sidi Bishr** is the most reliable beach in Alex, with surprisingly consistent sets during a swell. Facing the Ramada hotel, the break is open to all swell and wind, and therefore can become choppy. Parking can be tricky. A second **Cleopatra Beach**, accessible from the Montazah Castle Resort, has a potential righthand point; this is dangerous when stormy so best in a clean NW swell. At the east end of the Maamoura resort town, **El Farasa** is a shifty beachbreak with vicious currents.

SURF STATISTICS			
Spot	Size	Btm	Type
①	6/2		
②	8/1		
③	6/1		
④	6/1		
⑤	4/1		
⑥	4/1		
⑦	6/1		
⑧	6/1		
⑨	6/1		
⑩	8/1		
⑪	6/3		
⑫	6/1		
⑬	6/2		
⑭	4/1		

The 'Calendar of Storms' – a document based on 2000 years of experience by fishermen – indicates that between November 20th and June 18th there are 19 storms with 55 days of onshore winds. The majority of these storms occur in December, January, February and March. Over the winter, these cold fronts drive waves from the W or NW. The length of the eastern Med basin allows a potential fetch of 1500km from Sicily to Egypt so there can be 12-36h of clean offshore swell before the storms hit the coast. During the storm, it's mostly out-of-control except for the east-facing spots that gather a bit of swell and are still surfable with strong sideshore winds. During summer, the Greek "Meltem" blows a constant NNW wind over the Aegean Sea, which produces regular onshore 1-2ft (0.3-0.6m) conditions at the beachbreaks. There is probably 60 days of decent surf at the Corniche spots. Because of the absence of tides, it's fairly easy to be in the right place at the right time.

SURF STATISTICS	J F	M A	M J	J A	S O	N D
dominant swell	W-NW	W-NW	NW-N	NW-N	W-NW	W-NW
swell size (ft)	1-2	1-2	0	1	1	1-2
consistency (%)	40	30	10	20	30	40
dominant wind	SW-NW	W-N	W-N	W-NW	W-N	W-N
average force	F4	F3-F4	F3	F3-F4	F3-F4	F3-F4
consistency (%)	55	58	72	77	75	48
water temp.(°C)	17	18	22	26	25	21
wetsuit						

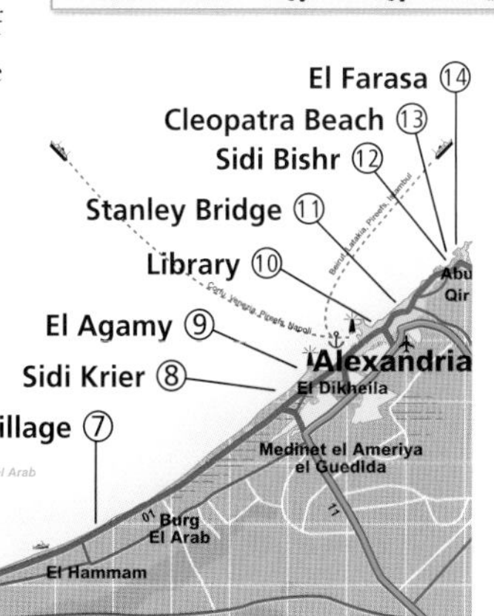

172. Tunisia

Cap Mérou

ALL PHOTOS YEP

Summary
+ High Med consistency
+ Wide swell window
+ Virgin pointbreaks and reefs
+ Cheap tourist destination
+ Easy access

– Short-lived swells
– Chilly winter weather
– Jellyfish plagues
– Rough north coast roads
– Very quiet in winter

When in need of a cheap escape from Europe, surfers traditionally go to Morocco or the Canaries, ignoring the Mediterranean Sea entirely. Tunisia, with cheap flights and 120 days of Mistral wind a year, offers a viable alternative destination with fairly consistent surf. Although Tunisia has been barely surfed for years, the wide swell exposure of the north coast and the potential for numerous lefts to break under the prevailing winter wind is attracting more French and Italian surfers. From the Algerian border to Ras Sidi Alik Mekki in the Bizerte area, the Tunisian coastline is characterised by a number of capes (such as Cape Zebib and Cape Serrat), rocky shorelines with sandy rivermouth beaches, and alluvial plains.

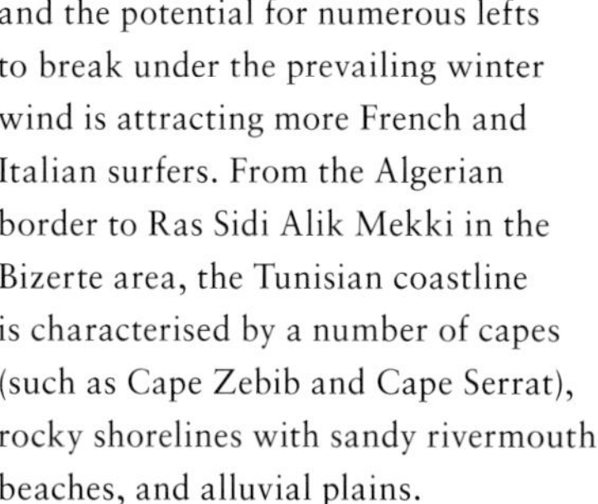

Fort Génois

Cap Méduse

In the Tabarka area, the lefts at the **Amphithéâtre de la Mer** on the Cite Larmel side are a consistent option, particularly as they are side/offshore in a NW wind. The next break heading east is a right pointbreak located beneath a magnificent Genoese fortress. Set at the end of a spectacular peninsula, **Fort Génois** needs size to clear the

TRAVEL INFORMATION

Population: 530,000 Bizerte
Coastline: 1300km (800mi)
Contests: none
Other Resources:
meteosim.com/waves/hs.html
meteotunisie.com

WEATHER STATISTICS	J/F	M/A	M/J	J/A	S/O	N/D
total rainfall (mm)	88	52	18	4	57	91
consistency (days/mth)	14	12	6	2	9	14
min temp (°C)	7	9	15	19	16	9
max temp (°C)	15	19	26	32	27	18

Getting There – Tunisia is popular with European tourists, especially the French. Fly to Tunis (TUN) as the more popular airports of Djerba or Sfax are too far from the surf. Some charter flights land in Tabarka (TBJ) during the peak season. Bizerte and Hammamet are 1h from Tunis, whilst Tabarka is 4-5h drive away. No visa is needed for most visitors.

Getting Around – Although Tabarka may have a concentration of quality spots, Bizerte serves as a better base due to services and proximity to the east coast. The old road from Bizerte to Tabarka is faster (3h) than the new road. Renting a car with Anouar (www.tunisiarentacar.com) costs $215/wk. Fuel is relatively cheap.

Lodging and Food – In winter there is little choice of places to stay, few hotels are open and most seaside guesthouses close. A 3-star hotel in Tabarka or Bizerte by the Corniche would be $30/dble. Nawas Montazah in Tabarka is $40/dble, but it is cheaper to stay in town. Food is good and cheap ($5/meal) but good restaurants on the road are rare.

Weather – Whereas most of Tunisia experiences sub-Saharan climate, with dry warm temperatures all year round, North Tunisia has a Mediterranean climate with wet, mild winters and hot dry summers. Because winter has the best surf, expect a few rainy days requiring winter-like clothing because of the wind chill. The wettest area of Tunisia can receive up to 900mm (36in) of rain. Because of the northern Atlas coastal range, there is a clear difference between Tabarka and Hammamet. More often than not, the lows bringing the surf will bring storms with strong winds and rain, but it won't last long. The water will start to get chilly in December, dropping to 14°C (58°F) in February, requiring a 4/3mm fullsuit. Take an extra wettie for multiple sessions during the same day.

Nature and Culture – In Tabarka, there's golf or scuba diving for red coral, but in the off-season, options shrink to visiting the Genoese fortress or strolling through town. Bizerte is much bigger, with better sightseeing potential, including the double Kasbah near the old harbour. Population is 98% Muslim but pretty tourist friendly, although it is not easy to buy beer.

Hazards and Hassles – The surf is fairly safe unless you hit a rock or wreck. The main problem is little purple jellies called *Pelagica Noctiluca*, which are quite numerous in winter. Bring light gloves and booties to avoid stings. Apart from rare Italian surfers and a handful of locals, there is never a crowd. The roads and towns are safe.

Handy Hints – Take a shortboard and a longboard for the smaller days. Take good walking shoes to walk through muddy fields. Internet facilities are rare and slow. Learn some French to get by at hotels & restaurants. Tabarka is much smaller and quieter than Bizerte.

rocks and clean conditions to reveal its potential, whilst back across the bay, near to Les Aiguilles, a short left also breaks in a solid swell. Along the **Route Touristique**, consistent beachbreak and coffee-rock reef options present themselves, between the hotels and golf course. Easy access to **Barboukech** leads to a beachbreak exposed to NW wind and swell. **Sidi Mechrig** is reached via a 45-minute detour off the main road and as well as ancient ruins, boasts exposed beach and reefbreaks. Driving west towards Bizerte, a 4WD helps access many of the coastal tracks leading to scenic bays like Cap Mérou where a long, hollow, lefthand pointbreak offers one of the best rides in Tunisia. Between Cape Blanc and Cape Bizerte is **La Grotte**, with several lefthand reef options favouring clean conditions, but if a swell is running, head further east for the lefts of **La Corniche**. Driving from Bizerte to La Corniche with a good swell running reveals multiple sectioney lefthanders breaking right by the coastal road. Try the juicy left at Pointe du Daouli next to 'El Bistro' restaurant. It is likely you will be surfing alone here, but unmarked gravel roads offer still more potential for seclusion. East of Bizerte signals a change of landscape, and a vast forest begins following a 20 minute crossing of the canal. The forest hides waves, including **Plage Remel** where three tankers have been shipwrecked. If the waves are clean they can be hollow. If the swell is too much for Corniche, drive eastwards towards Raf-Raf and be sure to check the **Metline Port**, very sheltered from NW winds but usually too small. **Raf-Raf Plage** itself offers powerful rights and an attractive resort village, coastal range and island. Near the city of Tunis and the ancient ruins of Carthage, **Gammart** sometimes has mellow waves, but energy is sapped by the Gulf of Tunis. A straight N swell and NE wind can light up the best right pointbreak in Tunisia, **Cap Méduse**, located near the Korbous ancient thermal station. Further up the cape lies **Sidi Daoud** and more wind exposed reefbreaks. Rounding the headland towards the Kelibia area, the impressive fortress at **El Mansourah** provides access to long, sandy beaches that pull plenty of swell. If an E-SE swell materialises, a drive

Mansourah

down the east coast to Hammamet could be worthwhile, with long, sweeping lefts at **Medina** and more consistent peaks at Nhoza Beach. If in the area with time to spare, also check the reefs at Sousse and Monastir.

Tunisia faces three different masses of water, with the majority of swell provided by the NW Mistral and N Tramontana winds. These strong winds blow down the Mediterranean for over 120 days per year, so this area is more consistent than many realise. Surfing in Tunisia generally involves a day of clean surf before the wind arrives, then finding shelter whilst the storm blows, and chasing gradually cleaner conditions as the swell fades. The Tyrrhenian Sea extends towards Italy, giving a northerly fetch of up to 600km (372mi). The third potential swell-generating body of water is the central Ionian Sea, which can create a SE fetch of up to 800km (496mi) down to Libya. This type of swell rarely lasts beyond 24 hours. Windswells of this nature usually don't carry enough power to create wrap-around waves, so places that are offshore can often be flat. Because Tunisia has tiny tides, if swell and wind come together there are waves all day. However, swells come and go fast, so stay alert to get the best waves.

SURF STATISTICS

Spot	Size	Btm	Type
1	6/2		
2	8/2		
3	8/1		
4	6/1		
5	6/1		
6	8/2		
7	6/2		
8	6/2		
9	4/2		
10	6/2		
11	4/1		
12	6/2		
13	6/2		
14	6/1		
15	4/2		

SURF STATISTICS	J F	M A	M J	J A	S O	N D
dominant swell	W-SE	W-SE	NW-N	NW-N	NW-N	W-SE
swell size (ft)	2-3	2	1	0-1	1-2	2-3
consistency (%)	60	50	30	10	20	60
dominant wind	W-NW	W-NW	W-E	W-E	W-E	W-NW
average force	F5	F4	F3-F4	F3-F4	F3-F4	F4-F5
consistency (%)	48	45	71	69	63	48
water temp.(°C)	14	15	19	24	23	17
wetsuit						

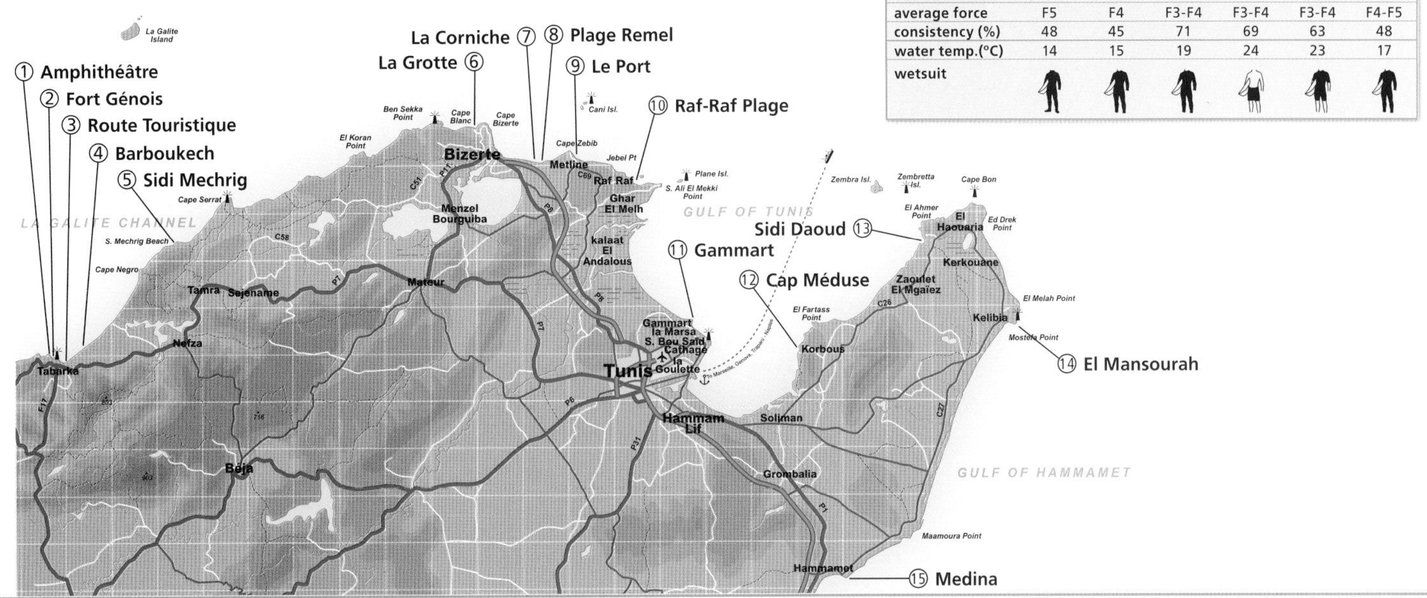

173. Western Sahara

ALL PHOTOS JOHN CALLAHAN/TROPICALPIX

Summary

+ Consistent winter conditions
+ Epic, empty right pointbreaks
+ Kitesurf and fishing hotspot
+ Friendly Saharaoui hospitality
+ Desert beauty and wildlife

– Mostly windy conditions
– Remote surf spots
– Chilly desert conditions
– 4WD rental necessary
– Lack of variety of hotels

Western Sahara is the former Spanish Sahara, a large, lightly populated desert country south of Morocco. When Spain pulled out in 1976, the territory was occupied by troops from Morocco and Mauritania. The Mauritanians withdrew in 1979, and Morocco has occupied all of Western Sahara since then. That annexation is not recognized by any other country and other African countries recognize instead the Republica Saharaoui, organized in exile in Algeria. Presently, Morocco is administering Western Sahara under a 1991 armistice agreement and pending a referendum on the future status of the country to be organized by the United Nations. This referendum has been postponed repeatedly. Security conditions in the country are currently quiet and the coast is open to adventurous foreign tourists.

Tarfaya is last major town in Morocco supporting 4,500 inhabitants but no quality hotel. **Casamar** is a decent beachbreak, facing NW, best on S winds, next to the scenic

TRAVEL INFORMATION

Local Population: 382,617
Coastline: 1,110km (684mi)
Time Zone: GMT
Contests: None
Video:
Les Fils du Pays (2005)
Other Resources:
taxisurf-maroc.com
saharasurfmorocco.com
dakhla-aventure.com
sahararegency.com
sahara-online.net

Getting There – Visa: same as Morocco. Best is to fly Casablanca (CAS) easily accessible from Europe. Then, national Royal Air Maroc flies 3 x wk to Dakhla with a Boeing 737 ($180 return). Régional Air Lines also operates flights. CTM bus company makes daily Agadir/Dakhla (15h, $110 return) or Marakkech/Dakhla (20h, $120). Or drive a rental car from Agadir.

Getting Around – Dakhla is 1200km (745mi) south of Agadir and Laâyoune is mid-way. From Laayoune to Dakhla (542km/336mi), the main road is paved but most spots access require 4WD, usually a Land Rover Santana. Hotels can provide one with driver at $80-90/day. Gas is pretty cheap. It's very easy to get stuck in the soft sand!

Lodging and Food – Try Nagjir in Foum el Oued or Josephina in Al Marsa ($45-59/dble). In Dakhla, best is Sahara Regency 4 star at $120. Cheaper is Dakhla hotel at $30/dble. Lots of new hotels like Bab El Bahar 4 star and Calipau Bay 5 star. Dakhla Attitude and Auberge des Nomades ($260/week) offer efficient tents. Food is a bit pricey at $15 per meal.

WEATHER STATISTICS	J/F	M/A	M/J	J/A	S/O	N/D
total rainfall (mm)	32	20	3	0	115	44
consistency (days/mth)	6	3	2	0	4	7
min temp (°C)	10	12	15	17	16	10
max temp (°C)	20	21	23	25	25	23

Weather – Western Sahara is a hot, dry desert and rain is rare, but flash floods do occur. Cold offshore air currents produce fog and heavy dew. Due to the inability of sand to absorb heat, harsh, cold nights are common. It's quite a moderate climate with temps varying between 18-26°C (64-79°F), heavily influenced by the oceanic trades and the coldish Canary's Current. Low-lying sand dunes cover the territory. The Azores High weakens from September, making the winds lighter and less consistent throughout the winter, when Atlantic lows pass over the Moroccan coast bringing rain fronts and S-SW winds. Take a light fullsuit for January to April and a springsuit the rest of the year. Take booties to avoid cuts from the shells.

Nature and Culture – It's a full on desert with dramatic landscape and not much around apart from a lighthouse and tiny urban areas. Climb Dakhla's 240 steps and get a good view. Many camps are set-up for surf-casters and anglers because the sea is teeming with fish. Kiteboarders love it and Tarfaya/Cap Juby is also the finishing line of "The Dash", a windsurf race from Lanzarote to Tarfaya, 72 nautical miles away (133km/82mi). Lots of birds, some seals. Forget about beers and nightlife.

Hazards and Hassles – No water, no cities, only dunes, dust, sand, strong winds, personnel mines and some military activities. Even at the main spots, you will feel very isolated. Waves aren't particularly powerful, but some reefs are nasty plus beware of sharp shells. Morning wind-chills can feel damned cold. Political situation still unsolved. Currency is Moroccan dirham.

Handy Hints – No surf shop anywhere but a handful of locals. Taxi Surf guide small groups at $180/day or $15/day per person - min 5 days from Agadir. Rent a board for $130/wk and take a course for $40. It's a muslim country, avoid Ramadan time (Sept-Oct until 2012, 10 days earlier each year).

Casamar Fort that protrudes into the ocean. A sketchy desert track leads to **Yoyo**, an excellent right pointbreak at Km25, that's shallow and cylindrical, quite exposed to the winds, but it holds big swells. Over the frontier, 100km (62mi) south is Laâyoune, the main city in the Sahara with 200,000 people. It's another 20km (12mi) to reach the coast and the 11km (7mi) long **La Corniche** of Foum El Oued, a kind of seaside resort with hotels. It's a long beachbreak, best with slack wind, high tide and small swells. Laayoune Beach is the main harbour at **Al Marsa** where 2 big jetties stick out up to 3km and along with several secluded beaches, provide some shelter from N winds. Roy is a right working with small swell while Jo Left holds size and barrels and Margot breaks along a rock spit. 20km (12mi) south of Laayoune is **Zbarat**, a small village, just off the main road with a really good right reefbreak. In **Tarf Noa**, there are reefs near a decent size village and a good right set-up, 4km (2.5mi) north towards Cap Cinq. Boujdour is interesting with it's old lighthouse, harbour and NW-facing Corniche road. **Msdoud** hosts fat, mushy waves over sand and reef, either at the port entrance or along the exposed beach extending north of town. It will take a lot of effort to find **Skaymat** near Garnet Bay, but the long pointbreak rights 2km north of a small farm are worth the effort in bigger swells and N winds. Dakhla is the main city of the Oued Ed-Dahab-Lagouira region plus it's one of the main fishing harbours. Dakhla's unique 37km (23mi) long bay, became the crossroads of kitesurfers from Europe in 2003 and it's been attracting surf-casters for decades, catching giant 45kg/100 pound sea bass! A good 60km (42mi) north of Dakhla is **Tarf Entayreft** or Uad el Cabiat, producing long wrapping rights, offshore in N winds, next to a huge fishing village, that's easy to find. Most of the kiters who stay in the camps (such as Dakhla Attitude) go wave-riding at **Pointe de l'Or**, both north and south sides can be surfed but a 4WD is required to get there. Close to town, **Foum El Bouir** was the site of the Windsurf Challenge 2006, yet a huge harbour development project seriously threatens the future of these very long rights, ideal for longboarders at the base of the cliffs. Right at the tip sits inconsistent **Ponta Negra**, sometimes giving powerful, wedging rights over a sandspit, with full protection from even NW winds. One hour drive south is **Lagtoua**, a killer set-up near a big fishing village where two long, right pointbreaks are sheltered from N winds by tall cliffs. Mauritania operate the east/west military border crossing 10km (6mi) north of the peninsula and Nouadhibou, which is shown on most maps as running north/south. Obtaining a visa in advance is a good idea in order to surf the spots in the abandoned ghost town of **Lagouira**. There are several right points between Faux Cap Blanc and Cap Dubouchage when small, or go further south when the swell gets over 4ft (1.2m). On a proper swell, these rights can be long, fast and flawless. **Cap Blanc** is the southern tip of the peninsula and holds a major shipwreck on the beach, along with a rare, steep-bottomed shorebreak. Rips can be pretty intense despite low swell exposure and minor tidal phases, but it's offshore in the regular NW winds.

The rule of thumb for surf trips to Morocco and Western Sahara is strong winds and small waves in summertime and the reverse in winter. Swells mostly arrive between September and May, with heights of 6ft (2m) quite common and a good chance of 10ft (3m) in the heart of winter, especially if the low pressure system is centrally located in the Atlantic, due west of Portugal. This desert coastline experiences the same trade wind pattern that influences the Canary Islands. Morocco is squeezed between the Azores High and the North African Desert Low, which together create a stable N-NE airflow during the summer months, further strengthened by local land sea thermals and venturi effects, especially around Dakhla. The wind is strongest and most consistent from June to the end of August, with 80% or more chance of Force 6 and often Force 7-8. Dominant direction is between N 350° and N 060°. The average tidal range is 4-5ft (1.2-1.5m), whilst the highest range reaches 6-7ft (1.8-2.1m).

SURF STATISTICS	J F	M A	M J	J A	S O	N D
dominant swell	NW-N	NW-N	NW-N	NW-N	NW-N	NW-N
swell size (ft)	4	3	2	1-2	2-3	4
consistency (%)	70	50	30	20	50	70
dominant wind	N-NE	N-NE	N-NE	N-NE	N-NE	N-NE
average force	F4	F4	F4	F4	F4	F4
consistency (%)	54	68	81	93	71	58
water temp.(°C)	18	18	19	21	22	20
wetsuit						

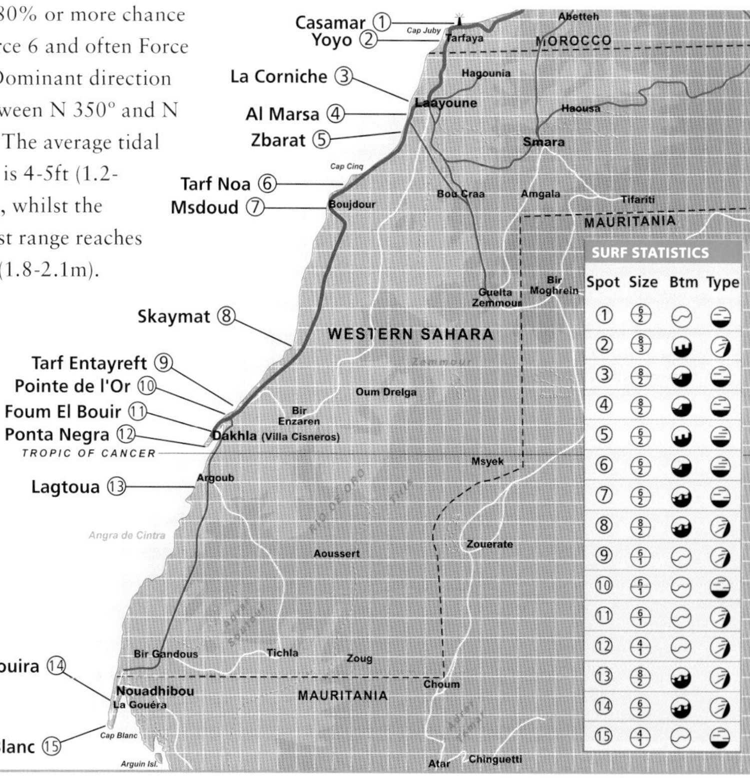

175. Togo and Benin

Lomé-Rivage

STUART BUTLER

Summary
+ Consistent, long range swell
+ No crowds
+ Friendly people
+ Exploration possibilities
+ Voodoo culture

– No epic spots
– Light onshores
– Rain in swell season
– Malaria
– Expensive flights

The West African countries of Togo and Benin are largely off the map for both surfers and travellers. The two tiny nations, home to voodoo and friendly beachbreaks, offer a tropical climate and consistent, uncrowded surf potential. Whilst both destinations are unlikely to warrant a surf trip on the quality of their waves alone, for visitors to neighbouring Ghana, Togo and Benin offer an escape into a unique and magical culture. The Togolese/ Beninese coast is made up of a series of steeply shelving beaches, almost entirely backed by lagoons that themselves sometimes play host to floating villages. The best waves break where a natural or manmade feature creates sandbanks, breaking up the endless shore-pound.

STUART BUTLER

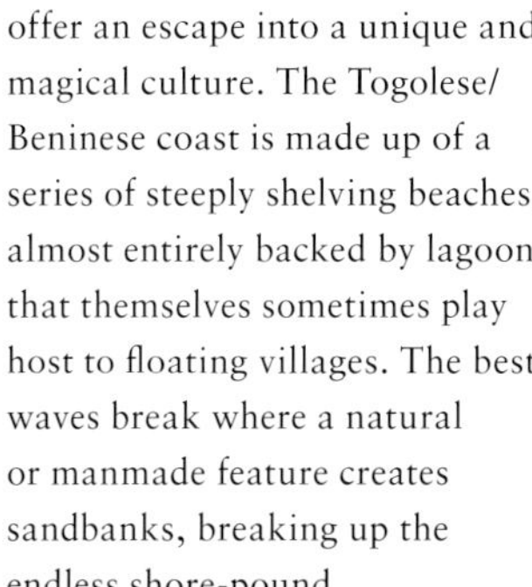

Benin

STUART BUTLER

In the west of Togo, **Lomé-Rivage** is located a couple of kilometres to the east of Lomé centre and may be reached in a taxi. The spot itself usually has decent sandbars held in place by a large jetty. Two other advantages are its exposure to swell and minimal crowds. Visitors should be aware

TRAVEL INFORMATION

Population: 7.5M Benin: 6M Togo
Coastline:
121km (75mi) Benin
56km (35mi) Togo
Contests: none
Other Resources:
oceansurfpublications.co.uk

Getting There – Expensive visas ($60) are required for both countries. Flights are usually costly. Air France and Royal Air Maroc are the most reliable airlines serving Cotonou (COO) and Lomé (LFW). Air Maroc is usually cheaper and more board friendly than Air France. The border crossing between the two countries is painless.

Getting Around – Car hire is not cheap, at around $80/d for the smallest car. It's much easier to just charter a taxi for the day. For city transport, hop on the back of a zemidjam (motorbike taxi), but be warned, they are dangerous at the best of times and treacherous with a surfboard.

Lodging and Food – Every major coastal town has somewhere to stay and standards are, for West Africa, good. Budget at least $20/day for a double room with a/c and a shower. Food is renowned as the best in West Africa, with lots of spicy sauces and plenty of variety. Rat is the local delicacy of the coast. Basic meals don't cost more than $1.

WEATHER STATISTICS	J/F	M/A	M/J	J/A	S/O	N/D
total rainfall (mm)	33	121	310	64	101	36
consistency (days/mth)	2	6	12	5	8	4
min temp (°C)	24	26	23	23	23	24
max temp (°C)	28	28	27	26	27	28

Weather – Bénin and Togo have hot, wet tropical climates, dominated by a strong southwest monsoon between April and October when heavy rainfall (1312mm/52in per year) can be expected every day. Even during the dry season, it still rains frequently near the coast. May-June and October are the rainiest months. Year-round temperature changes little and it's almost always hot. March and April (just before the main rainy season breaks) can be almost unbearably hot and humid, but it's worse inland than on the coast. The Harmattan is a strong, very warm and dusty wind that blows out of the desert between December and February. It makes perfect offshore conditions for the surf but swell is rare at this time of year. Dominant winds are SW and the water warm enough for boardies year-round.

Nature and Culture – Any trip is likely to leave the traveller with tales of encounters with the supernatural. The beautiful towns of Ouidah, Porto Novo and Anécho are all Voodoo centres, with plenty to experience. Don't miss the fetish markets of Cotonou and Lomé.

Hazards and Hassles – Most trips are trouble free. Pollution around Cotonou and Lomé is a problem and there have been cases of robbery and worse on both city centre beaches. There is some political tension in Togo. Bénin is one of the safest countries in Africa. Malaria is a major problem in both countries.

Handy Hints – Take everything you need as there is no surf industry whatsoever. A standard day-to-day beachbreak board is perfect and don't forget sunscreen and plenty of wax. The Capital city of Benin is Porto Novo, not Cotonou.

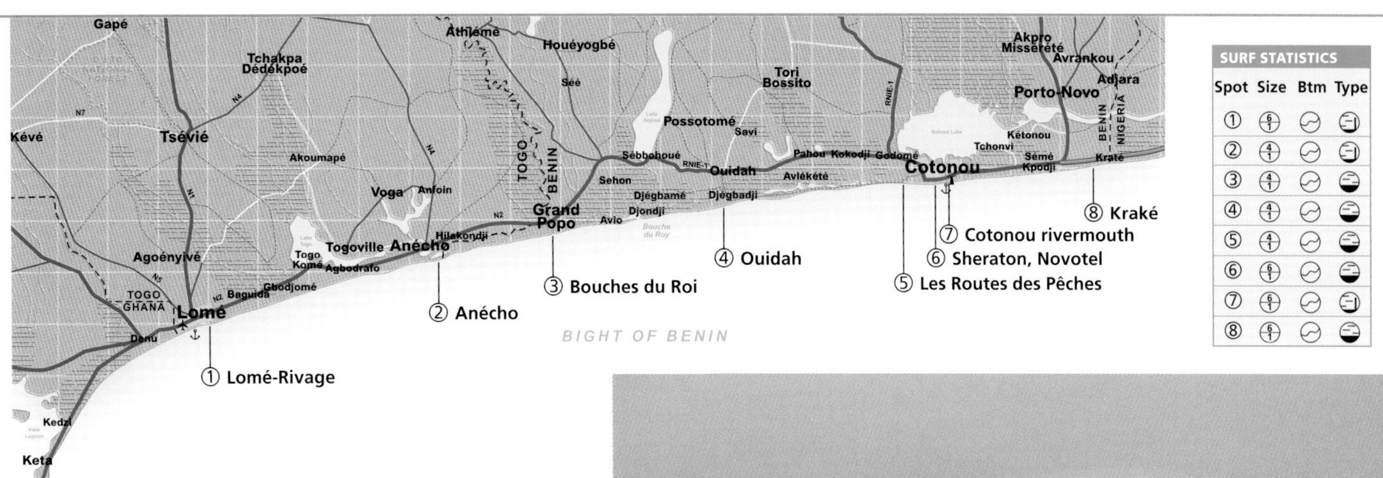

SURF STATISTICS

Spot	Size	Btm	Type
①			
②			
③			
④			
⑤			
⑥			
⑦			
⑧			

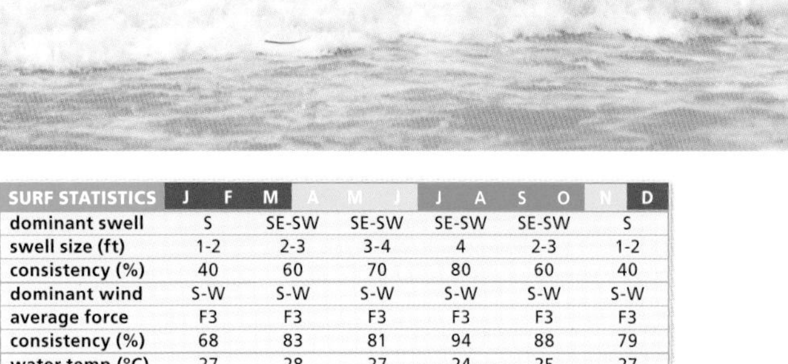

that this is a private beach with a resort and restaurant frequented by expats. Heading east, approaching the border of Benin, the beautiful German colonial town of **Anécho** hides one of the best waves in either country. A short walk from the town centre in the direction of Bénin can reveal long and hollow rights that break off a jetty. Be warned, it is a little fickle, exposed to the wind, and only breaks at low tide.

Crossing the border into Bénin, the first town is called Grand-Popo. The nearby beach, **Bouches de Roi**, offers low-quality closeout shorebreak, mostly unsurfable, with powerful and dangerous rips. At the fascinating town of **Ouidah**, a more attractive beach has marginally better potential, and becomes surfable at lower tides. The nearby snake temple is worth a visit if the waves aren't doing it. A track known as **Les Routes des Pêches** offers up more beachbreak surfing opportunities and the increased likelihood of encountering other surfers. Towards Cotonou, sandbars in front of the **Sheraton and Novotel** hotels will sometimes turn on, but pollution and beach crime can be an issue. Further west still, the best waves in Bénin often break in the **Cotonou Rivermouth**. Unfortunately, this spot is very polluted, and the top to bottom barrels usually go unsurfed due to the dubious water quality. To the west of Cotonou, approaching the Bénin-Nigeria border, Kraté receives more swell and can hold a good bank 50m (150yds) off the beach.

SURF STATISTICS	J F	M A	M J	J A	S O	N D
dominant swell	S	SE-SW	SE-SW	SE-SW	SE-SW	S
swell size (ft)	1-2	2-3	3-4	4	2-3	1-2
consistency (%)	40	60	70	80	60	40
dominant wind	S-W	S-W	S-W	S-W	S-W	S-W
average force	F3	F3	F3	F3	F3	F3
consistency (%)	68	83	81	94	88	79
water temp.(°C)	27	28	27	24	25	27
wetsuit						

The coastlines of Bénin and Togo receive surprisingly consistent swell, and during the May-Sept wet season there are usually rideable waves. The south-facing coastline means that both countries pick up long-distance southern-hemisphere swells, and having travelled halfway around the world they are super-clean and orderly, with long lulls between sets. The massive distance these swells travel means that there is a considerable decrease in swell size, and wave faces very rarely get above 6ft (2m). The main problem with the wet season is that the wind is a light onshore S-SW almost all the time. Perfect offshore conditions are a feature of the dry season, but swells are much rarer. Experienced West African surfers consider October or November to be the best months. Tides are small, but low tide can make a real difference to the quality of the beachbreaks.

Anécho

176. São Tomé

Radiation Point

JOHN CALLAHAN/TROPICALPIX

Summary
+ Quality, empty pointbreaks
+ Consistent summer swells
+ No rain during surf season
+ Untouched equatorial island
+ Beautiful scenery and wildlife

– Mostly small waves
– No access to west coast
– Expensive local prices
– Costly flights
– Malaria

JOHN CALLAHAN/TROPICALPIX

Approximately 270km from the western shores of Africa, São Tomé and Príncipe archipelago are composed of three islands: São Tomé is the largest, followed by Príncipe which is 30min away by plane, and finally the tiny islet of Rolas (3km/sq). São Tomé and Príncipe is a developing country, with an economy based on coffee, cocoa, small-scale agriculture and fishing. Principe was the first island where cocoa trees were planted in 1822 by the Portuguese, hence the nickname of the "Chocolate Islands". Many plantations were abandoned after independence in 1975, which wreaked havoc with the economy of the country for decades. The islands are still in reconstruction, but war is history and oil and tourism have taken over as the new way to give a better future for this secluded paradise. Besides Australian and American surfers, who visited as early as the '70s, and the odd French surfer from Gabon or the Ivory Coast, the first media surf trip to this area was in August 2000, when John Callahan/

Point Zero

JOHN CALLAHAN/TROPICALPIX

TRAVEL INFORMATION

Population: 146,000
Coastline: 209km (130mi): 136km (85mi) Sao Tome
Contests: None
Other Resources:
thelostwave.com
stome.net

Getting There – 30 day visa necessary ($65). Vaccination against yellow fever is mandatory. Sao Tomé (TMS) flights can be very expensive, although it's cheaper for flights from Lisbon. Weekly direct connections via TAP, STP Airways and TAAG from $980. Connections to Angola (Luanda), Ghana (Accra), Cape Verde (Sal) and Gabon (Libreville). Departure tax: $20.

Getting Around – Rental cars are very expensive. A basic car such as a Hyundai Electra costs $530/wk, or hire a private yellow taxi (no meter), close the deal first and be prepared to pay for 5 persons plus the journey back. Roads are getting better but remain slow and winding. Locals use motorbikes. Rolas is 20 minutes by boat. Island Tours are available: from $1050 with Club Maxel boat.

Lodging and Food – There are pricey luxury hotels, and some cheaper options. On Rolas, Pestana Equador Resort is a diving & fishing resort that costs $225/day/p: Jalé Beach Ecolodge bungalow for 2 is $35/day and just 3km from Porto Alegre, $8 per meal. "Roça" are ex-plantation houses. Roça de Sao João dos Angolares: $48 for dble. Pensão Turismo in ST is $75 for an A/C room.

WEATHER STATISTICS	J/F	M/A	M/J	J/A	S/O	N/D
total rainfall (mm)	94	140	81	0	66	103
consistency (days/mth)	7	9	5	0	6	8
min temp (°C)	23	23	21	21	21	21
max temp (°C)	30	30	28	28	29	29

Weather – Sao Tomé is fully equatorial but because of abrupt topography and oceanic SW winds, there is a great diversity of climates as well as rainfall, going from 2000mm (80in) in the coastal NW to 7000mm (280in) in the SW highlands. Northern and western zones are drier than the rest of the island. The eastern coast is semi-humid, cloaked with rainforest down to the sheltered beaches. The south is generally the most humid and rainy. The main rainy season is from February to May and again from October to November, when an almost constant southerly breeze blows at 10-25 knots. When it rains, the sea becomes muddy. Despite the moisture it is often sunny, and the rains are mostly thunderstorms. During "Gravana", from June to September, the sea becomes choppy, which makes it difficult to go out by boat. Divers prefer the rainy season for visibility. "Gravanita" is the name given to Dec-Feb, which is a lighter version of Gravana. Warm water year-round, with a vest in July-August.

Nature and Culture – A paradise for bird watchers, hikers and biodiversity lovers. Sao Tomé Pico is a volcanic cone at 2024m (6640ft). Don't miss Obo National Park. Check out Tchiloli, a weird form of theatre where men roam around Cao Grande, a mountain on Sao Tomé. Visit coffee or cocoa plantations. Sea turtles can be seen at Mikolo Beach.

Hazards and Hassles – Vaccination against yellow fever is necessary; full protection against chloroquine-resistant malaria with appropriate drugs and mosquito repellent is essential. To surf the SW coast means going prepared. Radiation Point can be quite shallow but rocks are ok. Rolas can be out of control with strong rips. Friendly locals on local wooden boards are becoming more common.

Handy Hints – Bring a longboard for the smaller days. Dollars and Euros are accepted for main payments. Dobras are used for local markets, taxis etc. Santomean cuisine is very rich! Refuse to eat dishes made of sea turtles (meat or egg), or other protected species (shark, earth snails, forest pigeons etc). Eat Calulu, Blabla, Cachupa and Feijoada.

Tropicalpix gathered a small crew including Randy Rarick, Sam George, Nuno Jonet and Tiago Oliveira, but travelling surfers remain rare.

Forte de São Tomé is the quickest check from the capitol, but the scenery is usually better than the short, dribbly, boulder rights that are often flat. **Lavaduro** could be a great right slab if it was not facing northeast, meaning the tubes are rarely big enough to clear the rocks. Further South, **Radiation Point** is at the easternmost point of the island. This wave is located in the grounds of the giant Voice of America transmitting station - look for the huge antennas. Before driving out to the point, ask permission at the gate (usually refused), otherwise paddle around. Radiation Point is fairly consistent, because even local windswell will wrap with enough size to ride, and the SW wind is offshore. Beware of shallow rocks and when the tide gets too high, waves will get fat and inconsistent. From there to Porto Alegre is an interesting set of right pointbreaks, which need a decent swell to start rolling. **Batismo** in Praia das Pombas is a great set up with long walls down the rocky point when a bigger S swings up the east coast. The same conditions will see hollower waves at **Dique**, a shallow, urchin covered reef/point north of Santana village. **Agua Izé** bay looks really nice and the right pointbreak set-up is obvious, but once again needs a strong pulse to fire. Check the large beach with average beachbreak waves known as **Baia Coqueiro**. There's another good point/rivermouth referred to as **Lo Grande**, which picks up a bit more swell and handles W winds. **Porto Alegre**, the African Nias, is the best wave on the island. It's a really long boulder/cobble right point but it needs a big S swell to work and it's the only place you will bump into the 15 or so locals who share seven boards between them. Ilheu das Rolas is a small islet straddling the equator off the southern tip of Sao Tomé. It's an amazingly beautiful island, home to a very upscale dive resort called Pestana Equador, better suited to divers and big game fishermen. To reach the island catch the Cariouco boat from São João dos Angolares and cheaper accommodation is available at a "Roça." The more serious wave is called **Point Zero Lefts** because surfers take off in the Southern Hemisphere, cross the Equator riding, and kick out in the northern hemisphere. Unfortunately this wave is usually sideshore and when big can suffer from strong currents. **Praia Pestana**, or Fishermen's Bay, is a Waikiki-style reform, ideal to have fun on a longboard. Local kids on wooden boards can sometimes be found surfing here. Back on São Tomé there is now a decent new road built by Taiwanese to access **Ecolodge**, a really nice place to stay with good-size lefts, but it's often onshore and the rocks can be intimidating. The west coast shows potential for long lefts, but there is no precise info to date because of very difficult access. Much further north is **Fim do Caminho** (end of the trail) near Santa Catarina unfolding a long wrapping left pointbreak over a bunch of rocks, but it's a 2h drive from São Tomé.

Ecolodge

GUILLAUME CAPETTE

Lo Grande

GUILLAUME CAPETTE

At this equatorial latitude, only solid S-SW groundswells produce surf. It's usually flat from October to March. The Austral winter brings several main swells a month, producing 2-8ft (0.6-2.5m) waves. Rolas is the most exposed island but it can't handle much size. Radiation Point also boasts consistency and will break on windswell. The SW wind is dominant throughout the year, but it is stronger from June-Sept, blowing 50% of the time as opposed to 35% from Oct-May. Porto Alegre rights need a good swell to break, and rarely reaches 6ft (2m). Access is a problem for west coast spots and other potential locations between Porto Alegre and São João dos Angolares. Check Buoyweather Gabon virtual buoys for forecasts. It takes 3-4 days for South African swells off Cape Town to reach São Tomé. Salinity might be lower in the Guinea Gulf during heavy rainy seasons. Tides are semi-diurnal with 4ft max of tidal range. This affects Radiation Point, which does not work at high tide when small.

SURF STATISTICS			
Spot	Size	Btm	Type
1	4/2		
2	4/2		
3	6/2		
4	6/2		
5	6/2		
6	4/2		
7	4/1		
8	6/2		
9	6/2		
10	10/2		
11	4/1		
12	8/2		
13	6/2		

SURF STATISTICS	J F	M A	M J	J A	S O	N D
dominant swell	S-SW	S-SW	S-SW	S-SW	S-SW	S-SW
swell size (ft)	1-2	2-3	3-4	3-4	2-3	1-2
consistency (%)	30	50	60	70	50	30
dominant wind	S-W	S-W	S-W	S-W	S-W	S-W
average force	F2-F3	F3	F3	F3-F4	F3	F3
consistency (%)	76	74	75	92	85	78
water temp.(°C)	28	28	27	25	26	27
wetsuit						

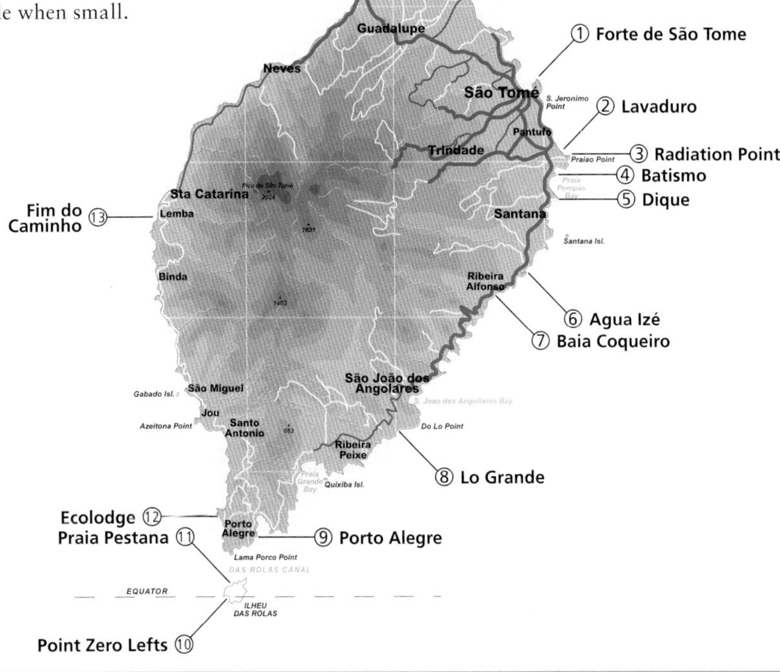

177. Pointe-Noire

Piege a Sable

ALL PHOTOS STEPHANE MIRA

Summary
+ Fairly consistent swells
+ Relatively safe
+ Tropical & uncrowded
+ Dry during the surf season
+ Amazing wildlife

– No world-class spots
– High costs
– Difficult travelling
– Often onshore
– Some health risks

Only expats working in the oil industry are likely to be in a position to surf in Pointe-Noire, so knowing someone who works there or at the very least speaking some French are essential to find waves in the Republic of Congo. Despite all the difficulties to get there, Pointe-Noire is one of the safest coastal cities in Africa and truly an oasis in a turbulent region and this short stretch of coastline provides a playground for ocean-lovers and wildlife alike. The warm, consistent waves have nurtured notable surfers like Jean-Luc Dupont or ex-WCT female Marie-Pierre Agraal, who learned their trade in Pointe-Noire. The Republic of Congo coastline measures 170km (106mi), compared to the short (37km/23mi) length of the often confused Democratic Republic of Congo's coast to the south. The Rep of Congo's shoreline is characterised

La Plage Sportive

TRAVEL INFORMATION

Local Population: Pointe Noire 600,000
Coastline: Rep of Congo 169km (105mi)
Time Zone: GMT +1h
Contests: None
Video: None
Other Resources:
twigahotel.com/surf/index.htm
congo-site.com
malondalodge.com/

Getting There – A visa ($100) is required along with a return ticket. Flights are expensive, Aero Benin, Air France, Gabon Airlines and Cameroon Airlines reach Brazzaville (BZV) or through Libreville in Gabon. Lina Congo (GC), operates from Brazzaville to Pointe-Noire (PNR), 512km (318mi) away. Trains used to take between 10h30 and 3 days but the inter-city railway has stopped running.

Getting Around – Roads are mostly earth tracks, sandy in dry season and impassable for all but the best 4WDs in the wet. Rental cars are really expensive, better to use local taxis ($2 local). There is a good new road southwards to the Angolan enclave of Cabinda. There are 2500km (1554mi) of inland waterways, navigable year-round. Loango is 20km (12mi) from Pointe Noire.

Lodging and Food – Stay at the mid-priced Twiga hotel facing the beach; the owners surf! Best hotels are Novotel or Azur ($120-180) and other options are Palm Beach ($20-40) near Cote Sauvage or Migitel downtown ($40-80); Malonda lodge in Djeno costs $205 for a bungalow for 2. No hotel at Pointe Indienne. Local food can be cheap ($5).

WEATHER STATISTICS	J/F	M/A	M/J	J/A	S/O	N/D
total rainfall (mm)	185	195	70	10	60	160
consistency (days/mth)	6	6	2	1	6	7
min temp (°C)	23	24	21	19	21	23
max temp (°C)	29	30	28	25	27	28

Weather – Since Congo is located just south of the Equator, the climate is hot and humid year-round. Jan-Feb is the short dry season, March-May is the short wet season, June-Sept is the long dry season while Oct-Dec is the long wet season. Temps are relatively stable with little variation between seasons. Much greater variation occurs between day and night, when the difference can range 15°C. Annual average temps range between 20°C and 27°C (68-80°F), although the cooling effect of the Benguela Current may produce lower temps (18°C/64°F). The resulting cooling and condensation of the evaporated air produces prolonged and heavy rainfall from October or November through to May. Annual average rainfall is 1200mm (48in) but often surpasses 1800mm (72in). Use a shorty during July and August and boardshorts for the rest of the year.

Nature and Culture – Sightseeing spots include the Wharf des Potasses and Conkouati lagunas, the harbour (old lighthouse), the railway station district, Notre-Dame Cathedral and the happening beach. 5h north by 4WD is Conkouati Chimp reserve and the Diosso canyon is nearby. Only 45min to Tchissanga Monkey World. Surf-casting and deep sea fishing, plus hang-gliding.

Hazards and Hassles – A yellow fever certificate and a really serious anti-malarial prophylactic, as some areas are chloroquine resistant. The heavy oil industry means you get occasional tar balls on the beach. Instability in the Pool Region has meant passenger trains between Brazzaville and Pointe Noire have stopped running.

Handy Hints – One all-round board will be enough. Bagatelle surf shop may have changed it's name, but it will still be expensive stuff! Don't get mixed up between Republic of Congo (Brazzaville) and the much larger Democratic Republic of Congo (Kinshasa) to the south and east. Check the nightclubs like Biblos, Colibri, Nels Club. Lots of cheap cyber-places. Speaking French makes life much easier!

La Plage Sportive

by a succession of shaded bays and lagoons bordered by mangroves and only Pointe-Noire and Pointe Indienne stick out from the monotonous, straight beaches. Since the civil war ended in 1999, Pointe-Noire is quite safe, yet some parts of the country still remain sketchy and some fighting continues in the disputed Angolan exclave Cabinda, just over the southern border. Surfing started in the early '80s, led by Russian-Congolese kids like Jannick Laforge, Ferdinand Yidika, Dimitri Mamouna or Edouard Serge and the small surf population is growing steadily with bodyboarder kids and expat surfers. Most of the fishermen don't know how to swim and are usually scared of entering the water. A lot of bodies have been found at Piège à Sable at the harbour lighthouse, inexperienced swimmers falling victim to the Atlantic rollers and rips.

Pointe Indienne looks promising, but it's an ill-defined left point, where swells don't quite wrap in because shallow outside sandbanks dissipate wave energy. Access from Plage de la Pointe Indienne is difficult and the line-up is fully exposed to the onshore wind with no action in the lee of the point. Bear in mind there are rumoured to be some quality lefts to the north towards Kouilou rivermouth on the way to Gabon. The **Piege à Sable** (literally the sand trap) aka Le Phare, is a left sand pointbreak and the place to be on big SW swells. Waves are hollow and fast, offering great rides, but there are heaps of currents. There is another section way inside when huge. Overland access is through a military zone, which might take a while even if you know the right people, so getting there by small boat or jet ski is preferable. The best thing about **La Plage Sportive** is that it's super consistent and the beachbreak peaks hold good shape thanks to some reef formations holding the sand in place. It's also a good hangout since there are beach restaurants, showers, music, beachgoers and a general fun vibe. The waves turn from fun to serious when it exceeds head-high, earning this stretch the Cote Sauvage name tag. **La Pyramide** is easy to find near an old derelict wharf that creates better banks, despite the frequent onshore winds, plus a few reefs add to the possibilities in this area that rarely sees a surfer. When Côte Sauvage gets out of control, especially in winter, it's an easy drive to **Djeno Point**, 30km (18mi) south of Pointe Noire, where lefts wrap in on big swells, over a rock and sand bottom. Djeno is an oil terminal owned by ENI, producing 250,000 barrels/day so expect some tar balls. Further south is the fabled **M'Vassa**, where quality reefbreaks fire when a big SW swell meets clean, E wind conditions. The area is beautiful and pristine with turtles gracing the line-up, but getting there is quite difficult.

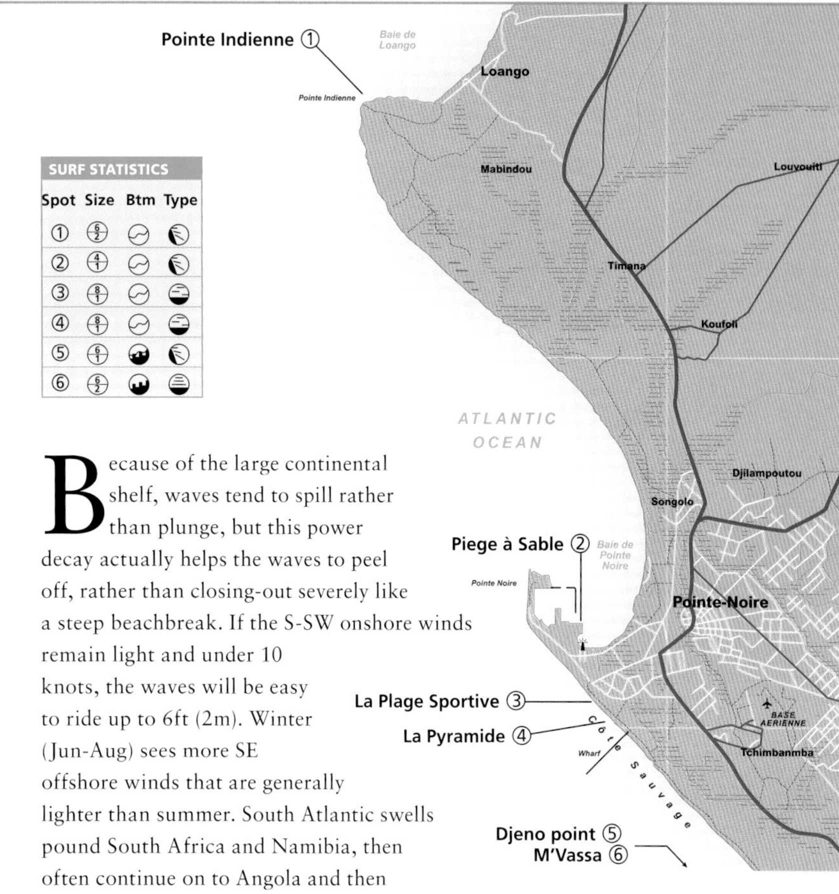

Because of the large continental shelf, waves tend to spill rather than plunge, but this power decay actually helps the waves to peel off, rather than closing-out severely like a steep beachbreak. If the S-SW onshore winds remain light and under 10 knots, the waves will be easy to ride up to 6ft (2m). Winter (Jun-Aug) sees more SE offshore winds that are generally lighter than summer. South Atlantic swells pound South Africa and Namibia, then often continue on to Angola and then

La Pyramide

Congo, aided by the Benguela Current which acts as a swell corridor. 2-3ft (0.6-1m) is the norm while 4-6ft (1.2-2m) swells happen several times a month during the winter season with 10ft (3m) days possible. The biggest swells just happen to coincide with the dry season, so June-August are the best months to surf the Congo. Semi-diurnal tides and a maximum tidal range of 6ft (1.8m).

SURF STATISTICS	J F	M A	M J	J A	S O	N D
dominant swell	S-SW	S-SW	S-SW	S-SW	S-SW	S-SW
swell size (ft)	1-2	2-3	3-4	4	3	1-2
consistency (%)	30	50	80	80	60	30
dominant wind	S-SW	S-SW	SE-S	SE-S	S-SW	S-SW
average force	F2-F3	F3	F2-F3	F2	F3	F3
consistency (%)	55	53	47	50	81	62
water temp.(°C)	27	28	24	21	24	26
wetsuit						

178. Skeleton Coast

Terrace Bay

STUART BUTLER

Summary
+ Virgin waves
+ Consistent, powerful swells
+ Exploration possible
+ Amazing scenery and wildlife

– Heavy, scary conditions
– Onshore winds and sea fog
– Cold water & difficult access
– Sharks and seals

Namibia is one of the last frontiers of the surfing world. It receives consistent swell, but aside from one or two small patches of coastline close to the few towns, it remains almost completely untouched by surfers. Extreme isolation, unfriendly terrain and virtually impossible access combine with cold water, strong currents, dense fog, unpredictable conditions and lots of very large sharks to keep much of the coast unexplored. The entire Namibian coastline, over 1500km (930mi) long, forms a part of the oldest desert in the world. The Namib Desert is characterised by huge red dunes in the south, making the coast completely inaccessible except around the crumbling German colonial town Lüderitz, which itself has several fickle breaks. The central zone and the major coastal towns of Swakopmund and Walvis Bay are the most commonly surfed areas. North is the Cape Cross

STUART BUTLER

STUART BUTLER

TRAVEL INFORMATION

Population: 2,050,000
Coastline: 1572km (977mi)
Contests: Nationals (Swakopmund)
Other Resources:
capecross.org
skeletoncoastsafaris.com

Getting There – Most nationalities don't need a visa, but all need to travel via South Africa. SAA operates daily flights from Johannesburg to Windhoek (WDH) with connections possible to Swakopmund (SWP). Flights also arrive straight from Cape Town to Walvis Bay (WVB). It is possible to drive up from Cape Town, but it's a 1800km (1120mi) journey.

Getting Around – Car hire is easily available and a 4x4 is not generally needed. Remember, visitors are not allowed to drive off-road. Permits are required for the Skeleton Coast National Park, whilst the Skeleton Coast Wilderness Area can only be visited as part of a fly-in safari.

The Weather – Namibia has a dry climate typical of a desert country. Days are mostly warm to very hot (20-35°C/68-95°F)), but the strong sea breezes can make the coast feel cold. It gets bitterly cold at night on the coast (down to 0°C/32°F). Inland areas become cooler with altitude and are generally much more pleasant than the coast. There is very little rainfall along the coast with most precipitation coming in the form of dense fogs, most common in the mornings. This morning fog occurs 340 days a year and can make the already scary surfing conditions terrifying. Occasionally, normally in winter, when the Berg wind blows offshore, the temperatures can soar. Surfers need a 3/2 full suit from Dec-April and something thicker through the winter.

WEATHER STATISTICS	J/F	M/A	M/J	J/A	S/O	N/D
total rainfall (mm)	3	6	0	2	0	0
consistency (days/mth)	1	2	1	2	1	1
min temp (°C)	15	14	10	8	10	13
max temp (°C)	23	24	23	21	19	22

Food and Lodging – Excellent accommodation is available at the Cape Cross Lodge for $120 per night. Terrace Bay has a range of cheap $20 per night huts, and camping is allowed at Torra Bay. Free camping is neither permitted nor a sensible idea anywhere else. Skeleton Coast National Park is a protected area, and travellers will not be allowed in unless they have booked a place to stay at Terrace Bay.

Nature and Culture – The Skeleton coast is home to unique wildlife and plant life, including desert elephants and 'dead' plants that live for 2,000 years. Don't miss the Etosha National Park, a long drive inland and one of the best wildlife spectacles in Africa. Other highlights include the sand dunes of Sossusvlei and the remote Damaraland in the northwest.

Hazards and Hassles – There are lots of big sharks, not to mention jackals, hyenas and occasional lions on the beaches. The wildlife danger is over-hyped and a seal bite is far more likely than a shark bite. The currents and general heavy surfing conditions are genuine risks.

Handy Hints – Take all surfing equipment, as nothing is available outside Swakopmund. Packing a pair of binoculars, and some prior knowledge of the plant and animal life, could be useful. Namibia is a stunning wilderness where human impact is minimal - an intimidating but pristine destination.

Ovahimba
GOOGLE EARTH ID YEP 511 4955

Seal Reserve - three classy left points that house the largest seal colony in the southern hemisphere. Sharks are drawn to the seals, but in truth the biggest obstacle to surfing these points are the National Park officials. After a small minority of surfers abused the rules and regulations, they have banned surfing anywhere within the park grounds.

North of Cape Cross, into the Skeleton Coast National Park, coastal access again becomes very difficult. This fragile ecosystem is characterised by flat gravel plains and patches of low dunes and though it might look uninhabited, wildlife flourishes here. This northern part of the Namib Desert can surprise the visitor with Oryx, springbok, hyenas, jackals and even elephants and lions strolling down to the beach to check the surf – some indication of the true wildness of this region. There are definitely a few spots hidden away in coves and around headlands. However, visitors cannot just go off-road in a 4x4 to check the waves. This is a very fragile ecosystem and a simple footprint really can last for years. The plant life, which forms the basis of the food chain, takes decades to grow and is easily destroyed by human interference. Under no circumstances are tourists allowed to leave the marked trails. In the middle of the reserve lies a left pointbreak of epic proportions. Impossibly long and hollow, tube riding records could easily be set at **Ovahimba**. Incredibly hard access via 4x4. Requires expert planning and surfing skills. **Terrace Bay** is about as far north as the average visitor will be permitted to go. There is an inconsistent left point here, and a more regular beachbreak, both of which are frequented by plenty of big sharks. Accommodation is available in basic blocks, which must be booked through the National Park office. Terrace is a popular fishing resort and offers the best beach shark fishing in the world. The left finishes up in front of the point where the fishermen gut their catches and throw all the entrails back into the sea! North of Terrace Bay there are certainly further good waves, but with no roads and access limited to scientists and those on expensive fly-in safaris, there is little opportunity to explore for waves. The next inhabited spot is **Torra Bay**, another average and often messy beachbreak. Small, glassy conditions offer the best chance of scoring waves. A highly fickle right point lines up at the southern end of the beach if the swell kicks in and the wind stays light. Camping is permitted here but must be booked in advance. There is also a mediocre but very consistent beachbreak located by the wreck of the **South West Sea**, a fishing vessel that ran aground here in the mid '70s.

Terrace Bay
STUART BUTLER

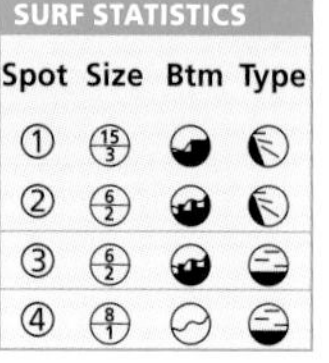

SURF STATISTICS	J F	M A	M J	J A	S O	N D
dominant swell	SW-W	SW-W	SW-W	SW-W	SW-W	SW-W
swell size (ft)	3	4	5	5	4	3
consistency (%)	60	70	80	80	70	60
dominant wind	SE-SW	SE-SW	SE-SW	SE-SW	SE-SW	SE-SW
average force	F4	F4	F4	F4	F4-F5	F4
consistency (%)	86	92	87	88	93	92
water temp.(°C)	21	19	17	16	16	17
wetsuit						

The coast of Namibia picks up even the smallest of South Atlantic swells and receives waves on an almost daily basis, year-round. The best season is from May to Sept, with consistent 6-10ft (2-3.3m) SW swells. Most spots are difficult to find and fickle. This is a windy stretch of coast and most spots are highly sensitive to the wind. To score anywhere but the Cape Cross points requires patience. The dominant wind is from the S, varying very little from 49% (August) to 62% (November), and S-SE is the prevailing annual wind direction. The tidal range can reach 6ft (2m), and tide tables are available in Swakopmund.

179. East London

Yellowsands

ALL PHOTOS LOUIS WULFF

Summary
+ Swells year-round
+ No crowds, often offshore
+ Heaps of long, right points
+ Close to J-Bay, but warmer water
+ Fairly cheap, good tourism services

– Noon summer ENE wind
– High shark attack stats
– Cool, windy winters
– Spooky, empty line-ups
– Long drive from anywhere

East London, South Africa's only river port, sprawls between the rivermouths of the broad Buffalo, Nahoon and Gonubie Rivers. Being the gateway to the Sunshine Coast and the Wild Coast, East London is a major hub for the region and attracts the adventurous and sporting to many international events. What isn't so obvious is the fact that East London is one of the best areas in SA to visit and surf. Since 1847, about 150 ships have been wrecked within a 5km radius of the Buffalo Harbour, the reason being that swells hitting the Eastern Cape are the most consistent for the whole South African coastline. Considering the warmer water and the number of legitimate right pointbreaks which have nurtured surfers like Greg Emslie or Nikita Robb, East London is a world-class zone that sharks have managed to keep quiet. To date, 20 shark attacks have been recorded in the past 18 years around East London. The worst incident was in 1994 when top local surfer Bruce Corby died as a result of

Kidd's Beach

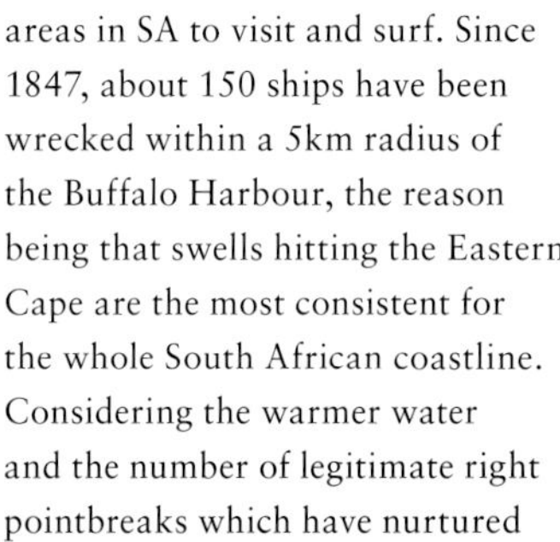

Nahoon Reef

TRAVEL INFORMATION

Local Population:
Eastern Cape - 6,436,761
Coastline:
Eastern Cape Province - 800km (500mi)
Time Zone: GMT+2
Contests: June (SA Chips, Nahoon), April (O'Neill SA)
Other Resources:
dawnpatrol.co.za
surfingsouthafrica.co.za
wavescape.co.za
zigzag.co.za
Video:
African Sensemilla
Pits & Pieces

Getting There – No visa. South Africa is remote but with direct flights from Sao Paulo, Miami, New York, London, Frankfurt, Dubai, Singapore and Perth. Most airlines hit Johannesburg (JNB). Daily flight to East London (ELS) costs $120-150 r/t. East London is 1037km (645mi) from Cape Town, 658km (409mi) from Durban, 294km (183mi) from Port Elizabeth and 961km (597mi) from Jo'berg.

Getting Around – The road network is very good and long drives are the only way to get around. Expect $32/day car hire (National). Transkei can be a bit sketchy to cross; only drive during daytime. It takes 4-5h drive from J-Bay. Access to most of the spots is easy, just don't paddle across rivermouths when they run out to sea. Seaside resorts are only busy during summer.

WEATHER STATISTICS	J/F	M/A	M/J	J/A	S/O	N/D
total rainfall (mm)	79	91	45	55	91	86
consistency (days/mth)	13	11	7	6	12	13
min temp (°C)	18	16	11	10	13	16
max temp (°C)	26	25	22	21	21	23

Lodging and Food – Expect modern amenities such as reliable communications and clean, drinkable tap water. Stay at Dawn Patrol camp near Nahoon Reef or the Sugar Shack at Eastern Beach ($25 dble, surf lessons available). Dolphin Hotel in Nahoon costs $21-35 dble. Expect $5 for a good meal. Wine and lobster are great and not that pricey.

Weather – East London enjoys a moderate subtropical climate, with few extremes in temperature and is generally sunny and pleasant. Winters are usually mild with temps between 10°C and 23°C (50°F-74°F) even if a brief cold spell can be expected. From September to April, the climate is cool and wet with temps ranging from 12°-25°C (54-77F) and higher precipitation than the rest of the year. East London's sweeping white beaches extend for miles; unpolluted, uncrowded and unspoilt. There is subtropical vegetation throughout the entire city. Boardshorts, shorty, spring suit or light steamer will cover the seasons.

Nature and Culture – Nahoon Fossil Prints, in Nahoon Bats Cave are the oldest homo sapiens footprints, 200,000 years old! Check the lion park where you can handle lion cubs. Go sandboarding or rock climbing in the Amatole Mountains, the EL Golf Club courses are amongst South Africa's best, while the Aquarium is the oldest. German settlement = Oktoberfest!

Hazards and Hassles – Records show that shark attack is the main threat at most rivermouth spots. Buy a Shark Shield ($645) to stop the Jaws theme playing in your head. Spots are fairly uncrowded and localism is rare. Wave power can be fierce in winter. Black & white differences are still apparent; don't underrate the problem.

Handy Hints – Dawn Patrol is run by Roger Smith & Louis Siebert, both well-known surfers and experienced operators. Because of the variety of spots and sharks, a guide can be crucial. 2 surfers pay $864 each for 7 days, or less if in a bigger group. When it's 6ft, use a thicker and longer board to avoid late take-offs. Custom boards are cheap around US$400.

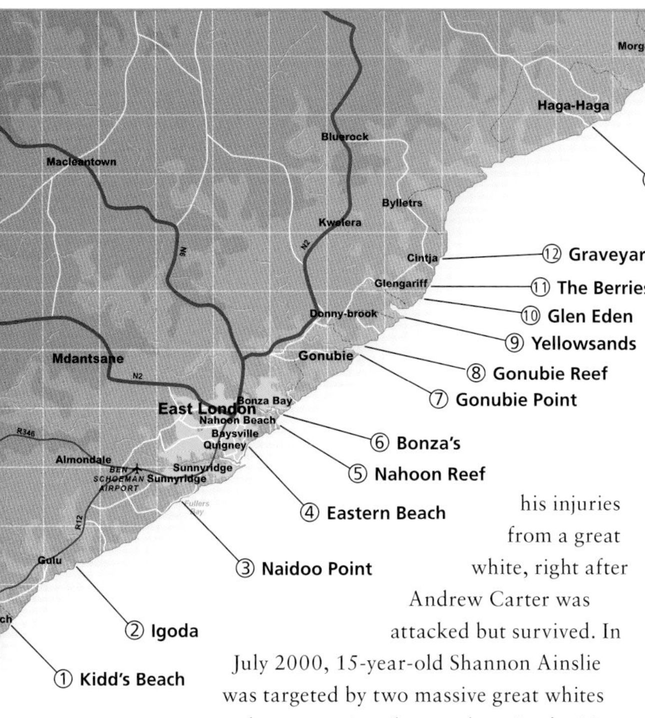

his injuries from a great white, right after Andrew Carter was attacked but survived. In July 2000, 15-year-old Shannon Ainslie was targeted by two massive great whites and you can view the attack on Surfer Mag (or youtube). At Gonubie Point, Anton Devos was killed by a great white while bodyboarding in 2004. Then in November 2007, local Lee Mellin, survived an attack at Bonza Bay by a monster shark, which left a 38 cm wound down his thigh. Locals advise not to enter the water in the early morning or late afternoon, when birds and dolphins are seen feeding, and on no account to go out alone.

Kidd's Beach is a popular holiday resort 35km (24mi) south of town, offering a half-decent beachbreak best on small to mid S swells. **Igoda** is a better bet, facing south and sucking in plenty of swell (and sharks) at the eastern end rivermouth in front of the rocks forming really good tubes and beachbreak walls that are best on light NE or NW berg winds. Gets crowded on small days. Nearby is **Naidoo Point**, producing nice tubular rights on small clean swells, or check Fuller's on the beachfront road nearby. In central East London, **Eastern Beach** delivers variable quality shifting sandbars, but on N winds and summer NE swells, it's the place to be. Countless contests are held at **Nahoon Reef**, the most popular right point in town. The outside section named Reef can handle very big swells, when huge drops and powerful bowl sections challenge the ever-present crowd. Corner, on the inside prefers E swells and any W wind and suffers less from the bad rips and bad shark attack record of Reef. Two rivermouths shape the sandbars to the north, but **Bonza's** is a below average spot needing berg winds and small peaky E swells. **Gonubie Point** is a fine right point, requiring a medium E-SE swell to create angular pits over slabs of reef at lower tides. Crowded when on, there is also a consistent beachbreak, a tidal pool and plenty of accommodation. On the other side of the bay is **Gonubie Reef**, a consistent left pointbreak, which is a rarity in these parts. Really long, fun bashable walls on any swell direction or size, but medium swells can be tricky sometimes. There's a fickle, high tide, right point at **Yellowsands**, but it's the transitory low tide rivermouth sandbars that dish up solid barrels, even when strong winter SW winds blow-out most spots. The fast, right sandbank into the river flow at **Glen Eden** is one of the only spots that works with summer NE winds. **The Berries** is a text book righthand point, with throwing lips and barrels out the back, bending into mellow shoulders on the inside. Needs NW winds not SW and Queensbury Bay has all sorts of accommodation from hotel to campsite. **Graveyards** near Cintsa is a fickle, uninspiring right that only reacts well to wrapping SW swell and W winds. The same conditions are needed for **Haga-Haga**, but it is rarely good at the left reef/point in front of the hotel and nearby beachbreak. Surfers will stay at quiet Morgan's Bay and surf **Barbel Point** rights when a large SW swell and wind front hits. **Wacky Point** at the Kei Mouth is somewhat fickle but an absolute gem when on. A couple of challenging, tubular sections unload over rocky shelves and it's rarely surfed by East London locals since it's a long drive along bad roads on the border of the Transkei.

SURF STATISTICS			
Spot	Size	Btm	Type
①	6 / 1		
②	8 / 1		
③	5 / 2		
④	6 / 1		
⑤	12 / 2		
⑥	6 / 1		
⑦	8 / 2		
⑧	8 / 2		
⑨	8 / 2		
⑩	8 / 2		
⑪	10 / 2		
⑫	8 / 2		
⑬	6 / 2		
⑭	12 / 6		
⑮	8 / 4		

The Berries

Swell patterns are a mix of Transkei/Natal and the cooler Western Cape coast and the transition occurs between Port Alfred and Port Elizabeth. The East London zone gets sheltered from the strong SW winds and cold rain squalls that affect most of the western part of the Eastern Cape Province. On clean winter days, it's offshore every morning so early sessions guarantee clean waves. In summer, it gets warm and humid as in Natal but with less of the surf-destroying NE wind. Most of the right points work well with SW swells & winds. At Nahoon Reef, expect occasional 2-6ft (0.6-2m) waves in spring/summer, 3-6ft+ (1-2m+) in autumn and 3-8ft (1-2.5m) in winter when it can get hairy. Gonubie lefts are rideable at 3-4ft (1-1.2m), but can hold 6-10ft (2-3m), usually in autumn and winter. Queensberry will be 2-4ft most of the time, but still rideable at 8ft plus. Tides are semi-diurnal and can reach 7ft (2.1m) on spring tides, which is medium range but quite significant at rivermouth breaks.

SURF STATISTICS	J F	M A	M J	J A	S O	N D
dominant swell	NE-SW	SE-SW	SE-SW	SE-SW	SE-SW	N-E
swell size (ft)	2-3	4-5	5	5-6	4-5	3
consistency (%)	60	70	90	90	80	70
dominant wind	E-SW	NE-W	SW-W	SW-W	NE-W	E-SW
average force	F4	F4-F5	F5	F5	F5	F4-F5
consistency (%)	40	55	45	43	55	41
water temp.(°C)	22	22	20	19	19	20
wetsuit						

180. Southern Kwazulu Natal

Scottburgh Point

ALL PHOTOS GARTH ROBINSON

Summary
+ Very consistent swells
+ Offshore every morning in winter
+ Hollow punchy right points
+ Uncrowded, warm water
+ Proximity to Durban

– Blown-out most afternoons
– Sharks, un-netted beaches
– Almost straight coastline
– Some dodgy neighbourhoods

The huge province of Kwazulu Natal is split by Durban and the 160km (100mi) of coastline to the south is well known as a sunny holiday playground. This "South Coast" also happens to be one of the world's most underrated surf zones. There are high quality, consistent waves everywhere, including hollow beachbreaks, heaps of righthand points and a few classic reefbreaks. Add the low crowd factor and it becomes obvious that scoring a few screamers here is more than likely! The continental shelf drops away sharply, so catching the plentiful, year-round, open ocean swells is easier, attracting a variety of wave riders like wave-skis, kitesurfers, kneeboarders and even ocean outriggers.

Warner Beach

T.O. Strand just north of Port Edward needs a big SW groundswell and land breeze to produce heavy, rights over a rock shelf. **Southbroom** has very good mainly sand-bottomed rights that need strong S swells and a light SW-NW wind. Easy access attracts occasional crowds - jump in from the rocks. Margate is the largest resort town along the

TRAVEL INFORMATION

Local Population: 9,426,019
Coastline: KZN 575km (357mi)
Time Zone: GMT+2
Contests:
ASP Africa Scottburgh (March 24-25)
SC Carnival Scottburgh & Kelso (Oct 27-29)
Other Resources:
africansurfaris.com
offshore.co.za
wavescape.co.za
zigzag.co.za
Video:
African Sensemilla
Pits & Pieces

Getting There – No visa. Johannesburg (JNB) gets direct flights from Sao Paulo, Miami, New York, London (overnight), Frankfurt, Dubai, Singapore and Perth. Fly then Durban (DUR) which cost $100 r/t. South African Airways, South African Express and Airlink fly between all the major cities. Kulula.com, 1time and Mango offer cut-price flights.

Getting Around – Rent a car at Southafricar and pay $225/wk. Durban Airport is 20min from Amanzimtoti and 170km (106mi) to Port Edward. Driving is easy along the N2 freeway/toll road up to Ramsgate then use R102 aka Marine Drive to Port Edward. High season is late March-April and Dec-Jan holidays.

Lodging and Food – Lots of great backpackers like Mantis & Moon in Umzumbe ($25-30/dbl) or Southbroom Backpackers ($30-40/dbl), Vulamenzi Lodge ($35-55) or The Beach (Banana). Expect $5 for a good meal. Good, cheap seafood.

WEATHER STATISTICS	J/F	M/A	M/J	J/A	S/O	N/D
total rainfall (mm)	118	105	42	37	89	116
consistency (days/mth)	10	8	3	4	8	11
min temp (°C)	21	18	12	11	15	18
max temp (°C)	27	27	23	22	24	26

Weather – The province has a warm, sub-tropical climate with temps moderated by the expanse of the Indian Ocean. Durban boasts an average of 320 days of sunshine a year. Summer months (September to April) are hot and humid with temps ranging from 23-33°C (74-92°F). Winters are mild to warm and dry with temps between 13°C and 25°C (56-77°F). Precipitation can be expected mainly from October to April and particularly in the summer months of December, January and February when one can count on strong tropical thunderstorms almost daily in the afternoons. Average annual rainfall is 1000mm (40in). Choose a really light fullsuit during winter and a shorty or boardshort during summer.

Nature and Culture – If you're into golf, there are dozens of courses. Dive Aliwal Shoal, Protea Banks and do tiger shark diving to see the beasts! Check the wildlife at Hluhluwe 'Big-5' Game Park. In Port Shepstone you can board the Banana Express old steam train which runs on a narrow gauge railway line. Plenty of bars & nightclubs in high season.

Hazards and Hassles – Most of the beaches have shark nets but Natal Shark Board remove them during the sardine runs whenever in June-August. No attacks recorded for the last 15 years. Don't park anywhere, car thievery is a problem. Crowds are fairly low, but tight-knit locals can be protective at some spots and high season gets packed.

Handy Hints – No need for a gun, but boards that can deal with barrelling point waves. 5 days with Vulamanzi/Kelso surf camp cost $475 (based on 4 pax). African Surfaris offer numerous packages that cover the N and S coasts of Durban, as well as Transkei and Mozambique (combo trips possible). Expect $1200 to $2000 for 10 day trips.

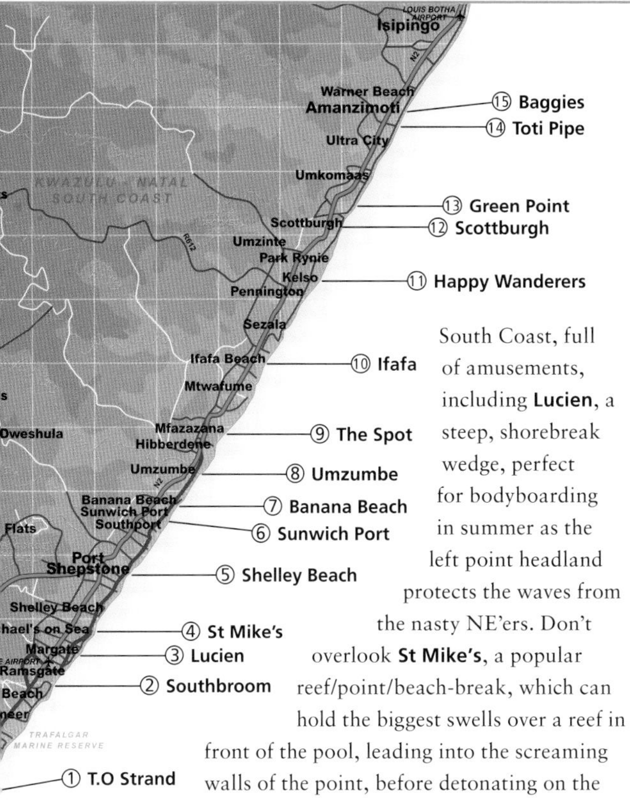

South Coast, full of amusements, including **Lucien**, a steep, shorebreak wedge, perfect for bodyboarding in summer as the left point headland protects the waves from the nasty NE'ers. Don't overlook **St Mike's**, a popular reef/point/beach-break, which can hold the biggest swells over a reef in front of the pool, leading into the screaming walls of the point, before detonating on the sand inside. If the rivermouth opens after rains, it will get murky and sharky, despite being netted. **Shelley Beach** near Port Shepstone is only an average beachbreak, best in summer. A finger of reef holds the sand at **Sunwich Port**, which then sucks the sand back up into gaping barrels when a solid SW swell meets a W-NW wind. **Banana Beach** is a fast, peeling, shredable right that relies on sand from the rivermouth and the rocks off the southern point of this long beach. Doesn't like much wind and needs any S swell. Very long rides are possible at **Umzumbe**, but the sandbanks vary a lot. Holds moderate SW winds and swells, plus a crew of protective locals. Among the most famed South Coast breaks is **The Spot** at the hard to find Mfazazana local village. Leg-burning rights appear if the sandbanks cooperate, with epic tubes and an inside bowl section, otherwise there's lots of close-outs. SW winds are OK, but there are no shark nets. Scottburg surfers visit **Ifafa** in small, clean swells for the several high tide reefs and beachies including a crazy ledge called Heavy, which breaks to the south of the caravan park. Another caravan park at Kelso has private access to the fun, rolling walls of **Happy Wanderers**, otherwise pay a fee or walk around. The Point at **Scottburgh** is one of the most consistent waves around, breaking in front of the pool on a mussel infested reef, before winding into the highly changeable rivermouth sandbanks on the beach. Any S swell, any W wind and any tide, but remember your manners with the local crew. Next to Clansthal lighthouse is the legendary **Green Point**, which like many KZN righthanders, needs the right sands to build up. On medium S swells and light SW or land breeze, there should be a combination of hollow and slopey walls. Car break-in hot-spot. Amanzimtoti boasts two famous beachbreaks next door to each other at Warner Beach. This stretch used to have the highest shark attack record in the

Green Point

world, before nets went in and a recent competition final was held up by a sighting in the line-up. South of Inyoni Rocks, **Toti Pipe** is a fickle, serious shorebreak wedge, breaking over an old effluent pipe below the sand at high tide. **Baggies** is punchy and consistent on head-high swells and SW winds, while Pulpit is the other spot to check in the area.

SURF STATISTICS			
Spot	Size	Btm	Type
①	8/4		
②	6/3		
③	6/1		
④	10/2		
⑤	6/1		
⑥	8/2		
⑦	8/3		
⑧	8/2		
⑨	8/3		
⑩	6/1		
⑪	8/2		
⑫	6/2		
⑬	6/2		
⑭	6/1		
⑮	6/1		

The most consistent surf happens in the winter months, from May to August, mainly due to the cold fronts that sweep up the coast from the Cape, bringing solid 6-8ft (2-2.5m) swells, lighting up all the pointbreaks along the KZN coast. There is clean surf most mornings during winter as a gentle land breeze blows straight offshore from the Drakensberg mountains. In summer, swells tend to be smaller with fun surf at most beachbreaks almost every day. Prevailing NE winds provide windswell along with the regular groundswells from the south. During summer months, offshore days are rare due to the dominant NE onshore wind. The big bonus may come from the summer tropical cyclone swells forming off the east coast of Madagascar before tracking south and often pushing in seriously big swell to the Mozambique and KwaZulu Natal coast. A lot of spots are at their best in these E swells although many of the points prefer SW. Tides are semi-diurnal, 8ft (2.4m) max tidal range.

SURF STATISTICS	J F	M A	M J	J A	S O	N D
dominant swell	NE-SW	SE-SW	SE-SW	SE-SW	SE-SW	SE-SW
swell size (ft)	3	4	4-5	5-6	4-5	3
consistency (%)	70	80	90	90	80	70
dominant wind	NE-S	NE-S	N-S	N-S	NE-S	NE-S
average force	F4	F4	F4	F4	F4-F5	F4-F5
consistency (%)	44	42	56	59	45	48
water temp.(°C)	26	25	23	21	22	24
wetsuit						

Happy Wanderers

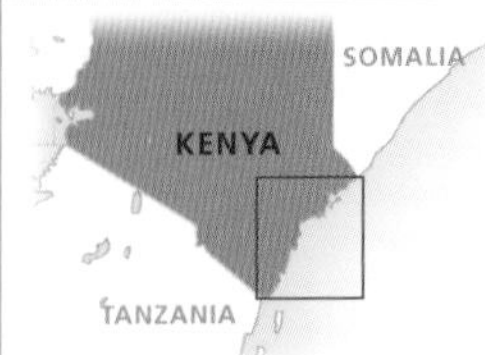

181. Kenya

Between Malindi and Mombasa

MICHAEL KEW

Summary
+ Semi-consistent during summer
+ Warm water
+ Virgin reefs & beachbreaks
+ Good hotels
+ Fascinating wildlife

– Lots of onshore mush
– Mombassa sharks
– Remote reefs with tidal flats
– Robberies and muggings
– Recent social unrest

Kenya and Tanzania have recently unveiled a few surfing secrets along their considerable Indian Ocean coastlines. Kenya is a prime destination for visiting big-game parks or climbing Mount Kenya, yet beach lovers have stumbled upon coastal Kenya and like what they have found. A small expat surfing community has been tapping the surf here for decades, but Kenya is now starting to attract inquisitive surfers to the fringing reefs that break consistently during the southern hemisphere winter, since Kenya lies just south of the Equator. Mombasa Island is the crossroads for four major routes, is the commercial centre for many businesses and makes sense as a base for surf exploration, since there's waves right on it's doorstep. South of Mombasa, newer hotels have set-up around Diani Beach, but the coastal area to the north features Arab and Portuguese forts, old towns and some of the finest beach hotels in Africa.

JOHN CALLAHAN/TROPICALPIX

Manda Left

JOHN CALLAHAN/TROPICALPIX

TRAVEL INFORMATION

Local Population:
Mombassa – 900,000
Coastline:
536km (333mi)
Time Zone: GMT +3
Contests: None
Video:
Blues 111 (Italy), Kite Surfing documentary
Other Resources:
prosurfkenya.com

Getting There – Visas upon arrival at Nairobi airport for $50 (single-entry). Nairobi (NBO) has many air connections with Europe, plus charter flights with package deals. Mombasa (MBA) direct, 500km (310mi) away, is much better. Daily flights from Nairobi with Kenya Airways or Air Kenya to Malindi (MYD). Planes to Malindi generally travel onto Lamu.

Getting Around – Malindi is 120km (74mi) from Mombasa, 2hr drive on tarmac. Mombasa to Nairobi takes 6-8hrs, road varying from excellent to poor. Car hire $120/day, so it's better to be picked up by hotel van and use local transports in the main places like Malindi or Mombassa. In Lamu, use dhows!

WEATHER STATISTICS	J/F	M/A	M/J	J/A	S/O	N/D
total rainfall (mm)	27	118	191	72	81	85
consistency (days/mth)	3	7	15	12	9	5
min temp (°C)	23	24	22	21	21	23
max temp (°C)	31	31	29	27	29	30

Lodging and Food – Cheap all-inclusive deals for Mombasa and Malindi. The Coconut Village in Malindi offers AC rooms for $70/pax in double rooms, Eden Roc is cheaper and only $8 for a basic backpacker room. Meals go from $2-8 with cheap Ugali or Githeri, a Tusker Lager beer is $1. Tamarind in Mombassa has the best seafood.

Weather – The climate is tropical dry tempered by the Indian Ocean. The coastline benefits from the effect of the monsoons (NE in winter, SW in summer) which make the temperature pleasant. Average temps range from 21-32°C (70-90°F) in January and from 20-29°C (68-84°F) in July. There are no seasons as such, but there are two main periods of rain. The "long rains" extend roughly from March to June and "the short rains" last from October to December. Rain usually arrives in violent downpours but tends to last for only a few hours. Annual average rainfall is about 1000mm (40in). The monsoon winds blow NE-SE onshore all year-round. Boardshorts only.

Nature and Culture – North of Mombassa has several world-class dive sites, Watamu Marine National Park being a well managed area. Check Gede Ruins, Crocodile and Snake farms and play at Malindi Casino. Safari Day trips to Tsavo Game Park; Nyali Golf & Country Club. Mombasa: Fort Jesus, Old Town, Yuls' Beach Bar, Pirates (Disco) or Mamba Village. Watersport is Malindi's prime tourist attraction with sailboarding, water-skiing, diving and deep-sea fishing.

Hazards and Hassles – Shallow live-coral reefs can be nasty and a shark encounter is likely, especially in the Mombassa Channel. Beware of weed patches in Malindi where thorns, logs, branches and crabs can stop you dead in the water. For security reasons, visitors to Lamu are advised to travel by air. Nairobi is notorious for robberies and muggings, be vigilant in Mombassa.

Handy Hints – No surf stuff available. Bring a board and you might sell it. Lots of British and Itlaian tourists. The areas bordering Somalia are all prone to banditry.

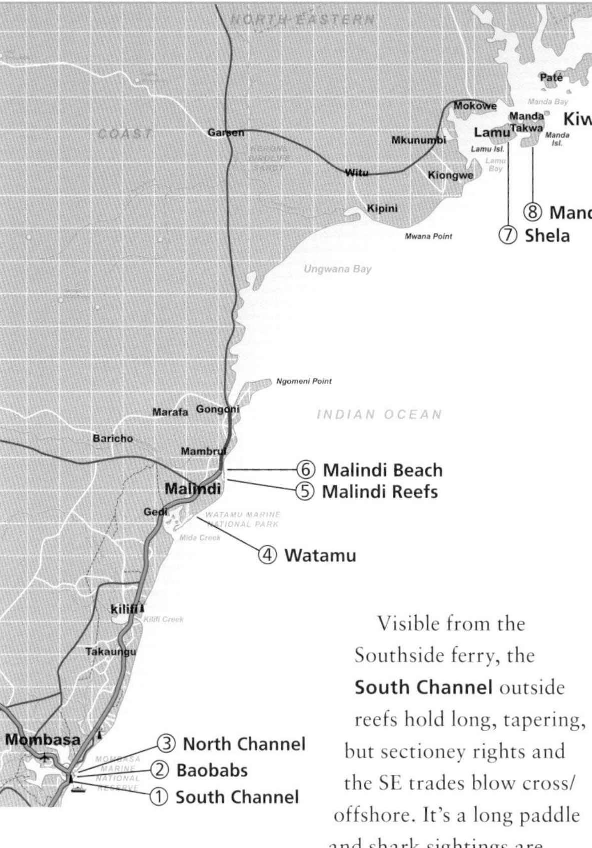

Visible from the Southside ferry, the **South Channel** outside reefs hold long, tapering, but sectioney rights and the SE trades blow cross/ offshore. It's a long paddle and shark sightings are frequent. Near the Florida Disco, within the Golf Course is **Baobabs**, where the local expats usually surf. These reefs are at the base of the cliffs and usually run left, but with backwash at high tide and quite shallow at low. Past Nyali bridge is the access to the **North Channel** outside shallow reef, sometimes called Leven Reef. Favouring lefts and usually plagued by onshore SE trades, it's a much shorter paddle and less sharky than the South Channel. North of the Nyali Beach strip lies the fascinating Mamba Crocodile Village and Marineland Snake Park with turtles, sting rays, hand-fed sharks and a multitude of serpents. Miles of white powdery sand with a reef 2km offshore provide a natural lagoon ideal for kitesurfing with Prosurf Kite. **Watamu** is set around Turtle Bay, a curve of aquamarine water with coral gardens and atolls including Whale Rock, a humpbacked piece of coral, next to below average southeast-facing reefs that are usually onshore and best at high tide. Malindi could be the surf capital of Kenya, thanks to a handful of expats promoting surf-tourism to take advantage of some semi-consistent, virgin waves.

Malindi

MICHAEL KEW

Malindi Reefs facing east, pick up any swell going and bend it around some quality righthand coral corners. The furthest of the 4 outside reefs sits 3km offshore, while it is only 1km from the long jetty to the most popular wave. From there, the large **Malindi Beach** extends north to a rivermouth, offering surprisingly consistent sandy peaks up to shoulder high, which are bigger at the north end and it's best at high tide. Go past Casino and park near Palm Tree Beach, preferably in a 4x4 able to tackle the deep, powdery sands. Driving to the island town of Lamu can be sketchy - ask around to find out if the road is safe. **Shela Beach** is lined with hotels and a virtually endless stretch of rolling sand dunes. It's one of the more consistent beachbreaks, bigger at the south end, but beware of currents and wildlife near the rivermouth. Because of its south-facing aspect, Shela is often onshore. Manda Island has wonderful beaches and even elephants have been known to swim across from the mainland to hang out. **Manda Lefts** can be long with racy sections over the live coral and it picks up and handles the most swell in Kenya, but is badly affected by the SE onshores. **Kiwayu** has some good set-ups with reefs and a decent beach, although outside reefs may filter the swell.

SURF STATISTICS

Spot	Size	Btm	Type
①			
②			
③			
④			
⑤			
⑥			
⑦			
⑧			
⑨			

Kilifi

MICHAEL KEW

The area is seriously affected by the monsoon patterns. The NE monsoon from December to March does produce occasional windswells but Kenya's exposure is far from ideal and while the Seychelles get a decent supply of NE swell, Kenya remains mostly flat during the high tourist season. Then, SW monsoon typically gives a strong high over Mauritius and the SE winds blowing on the edge of the high create a regular 6-12ft (2-4m) windswell, mostly from June to September, which diminishes to 3-6ft (1-2m) by the time it reaches the coast. Most of that swell arrives with the strong SE onshores, so rights wrapping around reefs create the only options for side/ offshore conditions. Tides are semi-diurnal with diurnal inequality reaching 13ft (3.9m) max, which is fairly significant at all spots. Most beachbreaks will be better at high tide.

SURF STATISTICS	J F	M A	M J	J A	S O	N D
dominant swell	NE	E-SE	E-SE	E-SE	E-SE	NE
swell size (ft)	1	1-2	3-4	4	3	1
consistency (%)	10	20	60	70	50	10
dominant wind	NE-E	E-SE	SE-S	SE-S	SE-S	NE-E
average force	F4	F3	F4	F4	F3-F4	F3-F4
consistency (%)	88	55	83	89	82	63
water temp.(°C)	26	28	27	25	26	27
wetsuit						

Indian Ocean

Politics rarely affects surfers, but anyone surfing this off-limits wave in Myanmar could be putting locals at risk of retribution from the heavy-handed military junta currently in power. Imaginatively named The Rock by a 2000 search party.

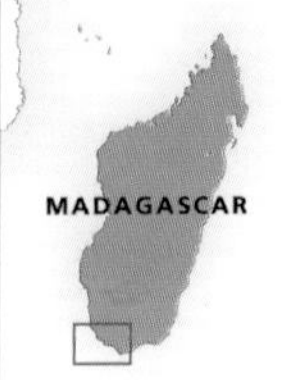

182. Southwest Madagascar

Lavanono Lefts

YEP

Summary
+ Quality left reefbreaks
+ Unique desert surroundings
+ Long, virgin, mellow waves
+ Perfect photographic light
+ Unreal "back in time" experience

– Strong SE trades
– Transport nightmare
– Extremely remote villages
– Lack of infrastructure
– Pricey domestic flights

While the airport accessible Fort-Dauphin and Tulear have appeared in the surf press since the '80s, the stretch of coast in between has long remained a mystery, thanks to the sheer degree of difficulty to get there. The main road RN 10, is no more than a dirt road full of potholes. It takes at least 40 hours for the Taxi-Brousse, the local bus, to go from Tulear to Fort-Dauphin, which is only 626km (389mi), but that's only if you're lucky and things go according to schedule.

Lavanono Beach

YEP

Itampolo

GILLES CALVET

Some nightmare trips have taken a week! Furthermore, to get to the coastal villages of Androka, Itampolo or Lavanono requires hitchhiking a lift with the water-tanker or lobster dealer trucks, otherwise there's only the zebu-

TRAVEL INFORMATION

Population: 18,606,000
Coastline: 4,828km (3000mi)
Time Zone: GMT +3
Contests: None
Video: Surf Session Madagascar
Other Resources:
lavanono.com
exittoafrica.com/madasurf/
chezalain.net

Getting There – Visa on arrival costs $30. Most flights go through "Tana" (TNR) usually from Paris via Air France or Air Madagascar. Fly to Fort-Dauphin (FTU) from Reunion Island for $600 return. From Tana, fly FTU or Tulear (TLE) but most transport is organized from FTU. Then, 6-8h by 4WD to Lavanono or rent a Cessna to land at the Lavanono airstrip; 3pax for $900 o/w.

Getting Around – Domestic flights are expensive FTU to TLE is $320 r/t and can be fully booked. Taxi-Brousse overland transport is amazingly slow (and cheap), only use it if you have lots of time. Renting a 4WD in FTU with a driver costs $300-350/day with Lavasoa. Beware of pirogue cruises, it can take days. Zebu cow cart trips are a classic!

WEATHER STATISTICS	J/F	M/A	M/J	J/A	S/O	N/D
total rainfall (mm)	82	28	14	6	10	51
consistency (days/mth)	7	4	2	2	2	5
min temp (°C)	22	18	16	14	16	20
max temp (°C)	32	31	28	27	29	31

Lodging and Food – In Itampolo, stay at Chez Alain at $20-30/dble, they know about surfing. Lavanono Lodge has a camp with 10 bungalows at $30-50 with lots of facilities, facing the spot. They provide all transports, even Cessna air transport from Fort-Dauphin. Truebluetravel.co.za do some Madagascan surf packages. Local food is dirt cheap, expect $2-3 for a meal.

Weather – The climate of Madagascar is generally sub-tropical with two seasons: a hot, rainy one from November to April and a cooler, dry one from May to October. Neither the trade winds nor the monsoons reach the southern part of the island, which consequently receives little rain and is, in places, a semi-desert. The dryness is aggravated by a cold offshore current. Annual average rainfall is 390mm (16in). Thunderstorms are common during the rainy season and tropical cyclones are an important climatic feature; the island has already been significantly damaged by their impact. Temps vary between 14-28°C (58-82°F) in winter and range from 20-32°C (68-90°F) in summer. Use a springsuit or light fullsuit from May to December and boardies for the other months.

Nature and Culture – Expect a full-on desert, Antandroy means the land of thorns! It's bushy, spiny everywhere with zebu cows and goats eating the meagre vegetation. It's a world lost in time, very remote, very basic facilities. Meet the friendly lemurs on the Berenty Natural Reserve. Some nightlife in Tulear, but it's often designed for sex tourists.

Hazards and Hassles – Sharks on this SW coast are rare. The reef in Lavanono is fairly flat, covered with seaweed but Androka and Itampolo are live coral. The SE wind can be a bother and it's coldish at night. Potential fleas in the beds! No mosquitoes but occasionally, small flies appear. Respect the local traditions.

Handy Hints – No need for a gun but kite-surf equipment would be useful. Take a beat-up board for the kids. There is no place on earth like Madagascar – be patient and open-minded and remember that all good things take time!

cow carts and they only go 5km/h. Don't try to use sailing pirogues between villages, as it might take days to cover dozens of nautical miles! Travel problems aside, there are undoubtedly some quality coral reefs and even a fun beachbreak to be savoured, along with the slow pace of life in this harsh, desert environment.

It's a good idea to get acclimatised by staying a few days in nearby Tulear or Anakao, before driving the 10-12h to **Itampolo Left.** These reliable, lined-up lefts in front of the village, wrap around a coral reef that is offshore in the prevailing SE'er. It's a 1km long paddle, so it's safer and more practical to use a local fishing boat. There are other reefs on the north side of the bay but the peaks are usually disorganized compared to the left. 48km (30mi) down the coast is **Androka**, where a large fringing reef shapes up some excellent bowling lefts that bend into the main channel, which is also flanked by wind-exposed rights on the other side. These waves sit about 3km (2mi) from the shore so getting a fisherman's help is essential. Just remember the whole process will takes heaps of time especially if you have to use the sail. Hardly anyone makes it to **Befamata**, an ultra-remote beachbreak with plenty of options, skirted by a long, sandy stretch eastward. Pristine water and surrounds, but it's cross-shore in SE winds. Most surfers only go to Lavanono, often travelling the long road from Fort-Dauphin and staying for as long as they can. Crowds are almost non-existent and the left is a long wave so this middle of nowhere village has become the region's No1 spot. A Reunion-based surfer, Jean-Jacques Arnouilh, aka Gigi, has set-up Sorona surf camp and helped the village install a crucial 3000l water tank. After a very slow start, the camp has become a reliable stopover for all passing travellers and a must-stop for travelling surfers, because Lavanono epitomizes the Malagasy experience. **Lavanono Beach** produces crystal clear waves and an especially long mellow right, breaking further out and rolling all the way to the shore. **Lavanono Lefts** are reminiscent of St-Leu on Reunion Island, as the reef starts with long racing walls, usually ruffled by side-shores, before bending into a hollow, dead offshore, end bowl section, offering the odd barrel for tail stomping stall masters! The bowl can be shallow but it's mostly flat, dead coral and covered with kelp. Despite being better at higher tides, on very low tides and small swell, the reef actually holds longish rights, zipping inside the reef if the trades are low. Further inside where the village sits, a reform left breaks, where the village kids take turns on a couple of beat-up boards, while the group sitting on the beach yell a warning whenever a set approaches. Those who travel by 4WD from Fort-Dauphin, may get to stop at the barely accessible **Cap Sainte-Marie** near Ankororoka, where there can be extremely long lefts, sheltered from the blustery SE winds.

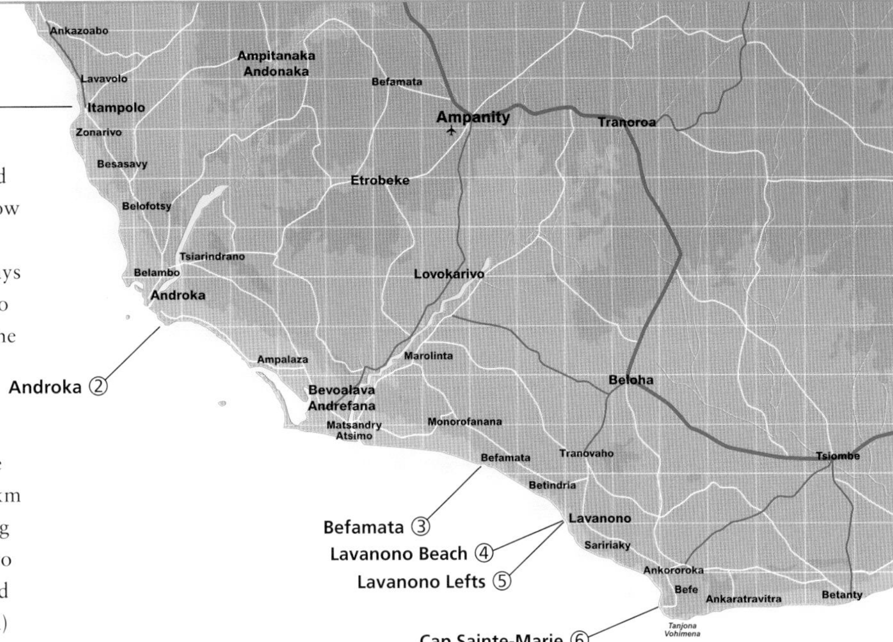

The same swells that hit Reunion island, sweep out of the S-SW off the top edge of the east travelling Roaring Forties lows as they head east for Australia. From April to September, expect regular 4-12ft (1.2-4m) swells on the SW exposed shores, where most breaks average 3-8ft (1-2.5m) waves. Because the prevailing wind is E-SE, most setups experience cross-offshore conditions and is better angled for the lefts. The SE trades can be accelerated by the venturi effect of the coastal mountain range, and sometimes shift onshore as cold front cells approach the coast in winter. Early winter season is best for gentle winds. A varatraza onshore wind spell is a real bummer and usually happens wintertime, while Sept-Oct are considered the windiest months. The tidal range is less than 2ft (0.6m) in the far south, but it becomes significant (6ft/2m) towards the Mozambique Channel, affecting navigation with local dug-outs to Androka or Itampolo reefs.

SURF STATISTICS			
Spot	Size	Btm	Type
①			
②			
③			
④			
⑤			
⑥			

SURF STATISTICS	J F	M A	M J	J A	S O	N D
dominant swell	S-SW	S-SW	S-SW	S-SW	S-SW	S-SW
swell size (ft)	2	3-4	4-5	5-6	4	2-3
consistency (%)	30	70	80	70	60	40
dominant wind	E-SE	E-SE	E-SE	E-SE	E-SE	E-SE
average force	F4	F4	F4	F4	F4	F4
consistency (%)	59	55	42	45	45	51
water temp.(°C)	25	25	22	21	21	23
wetsuit						

183. Anjouan

Dead Fishermen

ALL PHOTOS JOHN CALLAHAN/TROPICALPIX

Summary
+ Empty line-ups
+ Undiscovered waves
+ Beautiful landscapes
+ Variety of spots

– Onshore winds
– Political instability
– Diseases and poverty
– Inter-island transport

Located in the north of the Mozambique Channel, between Africa and Madagascar, the Comoros have hidden their surf potential for a long time, until a recent expedition found waves on Anjouan. The volcanic archipelago is made up of four islands; Grande Comoros, Anjouan and Mohéli form the independent Comoros Union, while Mayotte remains a French territory. Tourism is undeveloped thanks to political instability (18 coups in 24yrs, often led by the well-known mercenary Bob Dénard) and a lack of infrastructure. With a mix of African, Malagasy, Arab and Persian origins, it's hard to make a living for most Comorians in one of the poorest countries in the world, where poverty creates health problems like malaria and cholera. Grande Comoros, the biggest island of the archipelago and overshadowed by the 2361m (7746ft) peak of the Karthala volcano, holds a couple of low tide beachbreaks north of Moroni (Itzandra) sprinkled with a few coral heads. Also check the east coast beaches around Chomoni and the northern reefs near the salt lake. The little reef-fringed island of Mohéli has waves off Fomboni beach,

Vouani

TRAVEL INFORMATION

Local Population: 200,000 (Anjouan)
Coastline: Comoros – 340km (211mi)
Time Zone: GMT +3
Contests: None

Getting There – International flights via Dar es-Salaam (Tanzania), Nairobi (Kenya), Dubaï (Emirates), Johannesburg (SA), Madgascar, Mauritius, Sanaa (Yemen). Also flights from Reunion and Mayotte to Moroni in Grande Comoros. Going to Anjouan can be a hassle. Domestic flights between Grande Comoros and Anjouan, but with small planes (no boardbags allowed). The ferry from Moroni (and Mayotte) is irregular with no schedule, no fixed rates, and the comfort and safety of the passengers is a low priority.

Getting Around – The main road circles Anjouan with plenty of easy coastal access, but it is better to rent a 4WD, because many sections and bridges are damaged. Gas stations in Mutsamudu, Domoni and sometimes Moya. Both east and west coasts can be easily surfed in the same day. 4WD rental for $80-$100/d (+ fuel) with a driver (ask for Moustali).

WEATHER STATISTICS	J/F	M/A	M/J	J/A	S/O	N/D
total rainfall (mm)	188	132	4	3	11	130
consistency (days/mth)	16	8	2	1	3	7
min temp (°C)	23	23	19	18	21	23
max temp (°C)	31	32	31	31	32	32

Lodging and Food – Moya Pension Bungalows is probably the best place to stay ($20/nt) just in front of the reefbreaks and close to the beachbreak. To stay in Domoni, check Loulou Motel ($20/nt) or Mutsamudu (Al Amal). Few restaurants in Mutsamudu and Domoni ($5-15), or find cheap food in the street shops.

Weather – The archipelago has a tropical, warm climate with gorgeous vegetation, and a slight change between the 2 main seasons. East coast of Anjouan has a less humid climate than west coast (Moya) and the north coast (Mutsamudu). The temperature is a little bit more chilly when you go in the mountains. Water is boardshort warm year-round - take a rash or light wetsuit vest for when it's windy.

Nature and Culture – Covered by tropical forests, hiking inland should uncover the endemic fauna (lemurs, giant fruit-bats) and flora. Hike Mount Trindini from Domoni. Mosques and ancient monuments in Domoni show Arabic influences in the local architecture. Visit the old citadel of Mutsamudu at the top of the medina.

Hazards and Hassles – The Mozambique channel is known for it's shark factor. Lack of hospitals, many diseases and health problems. Drink only sealed bottled water. Domestic flights are on the European black list. Be careful at all times –don't travel alone.

Handy Hints – With the lack of real hospital infrastructure, bring your own first aid kit, anti-malarials and pills to purify drinking water. No surf shop, so take usual boards, a semi-gun, a spare leash, wax, sunscreen & a ding repair kit.

Goat Wash

SURF STATISTICS			
Spot	Size	Btm	Type
①	8/2		
②	6/2		
③	10/2		
④	6/2		
⑤	6/2		

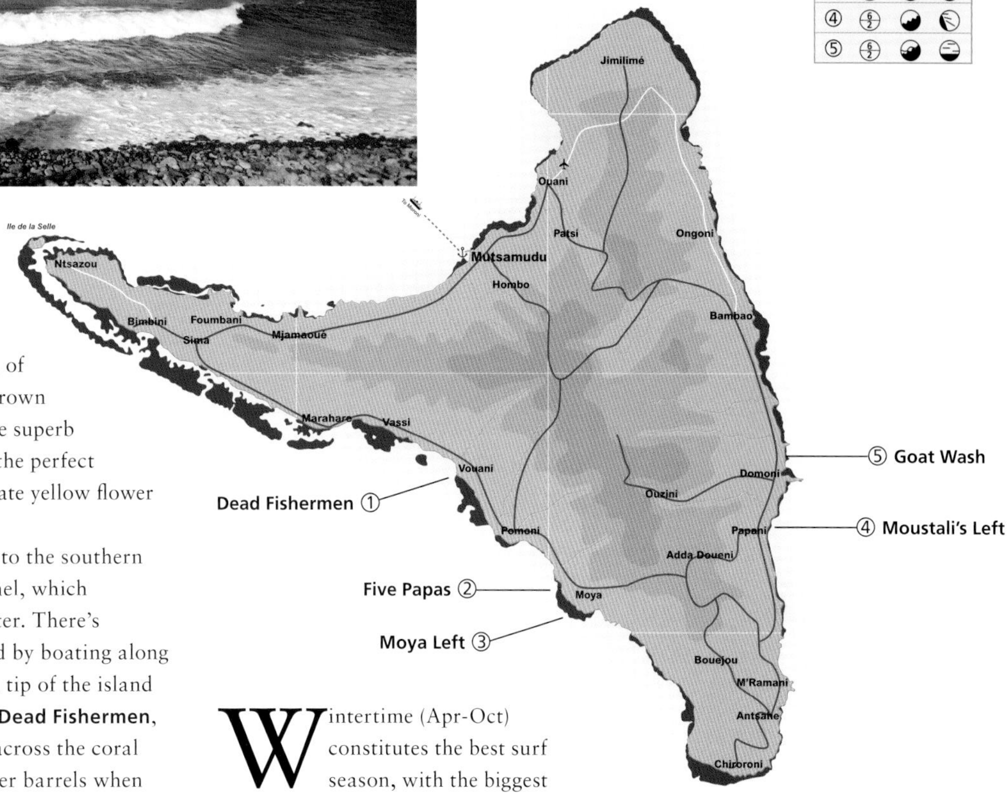

Ile de la Selle
Ntsazou
Bimbini
Foumbani
Sima
Mjamaoué
Marahare
Vassi
Vouani
Pomoni
Moya
Ouani
Patsi
Mutsamudu
Hombo
Jimilimé
Ongoni
Bambao
Domoni
Ouzini
Papani
Adda Doueni
Bouejou
M'Ramani
Antsahe
Chironoi
Dead Fishermen ①
Five Papas ②
Moya Left ③
④ Moustali's Left
⑤ Goat Wash

but Anjouan has the best potential for surf with a variety of spots and good exposure to the different swells. The island was in turmoil when they proclaimed independence from the Union of Comoros, but the separatists were overthrown by a military operation in early 2008. The superb tropical landscape of the island provides the perfect garden for producing ylang-ylang, a delicate yellow flower used for essential oils and fragrances.

The southwest-facing coast is exposed to the southern swells coming up the Mozambique channel, which sometimes show some decent size in winter. There's potential for more waves to be discovered by boating along the outer reefs between the northwestern tip of the island and Vouani. Just west of this village lies **Dead Fishermen**, a hollow, ledging right wall that sprints across the coral shelf in front of a big rock, offering proper barrels when it's clean. The surrounding waters are treacherous for outriggers and the wave packs a punch with heavy hold-downs. The little village of Moya is probably the best place to stay, with two spots breaking just in front of the hotel. **Five Papas**, a "V" shaped reef produces a longer walled left and short hollow right at mid-tide. **Moya Left** breaks on the outside coral reef, best at mid-high tide as the shallow reef drains down to dangerous levels at low and the strong current in the lagoon makes the paddle back to the beach tough. The long, black sand beach north of Moya offers nice peaks at low tide, with sandbanks stabilized close to the tunnel. Exposed to the NE windswell, the east coast can be regularly surfed in winter. **Moustali's Left** is the first spot accessible from the road south of Domoni, close to the filling station. The swell wraps around a bend in the coast covered in big black boulders and sometimes offers a nice wall. The place is exposed to the main onshore SE wind, so it needs to be glassy or NW to be any good. Just north of Domoni, **Goat Wash** is a peaky, punchy and occasionally hollow, black sand beachbreak. A good right appears at low tide, sheltered from S winds by the rocky point. Bambao can sometimes hold a decent fast right at the Tatinga rivermouth, but with many close-outs. The north coast of Anjouan between Mutsamudu and Sima doesn't pick up ordinary swell, but a few boulder reefs may pick up a northern cyclone swell in summer. One thing is for sure - this beautiful island has plenty more spots waiting to be discovered.

Wintertime (Apr-Oct) constitutes the best surf season, with the biggest S-SW swells produced by low pressures off the Cape of Good Hope and ploughing up the Mozambique channel. The eastern coast faces into the predominant NE-SE tradewinds and is the recipient of consistent swells, albeit with onshore winds.

SURF STATISTICS	J F	M A	M J	J A	S O	N D
dominant swell	NE	SE-SW	SE-SW	SE-SW	SE-SW	NE
swell size (ft)	1-2	2	2-3	3	2-3	1-2
consistency (%)	20	40	60	70	60	20
dominant wind	NW-N	SE-S	SE-S	SE-S	NE-S	N-NE
average force	F3-F4	F3-F4	F4	F4	F3	F3
consistency (%)	50	55	80	80	60	45
water temp.(°C)	29	28	27	26	25	27
wetsuit						

The Comoros is also in the road of the big summer cyclone swells, arriving from the N to NE, between December and March. The main winds blow from S-SE in winter, and from the N in summer. Tidal range can be very important and most of the beachbreaks are better at low tide.

Moya Left

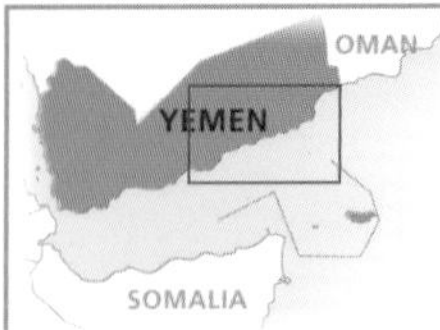

184. Yemen

Sheba's Wedge

TOBY ADAMSON

Summary
+ SW monsoon guaranteed surf
+ Powerful, virgin beachbreaks
+ Very warm water
+ Unique desert environment

– Messy windswell surf
– Lack of points and reefs
– Remote, difficult access
– Visas, permits and high costs
– Very hot

Yemen has an ill-founded reputation for feisty tribes, intent on war, kidnapping and bolstering the huge Al-Qaeda fan club in this fundamental Islamic nation. But, for those in the know, Yemen conjures up images of thunderous mountains, rolling desert dunes, ancient caravan cities and, most importantly of all, a warm-hearted and friendly people for whom pride, hospitality and honour are the pillars of life. So far only a handful of people have ridden the waves breaking along Yemen's long south-facing Indian Ocean coastline. A mid-summer 2003 trip by US expats Jay Quinn, Charlie Smith and Cole Estrada, found surf before British bodyboarder Stuart Butler unveiled 6-8ft beefy

STUART BUTLER

No Name

TOBY ADAMSON

TRAVEL INFORMATION

Local Population: 1.03M Hadhramaut
Coastline: 1906km (1185mi)
Time Zone: GMT+3
Contests: None
Other Resources:
oceansurfpublications.co.uk
hadmothtl.com.ye

Getting There – Visas required by all and can be collected on arrival at Sana'a if booked onto a tour package. Any evidence of a visit to Israel will mean refusal of entry. Almost all flights to Sana'a (SAH) are via the Gulf States. Prices tend to be cheap with Gulf Air probably being the best value. 2 daily flights from Sana'a to Riyan Mukalla (MKX).

Getting Around – Travel permits are required by all. An organised tour is really the only way of doing it. Try Future Tours Industries (http://www.ftiyemen.com) based in Sana'a or, Oceansurf who have in the past organised a surf tour to Yemen and may do so again in the future. Lots of desert driving under hot & dusty conditions. It is not possible to rent a car without a driver.

Lodging and Food – Plenty of hotels can be found in Mukalla and other towns with prices averaging around $10-18 for a mid-range double room. Exploring the coast means camping out on the beaches. A double room in 4 star Hadramaut Hotel in Mukalla costs $40. There is a diving centre. Food is cheap, but in the desert areas monotonous consisting of little but fish and rice.

WEATHER STATISTICS	J/F	M/A	M/J	J/A	S/O	N/D
total rainfall (mm)	3	2	0	4	0	3
consistency (days/mth)	1	0	0	1	0	1
min temp (°C)	22	24	28	28	26	23
max temp (°C)	28	31	36	36	35	29

Weather – Hot, hot, hot. During the summer surf season temperatures can average around 45°C with highs nearer to 50°C (113-122°F), but the monsoon winds have a moderating influence on the coastal areas and the temperature in Al-Mukalla hovers around 30°C (86°F). Though temps are a little lower the humidity is completely overwhelming. In winter, temperatures tend to be warm and range between 20-23°C (68-74°F). Afternoon winds can get strong and are very hot. Rainfall is unlikely but the eastern mountains catch a little cloud and mist from the monsoon. In summer, the climate of Hadhramaut is hot in the coastal areas and ridiculously hot on the plateaus, though not as humid. The water is in the high 20's to low 30's (85°F).

Nature and Culture – Where to begin? Yemen is stunning and unforgettable. It's every exotic Eastern fantasy brought to life. If the political situation ever calms down then Yemen will quite rightly become one of the biggest tourist destinations in the Islamic world. Highlights are the old town of Sana'a, the hundreds of fortified mountain villages, the ruins of ancient Kingdoms lost deep in the desert, the centuries old mud brick skyscraper cities of the Hadhramawt and simply mingling with the Yemenis and absorbing the culture and lifestyle of the worlds last remaining traditional Islamic society.

Hazards and Hassles – Heat, dust, lack of infrastructure, tribal tensions, travel restrictions, Al-Qaeda, high costs, sharks – the list goes on and on, but the truth of the matter is that Yemen is in fact one of the safest and most welcoming countries on the planet. There is almost no petty crime whatsoever and the dangers from Islamic militants are vastly over-inflated. Heat stroke and sharks (especially on Socotra) are the real dangers.

Handy Hints – Come prepared in every meaning of the word. There is no surf culture whatsoever, so bring everything. Respect the Islamic tradition and culture and keep an open mind. There are no tourist offices outside Yemen and the few in the country are of no real help. Lonely Planet's new Oman, UAE and Arabia guide contains the best information on Yemen written by Stuart Butler, one of the few people to have surfed Yemen.

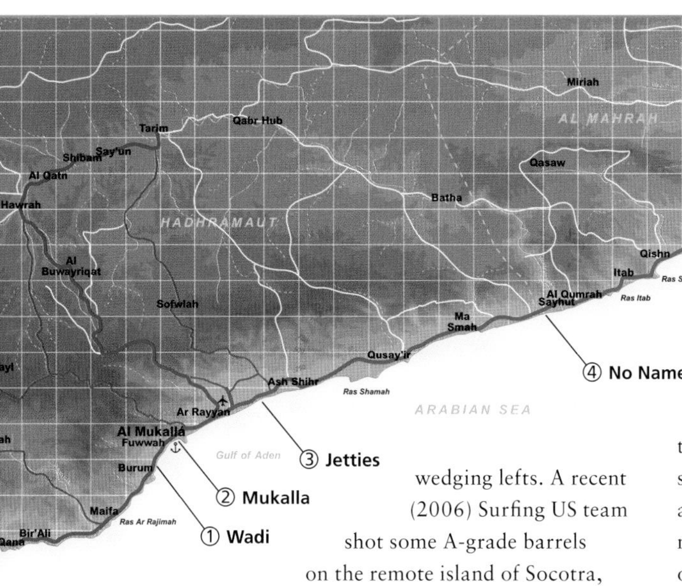

SURF STATISTICS			
Spot	Size	Btm	Type
①	8/2		
②	8/2		
③	8/2		
④	8/2		
⑤	8/2		
⑥	6/2		

wedging lefts. A recent (2006) Surfing US team shot some A-grade barrels on the remote island of Socotra, which holds a number of blown-out left pointbreaks and occasional beachbreak.

The best bet for mainland surf will be the provinces east of Mukalla, but be warned that this is not a trip to approach lightly. Ample time, determination and money are required to explore this coast and Yemen is totally flat for much of the year except between the months of late May and early September. The desert provinces of Hadhramawt and Mahra are a very long way from the beautiful capital, Sana'a, and Mahra in particular, is a very remote area indeed. Don't underestimate the difficulties of travel in this region. To get to the surf zone there are flights to Al Mukalla or Al Ghaydah or even go overland straight through the desert (sketchy). It is almost impossible to travel here independently as a surfer - there is little public transport, distances are long, tribes suspicious of strangers, access to beaches almost impossible without a 4WD, supplies virtually non-existent and a government travel permit is required. Due to the nature of the area where the surf is to be found, these permits won't be issued unless travelling with a recognised Yemeni tour agency. Such an agency should provide all permits, drivers, jeeps, armed guards, tribal escorts and all day to day supplies such as food, water and camping equipment, but of course none of this comes cheap and a two week trip here is going to cost in the region of US$2500 per person at a minimum. Yemen is primarily beachbreaks with a couple of reefs and points. **Wadi** is the name given to a dry river bed and this one 20kms (12mi) southwest of Mukalla leads to a bay with rights (Barbie's) and lefts (Hussain's) over volcanic rock. **Mukalla** has jetties with a small, polluted, right point breaking off one of them, but the old city has been surrounded by a wave-breaker since the late '80s, limiting the surf options. Check the rocky peninsula to the south of town. 15kms (9mi) west of Ash Shir, there is a village with huge circular oil storage tanks and 3 **Jetties**, which would provide good sheltered surf inside when it's stormy and big. Unfortunately, it is utterly out of bounds to everyone and heavily patrolled by army tanks and jeeps to prevent further suicide bomb attacks on the installation. A long expanse of exposed beach parallels the coast road and about 20kms (12mi) west of Al Qumrah, a mini headland offers some shape. Imaginatively called **No Name** the rights are generally hollower and faster than the fat mushy lefts on the other side of the point, which are exposed to more SW wind. **Haswayn** does not look like a great set-up but the village is amazing and waves break with angle really close to shore. In **Al Ghaydah**, check the village by the coast, there is a sloppy SE-facing beachbreak. All the accessible spots in between are just waiting for someone to discover and name them! With the swells coming out of the SW and much of the Yemeni coast being blocked from the open ocean by Somalia it doesn't take a genius to work out that the eastern parts of Yemen are the most reliable.

From June to August, it's never flat thanks to the SW monsoon, the world's most consistent weather system. As the Indian sub-continent and Arabia start heating up in April and May warm air rises over India and cooler, damper air rushes in off the Indian Ocean bringing with it torrential rains and strong winds. This depression generates gale force S-SW winds day in and day out for almost four months and creates the constant swells throughout the summer months. By the time this swell hits the Yemeni beaches, wave face height averages about 4ft (1.2m), rising to double this on big days and falling to 2-3ft on rare calmer days, but always the swells are fast moving and powerful. The wind that accompanied these swells out at sea largely dies away by the time the swells make landfall and, thanks to high coastal mountains strung along much of the Yemeni shoreline, the little remaining wind is often funnelled offshore - at least for the mornings. Tidal range is average reaching 6ft max. Check Aden tide tables.

SURF STATISTICS	J F	M A	M J	J A	S O	N D
dominant swell	NE	–	SW	SW	SW	NE
swell size (ft)	1	0	4-5	5-6	3	1-2
consistency (%)	10	0	80	90	60	20
dominant wind	NE-E	E-SW	S-SW	S-SW	S-SW	NE-E
average force	F3	F2	F3-F4	F4	F3	F3
consistency (%)	60	64	80	88	55	71
water temp.(°C)	25	27	29	25	26	26
wetsuit						

STUART BUTLER
Socotra

185. Baluchestan

Kabab

ALL PHOTOS OLIVIER SERVAIRE

Summary
+ Totally empty waves
+ Break diversity
+ Consistent monsoon surf
+ Warm water
+ Exotic culture

– Short swell season
– Painful heat
– Mild onshores
– Language barrier
– Risky country

Tucked between Iraq, Afghanistan and Pakistan, the political and geographical landscape of Iran isn't exactly perfect for a trouble-free surf trip. Yet Iran has coasts on three seas, and while the Caspian and the Persian Gulf are too enclosed to produce much surf, it's not the case for the Gulf of Oman, which connects with the Indian Ocean. The region of Baluchestan and its Makran coast continues into Pakistan (see Zone 99, WSG Vol2), offering endless opportunities to discover new waves in the bays and on the headlands of this sparsely inhabited, deserted seaboard. Inland, the narrow coastal plain rises rapidly into the mountain range, so most of the population work in fisheries located in a string of small ports and even smaller fishing villages, explaining the name Makran, meaning fish eater.

Bod

Boats abound in a village like **Tang**, but their operators rather stick to their routine than take curious surfers to the rights off the hammerhead peninsula, 2km from the

TRAVEL INFORMATION

Local Population: 2.29M
Coastline:
Sistan & Baluchistan
270km (168mi)
Time Zone: GMT +3.5h
Contests: None
Other Resources:
iranhydrography.org

Getting There – Getting a visa might be tough especially in the US. Iran's a big country and Chabahar (ZBR) is 2200km (1367mi) away from the capital of Tehran (THR) where international flights land. While a railway is planned, there are already regular flights ($150 r/t). On the way back surfboards will only get on the plane if it's not already loaded with fish containers.

Getting Around – The coastal road is usually fine and allows multiple surf checks. Local taxis can serve as guides and interpreters, but finding a reliable one may come at a price ($60-80 daily). Police roadblocks are common but not that much of a hassle. The road east of Chabahar is mainly coastal while the westward road sits inland. Petrol is dirt cheap.

WEATHER STATISTICS	J/F	M/A	M/J	J/A	S/O	N/D
total rainfall (mm)	18	9	5	55	8	7
consistency (days/mth)	2	1	1	2	1	1
min temp (°C)	12	19	26	29	24	14
max temp (°C)	25	31	36	35	33	29

Lodging and Food – Chabahar's best hotel is the 4* Lipar located in the Free-Zone ($80 double). Sepideh, Daryayi and Keshtirani are much cheaper options in town. Remember that AC is a must. Kababs served with rice are the national dish. No beer, try doogh, a fizzy drink made from yoghurt, spices and aromatic herbs. Cheap food, usually $2-3 a meal.

Weather – Chabahar is close to the tropic of cancer and in the route of the monsoon winds from the Indian subcontinent and the tropical fronts. Therefore, and because of its proximity to the sea, it has a tropical climate. The zone is the warmest part of Iran in winter with average temps of 19°C (66°F) and the coolest part in summer with temps around 32°C (90°F). The place is called "Char-Bahar" which means four springs due to its mellow warm weather and breeze from the Gulf of Oman. Average annual rainfall is 110mm (4.4in). The trees are always green during the year and it is one of the most beautiful areas of the province. Boardies are sufficient to go surfing except during winter when it's better to have a shorty.

Nature and Culture – The free zone provides shopping opportunities, but fishing villages don't. Check out the curiously eroded "Mars Mountains" or the GelFeshan mud volcano. For a real taste of Persian culture fly to Isfahan, the cultural capital. Budget-priced skiing in high resorts and fantastic rock climbing near Tehran.

Hazards and Hassles – Beachbreaks can hide some nasty rocks; remember you're a long way from everything. Heat is the main danger, don't go anywhere without water. Despite attractive surf consistency, the border area is a sensitive one. Iran is an Islamic republic, don't stray from the rules. Getting to Iran might be discouraged by family, embassy and insurance.

Handy Hints – English is seldom spoken. Persian (Farsi) is the official language, although locals mainly speak "Baluchi" which is derived from Hindi languages. Even though it's 40°C, dress codes require long sleeves. T-shirts on land and boardshorts in the water seem tolerated... only for men of course! Take plenty of wax and at least 2 boards.

village. A large offshore sandbank blocks swell from the beach. Access is an issue around Gurdin, requiring a good 4x4 to explore and also at **Pozm** where the lefts in front of the jetty break too close to the cliffs for comfort. The best waves are out the end of the Konarak peninsula but a naval base keeps the area shut down. Things get better going eastward from the airport thanks to a reliable coastal road. Negotiate with employees of the **Aab** water desalination plant to surf the perfect beginner's beachbreak either side of the breakwalls. Counting over 50,000 inhabitants, Chabahar is a fast growing city, thanks to being the biggest oceanic port in Iran and a free trade zone. The northern beaches are too sheltered from the swell, but on the other side of town, **Darya Bozorg** (Big Sea) lives up to its name. This easily accessible beach proves perfect for a surf check, but despite interesting reef setups, most waves end up on dry reef. For a safer surf, head east to **Lakposht** where a good beachbreak can be surfed with only turtles for company. A stop at the **Maahi** fish cannery offers a great view of what may be the best pointbreak around. Unfortunately there's no way down the 60ft (20m) cliffs and only a boat ride from Ramin can reach the lefts that peel below. **Ramin** probably offers the best combo of surf and access. West of the port, a beachbreak offers mellow, crumbly waves, at least till the heavy shorebreak turns on. To the east lies a left pointbreak dubbed **Kabab** since it offers several sections instead of a straight ride. The waves start as a heavy peak facing the point before flattening out and then reforming into the bay to offer some of the best barrel opportunities around. There's a longer pointbreak setup towards the shrimp factory, **Meygou**, but the lefts don't line-up that well and cliffs complicate the access. The road then follows a string of consistent beachbreaks with plenty of potential. **Bod** located in front of a metallic windmill may not be the best one, but it surely packs plenty of power and the windmill makes it easy to spot. Beachbreak action continues under the crazy shadow of the so-called **Mars** Mountains all the way to **Beris**, which features a large port and a couple of points. One of them offers a perfectly wrapping lefthander, but requires tons of swell to get going and only a boat or a very long paddle could get you to the bottom of the huge cliff. Neither Pusht or Pesabandar offer anything much different, but there's a last treat towards **Gwatar**. Water flows into the sea from a man made irrigation canal forming a rivermouth righthander that peels for about 100m in the muddy water.

Gwatar

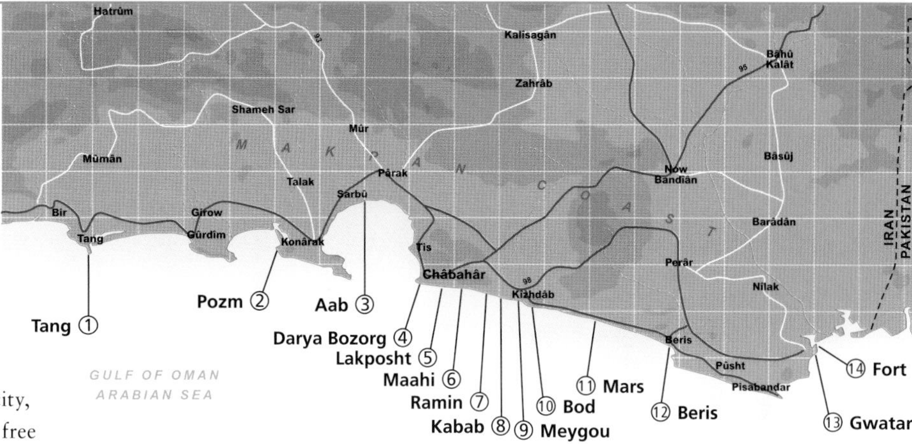

Since the water is discharged by a nearby shrimp farm factory, its quality is dubious at best, and so murky only a shark could enjoy it. Yet, it's hard to walk away after witnessing a head-high set roll in. The final option before Pakistan is a point where a couple of small right-handers break, but since it's occupied by a police **Fort**, these waves may not be worth the hassle and remain off-limits.

SURF STATISTICS			
Spot	Size	Btm	Type
①			
②			
③			
④			
⑤			
⑥			
⑦			
⑧			
⑨			
⑩			
⑪			
⑫			
⑬			
⑭			

Though the main Indian Ocean pulses could theoretically rush-in the narrow window of the Oman Gulf, swells are all about the monsoon. In June, July and August, regular SW winds will send constant 3-12ft (1-4m) swells, or tropical storms can occasionally create big wave conditions. In June 2007, Gonu, the strongest tropical storm ever recorded in the Arabian Sea, brought record breaking waves of 4 meters

Maahi

to the Chabahar area. However, the likelihood to score overhead waves is quite low, but there's surf everyday in summer where nearby Europe is often plagued by long flat spells. The Baluchestan province is located at the crossroads of the Nambi S wind and the Shomal or Gourich N wind, but during the surf season, the monsoon naturally takes over to produce mild onshores. Although the wind can temporarily blow out some spots, it also provides some much appreciated relief from the heat. Tides follow a semidiurnal tide pattern with diurnal inequality, reaching 10ft (3m) on spring tides.

SURF STATISTICS	J F	M A	M J	J A	S O	N D
dominant swell	S	S	S	S	S	S
swell size (ft)	0-1	1	3	4	2	0-1
consistency (%)	10	20	70	80	60	10
dominant wind	S-SW	E-W	S-W	SE-SW	S-W	SW-N
average force	F3-F4	F2-F3	F4	F3-F4	F3	F2-F3
consistency (%)	40	48	80	72	72	59
water temp.(°C)	23	25	29	29	28	25
wetsuit						

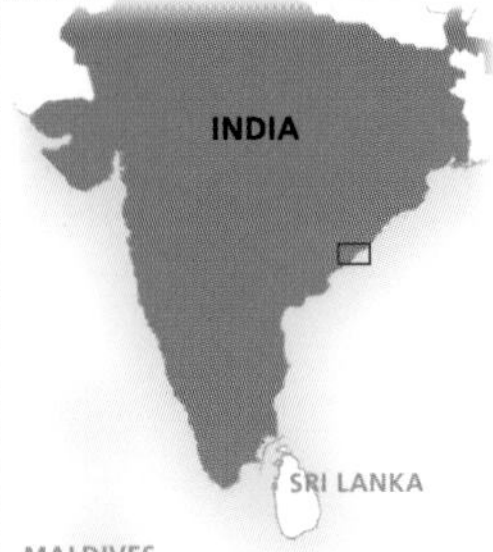

187. Andhra Pradesh

Lawson's Bay

ALL PHOTOS JOHN CALLAHAN/TROPICALPIX

Summary
+ Set of virgin right pointbreaks
+ Perfect longboard waves
+ SW monsoon consistency
+ Cheap beach hotels
+ Fascinating "surf city" culture

– Small waves
– Sideshore trades
– People shitting on beach
– Intense heat
– Crazy traffic

After 3 surf missions to the Andaman Islands, Asian-based photographer John callahan/tropicalpix turned his attention to the mainland, where he found some promising satellite pictures of the indented coastline around Visakhapatnam, backed up by good photos of Lawson Bay. Visakhapatnam, aka Vizag, boasts 3 million residents and it's large harbour is the focus for naval operations, steel production and other heavy industry. Tourists avoid the place and even today, there are only 10,000 foreign visitors, mainly businessmen rather than backpackers. Dubbed the "City of Waves", there are many aquatic icons like giga-size dolphins, mermaids and submarines along the busy Beach Road. Lawson Bay is the most obvious spot producing the longest and the biggest waves within walking distance from the Beach Road hotels. A huge fleet of 2,000 fishing pirogues punch out through the surf every day to hit the Bay of Bengal deep waters and then surf the boat on some long waves when they return. Only the kids are allowed to play in the surf and lots of them do on the inside, but these are the only locals to contend with in the long, empty line-ups.

Park Hotel

A long way north, **Sandy Point** reveals the most significant pack of kids playing in the reforms with

TRAVEL INFORMATION

Local Population: 75,727,000
Coastline: 970km (602mi)
Time Zone: GMT+5h
Contests: None
Other Resources: surfingindia.net
Video: Fuel TV On Surfari

Getting There – Pay for 6-month visa from Indian embassy prior to travelling. Visa valid from issue date, not arrival date and onward ticket required. Indian Airlines flies to Vizag (VIZ) daily from Mumbai, Calcutta, Hyderabad and Chennai. Domestic flights are fairly expensive ($300 r/t from Mumbai, cheaper from Chennai) but no extra charge for boardbags. Trains and buses are dirt-cheap, but journeys can take days. 30mins transfer to Park Hotel.

Getting Around – Andhra Pradesh (AP) is the 5th largest state in India; it takes 12h by train from the capital city Hyderabad. Once in Vizag, rent an Ambassador taxi ($25/day), a 4WD jeep if you're a group ($100/day) or just a rickshaw ($0.50/short trip) for nearby spots. Traffic is hair-raising, take a driver!

WEATHER STATISTICS	J/F	M/A	M/J	J/A	S/O	N/D
total rainfall (mm)	9	18	82	138	190	37
consistency (days/mth)	0	1	4	9	10	2
min temp (°C)	19	25	28	26	25	23
max temp (°C)	30	34	36	33	32	31

Lodging and Food – All the rooms in the 5 star Park Visakhapatnam Hotel have sea views and direct access to the beach. Full luxury facilities costs $110 with full board including safe, not-so-spicy food. Next door is Palm Beach; A/C double room is $20. Avoid street food, ice and un-bottled water!

Weather – Andhra Pradesh climate is subtropical dry with hot temps in spring. It rains in summer as well as in winter. The summer monsoon (June-Sept) is the SW monsoon which contributes nearly two thirds of rains (600 mm) in the state, while the winter monsoon (Oct-Dec), supplies the remaining one-third. On average, the coastal region receives the highest rainfall (1000mm/40in). Periodic droughts occur with heat waves (40°-50°C/104-122°F) that kill hundreds of people, usually in April-May, before the onset of the SW monsoon and violent electrical storms. During the SW monsoon, occasional floods in coastal Andhra may cause transport chaos. The monsoon rains are not as heavy as in Kerala and other western Indian states. It always feels really warm and there's no escape from the oppressive heat.

Nature and Culture – Visit some temples including the XIth Simhachalam. Beach Road is fairly entertaining. Climb Kailashgiri Park for Lord Shiva Parvathi statue and Lawson's Bay view. Check Dolphin's Nose, a huge rock promontory jutting out into the sea, sheltering the harbour.

Hazards and Hassles – Hundreds of shitters on the beach may cause bad smell, diarrhoea and possibly transmit disease. Favour rising tides! If you cut yourself, heal carefully and avoid infections. The flat rocks on the points don't require booties. Drink lots of fluids to withstand the intense heat. Be alert in the streets, more because of traffic than street crime.

Handy Hints – No need for a gun but a longboard will be useful for the smaller days. Take lots of wax and expect to surf long waves with no-one but your crew, so come in a group. Be ready to face poverty and infirmity. Wake up and surf early. May-June are the best months. Learn to understand the local way of saying yes, nodding the head sideways.

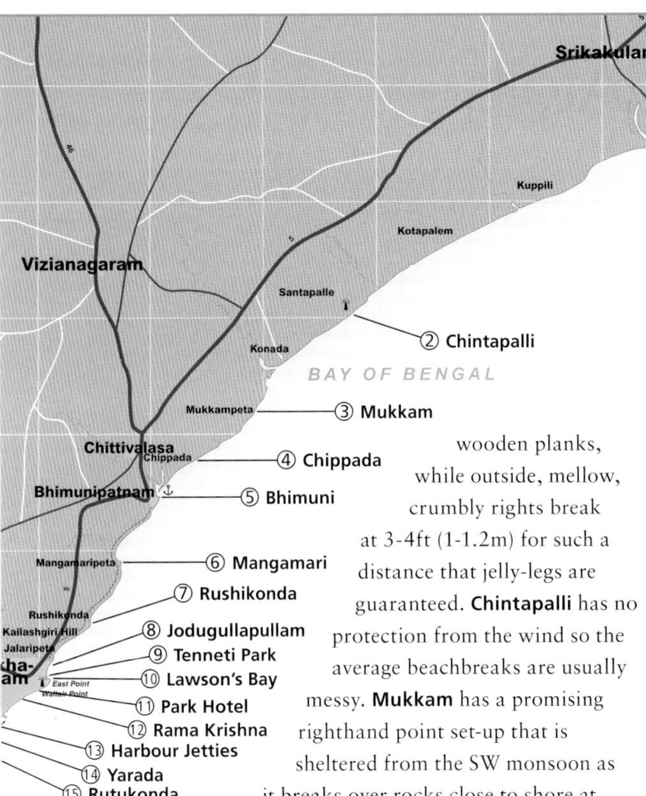

wooden planks, while outside, mellow, crumbly rights break at 3-4ft (1-1.2m) for such a distance that jelly-legs are guaranteed. **Chintapalli** has no protection from the wind so the average beachbreaks are usually messy. **Mukkam** has a promising righthand point set-up that is sheltered from the SW monsoon as it breaks over rocks close to shore at lower tides. Getting to **Chippada** is an ordeal via a half hour dirt road drive then a half hour walk along a dry river bed. It's an exposed rocky headland that has shallow banks and is probably a good small swell option. The scenic rights of **Bhimuni** have a sucky take-off leading into long sectioney walls that work best at high tide on bigger wrapping S swells. One of the best righthand points is **Mangamari**, where a rocky shoreline straddles a golden sand beach and waves peel for up to 800m (875yd) on big glassy days. When the lines start bending by Mangamari Peta point, there is still 90% of the swell size breaking on the first rock clusters. At high tide, despite some backwash, waves can unzip pretty fast with a real tubular wall, breaking in front of the rocks that cuts the wave in two at lower tides. Heavy refraction inside the bay means it is offshore all day in the SW monsoon and the fun sandbanks are perfectly suited to longboarding. Needless to say it's a long walk back, zigzagging between turds on the beach. **Rushikonda** is the number one tourist beach, with nice facilities, restaurants and no shitting on the beach rules, but the surf set-up isn't great, pushing the swell too wide onto ever shifting outside sandbanks. **Jodugullapullam** is an exposed beachbreak with difficult access and a potential left for the goofy footers. **Tenneti Park** is overlooked by a peaceful communal space filled with early morning meditaters and stretchers. It consistently holds the biggest waves wrapping in off Waltair Point, but it needs to be a clean, lined-up swell and SW-W winds. It's a flat submerged reef with quite a few big rocks, but most of them are well inside of the impact zone. More often than not, at least 1 or 2 waves per set are really hollow from the sucky take-off before filling into endless cutback shoulders. Effortless entry from the keyhole means dry hair paddle-outs. Visag's best right is **Lawson's Bay** in the town of Kailashgiri, another 500m+ (547yd) ride from take-off to the beach. The outside needs to be glassy to be rideable and the rock suck-outs can be intimidating but really give the wave some powerful sections. After a series of cutbacks, the wave reforms and there's some aerial action close to shore with the backwash! Aka E Point, the assorted peaks opposite the **Park Hotel** need light NW conditions and a bit of size to clear the many rocks lurking in a line-up that favours the lefts. The most popular beach along the Visag Beach Road is **Rama Krishna**, another rocky stretch that gets out of control in the NE-SW trades and disorganised wind swell. Also check Submarine Beach nearby. There's a large choice of **Harbour Jetties** with the pick being the south side of Dolphin Nose, but the serious pollution should be enough of a deterrent. **Yarada** is a long beach down Dolphin Nose lookout that is punchy but often closes-out, so high tide is better. **Rutukonda** is similar and also has a righthand point set-up and a rivermouth bringing pollution to a line-up that rarely looks inviting and the horrendous cross-town traffic is also worth avoiding.

SURF STATISTICS

Spot	Size	Btm	Type
①			
②			
③			
④			
⑤			
⑥			
⑦			
⑧			
⑨			
⑩			
⑪			
⑫			
⑬			
⑭			
⑮			

Tenneti Park

The Bay of Bengal is quite a deep (2.6km/1.6mi average) and vast oceanic mass, about 1,200km (745mi) wide from Chennai to Andaman and 1,500km (930mi) long from Bangladesh to Sri Lanka. There's at least 3 types of swells: SW monsoon windswells, long distance Indian Ocean straight S swells and rare (6 per year) cyclone swells pushing NE-E swells. SW wind-driven waves from Sri Lanka to Vizag usually push 4-8ft (1.2-2.5m) of ocean swell, especially from May to August, but they decrease markedly in size when refracting inside the points & capes, because windswells don't wrap as much as groundswells. Exposed shores will be a messy 3-6ft (1-2m), while protected north-facing bays break at 1-3ft (0.3-1m) with offshore conditions in S-SW winds. Mornings are often glassy while moderate SE-SW seabreezes usually blow after 10am. Southern hemisphere, long period swells are not so frequent, while during NE monsoons, there are occasional 2-3ft (0.6-1m) windswell mushburgers. The biggest tides reach 5-6ft (1.5-1.8m) so expect medium variations on some of the rocky sections and slight changes on the sandy spots.

SURF STATISTICS	J F	M A	M J	J A	S O	N D
dominant swell	NE-E	S-SW	S-SW	S-SW	S-SW	NE-E
swell size (ft)	1-2	2	3-4	3	2-3	2
consistency (%)	30	40	80	70	50	40
dominant wind	NE-E	SE-SW	S-SW	SW-W	S-W	NE-E
average force	F3	F3	F4	F4	F3-F4	F4
consistency (%)	57	82	81	86	53	82
water temp.(°C)	26	28	29	28	28	27
wetsuit						

190. Southeast Sri Lanka

Arugam Bay

ALL SHOTS YEP

Summary
+ Consistently clean and rideable
+ Various right sand pointbreaks
+ Laid-back friendly vibe
+ Amazing sightseeing and wildlife
+ Cheap

– Consistently small and mellow
– Crowded Arugam Bay
– Long access, slow driving
– Intense heat and insects
– Civil war bombings

Shaped like a teardrop below India, Sri Lanka divides the Arabian Sea from the Bay of Bengal. Famed for a warm welcome and laid-back atmosphere, this ancient culture is blessed with superb temples, rich wildlife, Ayurvedic massages, and some great tropical surf. Unfortunately, Sri Lanka is still being shaped by two modern catastrophic events: the civil war, which has been raging since 1983 (64,000 deaths) and the 2004 tsunami (35,000 deaths). For centuries, the Tamils have been claiming the north and eastern part of the island for the Sinhalese people and most of the bombings are aimed at government targets in northern Jaffna or Colombo, however, in September 2006, local unrest between Pottuville residents and security forces, sadly spilled over into peaceful Arugam Bay. An exodus of visitors followed and resulted in a travel warning. First surfed in 1964, Arugam Bay is no longer a surf secret, but on 26th Dec 2004, it was almost erased off the surfing map by the Boxing Day tsunami. Six waves, estimated to be 45ft (13m) high, struck this region with apocalyptic force, flattening the fishing

Okanda

TRAVEL INFORMATION

Local Population: 629,664 Ampara
Coastline: 1,340km (832mi)
Time Zone: GMT+6
Contests: National
Other Resources:
mambo.nu
ceylonsurfingtours.com.au

Getting There – 30 day visa upon arrival. Fly Sri Lankan to Colombo (CMB) from Europe. Daily flights with Singapore or Malaysian from SE Asia or USA. Airport is in coastal Negombo 45min north of crazy Colombo traffic. A-Bay is 9h drive away ($125 o/w by private van). Bus is 12-20hrs, twice daily ($3) Break up the scenic journey with an overnight stop in the "Hill Country", Kandy, or Ella/Haputale.

Getting Around – A-Bay is only 300km (186mi) away from Colombo so 40km/h is a good speed. Road network is light, potholed and there are multiple army checks. No traffic around A-Bay except Pottuvil. Hire a van ($50/day with driver) or use tuk-tuk (local ride $1) or walk. Boat rides are tempting but 4x cost and 2x time; A-Bay to Okanda is 2h by boat but 1h by tuk-tuk.

WEATHER STATISTICS	J/F	M/A	M/J	J/A	S/O	N/D
total rainfall (mm)	115	53	49	79	164	361
consistency (days/mth)	7	5	4	5	9	17
min temp (°C)	24	25	26	25	24	24
max temp (°C)	28	31	33	33	32	28

Lodging and Food – Cheap beach guest-houses like Hillton cost $10-20/day for room with fan. Medium priced Hideaway is $30/day, on the wrong side but great food. A/C places include Siam Hotel ($20-40), Tri-Star ($40-60) or Stardust Hotel ($26-67) for doubles. Food is tasty, sometimes spicy, & around $5 for a full meal.

Weather – Arugam Bay area is ideally located to avoid the ravages of the two annual monsoons that hit the island from opposite directions – the SW (May-September) and NE (Nov-Feb). This southeastern corner is the driest part of the country and it's stifling hot in the summer before the SSE sea breeze kicks in. The desert-like weather cools nights off, making sleep without aircon possible after 11pm. Average annual precipitation hits 1,900mm (75in), with thunderstorms and rainy days are rare apart from occasional NE storms, mostly during the off-season time of the year. Our Trincomalee weather stats from 200km north are wetter than A-Bay area. Weather records show an average of 330 sunshine days/year! Boardshorts year-round!

Nature and Culture – Yala National Park is the main wildlife sanctuary; enter from Okanda (cheaper than Tissama) but you need to rent a vehicle ($50-80/day). Check Kumana Bird Sanctuary. Many Hindu shrines close by like Katara-gama. Sri Lanka is a paradise: Sigiriya citadel, Kandy Perahera Festival, Ayurvedic massages. Full moon parties!

Hazards and Hassles – Besides the Tamil Tigers civil war bombings and rare local disputes, A-Bay is very peaceful. Main hassle is the slow roads. Very little shade at most spots, so take enough water and make sure your tuk-tuk driver will pick you up after surfing! July-Sept are the most crowded months.

Handy Hints – Air Taxi domestic flights have stopped summer 2007, because of Tamil Tiger rebels using light aircrafts to bomb civilian and military targets. Tourist numbers have dropped by 20% in 2007. Bring cash - The Bank of Ceylon in Pottuvil is a nightmare. You can rent NSP boards at Aloha and SurfNSun. Bring a fish type of board.

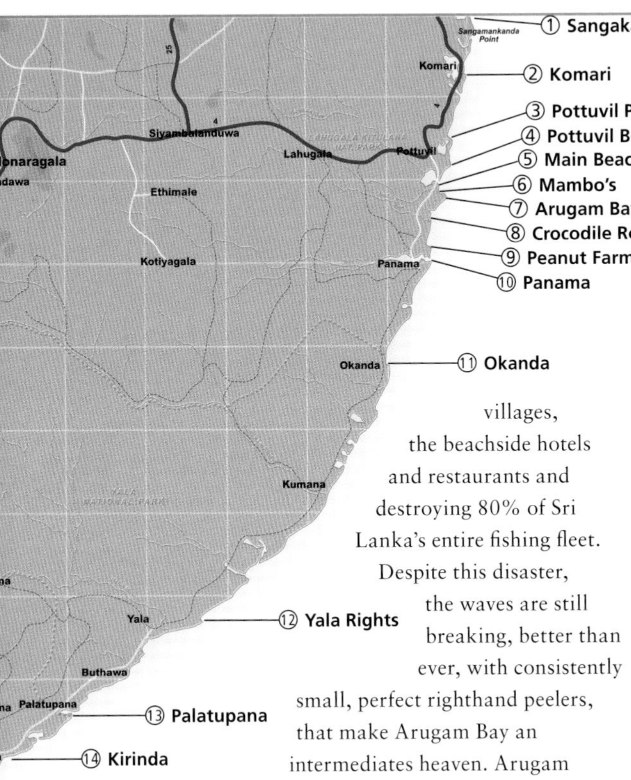

villages, the beachside hotels and restaurants and destroying 80% of Sri Lanka's entire fishing fleet. Despite this disaster, the waves are still breaking, better than ever, with consistently small, perfect righthand peelers, that make Arugam Bay an intermediates heaven. Arugam Bay (the 7 villages) is often compared to Kuta, Bali in the late '70s to early '80s, before the major developments and the civil war has contributed to keeping the village in its most basic form. A-Bay is the focus, but there seems an endless supply of sheltered sand-bottom pointbreaks along this southeastern coast.

Wave quality varies depending on sand build-up from point to point, which is heavily affected by river flows. **Sangakamanda** rivermouth is hardly ever surfed since access is difficult and wave quality not really worth it. **Komari** is a 20min walk from the end of the road to a small lighthouse on a rocky headland. Aka Green Point, it's hard to find and gets blown out in the afternoon sea breezes. The best northern spot is **Pottuvil Point**, which can have 800m (875yd) long rides from the tip to the beach, with a barrel in the middle in front of the huge granite rocks. Waves hug the shoreline and although small can be fun, A-Bay needs to be 4-6ft for Pottuvil to break, making it a low consistency break. Walk 700m north to ride a similar but shorter point away from the crowds. **Pottuvil Beach** has a scalloped cove with point-style rights pushing wide and deep, making it a perfect beginners zone only 20mins tuk-tuk ride from Arugam Bay. Despite being usually close-out beachbreak, the **Main Beach** at A-Bay should not be overlooked, especially near the bridge, where there can be a wedgy A-frame over the offshore rocks. The reform in front of **Mambo's** guesthouse can be a beginner's heaven, because it is always offshore, grooming tiny perfect walls, close to shore, making it simple to walk back up the beach. The southern point of **Arugam Bay** is a top-class wave breaking over an old coral reef, which can be dangerously shallow and sectioney at low tide. It's very consistent and often crowded with occasional barrels in front of the corner, but the afternoon SE sea breeze messes it up. South of the landmark **Crocodile Rock** is a sandy point with mushy rights, requiring a 20 min walk to get to, including crossing two rivermouths where the potential to bump into some wildlife is high. Semi-secret **Peanut Farm** is the best quality option within easy travel of Arugam, despite the 20min walk from Panama. Sucky rights break close to the rocks, while the beachbreak is perfect for beginners. **Panama** only works when the rivermouth is closed, offering rocky rights and a tiny reform by the boats. **Okanda**, is about 1h by tuk-tuk from A-Bay and picks up as much swell onto a sucky outside sandbar below a whale-shaped rock. The super-fun walls inside the cove are always offshorebut are also off-limits for now. The Yala National Park is now a war zone and the guards will even stop people from swimming let alone surf the sandy **Yala Rights**. Boat access used to be the go but is too dangerous now. **Palatupana** was wiped out by the tsunami and the surrounding surf seems to all be close-out shore-dump these days. **Kirinda** jetties hold small, sloppy and often polluted beachbreak. Surf potential increases further west around the coves and reefs of Tangalla.

SURF STATISTICS

Spot	Size	Btm	Type
①	4/1		
②	5/1		
③	6/1		
④	8/1		
⑤	8/1		
⑥	5/1		
⑦	8/2		
⑧	6/1		
⑨	6/1		
⑩	4/1		
⑪	6/2		
⑫	6/2		
⑬	8/2		
⑭	4/1		

Pottuvil Point

The main swell producer is the SW monsoon pushing constant 4-10ft (1.2-3m) SW windswell from May-August, along with long-distance S swells from the 20°-50° latitudes, mainly between March and November. Swell direction matters for those long distance swells and S-SE is obviously better than S-SW. Because of distance and angle, waves mostly break in the 2-6ft (0.6-2m) range and 3-4ft (1-1.2m) is the perfect size for A-Bay. Above this size, A-Bay becomes sectioney, so it's best to ride other spots like Pottuvil, Peanut Farm or Okanda. Bengal Bay does produce some rare NE swells in the 2-4ft (0.6-1.2m) range, but it's mostly onshore with overcast skies, rainy weather and running rivermouths. During the SW monsoon, the day starts with a bit of early morning sickness, then light offshore up to 11-ish, before the low to moderate S-SE sea breeze starts messing up the outside sections. Tidal range is only 2ft (0.6m) max, but A-Bay's sand-covered reef gets shallow and getting in and out at low tide is a bit tricky. Only slight changes for the neighbouring spots.

SURF STATISTICS	J F	M A	M J	J A	S O	N D
dominant swell	N-E	SW-W	SW-W	SW-W	SW-W	N-E
swell size (ft)	1-2	2	4	4	3	1-2
consistency (%)	30	40	80	80	60	20
dominant wind	N-E	N-E	SW-W	SW-W	SW-W	N-E
average force	F3-F4	F3	F4	F4	F4	F3
consistency (%)	85	40	88	89	79	52
water temp.(°C)	27	28	28	27	27	27
wetsuit						

191. Rakhine & Ayeyarwaddy

The Rock

JOHN CALLAHAN/TROPICALPIX

Summary

+ Exploration possibilities
+ No crowds
+ Consistent monsoon swell
+ Unique people and countryside
+ Independent tourism good for local economy

– Wet and onshore swell season
– Repressive dictatorship
– Coastal access restrictions
– Gov. tourism funds regime
– Opposition party wants tourism boycott

Locked away on the eastern shores of the Bay of Bengal is the secretive Buddhist nation of Burma. Given the opportunity, this beautiful country could be a main tourist destination in Asia, thanks to its plentiful supply of natural resources, but it has never had much of a chance under the repression of the State Peace and Development Council (SPDC). This military led dictatorship has re-christened the country Myanmar, but despite being the biggest geographical area in SE Asia, many western governments refuse to recognise the new name and continue to use Burma. Regardless of what you call it, the biggest obstacle to travelling to and experiencing this fabulously exotic culture is one of conscience. Tourism is in it's infancy and the government controls almost all facets, which often have a very negative

STUART BUTLER

Gottaung Beach

EMI MAZZONI

TRAVEL INFORMATION

Local Population: Yangon 4M
Coastline: 1930km (1200mi)
Time Zone: GMT +6.5
Contests: None
Other Resources: oceansurfpublications.co.uk

Getting There – Visa costs about $30 and only lasts 28 days. Most south Asian airlines fly into Yangon (RGN) and from there you can travel by bus or privately hired car (always with a driver) to the west coast beaches (about 6h away). Note that the capital city has been moved to remote Pyinmana.

Getting Around – Roads are often in a terrible state or non-existent since the cyclone and distances are long. Due to restrictions on where you can and cannot stay, it is perfectly feasible to get by on public transport, but a private car and driver would at least enable you to surf those beaches on the edge of the 'open' areas. Internal flights with government run airline are not recommended.

Lodging and Food – Avoid government run hotels and restaurants at all costs. There are now an increasing number of small, and often basic, locally run hotels where a room won't cost more than a few bucks. Every village has an abundance of basic restaurants serving very cheap and tasty Indian and Chinese influenced food.

Weather – Coastal Burma has a typically hot and sticky tropical climate and temperatures vary little throughout the year, but reach a peak around April when average highs are above 30°C (86°F). The rains begin around mid-May, peak in July and die away in early October. Throughout this time which unfortunately coincides with the swell season, expect daily torrential rain, normally confined to afternoons and evenings. Temperatures are slightly lower at this time of year, but humidity is intense. From late Oct to Feb, much of the country is dry and sunny with pleasant temperatures in the high 20's and low 30's (80-90°F). Water is boardies warm year-round, especially in SW monsoon. Cyclones are rare, but the cyclone and tidal wave of 2008 killed over 100,000 people, displaced millions and devastated the region.

Nature and Culture – Burma is stunningly beautiful and fairy tale exotic. The country literally glows in greens and blues and everywhere you look are the golden poems of Buddhist Stupas. The two biggest highlights have to be the Shwedagon Paya in Yangon and the temple ruins of Bagan, quite remote from the coast. It's also a frontier of global biodiversity in the world.

Hazards and Hassles – Very safe destination with crime of any sort against foreigners being almost unheard of. There are innumerable and constantly changing rules as to where you can and cannot go. Avoid all talk of politics. Do not put Burmese people into situations that could compromise them, it is rumoured that there are government spies everywhere. Beware with snakes.

Handy Hints – Take all surfing equipment with you as none is available anywhere in Burma. There are very few guidebooks available Lonely Planet being the main one. Before you choose to go you should look at www.amnesty.org and www.burmacampaign.org.uk. There is rebel-held territory in northern Myanmar. Check Seal Asia for boat deals.

WEATHER STATISTICS	J/F	M/A	M/J	J/A	S/O	N/D
total rainfall (mm)	4	30	394	555	287	40
consistency (days/mth)	0	1	18	25	15	2
min temp (°C)	18	23	24	24	24	21
max temp (°C)	33	36	32	29	31	31

impact on the local population. Displacing villagers to build new hotels in prime locations is an obvious consequence, but behind the scenes, it is claimed that the Burmese tourist industry is built on slave labour and funded by illegal heroin and jade mining. Villagers are given little choice in the matter and human rights abuses are common, so most western governments advise their nationals not to visit or invest in Myanmar. If visiting Burma, it is almost impossible to avoid financing the military junta, therefore enabling them to continue to suppress the Burmese people. Even the imprisoned leader of the opposition party implores foreign tourists to stay away, so we are publishing this information from an education and "what could be" standpoint, in the hope the political situation improves. The true extent of the tragedy of the 2008 cyclone Nargis will probably never be known and the governments refusal of western aid will cost many more thousands of lives. Rebuilding this region will take a very long time and much of the coast will be even more inaccessible than usual.

The Myanmar coastline is 1900km (1180mi) long and can be divided into three parts: the Rakhine coastal area to the west, the Ayeyarwaddy delta in the middle and the Tanintharyi division with the Mergui Archipelago to the south. Weaving through the mass of government imposed restrictions and finding a suitable surfing beach is easier said than done as visitors have little choice as to where they can and cannot go. What this essentially boils down to is that only a handful of the thousands of swell exposed beaches along this coastline are open to foreigners. So far, there have only been two media surf trips, firstly by John Callahan, Randy Rarick and Tor Johnson in March, 2000, to the offshore island of Cheduba (now Manaung) via Ngapali. The second trip was undertaken by Stuart Butler and the Italian crew of Surfnews, searching along the Rakhine State coastal road in Sept, 2003. Every spot surfed so far, bar one, is within a kilometre or so of the handful of west coast beaches currently open to foreigners. Though nothing is likely to happen to any tourist who manages to visit and stay on a closed beach, the consequences for any Burmese perceived to have helped a foreign tourist can be severe. Nowadays, Burma does contain a small privately run tourist industry, including a few simple hotels, restaurants, tea houses and transport companies that should be favoured ahead of the government run establishments. It's normally fairly easy to tell them apart because the government places are always bigger, brighter and largely empty. **The Rock** is a little islet off the southern tip of Cheduba Island discovered on the Callahan trip and shown in The Surfers Journal Vol 10 no.1. It's officially off-limits to foreigners. Ngapali Beach is the largest and oldest resort open to foreigners and is the easiest place for surfers to head to. The main beach gets poor quality waves but **Gottaung Beach**, 2kms to the north, can be wedgy and hollow, especially at low tide, but don't expect much above chest-high peelers. 30km (18mi) south of Ngapali, **Peninsula Left** is clearly visible on Google Earth, but is hard to get to without a boat and Stuart Butler came up empty handed when he went looking for it. **Kanthaya**, a newly opened tourist beach 120km (75mi) south of Ngapali, has a rivermouth to help create some sandbanks, but it's a slow, arduous road journey to get there. Just down the coast at **Gwa** an airfield makes it theoretically possible to fly from Yangon in 50mins (if there were flights!) but the curved beach is fairly protected at the southern end and is usually quite small. Another popular beach is **Chaungtha**, only 5hrs drive from the capital, attracting droves of middle-class holiday makers on the weekend to this northwest-facing beach with consistent waves, even in the regular onshores. **Ngwe Saung** is a recently developed area with 9km (5.5mi) of consistent beachbreak and plenty of empty resort hotels (many with government connections) and not a surfer for miles.

Burmese surf comes from two swell sources, the first are the super long distance southern hemisphere swells generated by storms off Antarctica. Having travelled halfway across the world these swells are very clean with long lulls. On the minus side they rarely get above 4-5ft (1.5m). A much more likely scenario for waves occurs between mid-May and late September when the Indian SW monsoon sweeps across the northern Indian Ocean and into the Bay of Bengal where winds blow close to gale force on a daily basis and generate big, but messy, short period swells for the coasts of Burma. In the heart of this period, there's swell almost every day, but also plenty of onshore wind and rain, so better to come at the start or end of the season when there's still plenty of swell activity. Interspersed with the wet and wild days will be calm, sunny offshore periods with, hopefully, great waves. Tides are semi-diurnal and hit 7ft (2.1m), which have a significant effect on most coastal areas. Many areas remain off limits to foreigners since the 2008 cyclone inundated the southern delta with a storm surge up to 25ft (8m) high.

SURF STATISTICS

Spot	Size	Btm	Type
①	6 / 1		
②	8 / 1		
③	6 / 2		
④	5 / 1		
⑤	4 / 1		
⑥	6 / 1		
⑦	5 / 1		

SURF STATISTICS	J F	M A	M J	J A	S O	N D
dominant swell	SW	SW	SW	SW	SW	SW
swell size (ft)	0-1	1-2	4-5	5-6	3	0-1
consistency (%)	10	30	70	80	60	10
dominant wind	N-NE	SW-N	S-W	S-W	S-W	N-E
average force	F3	F3	F3-F4	F4	F3	F3
consistency (%)	71	81	85	95	56	82
water temp.(°C)	25	27	29	28	28	27
wetsuit						

EMI MAZZONI
Ngwe Saung

Rasdhoo Atoll
ARI ATOLL
NORTH NILANDHE ATOLL
SOUTH NILANDHE ATOLL
KOLHUMADULU ATOLL
NORTH HUVADHOO ATOLL
SOUTH HUVADHOO ATOLL
ADDU ATOLL

Surf culture meets stone-age culture on megalithic Sumba, where the exclusive Nihiwatu surf resort controls access to the powerful lefts.

East Asia

PAUL KENNEDY

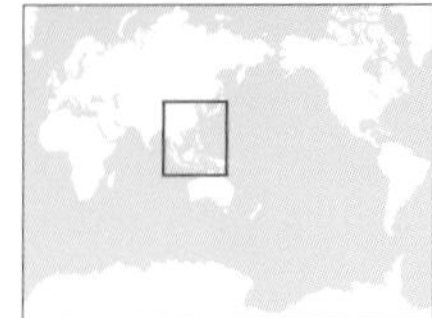

Surf Culture

The cultural melting pot that is East Asia has seen surfing evolve in a haphazard fashion, radiating out from the two focal points of Indonesia and Japan. Both countries have a deep rooted relationship with the sea and may have ridden waves on crude wooden bellyboards, possibly as far back as the 12th century in Japan. American servicemen brought their boards not long after WWII, then Bruce Brown scoped out Honshu for the *Endless Summer* in 1963, followed by Tak Kawahara, who shared his shaping skills and Californian industry contacts to kick start the local formation of a surfing association and national championships by 1965. Soon after, trailblazing surfers began clearing a path through the jungles of Indonesia for mass tourism to follow. Bali is a perfect example and while the well-heeled travellers of the 1930's were first to ride the warm Kuta beachbreaks, it wasn't until the early '70s that Uluwatu footage in the seminal film *Morning of the Earth* (1972) instantly transformed Bali into the ultimate surf destination. This sparked a search that resulted in some of the most notable wave discoveries of the century, starting with Grajagan (Laverty, Boyum, Jones; 1974), Nias (Troy, Geisel, Lovett: 1975) and the Mentawaii (Wakefield, Goodnow, Fitzpatrick; 1980), which in turn spawned the first surf camp and surf charter businesses. GI's like Derek Bailey started body surfing Big Wave Bay, Hong Kong in the 1960s, but the Chinese government has often arrested surfers for paddling out and is only now relaxing their stance in HK, Hainan, Guangdong and beyond. Taiwan has been less draconian, with a heritage dating back to 1965 and local pioneers like Mao Guh and his brothers ignoring the government ban and surfing Jin Shan beach with US soldiers. China Beach provided some essential beachbreak R&R for the US military during the Vietnam war, which in turn led to the establishment of surf culture in the Philippines, when the cast of war flick *Apocalypse Now* (1976) left their boards for the local kids in Baler, who now dominate national competitions. US airmen introduced surfing a few years earlier at the South China Sea breaks on Luzon, but it took another 17 years for legendary explorer Mike Boyum to discover the aptly named Cloud 9 and political instability has stunted the growth of surfing in the Philippines. The same can be said of South Korea who confiscated boards from the first surf mission in 1992, but 12 years later, Callahan scored super-typhoons, avoiding nervous lifeguards, who keep a non-swimming population out of the water. Less obvious Asian surf countries such as Thailand and Malaysia have been opened up courtesy of the ubiquitous travelling Antipodeans between 1980 (Phuket) and 1990 (Cherating). Other late blossoming regions include Papua New Guinea, which is arguably more Melanesia than Asia, where inquisitive Aussie's have spent the '90s discovering the treasure trove of reefs on the eastern islands and mainland surf towns like Vanimo and Wewak which are now developing a local surf population.

JOHN CALLAHAN

After decades of exposure to western surf culture, it's little wonder that Asian surfers have built their own scene, holding local competitions in some of the world's finest waves. Padang Padang recently hosted The Search.

Right – **As China awakens to it's extensive surf potential, police and lifeguards nervously enforce a swimming ban, especially when a typhoon swell hits.**

Today

Wedged between two great surfing oceans and home to the densest populations, Asia is an emerging surfing superpower in terms of wave resources and it's manufacturing supremacy, which now sees the world's largest surfboard building operation based in Thailand. It's also the base for most wetsuit manufacturers and of course China (and to a lesser extent Indonesia) is the source of just about all surf fashion and accessories. Bali alone has over 115 surf outlets to service the constant stream of tourists and an ever-growing local population that is starting to produce world-class surfers capable of taking on the top 44. International competitions have been run at all the world-class breaks including Uluwatu (1981), Nias (1994), Grajagan (1995) and Lakey Peak (1997), but even better mileage has been gleaned by endless media boat trips to the Mentawaii islands, showcasing the plethora of perfect waves in every surf mag on the planet. The Mentawaii indigenous tribes have benefited from the surfing invasion thanks to the dedication of the surfing doctors who set up Surf Aid, focussed on reducing some of the devastating yet treatable diseases like malaria. Natural disasters are common in the region with tsunamis, earthquakes, mudslides and typhoons, but the 2002 Bali bombings shook the surfing world as the terrorists targeted a surfers favourite night club. Japan's surf scene blossomed in the late '70s, attracting industry brands to milk the large population, willing to pay big bucks for boards, clothing

YEP

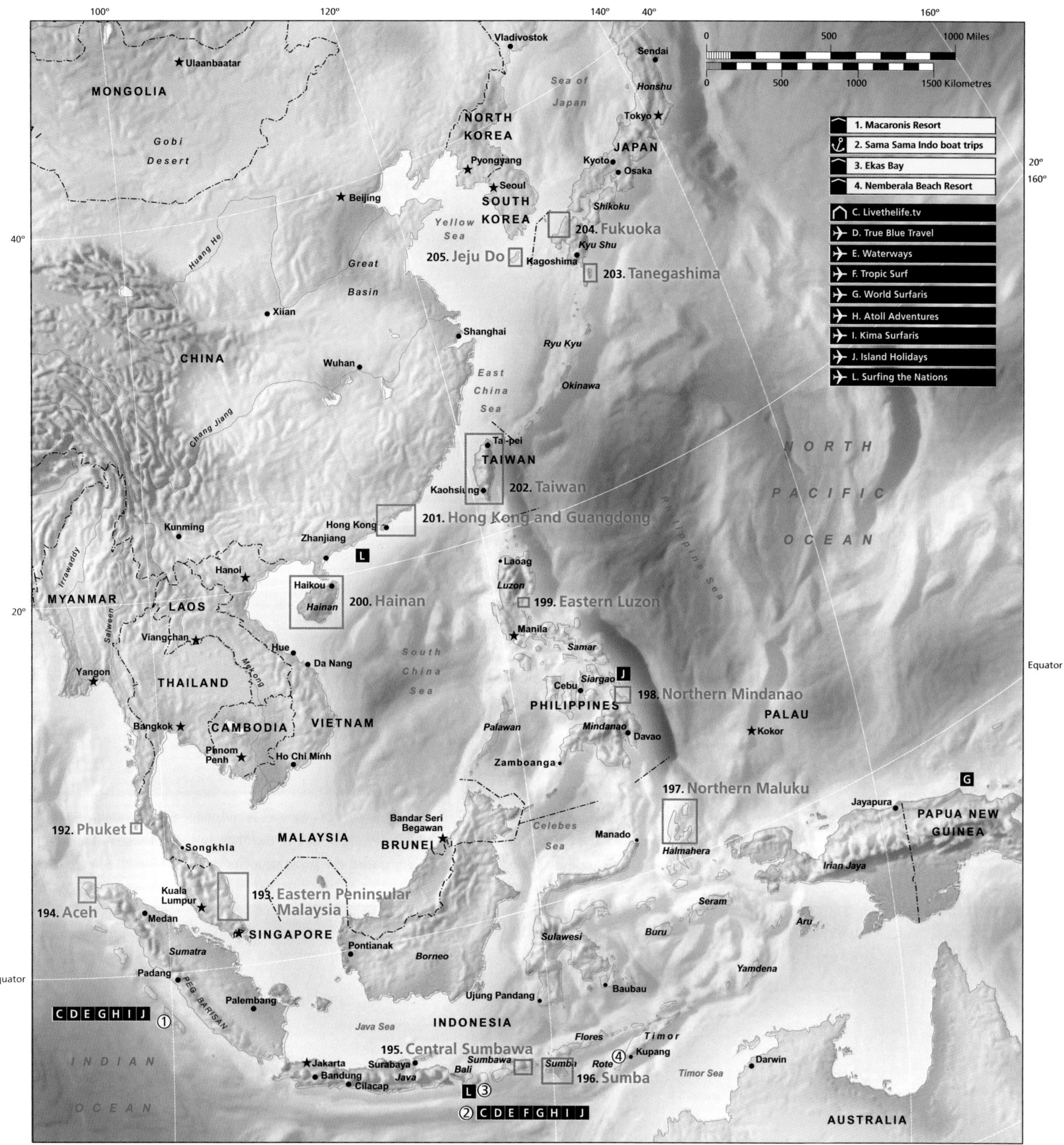

and accessories from abroad. Many a shaper got rich quick and big department store Marui sponsored more pro surfing events in Japan than either Australia or Hawaii hosted. The Miyazaki Ocean Dome wavepool cost $100M, yet despite the investment and huge numbers of surfers (approx 1M), the Japanese have failed to make an impact on the world circuit. In 2003, the 720 surfing contest saw Japan's Shinichi Yoshida become the first surfing champion of China, which is just awakening to the surf possibilities around it's extensive coastline. Localism is restricted to the busier breaks of Bali and some spots in Japan, but generally speaking East Asia has been a welcoming region to the hordes of foreign surfers who invade each year. Bad vibes at boat access banner breaks, particularly in the Mentawaii, is on the increase, as punters feel they have bought the exclusive rights to the waves, but with dozens of charters and increasing land-based surf camps, surfing alone is truly becoming a luxury few can afford.

193. Eastern Peninsular Malaysia

Cheriting

YEP

Summary
+ Frequent NE monsoon swells
+ Plenty of mellow beachbreaks
+ Small, friendly local surf population
+ Cheap and safe country
+ Good tourist infrastructure

– Short swell season
– Mainly messy windswell
– Lack of reefbreaks
– Murky monsoon waters
– Rainy swell season

Malaysia is made up of Peninsular Malaysia and East Malaysia located on the northern part of Borneo island, which the Indonesians now call Kalimantan. Peninsular Malaysia abuts the South China Sea on the east and fringes the Straits of Malacca on the west coast. The east coast comprises of mainly sandy beaches (91%) exposed to South China swells from the N and E. These exposed beachbreaks seemingly work best in the early monsoon season, when the sandbars have built up during flat summers. The weirdest fact about Malaysian locals is that most of them have learned to surf at Sunway Lagoon in Petalin Jaya, between the airport and KL. No personal or fibreglass boards are allowed, only softboards alternating 1h for bodyboards then 1h for surfboards. It costs $8 for entry plus $7 for board rental. Quiksilver organizes an international contest on December 31st and in 2003, Indonesians won the event boosting airs and tail slides and the pool got pretty popular after many pros did jet ski tow-ins.

Sunway Lagoon

YEP

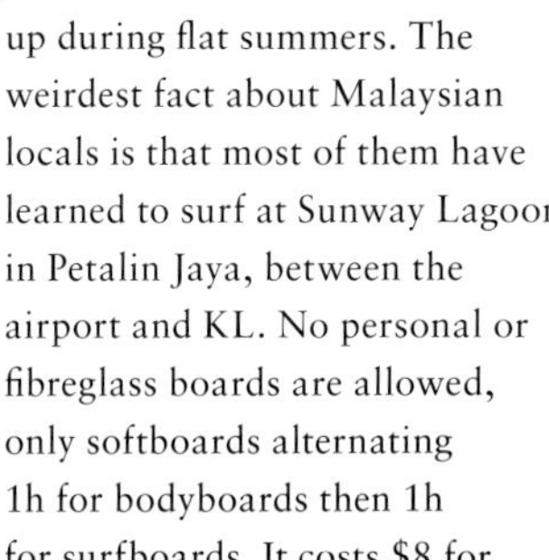

Quarry

YEP

Marang may be the only right pointbreak in Malaysia, but it's rarely surfed and needs specific conditions to work. The offshore resort islands like Perhentian, Redang, Gemia

TRAVEL INFORMATION

Local Population: Kuantan 450,000
Coastline: Malaysian Peninsular 2068km (1285mi)
Time Zone: GMT+8
Contests: Teluk Chempedak Malaysia (Nov 2006)
Other Resources: cheratingblue.com ecsurf.com
Video: Fair Bits (2006)

Getting There – 30 or 60 day visa on arrival. Malaysian is an excellent airline not charging for boardbags. KL airport is in Sepang, 75km (47mi) from Kuala Lumpur (KL), it takes 1h+ to get to town. From Singapore, cross the causeway at Johor Bahru, catch a ferry or take the train. 3 ferry lines between Malaysia and Indonesia. Penang-Medan is the most popular.

Getting Around – Rent a Malaysian Proton ($50/day, Orix). It's a 4-5h drive to Kuantan on the C4. Long distance taxis are twice the price of buses, but they're a comparatively luxurious and efficient way to travel. KL has a notoriously bad public transport system and avoid peak-hour city travel.

WEATHER STATISTICS	J/F	M/A	M/J	J/A	S/O	N/D
total rainfall (mm)	203	150	172	206	246	548
consistency (days/mth)	9	12	16	15	19	20
min temp (°C)	22	23	23	23	22	23
max temp (°C)	29	32	33	33	32	30

Lodging and Food – In Cherating, surfers go to Mimi's Guesthouse ($15/rm). Duyung Beach Resort, closest to the point ($18/chalet). Palm Resort family rooms ($27/nt). Many resorts closed from Nov to Feb monsoon season. Food is cheap and varied.

Weather –The tropical monsoon climate brings uniform temps of 21-32°C (70-90°F) throughout the year and average temps of 24°C (75°F) during the night. January through April are less humid and warm, while the months of May to December are the wettest. Rainfall generally occurs Oct/Nov and end of Feb with average annual rainfall about 2200mm (88in), coming in the form of a shower every 15 minutes. Malaysia is a maritime country with abundant sunshine, but it is very rare to have a full day with completely clear skies, because of the constantly moving cloud cover. Boardshorts only.

Nature and Culture – In KL, check Petronas Towers, KLCC shopping mall, the Loft pub and nightclubs like Zouk, Passion or Beach Club. Sepang Grand Prix is in March. Visit the Cameron Highlands (jungle walks, waterfalls, tea plantations, gardens), Batu Caves towering limestone outcrop or Taman Negara jungle.

Hazards and Hassles – Malaysia is one of the most pleasant, hassle-free countries to visit in SE Asia. Frequent rains can be a bummer during swell season, but that keeps the numbers and prices down. Water is murky and tidal rips can be heavy, but it's fairly safe, sandy surf. Local surf population is still small and very friendly.

Handy Hints – No need for a gun, but maybe a longboard. It's possible to buy some equipment in KL and rent boards at Satu Suku surf shop in Cherating. Lots of potential for discovery.

or Kapas maybe worth investigation. There are rumoured lefts at **Tanjong Jara** not far from the airport and a golf course and a bit further south check out the rocky headland of Pantai Teluk Bidara. **Kertih Resort** beach suffers from offshore banks killing the swell size and strength. The jetty to the south of the resort can create some shape to the banks, but it's rarely bigger than waist-high. The ivory sands of **Pantai Kemasik** hold small beginner or longboard waves south of the island. Further south is **Star Jetty Cruise**, a 500m long pier on stilts, which affords little or no wind protection. It needs a big swell and early season sandbars to be worth it. The most reliable beachbreak is **Kijal**, spreading the peaks along a 1km long coastal road and it's often best near the rocks at the south end. **Strawberry Resort** used to be the local's secret spot, boasting long walls and bowly sections down a sandy lefthand point, but access is often refused by the resort guards. It's best at low tide with no wind as it is fully exposed to the NE. **The Quarry** used to hold world-class lefts, but two rock jetties built in 2002 cut the spot in two. There's a short ride off the jetty's tip and then the wrapping pointbreak section on the inside. Still a good place to surf plus there are some rights to the south. It's hard to get access to the rocky pocket beaches on either side of the big industrial zone and harbour at Kemaman, but **Teluk Mengkuang** offers a little N wind protection in a big swell. On low tides and big swells **Chendor Beach** can hold wrapping lefts with many sections over estuarine sandbars, but swell energy is less focused than Cherating. It's down a long sandy track, followed by a 1km walk. It's a long walk and paddle to **Club Med**, visible from the Cherating line-up, sporting mellow, refracting lefts next to an island. There's always a pack on the sandspit lefts of **Tanjung Cherating**, Malaysia's best wave, which is about 5h from KL. This long, protruding sandbank takes the NE breeze side-on and although it is not so powerful, Cherating peels for a long way through the brown, rivermouth water. Take-off section can be hollow and it is always better at low tide. Intense rips require constant paddling to stay in position, but after a wave it's a walk back up the beach to access the peak. **Baluk Beach** hosts the Monsoon Madness windsurf event, but the flat beach slope means the waves are junky, catering for beginners from the surrounding resorts. Surfers from KL usually hit **Teluk Cempedak**, where fast-food restaurants and shops attract crowds to the attractive beach, peppered with granite boulders. The waves are often sloppy, but good enough to hold the occasional surf contest. Singapore surfers are often seen at Desaru in the very south, riding slow mushburgers or on idyllic Pulau Tioman, where a small surfer's community enjoy a semi-right point and a protected deep bay beachbreak at **Pantai Juara**.

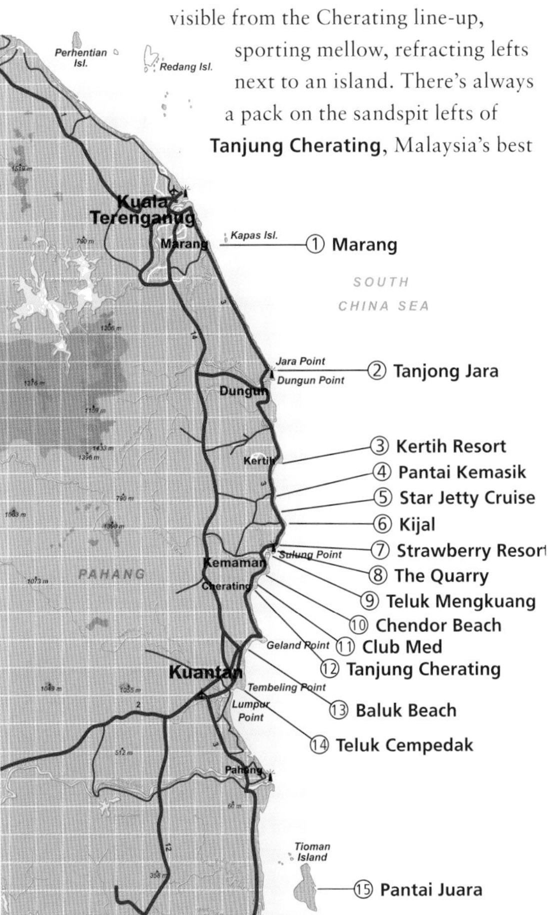

Quarry

YEP

SURF STATISTICS			
Spot	Size	Btm	Type
①			
②			
③			
④			
⑤			
⑥			
⑦			
⑧			
⑨			
⑩			
⑪			
⑫			
⑬			
⑭			
⑮			

During the NE monsoon from November to March, an atmospheric high pressure centres over China, a low pressure establishes over Japan and the winds blow from the NNE, bringing lots of stormy weather and swells down the South China Sea. The NE monsoon is subject to surges or rapid increases in strength, quickly producing rough seas upon reaching shallow water. Between Nov and Jan, consistent 6-12ft (2-4m) swells produce waves in the 2-6ft (0.6-2m) range on exposed beachbreaks, which seemingly only work before or after the heart of the NE monsoon like October or February-March. Locals don't count their experience in years but in seasons, as from April to October, there is not a single wave to be ridden, apart from rare late summer typhoon swells. Tides have irregular semi-diurnal cycles and reach 6ft on springs, which significantly affects the waves through all tidal stages.

Pantai Juara

JOHN CALLAHAN/TROPICPIX

SURF STATISTICS	J F	M A	M J	J A	S O	N D
dominant swell	N-NE	N-E	N-E	N-E	N-E	N-NE
swell size (ft)	4	1-2	0-1	0-1	2	3-4
consistency (%)	70	20	0	10	20	60
dominant wind	N-NE	N-NE	SE-S	SE-S	E-SE	NW-NE
average force	F3	F2-F3	F2-F3	F3	F2-F3	F3
consistency (%)	50	33	40	56	34	59
water temp.(°C)	29	31	31	29	28	27
wetsuit						

194. Aceh

A-Frame

BERNARDIN

Summary
+ Indo off-season conditions
+ Tsunami recovery help
+ Uncrowded waves
+ Wild Sumatra
+ Pulau Weh diving

– Lack of very consistent swells
– Separatist region
– Not quite Indo world-class
– Malaria, post tsunami havoc
– Basic accommodation & transport

Aceh, Indonesia's most western province, lost 100,000 people or 25% of it's whole population in the 26th December 2004 tsunami, out of a death toll of almost 300,000 people from 42 different countries. Worst hit was Indonesia with 220,000 victims and near the epicentre, the 30-35ft (10-12m) waves left waterlines up to 60ft (20m) above sea level. Aceh boasts 1,500km (932mi) of coastline and more than half of it was hit by the tsunami. Sumatra is the sixth largest island in the world and the third largest in Indonesia. The Aceh province has historically been more Muslim than other regions of Indonesia, but when Indonesian president Suharto pressured Aceh to come closer to the centre, it sparked off the Free Aceh Movement (GAM), which meant assassinations,

Galetzka devastation 10/2/05

CORNISH TRAVELLERS

BERNARDIN

TRAVEL INFORMATION

Local Population: 260,000 Aceh - 40M Sumatra
Coastline: 4,870km (3026mi) - Sumatra
Time Zone: GMT +8
Contests: Oceanzonesurf "Surf For Peace" at Ujung Batee Beach September, 10 2006.
Other Resources: oceanzonesurf-aceh.blogspot.com/ surftravelonline.com rubiahdivers.com
Video: Indo.doc

Getting There – Banda Aceh's airport is not a Visa-on-Arrival entry; apply for 30 day visa before arrival. 4 airlines offer daily flights between Jakarta, Medan and Aceh. Besides Garuda, there are 3 low cost carriers: Lion Air, Sriwijaya Air and Adam Air; (o/w from $40). Air Asia 3 x wk from Kuala Lumpur direct or fly Singapore Airlines to Medan.

Getting Around – Buses from Medan to Banda Aceh take 10hrs. There are 2-3 ferries a day between Ulee Lhe and Pulau Weh. It's only 30min from Banda Aceh to Lhok Nga by "labi-labi" bus so commuting every day to stay in better hotels is an option. Roads are still in post-tsunami trauma.

Lodging and Food – Mami Diana's Losmen at Pantai Camara is a good base. Surf Travel Online sells Aceh surf camp: 6nts/$700 or $1000. Staying in Meulaboh is decent, although all village accommodation will be very basic losmen, but that will help local population and it will be dirt cheap. Aceh coffee is amongst the most flavourful in the world.

WEATHER STATISTICS	J/F	M/A	M/J	J/A	S/O	N/D
total rainfall (mm)	121	107	113	92	162	192
consistency (days/mth)	6	9	8	7	10	11
min temp (°C)	23	23	23	23	23	23
max temp (°C)	30	31	31	31	30	30

Weather – Sumatra has a tropical humid climate and experiences relatively little change in temps from season to season. The weather is warm to hot with temps ranging from 23-30°C (74-86°F). There is a dry season that generally lasts from March through August influenced by the Australian continental air masses and a rainy season from October to January, when the Asian and Pacific Ocean air masses mix. Northern Sumatra experiences the most precipitation when monsoon clouds unleash heavy downpours and average annual rainfall is 1600mm (64in). Winds are moderate and generally predictable, with monsoons usually blowing in from the south and east between June and September and from the northwest during December to March. Boardshorts are sufficient with rashies for protection from the sun & reef.

Nature and Culture – Neat ancient architecture like The Great Baiturrahman Mosque, Museum Negeri, Kerkhof Churchyard, Syiah Kuala Grave. Takengon near Lake Laut Tawar in the central area of Aceh is cool (2O°C - 68F) for a change with shoreline cliffs ideal for rock hiking and the lake is stocked with trout.

Hazards and Hassles – Aceh was the worst hit place by 2004 Tsunami and despite reconstruction, there are still major scars from the mayhem. Serious travellers only as reliable medical help is far away. Aceh is in chaos caused by separatist conflict. There is rarely open armed conflicts, but transport can become difficult because of road blocks and bombed buses. Malaria is rampant.

Handy Hints – Oceanzone surfshop in Lhok Nga may have some stuff, but better plan to leave things behind than to buy. Remember to dress appropriately, local women swim fully clothed. West Sumatran coastline stretches 375km (233mi) from North Sumatra province in the northwest to Bengkulu in the southeast.

Lam Tadoh Lefts
YEP 511 4955/GOOGLE EARTH

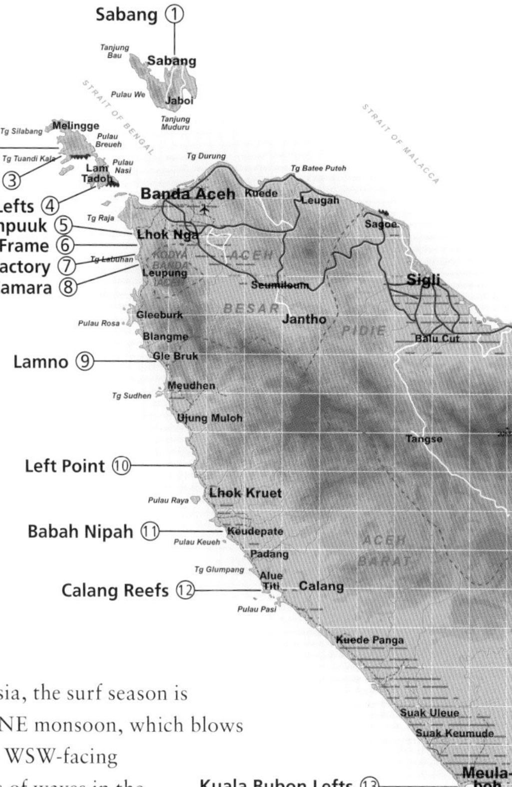

torture and alienation to the general population. The guerrilla war continued through the '90s, with an estimated 15,000 casualties on both sides, before an army offensive from 2002 - 2004 killed half of the GAM forces.

The surf around the capital of Banda Aceh on the northern tip has been documented by stoked adventurers since the 1980's. Pulau Weh, better known for diving (whale sharks and turtles) than its waves, has some mushy onshore beachbreaks around **Sabang** with some NE windswell. Surfers have even made their mark on Pulau Breueh at breaks like **Blangujung Rights** or the longer, more challenging right reef at **Lambaro**, which is easier to get to. Pulau Nasih is well worth the effort for long, hollow **Lam Tadoh Lefts** in a SSW-facing bay. Both islands are accessible by ferry from Banda Aceh and Weh has some of the most beautiful palm-fringed beaches in Sumatra with basic accommodation available. Aceh's west coast has a makeable road that flirts with the coastline all the way from Banda Aceh to Meulaboh (250km/155mi). Just to the west of Banda, **Lampuuk** aka Ujong Batee Beach is the place for easy, black sand beachbreak. Pro-surfers Rizal Tandjung, Marlon Gerber, Benji Weatherly and Ian Walsh visited Lhok Nga in April 2007, meeting local surfers Taufik and Agus, who have become Aceh's first-ever lifeguards, protecting locals who have an understandable fear of the ocean. Only 15km (9mi) south of Banda, a beautiful little village holds a consistent, perfect **A-Frame** reefbreak out in front. South of A-frame is **Cement Factory**, producing great rights near Lafarge's huge cement extraction works and harbour jetty. **Pantai Camara** can have perfect, long rights off the rivermouth north of Leupung, but it needs swell. South of Mount Gurutee, where a new island has emerged with the uprising reef, fickle but good wet season rights peel at the rivermouth near **Lamno**, plus there's a quality right point. On the way to Lhok Kruet, about 10km (6mi) north near Keudeunga, look for the long **Left Point** in a deep bay facing WNW that are offshore in SE winds. Further south is **Babah Nipah**, not easy to reach, but the rivermouth line-up promises long rides. Before **Calang**, have a look at the assorted reefbreaks facing west about 10km (6mi) north. After Calang, the shoreline becomes a straight sandy beach, dotted with various rivermouths and scattered rocks and reefs. On the other side of **Kuala Bubon** cape, there are also some good lefts over rock and sand, facing WNW. Once in Meulaboh, it will probably be polluted by the headland and the **Ujong Karang** reef quality is questionable. Beyond Meulaboh towards the ferry town of Susoh (for Simeulue), and Singkil (for the Banyaks), lies possibly the most uncharted surf territory in Indonesia.

Unlike the rest of Indonesia, the surf season is Nov-March during the NE monsoon, which blows straight offshore on the WSW-facing coastline. There is obviously lots of waves in the austral winter season, but it's plagued by almost constant WSW onshore winds so wave shape and quality won't be optimum. Of course, there is less swell during summer, but the regulation 2-5ft conditions will provide clean fun intermediate style waves for surfers looking for friendly size surf and the adventure of mainland Sumatra travelling. There is 400km (250mi) of potential fetch in the Andaman Sea and the NE monsoon kicks up mushy 1-3ft (0.3-1m) windswells on the east coast. If the West coast goes flat, there's always a chance of rideable, unchartered waves in Banda Aceh or Lhokseumawe. With 2ft (0.6m) maximum tidal range, tides are rarely a problem, but winds really need to be right.

Melingge
YEP 511 4955/GOOGLE EARTH

SURF STATISTICS		
Spot	Size	Btm	Type
①	5/1		
②	8/2		
③	8/2		
④	10/3		
⑤	5/1		
⑥	8/2		
⑦	6/1		
⑧	8/2		
⑨	6/3		
⑩	8/2		
⑪	8/2		
⑫	8/2		
⑬	8/2		
⑭	6/2		

SURF STATISTICS	J F	M A	M J	J A	S O	N D
dominant swell	S-SW	S-SW	S-SW	S-SW	S-SW	S-SW
swell size (ft)	2-3	3	4	5	4	3
consistency (%)	70	50	40	40	60	70
dominant wind	NE-E	NW-E	SW-W	SW-W	SW-NW	NE-E
average force	F3	F2-F3	F3-F4	F3-F4	F3-F4	F3
consistency (%)	58	45	45	47	60	44
water temp.(°C)	28	29	29	29	28	28
wetsuit						

195. Central Sumbawa

Periscopes

JOHN CALLAHAN/TROPICALPIX

Summary
- + Density of world-class spots
- + Consistent conditions
- + Lefts and rights
- + Dry surf season
- + Cheap, exotic, low traffic Indo

- – Sometimes very windy
- – Long paddles & tricky low tides
- – Crowds
- – Tough public transport access
- – Not much around

While many of the charter boats leaving Bali head east towards Nusa Tenggara, they usually only make it as far as the west coast of Sumbawa, so to get to the fabled waves of Teluk Cempi Bay in Central Sumbawa means a long, tedious journey by plane and taxi from Bali. Just south of Hu'u, Lakey (Lakai) Beach, is a long, wide, palm-lined stretch of ivory sand, fronted by reef. Since its discovery by Australian surfers in the mid '80s, Hu'u has been known to offer a varied selection of waves for every ability & taste. This area has produced some local stars like Dedi Gun, Joey Barrel and 2006 National Indonesian GromSearch winner, One Anwar. The total number of visiting surfers in the area can hit 150-200, especially when early morning high tides are happening, producing the best waves in glassy conditions. An extensive 500m wide lagoon needs to be negotiated to get out to the reef, and at low tide some more rock-hopping is required.

Lakey Peak

JOHN CALLAHAN/TROPICALPIX

Lakey Pipe

DUSTIN HUMPHREY

TRAVEL INFORMATION

Local Population: 1,540,000
Coastline: 1309km (813mi)
Time Zone: GMT +8
Contests: Quiksilver Open Lakeys, July
Other Resources:
amangati.com
isctour.com/2007/index.php
lakeypeak.com
baliwaves.com
Video: Indo Insane

Getting There – 30 day visa in Bali. Don't bring in more than 3 boards - heavy fines. Sumbawa ferries depart from Labuhan, Lombok and reach Poto Sano in 2h, but it's unreliable. Best is by plane using the 5/wk Merpati flight, which wont carry big boardbags. Bima r/t flight costs about $165. Best to get a pick up from your hotel.

Getting Around – Land transport is much more difficult to get than in Bali. Take a taxi-bemo or a bus from Bima (5h from Sumbawa Besar) to Dompu's Ginte Bus Terminal then take a cidomo (horse cart) to the Lepardi Bus Terminal. Or charter a bemo from Bima to Hu'u (3h) for about $35 per person, or private transfers $70-80 per vehicle one way.

WEATHER STATISTICS	J/F	M/A	M/J	J/A	S/O	N/D
total rainfall (mm)	299	177	105	55	77	172
consistency (dys/mnth)	18	13	8	5	7	13
min temp (°C)	23	23	23	23	23	23
max temp (°C)	29	31	31	31	30	30

Lodging and Food – 8 places to stay in Lakey, 3km south of Hu'u. Aman Gati Hotel has 40 rooms set in modern and local architecture; $45/dbl with aircon, $30 with fans. 7nt package from Bali; $425. The original 22 room Mona Lisa Bungalows with well-maintained places ($15/nt). Food is dirt cheap.

Weather – Sumbawa is a transitional volcanic island and it has a tropical monsoonal climate. The wet season generally occurs from November through February with heavy monsoon rainfall and clouds. The dry season, from May to October, can still experience rain but is generally fine, clear and hot. Average annual rainfall is 1350mm (53in). Temps are relatively warm, ranging from 23-32°C (74-90°F) all year-round. It can be breezy around August and September, but boardshorts and a rashie should do.

Nature and Culture – Not as lively as Bali. Visit Bima Sultan Palace on 99 old teak stilts, see Raba Dompu weaving village and Doro Bata relics in Dompu. Dompu is used by tourists as a stopover point to Mount Tambora. The trek takes 2 nights camping in a rain forest and 1 night to the 2,851m (9354ft) summit. Check Komodo island for its famous dragons.

Hazards and Hassles – The reef at Lakey Pipe can be nasty and long walks on low tide reef make booties almost compulsory. Surfing has 30 years of history, so there are now 2nd generation locals. It can be a bit aggro for the best conditions. Walk to the more remote spots – take good shoes and enough water. Low malaria risks.

Handy Hints – There are no surf shops around Lakey apart from wax at some of the hotels. A gun could be necessary for the 6-10ft (2-3m) days. There are rarely boat trips to Lakey area as boats go Bali - West Sumbawa or Sumba - Rote.

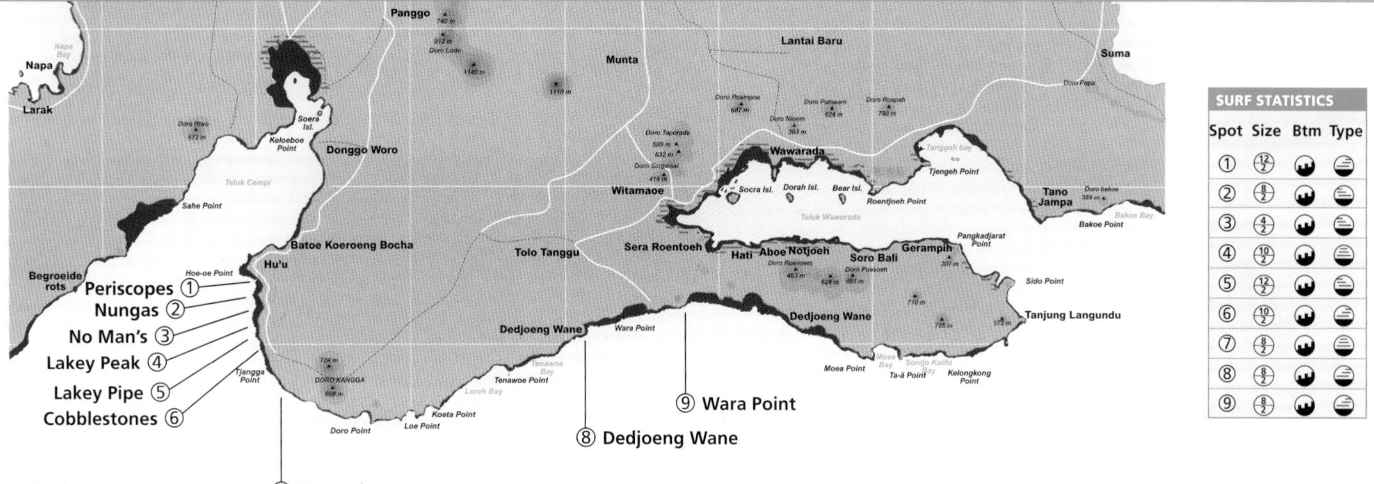

SURF STATISTICS			
Spot	Size	Btm	Type
①	12/2		
②	8/2		
③	4/2		
④	10/2		
⑤	12/2		
⑥	10/2		
⑦	8/2		
⑧	8/2		
⑨	8/2		

Periscopes is a 40 minute walk, but only a short 100m paddle-out. This wave requires a big swell with more S in it and can hold up to double overhead. Hit it early in the morning with a coinciding high tide, as this wave needs plenty of water over the reef to make it out of the barrel onto the shoulder. This is a natural footers tube riding paradise so expect crowds of 'em! **Nungas** can peel off like a mini version of G-land, grooming 200m long lefts with alternating shack and whack sections to play with. Many surfers get diverted on the long walk to Periscopes, opting for long ride, short walk. Nungas bends into a big calm bay, happily accepting more size than the Peak and not too much S in the afternoon trades. 300m right of Lakey Peak is a shut down section of reef called **No Mans** that may have a short shallow ride in small, lumpy swells. Perfect **Lakey Peak** peels off short, 30-40m lefts and rights into channels either side. The right will often throw up backdoor tube rides but gets too shallow at low tide, when the left is churning out predictable, ideal speed barrel rides. Mid tide lip-smacking sessions will appeal to intermediates and the flattish reef is user-friendly, except during full or new moon phases. Getting out to the Peak is easy by either paddling the 450m or taking the zodiac for around $2 return. Lakey Peak can hold juicy sized waves, but the optimum time to hit it is when it's in that perfect headhigh plus range. Just 400 meters to the south is **Lakey Pipe**, a gnarly reef with a fairly sedate take-off, which then hits the shelf and throws out a solid backdoor barrel that leaves enough space to drive a small car through. Optimum at mid to high tide and double overhead, but the Pipe can also take it from tiny to triple. Walk 45mins (or rent a zodiac) to escape the Lakey crowds at a deep reef channel called **Cobblestones**. Nice walled-up rights on one side and lefts barrelling into the channel opposite, pick up more swell and handle some solid size at mid to high tides. Arrange a lift on a motorbike to get to **Nangadoro** that offers both a spinning left and two right reefs, which pick up more swell than any other spot. Enjoy the hot springs. On small days with NW winds, venture to the south coast where great rights occasionally hit **Dedjoeng Wane** during the off-season. In the same conditions, check the outside reefbreaks at **Wara Point**, 4km south of Sondo and a very long paddle.

Lakey Peak

JOHN CALLAHAN/TROPICALPIX

Winter (May-September) is prime surf season, overloaded with 3-12ft (1-4m) swells, but plagued by sideshore afternoon trades. The SE trade winds start in April and the skies begin to dry. Mornings are often light offshores. The really windy season starts from the end of July until middle of November with 13-25 knots trades and the wind is cross-shore on the beach. Being the wet season, the official Indo off-season, November through February is not the best time of year for surf, but there is the chance of some cyclone swell and south coast spots will be offshore in the W-NW winds. The diurnal tide (one radical change per day) is a factor, so get a tide chart to plan your trip around AM highs.

SURF STATISTICS	J F	M A	M J	J A	S O	N D
dominant swell	S-SW	S-SW	S-W	S-W	S-SW	S-SW
swell size (ft)	4	5	6	7	5-6	4
consistency (%)	60	80	90	90	90	70
dominant wind	W-NW	E-NW	E-SE	E-SE	E-S	SE-NW
average force	F3	F2	F3	F3	F3	F3
consistency (%)	65	88	74	80	79	72
water temp.(°C)	29	28	28	27	27	28
wetsuit						

Lakey Pipe

JOHN CALLAHAN/TROPICALPIX

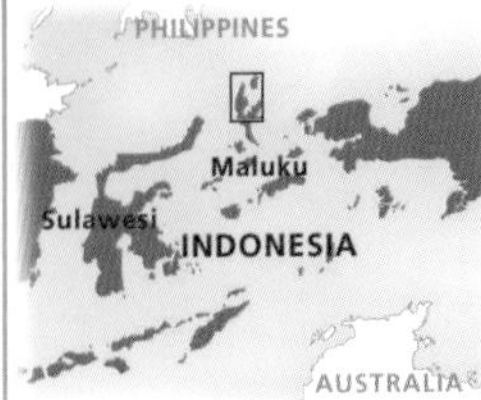

197. Northern Maluku

Serenade

ALL PHOTOS JOHN CALLAHAN/TROPICALPIX

Summary
+ Regular N monsoon swell
+ Quality, mid-sized waves
+ Calm winds, small tides
+ Totally virgin surf area
+ Super scenic and wild

– Short surf season
– Long distances between spots
– Equatorial wet
– Lack of organised boat trips
– Civil unrest

The original Spice Islands, the Maluku (Moluccas or Molluques are alternative names) are part of the easternmost archipelago of Indonesia, and the only Indonesian island chain in the Pacific. The Magallenes expedition, which took a ton of spices back to Spain in 1521, first put Maluku on the map. Despite waves as good as the Philippines, these islands remain largely ignored by travelling surfers. Occasional forays into the region by boat have revealed an outstanding variety of breaks, most of which go unsurfed.

The east coast of Morotai and Halmahera is only likely to come to life in a major N swell, or in an ENE typhoon. Reports on this area indicate that the **Atoll Reefs** off islets near Tobelo could go off, with two lefts witnessed but not surfed. **Pulau Kecil**, an island off the east coast town of Berebere, does have a long, wrapping righthander. Both these spots have great potential, but are very fickle. Sopi, the northernmost bay on Morotai, is an obvious swell magnet for consistent north monsoon swells. **Indo Jiwa**, named after one of the first boat trips to the area, is

Paniki Point

TRAVEL INFORMATION

Local Population: 2.1M
Coastline: 54,716km (34,000mi)
Contests: None
Other Resources: navo.navy.mil

Getting There – A 30-day visa costs $25. Fly to Manado (MDC) in Sulawesi, best routed from Jakarta or straight from Kuala Lumpur (Malaysian) via Kota Kinabalu or from Singapore (Silk Air) or Davao, Philippines. Apart from those on boat trips from Manado, flights run with Merpati to Ternate (daily), Galela (3/week) or Daruba (weekly). International departure tax costs IDR75,000.

Getting Around – The best bet is to get a group of 10 people together and hire a live aboard boat from Manado. Expect to pay $150/d for an A/C modern boat. The distance between spots can be long and the sea can be rough, so a good boat is essential. Land access is not a solution, as there is nowhere to stay in reach of the spots.

WEATHER STATISTICS	J/F	M/A	M/J	J/A	S/O	N/D
total rainfall (mm)	123	207	577	501	198	123
consistency (days/mth)	13	17	23	21	14	12
min temp (°C)	24	24	23	23	23	24
max temp (°C)	31	30	28	27	28	31

Weather – With a thousand odd islands, the climate in Maluku is heavily influenced by the monsoon trends, elevation, proximity to volcanoes, and coastal exposure. The weather varies from one island to another. However, humidity is the rule with over 2.5m (100in) of rain a year. Usually, north of the Equator, Nov-March NE monsoon clears up the skies while April-Oct SW monsoon brings downpours. Wind squalls are frequent and thunderstorm activity is amongst the highest on earth. Transition months like October or April are characterised by heavy rainfall as well. Fortunately, the surf season is somewhat clearer. Daytime temperature variation is small; expect it to be hot and humid year-round. Water is amongst the warmest on earth, at 29°C (84°F).

Food and Lodging – In Manado, stay in town for $30-110/d, at hotels catering for divers. Most hotels are 30-45min from Manado, but the best resorts are on the small Siladen Island in Bunaken Marine Park. There are cheap hotels ($5-10) in Ternate, Daruba or Tobelo. Food is fresh and cheap, boat menus have lots of fresh fish (yellow fin tuna). Expect to pay $3 for a meal in town.

Nature and Culture – Apart from old rusty jeeps and remnants of WW2, there is not much on Morotai except thick jungle. In 1988, most of the rusted remnants were removed. Underwater, there remain sunken ships and bombed planes for divers to visit. Halmahera has more WW2 evidence, and Ternate and Tidore are popular sightseeing spots.

Hazards and Hassles – This is a virgin area with a really low population. For the rare traveller opting for land access, be aware, malaria is present and humidity levels are high.

Handy Hints – Take at least 2 everyday boards and a semi-gun in case of a bigger swell. A longboard opens up a variety of long, fast, peeling waves. The water is extremely warm, so pack plenty of wax.

Serenade

SURF STATISTICS			
Spot	Size	Btm	Type
1	6/3		
2	6/2		
3	10/2		
4	4/2		
5	10/2		
6	6/2		
7	8/2		
8	8/2		
9	6/2		
10	8/2		
11	8/2		

an epic right with fast outside sections and hollow walls. Inside, the **Village Reform** is a super-fast right, which is on the shallow side of rideable. A few other reef options exist. Heading South, **Serenade**, also named after a pioneering boat, is a stunning left. Breaking on all tides, almost every day, this spot has a ledgy takeoff and flawless, 80m (264ft) walls. The reef is also safe, with an easy channel. The nearby **Short Ledge** right is a thick barrel on the east side of a deep bay. Land access is impossible. The western shores of both Morotai and Halmahera are largely steep cliffs, meaning no surf, but luckily, a few bays have the right topography to hold swell and a cluster of spots. The first spot on Halmahera is **Heavy's**, a long and sucky left that needs perfect SE winds to be makeable and may still be unsurfed. Nearby **Double Dome** is the only place at which local surfers can sometimes be found – kids from the village have shaped wooden planks to ride the waves. The channel here offers sectioney lefts. Offshore, islands known as Loloda Utara have many surf spots. At **Coconut Swing**, a savage left breaks, but few waves are rideable. The main attractions in this area are at Salandageke Island. **Sidewalk** is a perfect, long and mellow righthander. This spot breaks down a natural rock spit, is ideally exposed to the NNE, and is a lovely longboard wave when small. The **Racing Lefts** across the channel are long and sectioney. Both waves are super fun, with many different sections.

Although the NW Pacific typhoon season must give rise to some epic days, it's much safer to hit these islands at the heart of the North Monsoon season (Nov-March) for maximum consistency. Sept-Oct is the ideal time of year for a low latitude typhoon developing off Mindanao, Philippines. During winter NE monsoons, the usual size is 3-6ft (1-2m) of wind-driven waves, with potential for bigger days at the more exposed spots. Wind patterns at this equatorial "doldrums" latitude are very light and variable and glassy days are the norm, apart from the frequent rainy squalls. Some offshore ENE winds do occur, shifting NNW if the sun is shining. Transition months of April-May and September-October are usually calm with light winds but hardly any swell. The question of whether the Maluku straight produce SW windswell from July to Sept is yet to be answered. Tidal range varies up to 3ft (0.9m), and affects the shallowest spots.

SURF STATISTICS	J F	M A	M J	J A	S O	N D
dominant swell	N-NE	N-NE	NE-E	NE-E	NE-E	N-NE
swell size (ft)	4-5	2-3	0-1	1-2	2-3	4
consistency (%)	90	60	10	20	40	80
dominant wind	N-NE	N-NE	S-SW	S-SW	S-SW	NW-NE
average force	F3	F3	F2-F3	F3	F3	F2-F3
consistency (%)	65	54	40	66	49	48
water temp.(°C)	28	28	29	28	28	29
wetsuit						

Indo Jiwa

199. Eastern Luzon

Cemento

KAGE GOZUN

Summary
+ Frequent NE monsoon swells
+ Variety of reefs & beachies
+ Scenic Sierra mountains
+ Really cheap & entertaining
+ Pinoy surf culture

– No world-class waves
– Occasional crowds
– Onshore beachbreaks
– Tough overland access
– Landslides, rains, robbery

The Philippines are notorious for long, arduous journeys to way out there coastal villages, where fickle reefs await just the right typhoon swell to ignite. Despite being located on the main island of Luzon, the town of Baler is no exception, taking the adventurous over the rolling Sierra Madre mountain range in the province of Aurora. This nerve jangling road trip is a spectacular visual delight passing waterfalls, rivers and a lush cloak of tropical forest full of biodiversity. The surfing scene in Apocalypse Now was filmed in Baler at Charlie's Point and when the film crew departed, they left their surfboards behind. The locals took to surfing with a passion and it is no surprise that Edmund Mendoza, the first national surf champion, came from Baler, the birthplace of

Charlie's Beach

KAGE GOZUN

Sabang Beach

JOHN CALLAHAN/TROPICALPIX

TRAVEL INFORMATION

Local Population: 173,797 – Luzon
Coastline: Luzon 3250km (2020mi)
Time Zone: GMT+8
Contests: Aurora Southport Longboard (April)
Other Resources: tuasonsurf.com surfpinoy.blogspot.com waypoints.ch
Video: youtube.com

Getting There – No visa required for less than 21days. Extensions are really easy. Manila (MNL) has 2 direct flights from Australia, Qantas or Philippine Airlines. It's 12h from San Francisco. Most of the European flights will require a change at Singapore, Bangkok or Hong Kong. $15 departure tax and $4 for domestic.

Getting Around – It takes 7-9h by jeepney (bus) from Manila to Baler along beat-up mountain road. There are 2 bridges across rivers that typhoons can damage. Travel can be cancelled during rainy season because of landslides. If you want to rent a car (crazy idea), try RentaCar Manila (from $250/wk and $390 for a van). Manila traffic is heavily jammed.

WEATHER STATISTICS	J/F	M/A	M/J	J/A	S/O	N/D
total rainfall (mm)	182	221	256	228	342	370
consistency (days/mth)	13	10	10	10	15	17
min temp (°C)	20	21	23	23	23	21
max temp (°C)	29	31	33	33	32	30

Lodging and Food – Formerly known as Ocean View, the Bay Inn Resort on Sabang Beach has accommodations for up to 32 guests. Rates are $8 to $10 per night. MIA Surf & Sports Resort offers 5 VIP rooms with their own flush toilets, showers and electric fans. Pricing similar to Bay Inn. Sabang Beach is action central. Expect $3 for a really good meal.

Weather – The Philippines have a tropical marine climate, hot and humid throughout the year. Since it faces the Pacific Ocean and has no barriers to shield it from typhoons coming from the east, Baler experiences heavy rainfall evenly distributed through the year. Annual average rainfall is 3250mm (130in). Typhoons known as "bagyos" blow across the island about twenty times a year usually lasting 3 or 4 days. The province experiences two main wind currents. E-NE trade winds blow from November to April, then switches to a SW direction for the rest of the year. Temps vary little during the year, averaging 25°C (77°F). Water is boardshort warm, year-round.

Nature and Culture – Sierra mountains make for a beautiful tropical background. Check the small hot springs at Digisit near Cemento or Pimentel Falls near San Luis. Dilasag near Casiguran in the north is 8h away. Check the Banaue rice terraces in Isabela Province. Pinoys love partying and people come from Manila adding to the lively scene.

Hazards and Hassles – The Cobra section at Cemento can snap boards and smash bodies on the reef. Besides bugs and monsoon rains, watch out for thievery as there is much poverty. The journey from/to Manila can feel like a hassle but is often an adventure! Typhoons can be pretty destructive over Aurora Province.

Handy Hints – Bay Inn and MIA Surf & Sports rent surfboards for $3/day and bodyboards for $1.50/day. Locations are named after barangays or local districts. Landslides, earthquakes, volcanic eruptions, floods, typhoons, plane crashes; the Philippines competes with Indo for catastrophes! Pinoys speak good English.

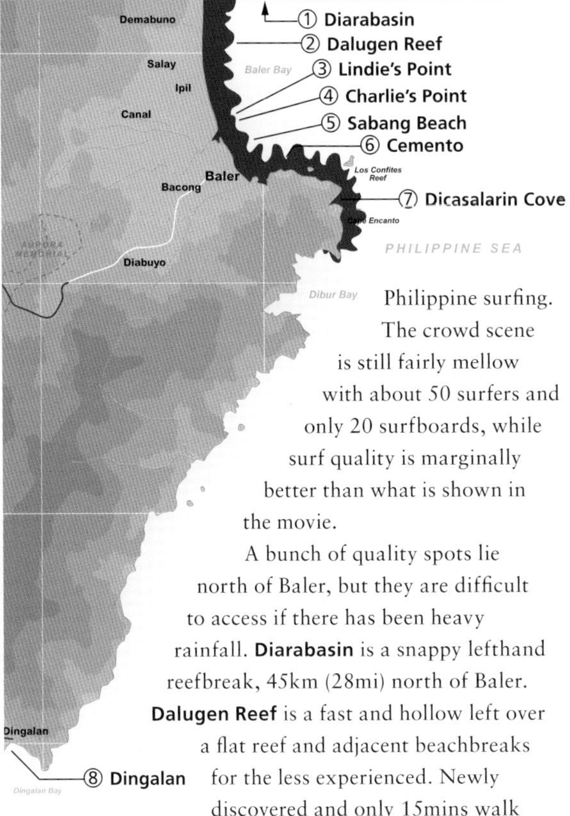

Philippine surfing. The crowd scene is still fairly mellow with about 50 surfers and only 20 surfboards, while surf quality is marginally better than what is shown in the movie.

A bunch of quality spots lie north of Baler, but they are difficult to access if there has been heavy rainfall. **Diarabasin** is a snappy lefthand reefbreak, 45km (28mi) north of Baler. **Dalugen Reef** is a fast and hollow left over a flat reef and adjacent beachbreaks for the less experienced. Newly discovered and only 15mins walk from the Bay Inn is **Lindie's Point** where waves were "artificially" created when local government engineers opened up the mouth of the estuary to prevent floods during the rainy season. Left and right rivermouth sandbanks have formed, but the rips are strong. Within walking distance from Baler is **Charlie's Point**, the *Apocalypse Now* spot where average quality peaks break lazily over a sand/gravel bottom. Baler sits on the south end of a 10km (6mi) long crescent beach where a rocky peninsula runs into the sea. In many places, the beach shelves a little too steeply so waves tend to close out quickly. Located on this long stretch of grey sand beach are several resorts like Angara's Beach House, Bay's Inn Resort or MIA Surf and Sports. The most popular surf spot **Sabang Beach** is found right in front of Bay's Inn, where beginners brave the soft beachbreak and regular surfers practice in the dumpier waves. It would be a decent longboard spot, but most of the locals have beat-up shortboards. The best spot around is undoubtedly **Cemento**, a righthander over a sharp coral reef, 40min walk (20 min by tricycle) from Sabang, or a quick 10min by motor boat. Exciting, heart in mouth take-off at this excellent wave, but the ride is short. Also known as "Cobra Reef" since the wave resembles the shape of a cobra snake about to strike. White sand, seashells, and crushed corals carpet the stretch of Cemento Beach, a popular haven for lobsters and other marine species. Although it's a semi-secret, you will hear about **Dicasalarin Cove**, a secluded white sand beach, with no facilities. It's a punishing 45 minutes by boat usually through rough seas to ride these exposed beach peaks over dead coral and sand. It's a bit of a trek down to **Dingalan**, a long expanse of southeast-facing beach with uninspiring random peaks, but there is some NE wind protection and the promise of uncrowded surf.

Cemento

JOHN CALLAHAN/TROPICALPIX

From March through June, the waves are relatively calm providing a good beachfront for swimmers. The typhoon season coincides with the wet season from mid June to November and sometimes even December. Aurora province is hit by typhoons at least 3 or 4 times a year. The typhoons blow in from the Pacific during the SW monsoon, bringing good swells, but it can mean 3 or 4 days of high winds, heavy rains and a tough time to travel. The best surf season runs from October to March, when the NE monsoon blows down from China, producing larger waves in the 3-8ft (1-2.5m) range. Winds will be onshore NE-E in the afternoon but mostly calm in the mornings. Tides are semi-diurnal with diurnal inequality, never exceeding 3ft (1m) tidal range, even on spring tides.

SURF STATISTICS			
Spot	Size	Btm	Type
①	6/2		
②	6/2		
③	6/2		
④	4/2		
⑤	4/1		
⑥	10/2		
⑦	6/2		
⑧	6/2		

SURF STATISTICS	J F	M A	M J	J A	S O	N D
dominant swell	N-E	N-E	N-E	N-E	N-E	N-E
swell size (ft)	4-5	3	1	1-2	2-3	5
consistency (%)	70	50	10	20	50	80
dominant wind	NE-E	NE-E	S-SW	S-SW	NE-E	NE-E
average force	F4-F5	F4	F3-F4	F4	F4-F5	F4-F5
consistency (%)	63	53	38	44	50	72
water temp.(°C)	26	27	29	29	28	26
wetsuit						

Lindie's Point

JOHN CALLAHAN/TROPICALPIX

200. Hainan

Yarakawa

ALL PHOTOS YEP

Summary
+ China's best surf
+ Quality left pointbreaks
+ Consistent during NE monsoon
+ Very warm water and tropical
+ Cultural adventure

– Lack of power
– Average beachbreaks
– Rare typhoon swells
– Difficult travel without guide
– Some areas off-limits

Hainan, the second largest of the Chinese islands after Taiwan, extends 1,500km (930mi) of coastline into the South China Sea. In China, Hainan is advertised as the perfect tropical holiday destination, attracting around 10 million Chinese tourists every year. Regarding surf potential, the coastal zone is still relatively unexplored, with hundreds of beaches and regular points. Long stretches of sand are divided by occasional headlands, with a backdrop of volcanic mountains. The pointbreaks, which have been ridden by visiting Australian and Japanese surfers for decades, are generally long, mellow lefts.

Rihue Bay

Yab-J

Between Haikou and Sanya, a 320km (200mi) long expressway skirts the coastline. However, once off this major route the road network is poor, so exploring is time-consuming. The NE coast of Hainan, around Wenchang, is hard to access. Tonggu Ridge is more of a sightseeing area than a surfspot, but the islet in the rivermouth at **Moon Bay**

TRAVEL INFORMATION

Local Population: 7M
Coastline:
1580km (981mi)
Contests: 720 Contest (mid-Nov)
Other Resources:
hnsurf.cn
surfinghainan.com/blog

Getting There – Get a visa at Hong Kong airport in less than a day. HK flights are more expensive and less regular than those from Shenzen, so take the ferry to Shekou from HK, then a cab. Hainan Airlines and China Airlines fly many times daily, although some aircraft might not take surfboards. Fly from Shanghai, or choose a direct flight from Osaka with Hainan Airlines.

Getting Around – The capital city is Haikou, but visitors can also fly to Sanya, closer to the main surf area. Individual tourism is still a strange concept, and tourists are not allowed to drive a car without a Chinese driving license.

Lodging and Food – Stay in 4 star accommodation at Sandalwood in Xiangshui Bay or Guangzhou Ocean Club in Rihue Bay. Chinese cuisine is quite different so be prepared with a Chinese speaking guide. Try Wenchang Chicken, Jiaji Duck, Dongshan Mutton, Merry Crab. There is lots of fresh seafood available. Food can be really cheap in restaurants.

Weather – Hainan is a tropical monsoon zone, with average temperatures between 22°C and 26°C (72-79°F). Annual rain is 1,639mm (66in), but much less in the leeward coasts around Niuling. Forest cover exceeds 50%. Surf without a wetsuit is possible in the early season because the water remains warm (25°C/77°F), but N winds can get chilly so take a springsuit in Nov-Dec and maybe a light fullsuit in Jan-March. Because of the fairly shallow South China Sea, the water is a bit murky.

Nature and Culture – There is plenty to see and do: Nanwan Macaque island and a Buddhist statue 108m tall, Xinlong Botanical Garden with 1200 plant species, Hainan Marine Tropical World in Haikou, the Hot Spring region, Yalong bay near Sanya, Tinanya Haijiao rocks, and the Sanya Zoological Garden. There is no nightlife, but karaoke and massage are commonplace.

Hazards and Hassles – There are few local surfers, so localism is not an issue. Pay respect to the Japanese surfers who have visited Hainan for years, either from China or Japan. There are some sea-lice and low tide rocks to stay aware of. Hiring a cab can be difficult. Some beaches are off-limits and guards may prohibit surfing in some areas.

Handy Hints – Very few people speak English or Japanese, only Mandarin. Internet facilities are very limited. Surf is mellow so take a shortboard and perhaps a longer, thicker board for small days. During typhoon season, it's really hot. Bring all surf supplies, including wax.

WEATHER STATISTICS	J/F	M/A	M/J	J/A	S/O	N/D
total rainfall (mm)	7	21	150	180	240	25
consistency (days/mth)	11	12	13	13	12	12
min temp (°C)	19	21	24	25	24	20
max temp (°C)	24	27	32	32	31	25

sometimes holds some close-outs. Getting to **Buddha Beach** is a mission, but the 16m (50ft) statue lends a unique feel to the place. Like the next spot south, **Dao Ao Bay**, Buddha Beach is generally surfed on typhoon swells with SW winds, as the NE monsoon is onshore. Further south, **Da Hua Jaio** breaks near a military camp under similar NE conditions. More spots around Wanning may be worth investigating, such as **Xing Tan Wan**, an exposed beach with difficult access. South of here the east-facing coast bends ESE, and the likelihood of consistent, offshore surf soars. **Rivermouth Bridge** can produce peeling rights with good access. The next three bays – Shimei Wan, Rihue Bay and Xiangshui Bay hold major surf potential. **Golf 14** is a long, mellow left breaking by a golf course. This point is consistent, a big paddle, and often most suitable for longboarding. At **Kani Rock**, powerful, low tide lefts throw out close to shore and the tourist lookout provides good access. **Kame Rock** is a hollow beachbreak with a good right, whilst Yarakawa is the most consistent wave in the area. **Yarakawa** can offer a low-mid tide 100m (330ft) left with a sucky take-off and hollow sections. If the swell is solid, head to Rihue Bay for

Buddha Beach

some beachbreaks and **Yab-J** (reverse J-Bay!). This long, zippy left point spins along a mussel encrusted rock bottom, with the potential for barrels when on. From **Niuling** Bay it is possible to get the ferry to Wuzhizou Island, where good lefts break next to the channel jetties. If the wind is up from the NE, **Abalone Farm** offers sheltered lefts tucked into a cove. At **Sandalwood**, a four star hotel caters to luxury seekers, and a good beachbreak is easily accessible from the highway. Further south near Sanya and Yalong Bay, **West Beach**, will work in SW swells. Unfortunately, access is yet to be constructed.

There are two imprecise surfing seasons in Hainan. The typhoon season runs from August to October while the NE monsoon extends from November to March. November is the best month, producing both early N swells and potential late season typhoons. The Taiwan Straight also produces regular NE swells while the Luzon Straight gets direct but occasional E swells. The NNE wind becomes side/

Yab-J

offshore on the ESE facing shorelines, and can get strong at times. Winds shift a bit ENE in the afternoon but remain fairly offshore for the spots in the SE. During SW season, from May to September, waves are rare. Typhoons can send some SW swells, and sometimes the SW monsoon will produce 2-3ft (0.6-1m) of windswell on the south coast. Coastal waters here are known as the Paracel zone. Tide phases can get up to 5ft (1.5m), with very irregular changes between the two tides. A general rule of thumb is to favour the beachbreaks on high tide and the points on low tide.

SURF STATISTICS	J F	M A	M J	J A	S O	N D
dominant swell	NE-E	NE-E	NE-SW	S-SW	NE-E	NE-E
swell size (ft)	3-4	2	0-1	1-2	3	4
consistency (%)	70	30	10	20	60	80
dominant wind	NE-E	NE-S	SE-SW	S-SW	N-E	N-E
average force	F4-F5	F4	F4	F4	F4	F4-F5
consistency (%)	77	91	74	61	62	95
water temp.(°C)	24	26	29	29	29	25
wetsuit						

SURF STATISTICS

Spot	Size	Btm	Type
1	4/1		
2	6/1		
3	6/1		
4	6/1		
5	6/1		
6	6/1		
7	8/2		
8	8/2		
9	6/2		
10	8/1		
11	8/2		
12	6/1		
13	6/1		
14	6/1		
15	6/1		

201. Hong Kong and Guangdong

88

ALL PHOTOS YEP

Summary
+ Consistent NE monsoon swells
+ New spots to discover
+ Offshore mornings
+ Close to Hong Kong
+ Main access point to China

– Mostly flat in spring & summer
– Few spots, mainly beachbreak
– Long journey to Tai Long Wan SK
– Language barrier in Guangdong
– Pollution

Surfing in Hong Kong is far removed from the big city shopping, skyscrapers, crowded streets and junks jostling in the harbour. Set in a much more peaceful rural setting at least an hours drive away, the relatively consistent beachbreaks and fickle, secret reefbreaks can produce some quality waves, in seasonally specific conditions. GI's like Derek Bailey were the first to surf Big Wave Bay, Hong Kong in the 1960's, becoming one of a dozen local surfers including lifeguards, but when Australian expatriate Rod Payne tried to paddle out there in 1979, he was removed from the water by police. The national government contracted Peter Drouyn in 1985 to give lessons to a group of Chinese students/ gymnasts in Hainan. Californians and Hawaiians followed the mainland trail and meanwhile surfing had taken root in Hong Kong, culminating in the founding of the HK Surfing Association in 1997.

88

Tai Long Wan is Cantonese for Big Wave Bay, but confusingly, there are three spots bearing this name. **Big**

TRAVEL INFORMATION

Local Population: Guangdong 91,940,000
Coastline: Hong Kong 733km (455mi), Guangdong 3368km (2093mi)
Time Zone: GMT+8
Contests: HK Surfing Cup (mid Dec)
Other Resources: cathayseas.com underground.org. hk/marine.html groups.msn.com/ sixrounds

Getting There – You don't need a visa for HK. You can get a 30 day visa for China mainland in 1 day from HK airport. Flying to HK's Chek Lap Kok (HKG) is often cheap, Cathay Pacific sometimes charges for boards. If you go to China direct, fly to Shenzhen (SZX), avoid the overland crossing and take the 30min ferry straight to Shekou. From there it's 3h to Shanwei.

Getting Around – Don't even think of renting a car! Traffic can be mad and orientation a main issue. Renting a van to Tai Long Wan HK will take 1h (about 2h from Lantau airport) and 2h (at least) to Tai Long Wan in Sai Kung. Access to some reliable surf spots is difficult because of lack of roads. Public transport will be a hassle with boards.

Lodging and Food – As most visitors to HK are business executives, hotels are relatively expensive, with many top-end hotels. As tourism takes off, a mid-range market is developing. Stanford Hotel in Mongkok is $120/ night, a good deal. Meals are cheap. China is all different, Zhelang has 3-star hotel for $30/ night. Chinese dishes are quite different from a western Chinese take-away!

WEATHER STATISTICS	J/F	M/A	M/J	J/A	S/O	N/D
total rainfall (mm)	39	106	343	374	185	37
consistency (days/mth)	4	7	15	16	9	2
min temp (°C)	13	17	24	26	24	16
max temp (°C)	18	22	29	31	28	22

Weather – South China Sea coasts enjoy a subtropical monsoon climate with adequate rainfall, long summers and warm winters. Annual precipitation is about 1,770mm (71in), the sun shines for 1,785h, while annual average temp is 22°C (72°F). October to January is the dry season, which is also the best time for swells. Jan - Feb is winter, dropping to 10-16°C (50-61°F) with occasional cold fronts followed by dry northerly winds. Feb - May is like the second winter with warmer but more humid weather, full of thick fog and rain. June to September is the monsoon season with warm, sticky, sunny days, sudden rains and heavy typhoons tracking low sometimes. On average, 31 tropical cyclones form in the western North Pacific or China Seas every year, and about half of them reach typhoon strength. You need a springsuit in winter for 2-3 months and maybe thicker on rare cold days.

Nature and Culture – Squiggly signs stacked in grimy alleys; ears reverberating to blaring taxi horns. Chrome and glass skyscrapers, like space-age cathedrals, sprout from drab apartment blocks, dizzy spires tickling the sky. HK is the events capital of Asia for arts, sports, theatre, festivals and concerts. It's a vibrant city, but nature escapes are close by.

Hazards and Hassles – BWB HK, Shek O and Cheung Sha can have lots of local surfers and expats but other spots are seldom surfed. E-coli and other toxic cauliflowers float nastily in a frothing sea, courtesy of cretinous ship captains, antiquated sewage disposal systems and apathetic officials – ear plugs and keeping your mouth shut is a good idea. Traffic can be pretty awful.

Handy Hints – Rent or buy boards at Eric's Shop on Big Wave Bay HK beach; rental boards $8/d and bodyboards $3/d, or store your own boards. 3 shops in HK sell boards. In China, driving and cycling are illegal for gweela's (foreigners). Shenzhen is a Special Economic Zone (SEZ).

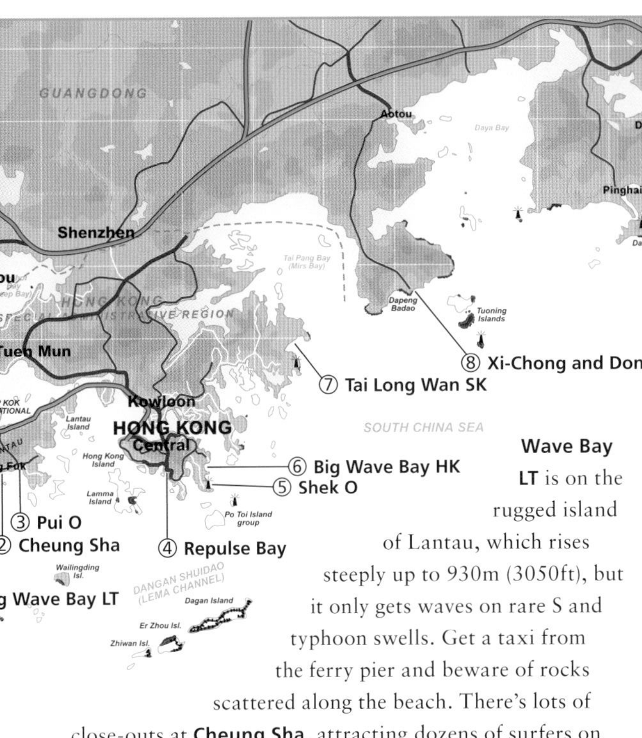

SURF STATISTICS			
Spot	Size	Btm	Type
①			
②			
③			
④			
⑤			
⑥			
⑦			
⑧			
⑨			
⑩			
⑪			

Wave Bay LT is on the rugged island of Lantau, which rises steeply up to 930m (3050ft), but it only gets waves on rare S and typhoon swells. Get a taxi from the ferry pier and beware of rocks scattered along the beach. There's lots of close-outs at **Cheung Sha**, attracting dozens of surfers on occasional 2-4ft days. It's a mini bus ride from the ferry, boasts one of Hong Kong's longest beaches and a small store that rents boards. There's more mushy waves at **Pui O**, a short taxi ride from the Mui Wo ferry and the site for a QS summer surf camp. The seven million residents of Hong Kong benefit from a modern, efficient road network, but it takes a while to get to the east-facing spots in quiet, bucolic areas. **Repulse Bay** is a popular tourist beach, surrounded by hi-rises, but it's rarely worth the trip because it faces southwest, is a shallow bay and offshore islands filter swell. **Shek O** is usually only a wild, close-out shorebreak, but it can be rideable outside when big swells have messed up the main wave at Tai Long Wan HK. **Big Wave Bay HK** is the centre of the surfing scene, attracting crowds of up to 100 surfers as well as plenty of swimmers, since it is patrolled by lifeguards and shark-netted. Shifting peaks will break in any swell from N to E, and a strong NE typhoon will create some barrel sections providing it doesn't get too near and close-out the bay over 6ft (2m). Dangers include rocks at either end, strong rips, pollution and too many bodies in the water! In the New Territories, known as Sai Kung province, the 3rd Big Wave Bay is **Tai Long Wan SK**, which has the biggest, most consistent and best shaped waves around. Consisting of four beaches facing NE to SE in a giant horseshoe bay, the long, white sands of Fung Bay and Sai Wan are probably the best, catching any swell on offer, while Ham Tin offers a little protection at the north end. Can get big, hollow and rippy, so not for beginners when a strong NE or typhoon swell hits. In winter, there is plenty of swell in the 2-4ft (0.6-1.2m) range and the sandbars shift around less. It is not uncommon for waves to break 4'-6' (1.2-2m) for a week. The best tide is mid to high and there are a couple of small-scale rivermouth setups, but the ride is short and the waves are usually no bigger than 3ft (1m). During a big swell, a classic little 3' left shorebreak can be ridden right in front of the store at Ham Tin. Most surfers camp overnight, since it is 2hrs from the city, eating at Hoi Fung store, nestling among trees on the beach. On the mainland in Guangdong province, spots are few and far between as the sea has only recently receded, leaving a super indented coastline with flat rocks and myriads of granite islets. Eastwards, at **Xi-Chong** and **Dongchong**, good longboard waves peel lazily down some rivermouth sculpted sandbars, plus there is lots of rocky coast to explore. There's also good clean beach-hut accommodation and restaurants at Dongchong. **Pinghai Point** is a bit more accessible, holding some rights just near the Dongchong Hotel. Zhelang area or Hong Hoi Wan is the best bet with powerful, peaks near a series of jetties, but be aware this area sits next to a power plant and new industrial zone so pollution is a problem. The jetties have sculpted some excellent sand banks at **88**, sheltered from sideshore N-NE winds and it's usually offshore in the morning with a left breaking off the northern jetty and beautiful A-Frames inside. **Cherry Point** lefts only work on the bigger swells and are usually quite mushy.

88

Typhoon season is best from Aug-Oct, but it's very inconsistent, whereas the NE monsoon, from Nov to March registers 80% surf day consistency, mid-season. The best month is November with early NE swells and potential late season typhoons. The Taiwan Strait produces NE swells while the Luzon Strait gets direct E swells. Winds tend to blow from the N, because of the continental mass, shifting to light to moderate onshore NE-E later in the day. During SW season from May to September, waves are rare. Tides have unequal semi-diurnal cycles, reaching 8ft (2.4m) and waves are often better at higher stages of tide.

SURF STATISTICS	J F	M A	M J	J A	S O	N D
dominant swell	NE-E	NE-E	SE-SW	SE-SW	NE-E	NE-E
swell size (ft)	3	1-2	0-1	1	2-3	3-4
consistency (%)	60	20	10	20	60	80
dominant wind	NE-E	NE-E	E-S	SE-SW	NE-E	NE-E
average force	F4	F4	F3-F4	F3	F4	F4
consistency (%)	76	66	59	59	64	81
water temp.(°C)	19	21	27	28	27	22
wetsuit						

202. Taiwan

Secret spot

ALL PHOTOS TAKAHIRO TSUCHIYA

Summary
+ SE typhoon & NE monsoon swells
+ Large tropical island
+ Powerful beachbreaks & left points
+ Cheap, easy access from Asia
+ Beautiful east coast

– No world-class breaks
– Suffocating summer heat
– Densely populated Taipei
– Risk of destructive typhoons
– Access banned during typhoons

When Portuguese sailors stumbled upon Taiwan in 1547, they named it "Ilha Formosa" meaning "Beautiful Island". Taiwan is only 160km (100mi) from the mainland where the government of the People's Republic of China (PRC) have ruled since winning the civil war against the Republic of China (ROC) in 1949. The ROC government withdrew to Taiwan and continue to dispute the political rights of the PRC and maintain some sovereignty over Taiwan and the 90 small islands of Penghu (Pescadores). Despite the confusing situation, surfing in Taiwan has a long history and surf arrives from a generous 225° swell window hitting all sides of the island. US soldiers were the first to ride the north coast beach of Jin Shan in 1965 and local pioneers like Mao Guh and his brothers ignored the Taoist suspicions of the sea and government ban on access to the ocean, to take up surfing. Mao Guh opened the original and still popular Jeff's Surf Shop near Honeymoon Bay and with the lifting of Martial Law in 1987, surfing clubs popped up across the island and Jung Wen-Chen, founder of R.O.C Surfing Association, estimates that there could be 25,000 people riding waves across Taiwan. While coast

Nanwan

TRAVEL INFORMATION

Local Population:
22.5M
Pingtun County 910,000
Coastline:
1,566km (973mi)
Time Zone: GMT +8
Contests:
Kenting Cup (late July)
Video: Sprout;
typhoon2000.ph
Other Resources:
taiwansurftours.com
spidersurfing.com
kentingsurfshop.com.tw
afei.com.tw
oceansmagazine.net
tealit.com/surfing.htm
tbay.com.tw

Getting There – Most countries get 30 days without a visa. Major carriers are China Airlines and EVA Air. You can fly to Taiwan from almost anywhere and Kaohsiung Airport (KHH) is a good option rather than Taipei (TPE). Airport transfer to Kenting (1h30) is $180r/t.

Getting Around – Once you get out of Taipei or Kaohsiung, traffic is smooth and parking is ok. Get used to lawlessness on the roads! No boards on public buses from Taipei to any surfing beach. Car rentals cost $84/day for a car and $106 for a 9pax van. Many east coast surfers ride trains. Stay in Kenting, use local transport.

Lodging and Food – Dorm rooms for $10/night and $20-30 in hotels in off-season, but typhoon season is high summer season. Stay in Fu Dog Surf House in Nanwan, backpacker style ($15). Stay with Spider surf club hotel: $10/night in summer (A/C), and $8 in winter. Motels and hotels price range is $45 to $120. Food is cheap: $3-10 per meal.

Weather – Kenting has a warm tropical climate with rich and fertile vegetation. There is little change between seasons. Summer weather is cooled by the afternoon sea breeze and although winter winds are cooler, it is still warm. Temps are generally between 19°C and 28°C (66-82°F) all year-round. Annual average rainfall is 2200mm (88in) mostly caused by summer typhoons. Springtime sees afternoon thunderstorms, while autumn and winter have a windy season with the "Lo-Shan-Fong", a violent wind that causes sandstorms. A springsuit is good enough the entire year except for a few weeks in January and February when air temps may dip to 10°C (50°F). Boardshorts from April to November.

Nature and Culture – Lots of sightseeing near Taipei – museums, temples (Shihtoushan Buddhist) and waterfalls (Wulai). Go-Tamsui Grass skiing resort near Paishawan. Many mountain peaks reach 3000m+, try hiking near Chushan or rafting on Hsiukuluan River (east coast). Kenting National Park hides beautiful forests.

Hazards and Hassles – Waves hardly ever reach dangerous size except during typhoons. Some volcanic reefs can be treacherous. Beware of concrete tetrapods! Crowds only happen near Taipei, riding skills are still fairly low and localism is rare. Big cockroaches and aggressive mosquitoes. The "9-21" earthquake in Sept 1999 killed 2500 people.

Handy Hints – There's good gear among the dozens of surf shops. Expect $600 for a shortboard and $900 for a longboard. Rentals are $20/d. In Taipei (Johnny Rose, Tube Factory), Ilan (Blue Ocean, Cool), Kenting (Hotel California, Beach House) or Jialeshuei (Pintung), will all help find lodgings, surf tour, school, rentals, etc.

WEATHER STATISTICS	J/F	M/A	M/J	J/A	S/O	N/D
total rainfall (mm)	15	48	244	381	195	42
consistency (days/mth)	2	4	7	8	5	2
min temp (°C)	13	17	22	23	21	15
max temp (°C)	23	27	30	31	30	26

guard towers are more interested in illegal immigrants landing by boat, when typhoon swells hit, the main beaches will be closed and surfing is still illegal along the coast south of Hualien. A steep central mountain range means the east coast is much less developed than the overcrowded west coast, which makes Taiwan second only to Bangladesh in population density.

North and east of Taipei, there is a bunch of consistent, crowded and sometimes polluted spots that are easily accessible, many by public transport. **Paishawan** is consistent in winter N swells, often offshore and easy to get to on the metro train system. **Jin Shan** aka Green Bay or Golden Mountain is super popular in summer with huge crowds of beginners and a beach party vibe, but the rivermouth brings pollution. Also check Wan-Li. The eroding golden sands of **Fulong Beach** are split by the large Shuanghsi rivermouth, which often floods the end of the access bridge. Weak, shifting peaks so surf next to the harbour wall for cleaner conditions. **Dashi**, aka Honeymoon Bay, benefits from clean water and some good, but unreliable sandbanks. Just north of Toucheng is **Wushi**, a decent black sand beach with south end jetties and some localism. Steep headlands, forested bays and a limited number of beaches make the east coast from Hualien to Taitung an explorer's paradise, with a lot of quality, isolated, left pointbreaks. **Gongs**, 3km south of Yan Liao, is a low to mid tide outside reef, near a county park at the harbour with parking, camping and toilets. Nearby is Chichi or **Jici**, the sandiest beach in rocky Hualien, serviced by Hualuan Surf shop and plagued by heavy traffic between Suao and Hualien. **Fongbin** is a rivermouth beach with good form, but watch out for rocks and the vicious shorebreak. Catching classic **Bashien Dong** lefts, at Eight Fairy Cave, will convince visitors of the power of Taiwanese surf. It's a long, boulder pointbreak that lines up great walling lefts on big NE swells, combined with NW winds. The rivermouth can create intense rips and some rights to the north. South of Three Fairy Platform is **Cheng Gong** an epic left reef/point, breaking close to shore, but only on typhoon Category 4 or 5 from the E-SE. Further south the number of sandy beaches and reefbreaks increases, but the swell is less consistent. However, the 1km wide beach at **Jialeshuei** may be Taiwan's most reliable spot for power and clean surf. There's shapely rights near the rivermouth while the lefts are almost always breaking, even in the regular onshores. Kenting area has a number of breaks, working on different conditions. Facing SE, **Nanwan**, aka Binglang Beach, stands out as a testing right reefbreak, but only on low-mid tide and SW swells. Crowds and barrels are a given when on. In front of the nuclear plant discharge pipes! In Kaohsiung, go to **Sunyatsen Beach** facing the university for a short, bodyboard style shorebreak. Escape to the Penghu Islands (64 tiny dots) on a good S swell – it's easy to fly there with boards. **Sanshuei** is one of those picture-perfect beaches, ready to catch the occasional SE-SW summer swells. Back on the heavily populated and usually flat NW coast of Taiwan is **Chu Nan**, a slow, mushy, beginners beachbreak that's protected from NE winds by the harbour wall, just avoid lower tides.

Jialeshuei

Chuupon

Taiwan sits smack dab in the middle of Typhoon Alley and the biggest swells of 8-12ft (2.5-4m) usually occur from July to October. Category 1-3 storms can appear in less than 24hrs, while super-typhoons Cat 4 and 5 usually take days to wind up, with potential for destruction, depending on the storm's track. Any violent storm activity far off in the southeast area of the Pacific Rim can create some waves. In the summer, knee to waist high is the average surf height pushed in by the SW monsoon winds without any typhoon activity. The most consistent surf is generated in winter from NE monsoon winds, which bring chest to head high waves almost everyday with potential 8-10ft (2.5-3m) peaks. North and east Taiwan has many spots that pick up even a sniff of swell (Yilan, Hualian) while the southern region has a myriad of breaks that need a bit of a look around to find (Taitung). Tides are semi-diurnal with diurnal inequality but hardly reach more than 3ft (1m).

SURF STATISTICS

Spot	Size	Btm	Type
1	6/1		
2	6/1		
3	6/1		
4	6/1		
5	6/1		
6	8/2		
7	6/1		
8	8/2		
9	8/2		
10	8/2		
11	8/1		
12	8/2		
13	4/1		
14	6/1		
15	6/1		

SURF STATISTICS	J F	M A	M J	J A	S O	N D
dominant swell	N-E	N-E	N-E	SE-SW	NE-SE	N-E
swell size (ft)	4-5	2-3	1-2	3	3-4	4-5
consistency (%)	80	50	30	60	70	80
dominant wind	N-NE	N-NE	S-SW	S-SW	N-E	N-E
average force	F5	F4-F5	F4	F4	F4-F5	F4-F5
consistency (%)	64	51	40	38	74	91
water temp.(°C)	23	24	27	29	28	25
wetsuit						

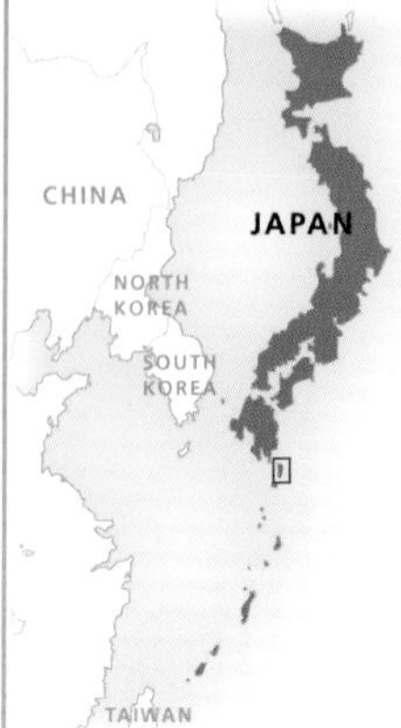

203. Tanegashima

Rock

ALL PHOTOS TSUCHIYA TAKAHIRO

Summary
+ Most consistent surf in Japan
+ Warm water year-round
+ Quality reefs & rivermouths
+ World Heritage nature on Yakushima

– Rarely world-class
– Limited access
– Often onshore
– Super expensive

The island of Tanegashima, located about 40km (26mi) off the southern tip of Kyushu in Kagoshima Prefecture, is one of the finest surf destinations in Japan. With the island's long, narrow shape and good exposure to both Pacific and East China Sea swell, the probability of scoring waves at any time of year is high by Japanese standards. There are a variety of breaks to suit all levels of surfer and the water is relatively warm all year-round. Many surfers have moved to Tanegashima simply for the surf, which can get really good on both coasts, particularly when a typhoon roars past the region.

Rock

The furthest break north, **Chinbotsu**, breaks in front of a shipwreck and can hold some size on a NE-SE swell. Consistent and shallow inside, it is better when higher tides cover the boulders. **Kazamoto** is a fun rivermouth break that can be good when everywhere else on the Pacific coast is closed-out. Long rides over the boulder sand combo

TRAVEL INFORMATION

Local Population: 34 500
Coastline: 150km (93mi)
Time Zone: GMT +9
Contests: None
Video:
A scene at the Sea. 1991, Drive Thru Japan
Other Resources:
keep-smile.blog.ocn.ne.jp/surf/2008/03/index.html
tanegashima-air.jp
jnto.go.jp/eng/location/regional/kagoshima/tanegashima.html
god.tksc.jaxa.jp/slrsub/tane.html

Getting There – No visa 90 days. Fly to Tanegashima (TNE) from Tokyo's Haneda Airport via Kagoshima (3h) and direct from Osaka's Itami Airport (1hr 20 mins). It's also accessible by boat from Kagoshima on the 'Rocket' and 'Toppy' high-speed boats (1hr 30mins) and the 'Princess Wakasa' ferry (3hrs 30mins). Boats from neighbouring Yakushima take 50mins.

Getting Around – Public transport on Tanegashima is limited and infrequent. Taxis are available but are quite expensive because of the relatively long distances between breaks. The best option for maximum access is rental car. Rates begin from around $50/day.

Lodging and Food – Choose from western-style beds or Japanese-style roll out futon mattresses in self-contained units to family-run minshuku guesthouses and standard hotels. Surf Villa Narai and Mauna Village cater specifically to surfers. Sushi, sashimi and sweet potatoes, are a prominent feature of the island's cuisine. Expect $15-20 for a meal.

WEATHER STATISTICS	J/F	M/A	M/J	J/A	S/O	N/D
total rainfall (mm)	124	158	173	392	60	83
consistency (days/mth)	10	12	13	11	11	9
min temp (°C)	9	12	19	25	22	13
max temp (°C)	15	19	25	30	26	20

Weather – Despite its sub-tropical location, Tanegashima is a relatively flat and dry island compared with its neighbour, Yakushima, which receives '35 wet days a month' as passing clouds collide with its lofty peaks. Nevertheless Tanegashima is located in Japan's typhoon alley between Okinawa and Kyushu so it does receive considerable rainfall in summer as the tropical storms pass. Typhoons and winter low-pressure systems provide the main swell seasons from July to October on the Pacific coast and from December to February on the East China Sea coast respectively. The weather is very hot and humid during summer but warm clothes are needed during winter and at night in autumn or spring. Annual average rainfall is 1200mm (48in). Boardshorts during summer, a shorty during spring and a 3/2mm fullsuit in the depths of winter.

Nature and Culture – Expect a relaxed island lifestyle offering a welcome escape from drab Japanese suburbia. Large limestone caves (Chikura and Matate-no-Iwaya) border the white sand beaches on the SE coast. The Teppo (gun) Matsuri, commemorates the arrival of the first guns in 1543. Visit the Tanegashima Space Centre outside of launch times.

Hazards and Hassles – The best surf generally results from summer typhoon swells however at such times access can be difficult with flights and ferries often cancelled. The line-up can get intense when the surf gets big and locals assert their priority, but you shouldn't have a problem if you are polite and friendly.

Handy Hints – It's possible to find some boards to rent but prices will be really high. There's a surprising array of ethnic cuisine, catering to the palates of well-travelled surfers. English knowledge is higher than the rest of Japan, but if you don't speak any Japanese, you might have a tough time communicating.

when it's overhead, incoming tide and offshore wind from the SW-W. Another rivermouth is **Azakou**, best on a rising tide, any E swell and is a good place to try when other spots are crowded. Fast take-offs and occasional tubes. When there's not much swell around on the Pacific coastline, the reliable winter beachbreaks like **Kanehama** are powerful enough to have fun waves, even when the surf is small, plus easy parking, showers and toilets make it very convenient. Rock and Hungry are located very close to each other just south of Kanehama. **Rock** is a less consistent righthand barrel, that breaks off Anjou Port on a big E-SE swell. **Hungry** is a consistent and quality offshore reefbreak with long walls offering up to 200m long rides. It's usually a lefthander, but it also breaks right when it gets big. Best on a low tide and any E swell. The sheltered break of **Injou** is often glassy and handles wind from S round to NW. It's usually a long, righthand wall, but will break left too when it's big from the E. Beware of rocks on the shallow inside. **Nakayama** is a beautiful, long beach with 3 breaks; Minato (port) to the north, Center in the middle and Takeyano to the south. Generally best on an incoming tide, an E-SE swell and a W-NW offshore. In the south, there are 3 picturesque beachbreaks to choose from. **Toudai-shita** is located below the lighthouse near the Space Centre. This exposed, scenic beachbreak catches a lot of swell from March to October and can be quite powerful. Ideal conditions are a pushing tide, an E-SE swell and a NW-N offshore wind. Around the cape on the southern tip of the island in front of the Iwasaki Hotel is **Hotel-Mae**. This year-round beachbreak gets crowded because it is offshore in the regular NW-NE winds. Generally, the lefthander on the left side of the beach is the most consistent spot in any S swell. Also on the south coast, a little west of Hotel-mae is **Takezaki**. There are numerous A-frame peaks along this beachbreak such as 'Stack' and 'Pavilion-mae', that offer long rides when the sandbanks are good. A 4WD vehicle is needed to pass through the 'jungle', which helps keep crowds down. The west coast facing the East China Sea is less consistent and has fewer breaks than the east coast. **Yakutsu** is a fun beachbreak that will catch typhoon or winter SW-W swells up to a solid size. **Nagahama** is a long beach on Tanegashima's west coast. At the northern end of the beach is a fickle, boulder and sand bottom rivermouth peak. The lefts in particular can offer long walls and even tubes when it's pumping on a W swell and SE wind. Check out Sumiyoshi, a heavy reefbreak off **Sumiyoshi** Port. Legendary for its big tubes and ability to handle the biggest swells, the peaks work best in a SW swell, NE wind combo. Wipe-outs at this experts only break are potentially dangerous as it's very shallow on the inside. **Yokino** is a little south of Nishi-no-omote, the main settlement of Tanegashima. Various hollow peaks, plus there are reefs in the centre and at the southern end of this picturesque, white sand beach. The reefbreaks on the northeast coast tend to hold larger swells, so usually work best during the typhoon season from July to October.

① Chinbotsu
② Kazamoto
③ Azakou
④ Kanehama
⑤ Rock
⑥ Hungry
⑦ Injou
⑧ Nakayama
⑨ Toudai-Shita
⑩ Hotel-Mae
⑪ Takezaki
⑫ Yakutsu
⑬ Nagahama
⑭ Sumiyoshi
⑮ Yokino

Kunigami
Iseki
Guniwa
Nishinoomote
Anno
Tanowaki
Sumiyoshi
Anju
Hirayama
Tanegashima Island
East China Sea
Cosmo Airport
Masuda
Noma
Shimama
Minamitane
Kukinaga
Cape Yoshinobu (Space Center)
Kamiyaku, Yakushima Islands
Anbo, Yakushima Island

SURF STATISTICS			
Spot	Size	Btm	Type
①	8/2		
②	8/3		
③	6/2		
④	6/2		
⑤	8/3		
⑥	8/3		
⑦	8/3		
⑧	5/1		
⑨	5/1		
⑩	5/1		
⑪	4/1		
⑫	6/1		
⑬	6/2		
⑭	8/3		
⑮	5/1		

Tanegashima offers opportunities for surfing in two different seas with plenty of seasonal options. The Pacific Ocean on the east coast provides NE-SE swells all year-round, but the main surf season is from July to November when the summer typhoons can bring strong SE-SW swells. These swells can also hit the west coast of the island in the East China Sea as well as winter low pressure systems bringing SW-W swells from December to February. Most of the surf is 2-6ft (0.6-2m) with occasional super-typhoon swells reaching 10-12ft (3-4m). Tides are semi-diurnal with daily inequality, reaching 7ft (2.1m) max on spring tides.

SURF STATISTICS	J F	M A	M J	J A	S O	N D
dominant swell	NE-SE	NE-SE	NE-SE	SE-SW	SE-SW	NE-SE
swell size (ft)	2-3	2	1-2	2-3	3-4	3
consistency (%)	50	40	30	50	70	60
dominant wind	NW-N	NW-NE	NE-SW	E-SW	N-NE	NW-N
average force	F4	F4	F3-F4	F3-F4	F4	F4
consistency (%)	53	49	43	48	42	47
water temp.(°C)	19	20	22	28	27	23
wetsuit						

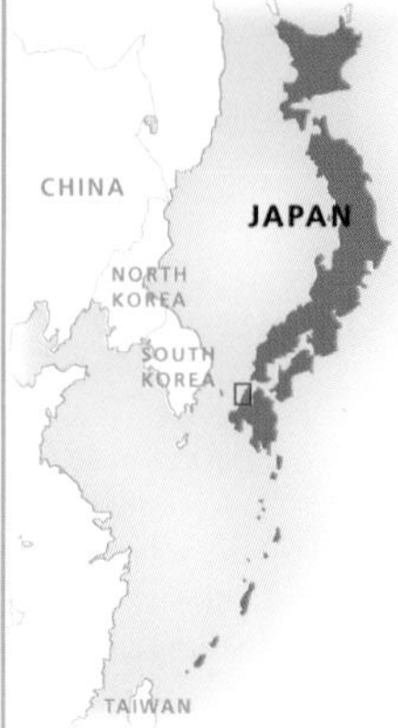

204. Fukuoka

Nishi-No-Ura

ALL PHOTOS BY TSUCHIYA TAKAHIRO

Summary
+ Some quality spots
+ Uncrowded surf for Japan
+ Pacific coast proximity
+ Relatively warm in winter
+ Cosmopolitan city

– Narrow swell window
– Cold winters
– Inconsistent Genkai Sea
– Expensive local costs
– Language barrier

Fukuoka is situated on the northwest coast of Kyushu, Japan's westernmost island. Its coastline faces the Genkai Sea, a small body of water at the southwest tip of the Sea of Japan. Picking up northerly swells coming out of the Sea of Japan, this narrow swell window is offset by warm water and low crowds, compared to the surf zones further north and offers visitors a real taste of the Japanese surf experience.

During winter when other nearby breaks are closing-out, **Waita** beachbreak can be a good, mellow option. After a session warm up at the nearby local onsen hot spring baths. Near the lighthouse at Tominohana

Shika-no-Shima

is **Iwaya**, a fun contest site beachbreak with all facilities of parking, toilets and showers. **Same** (Sa-may) handles NE wind and gets bigger waves than neighbouring Iwaya, but is still suitable for beginners. Past the Onga River is

TRAVEL INFORMATION

Local Population: Fukuoka region 5,057,932
Coastline: KyuShu - 1951 km (1212mi)
Time Zone: GMT +9
Contests: Fukuoka Cup, Keya, held in March
Video: A scene at the Sea. 1991, Drive Thru Japan
Other Resources: radix-sf.com/ ragesurf.com/ missionsurf/

Getting There – 90 days entry. As a gateway to western Japan, Fukuoka (FUK) has easy access. Flights from all over SE Asia plus connections with South Korea, Mainland China, Taiwan and Hong Kong. There's a ferry to / from Busan in South Korea. Hakata Station connects Fukuoka to the Shinkansen high-speed rail network.

Getting Around – Renting a car will cost about $300/wk at Tocoo Travel. Fukuoka's efficient public transport provides access by train to breaks north of the city from Shika-no-shima to Tsuyazaki. For west coast breaks between Nishinoura and Keya take the Chikuzen Railway to Imajuku and then take a bus. You can also take buses to get to northern breaks between Tsurigawa and Waita.

Lodging and Food – Anything from cheap 'capsules' ($40-60 a day) to 5-star hotels. Centrally located Khaosan Int'l Hostel in Fukuoka suits the budget traveller. There's a peaceful campsite on Nokonoshima island or near Keya and Iwaya breaks. Try mentaiko cod-roe (spicy fish eggs) or hakata ramen (salty, oily pork noodle soup). Eat out at the night stalls known as yatai, in the Tenjin and Nakagawa districts.

WEATHER STATISTICS	J/F	M/A	M/J	J/A	S/O	N/D
total rainfall (mm)	54	78	52	280	80	53
consistency (days/mth)	9	11	10	10	9	8
min temp (°C)	5	9	18	24	20	8
max temp (°C)	12	17	26	31	28	15

Weather – Fukuoka is bordered on three sides by mountains and opens north to the Sea of Genkai. It has a moderate climate with humid and fairly hot summers (August hits 32°C/90°F). Winter temps rarely drop below 0°C/32°F and it is generally rainy with occasional, brief snowfalls. Spring is warm and very sunny and autumn, often considered as the best season for tourism, is mild and drier. The rainy season lasts for approximately 6 weeks through June and July and the typhoon season runs between August and September. Annual rainfall is about 1600mm/64in). Use a 3/2mm fullsuit from November to April and a springy or boardshorts for the rest of the year.

Nature and Culture – Visit Dazaifu, Kyushu's old capital: the grand Tenmangu Shrine and the nearby Zen temple contrast differences between Shinto and Buddhist styles. For modern attractions, check out Robosquare near Fukuoka Tower. Don't miss Japan's largest basalt cave, Keya Oto and Uminonakamichi Marine Park. Most mountains are a bit over 1000m (3280ft) high.

Hazards and Hassles – Beware of stinging jellyfish in the water in late summer and early autumn. Car break-ins have been reported at Keya. Fukuoka surfers have a reputation for friendliness, but they can become territorial when the surf gets good so always remember to be respectful and wait your turn in the line-up.

Handy Hints – Plenty of surf shops around, but gear is expensive. Better bring your own surfboards like a standard thruster and something thicker or a longboard for mellow waves. Most of the road signs are in English, but if you don't speak any Japanese, you might have trouble finding your way.

Shiorigawa

another beachbreak at the **Shioirigawa-Kakou** rivermouth. Although the waves are a bit weak, this long, shallow beach will break cleanly even on small swells from the W-NE. **Hatsu-Gyokou** works in SW winds, which groom weak rights, unless it is pumping, when the left offers a longer ride, but look out for the backwash on the full tide. The premier venue in Fukuoka prefecture is **Kanezaki** beachbreak, offering tubing lefts and rights at each end of the beach. Kanezaki has waves constantly throughout winter and is usually bigger than other nearby breaks. Fukuoka surfers often check Tsuri rivermouth before going to nearby Kanezaki. Even if **Tsurigawa-Kakou** is usually much smaller, it's possible to get some decent barrels when the sandbanks are good. Next to Tougou Park and Kitakyushu Hospital, inconsistent **Tsuyazaki** right pointbreak is a quality wave, with a tube on take-off, then a playful wall up to 100m long. Near **Shingu** fishing port on the left side of the beach is a rivermouth where a long, fun lefthander breaks beside a seawall. Between the concrete tetra blocks, there's a shifting right and left peak. The left is usually smaller, but much faster than the longer rights. **Mitoma** is a typical beachbreak with a thriving surf scene and many surf shops. Being such a well-known spot, Mitoma is often crowded. Normally, it's easy rights and lefts ideal for beginners, but when it's bigger, long rides can be had for those that make it out the back. The island of **Shika-No-Shima** hosts three beachbreaks suitable for all levels, but there are plenty of close-outs and it's more suited to windsurfing. The main attraction is the eastside reefbreak where difficult, rocky, slow lefts gradually build up speed to form long walls when conditions are ideal. Fukuoka is located on the protected waters of Hakata Bay, but west of the city there is surf on the headland jutting out into the Genkai Sea. When **Nishi-No-Ura** is on, this rocky, lefthander tubes and peels for a long way. North of the tall torii shrine gate, is the highly consistent **Mitami-Ga-Ura**, often used for contests. The beachbreaks are usually slow and fat when small, but when it gets overhead, powerful waves break a long way out and a useful current runs out to sea from the right side of the beach. With small waves on the inside and big waves out the back, there's something for everybody on a good day. **Oguchi Bay** holds good reef-bottomed rights next to the rocks, plus a fun beachbreak with some power. When it's big, the quality right offers long rides, if you can make the steep take-off. Hazardous on a low tide, when the rocks become exposed. Last is **Keya**, the main surfing break in western Fukuoka, which can handle some size. It's consistent like Mitami-ga-ura but the waves are more powerful.

SURF STATISTICS			
Spot	Size	Btm	Type
①	4/1		
②	5/1		
③	5/1		
④	6/1		
⑤	6/2		
⑥	8/1		
⑦	5/1		
⑧	5/2		
⑨	5/1		
⑩	5/1		
⑪	5/1		
⑫	6/2		
⑬	6/2		
⑭	8/2		
⑮	8/2		

The best seasons for Fukuoka are autumn and winter (September to March). There can also be surf in summer if a typhoon deviates northwest from the

Shiorigawa

usual northeast path. Autumn is preferable as winter can be very cold and windy with occasional snowfalls. It is also the most consistent season for surf. In comparison with the Japan Sea coastline on the main island of Honshu, it is relatively warm. Generally speaking, all of the breaks in Fukuoka are best 3 hours either side of high tide. Tides are semi-diurnal and rarely exceed 5ft (1.5m).

SURF STATISTICS	J F	M A	M J	J A	S O	N D
dominant swell	NW-NE	NW-NE	NW-NE	NW-NE	NW-NE	NW-NE
swell size (ft)	2-3	1	0-1	1-2	2	3
consistency (%)	60	20	10	30	50	70
dominant wind	NW-N	NW-NE	E-SW	E-SW	N-NE	NW-N
average force	F4	F4	F3-F4	F3-F4	F4	F4
consistency (%)	53	49	30	48	42	47
water temp.(°C)	15	16	21	26	24	19
wetsuit						

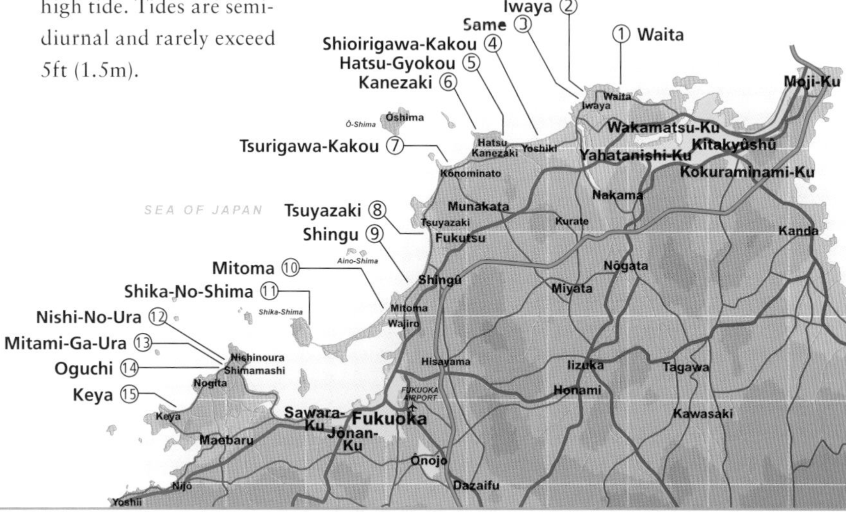

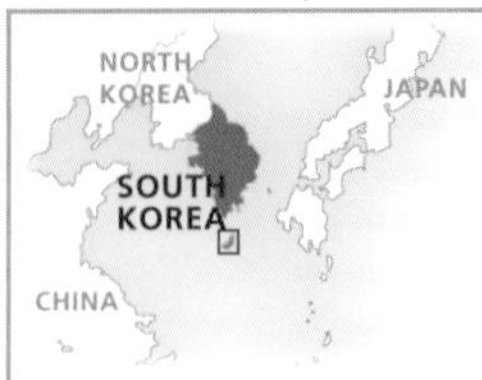

205. Jeju Do

Squid Point

ALL PHOTOS JOHN CALLAHAN/TROPICALPIX

Summary
+ Powerful typhoon waves
+ Beaches & lava reefbreaks
+ Uncrowded surf
+ World Heritage island
+ Great tourism facilities

– Inconsistent swells
– Short surf season
– Unpredictable typhoon tracks
– Expensive local costs
– Over-protective lifeguards

Lying off the southwest coast of the Republic of Korea, volcanic Jeju Island (Jejudo) is a UNESCO listed World Natural Heritage site. The lofty 1950m (6397ft) peak of Halla mountain in the centre of the island, slopes steeply down to the north & south coasts, surrounded by 368 smaller volcanoes called 'oreum'. Manjang cave is regarded as the longest lava cave in the world, at 13.4km (8.3m) long. The island's warm, sunny climate and myriad leisure facilities mean that it is one of the country's most popular tourist and honeymoon destinations. South Korea has cautiously opened it's doors to the world and in May 1992, Flip Cuddy from Hawaii surfed there with Grant Shoemaker and Donald Takayama on a longboard sprayed in Korean colours, although customs agents held the surfboards because they had never seen them before. When John Callahan visited in 2004 with an international crew of surfers, he stumbled into 8-10ft (2.5-3m) surf and constant swell during the whole trip, thanks

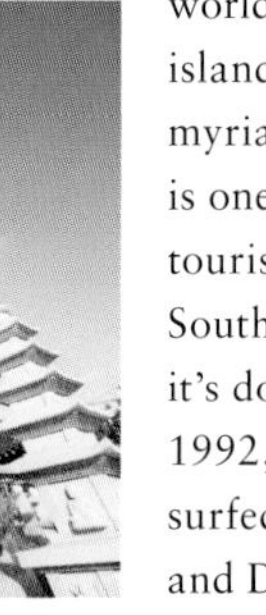

Old Ladies

TRAVEL INFORMATION

Local Population: 560,000
Coastline: 263km (163mi)
Time Zone: GMT +9
Contests: Jungmun
Other Resources:
oceanography.navy.mil/legacy/web/cgi-bin/animate.pl/metoc/101/21/0-0-1/6
chejuinfo.net
letsgojeju.com
tour2korea.com

Getting There – 30 day visa issued on arrival. All flights arrive in Gimpo airport (SEL), 60km from Seoul (apart from Tokyo, Osaka, Nagoya, Fukuoka or China direct to Jeju). Jeju (CJU) is 1h flight from Gimpo ($70) with Korean Air and Asiana Airlines. Ferry from Pusan, Inchon, Wando, and Mokpo. Wando - Jeju is 3h by Hanil Car Ferry. Deptax: $10

Getting Around – There is a good road system encircled by the 182km (113mi) coast road. Rental cars: Elantra 1.5 costs $75/d at Grand Rent Car. Most of the road signs are in western alphabet. Best to stay in Jungmun (if you can afford it!) and drive from there or stay in Seogwipo.

Lodging and Food – Shilla Cheju Hotel (super deluxe) with ocean view is $250/night. In Seogwipo City, Daemyung Green Ville, New Kyongnam, Kal Seogwipo or Paradise Hotel are cheaper at $70-120. Jeju Guest-house, 25min N of Jungmun is $30/day. Meals are cheap: $5-7 for a full meal. Try kimchi, pickled fermented cabbage.

WEATHER STATISTICS	J/F	M/A	M/J	J/A	S/O	N/D
total rainfall (mm)	60	82	130	227	119	66
consistency (days/mth)	4	5	7	12	7	5
min temp (°C)	3	6	14	23	15	5
max temp (°C)	8	16	24	29	25	15

Weather – Jeju is a volcanic island and experiences aspects of both subtropical oceanic and temperate climates. Because of the ocean current around the island and the geographical conditions, a wide change of temperature occurs and the winters are generally long, cold and dry thanks to the seasonal N winds. Summers are short, hot and humid, bringing downpours that are usually caused by high temps and humidity. Spring and autumn are pleasant but short in duration. Temps range between 15°C and 30°C (59-86°F) in summer and vary between 3°C and 16°C (37-61°F) during winter. Average annual rainfall is 1570mm (63in). Use a 3/2mm fullsuit from November to June and a springy or boardshorts from July through October.

Nature and Culture – Lava stones are piled on the ocean-side roads as wishing-good-luck monuments. Visit the incredible lava tunnels. Women divers (Haenyeo) with ancient wetsuit and goggles, collect seaweed, shellfish and sea urchins, then sell them on the roadside. Sungsan's Sunrise Peak is the main tourist site. Many trails (Yongshil, Orimok) to walk.

Hazards and Hassles – During typhoons, waves can reach spectacular sizes at Jungmun. Beware, lifeguards may stop you from entering the water. Police know surfing at Jungmun, but still might cause problems at other spots. Some lava reefs can be pretty nasty. Jeju is becoming known to Japanese surfers as a summer option.

Handy Hints – No surf shop so bring everything and leave your gear with locals. Locals don't speak Japanese. The phallic Harubang, or grandfather stone is carved from basalt and dotted across the island. Jeju has kept the traditional Korean cultural identity in houses and lifestyle.

Squid Point

to 2 super-typhoons. Koreans rarely swim in the sea, even when it's flat, so most lifeguards don't want anyone near the water, let alone play in the surf when there is typhoon swell, but a nucleus of local surfers are slowly altering these over-cautious attitudes.

Below the impressive Mt. Songaksan, **Squid Point** can offer a long left point on those all too rare typhoon swells from the SE-SW. Difficult access means it is hardly ever surfed. In front of the **Hyatt Regency**, a boulder reef holds the sand and some decent low tide rights on any S swell variation, plus offers a bit of protection from W winds. **Jungmun Beach** is the most popular spot in Jeju and was named among "Asia's Top 10 Beaches". It's frequently used as a location for movies, thanks to the dramatic backdrop of towering, black basalt cliffs against the blue sea. The Jungmun Tourist Complex provides top-quality accommodations and facilities complete with golf course, a Pacific themed leisure centre and the best concentration of surf spots on the island. Locals have a shack on Jungmun Beach called the 'Wave Club" where more and more Koreans come to learn and an annual surf contest has been held since 2005. The Centre Peak is the inside wave with lefts and rights, which can get very hollow and sucky when hitting the sandbar. The Outside is a mushier peak and shoulder that will roll through to connect with the inside and get hollow if the swell is bigger than 5ft (1.5m). Beware of very strong currents and while it is mainly sand there are patches of reef underneath. Centre and Outside are quite consistent, usually better at low tide and pretty much protected from the cross/offshore winds by the high cliffs. On the eastern headland is **Shilla Point**, a reefbreak peak that's fast and hollow. The lefts are usually smaller, but peel nicely and can lead into the hollow sandbars on the beach. Beware of the big rock in the middle of the righthander that often gets in the way and can only be seen at low tide. Going eastward check **SGI**, a very inconsistent right reefbreak that needs SW swell and NE winds to be any good. **Old Ladies** is not far from the World Cup venue Seogwipo Soccer Stadium and Chungbang waterfall. This quality right reefbreak is deep in a bay behind an island and affords good W wind protection. It's hard to find but there are other waves along this coast that probably work when a typhoon swell hits from the SW. Further east is a left slab at **Nanwon**, which only turns on in special conditions of SE swell, NW wind. During winter, NE winds can kick up some short-period windswell on the north shore beachbreaks like Iho, Hamdeok or **Gymnyeong**, which is at best, an average beachbreak that's usually onshore, but a trip to the labyrinth and lava tunnels will make it worth the drive.

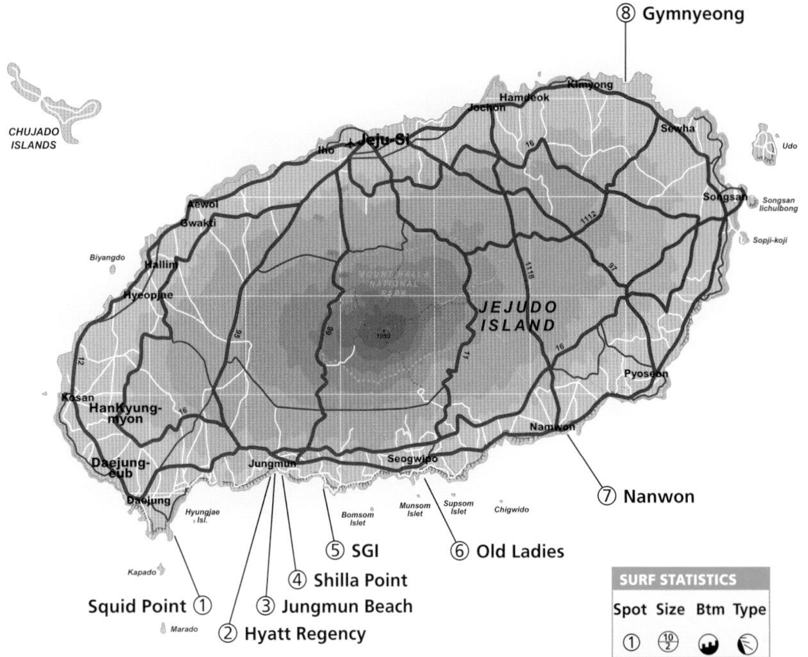

SURF STATISTICS			
Spot	Size	Btm	Type
①	10/2		
②	8/2		
③	6/1		
④	8/2		
⑤	8/2		
⑥	8/2		
⑦	6/2		
⑧	4/1		

Most swells are generated by lows in the Yellow Sea. Swells are short (2 days) but frequent (every 3-4 days) during the summer and there's always the possibility of the occasional typhoon with the right tracking. Winds are often strong and can change directions many times during the day. Most beaches are made of black lava stones and only some are sand covered. The waves are very, very inconsistent, but occasionally Jeju gets some excellent, powerful surf rolling in, and there are a couple of fine, thick reefbreaks along the south coast. The NE swells are not worth bothering with so really the only time to guarantee any wave action is from June to October. Tides are semi-diurnal with diurnal inequality and spring tides rarely exceed 6ft (1.8m). Download a tide chart online before the trip as it will be impossible to read the info in the Korean newspaper.

SURF STATISTICS	J F	M A	M J	J A	S O	N D
dominant swell	N-E	N-E	SE-SW	SE-SW	SE-SW	N-E
swell size (ft)	2	1	1-2	2	2-3	2
consistency (%)	30	20	10	40	50	30
dominant wind	NW-N	NW-N	NE-SW	S-SW	N-NE	NW-N
average force	F4-F5	F4	F3-F4	F3	F4	F4
consistency (%)	66	44	41	36	50	57
water temp.(°C)	12	13	18	24	23	17
wetsuit						

Shilla Point

The quintessential desert wave experience requires real determination to reach and even more to ride, since Red Bluff is as notoriously uncompromising as the surrounding environment.

PHOTO: SERGIO VILLALBA
O'NEILL

A Melanesian curtain cracks the coral in the Solomon Islands.

Pacific Ocean

STEPHANE ROBIN

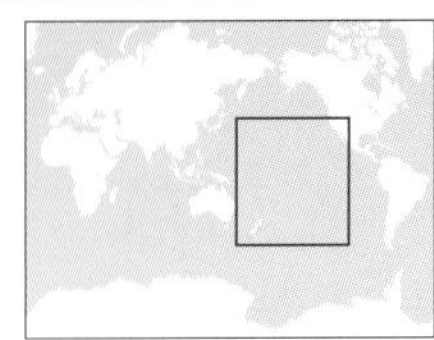

Surf Culture

After Captain Cook's discovery of the Sandwich Isles, Christian missionaries spread throughout the Pacific region and generally frowned on the act of surfing, despite it's long cultural heritage and integral social role in Hawai'i. By the late 19th century, when the USA finally annexed Hawai'i and jailed Queen Lili'uokalani, the population had been decimated by haole diseases and only 40,000 survived from an estimated 400,000 a century earlier. Surfing had almost disappeared except for isolated pockets of activity, one of which was based at Waikiki and had begun to pass on the ancient knowledge to a new type of visitor – the tourist. Amongst these travellers was Alexander Hume Ford, who instantly identified with surf-riding, promoting the activity through notable author Jack London in 1907, then forming the Outrigger and Canoe Surf Club, before the Waikiki beachfront was swallowed by hotel developments. Three years later (1911), the predominately Hawaiian Hui Nalu club was co-founded by a young local surfer and phenomenal swimmer, Duke Kahanamoku, who was honing his stroke to become the 1912 Olympic Champion in the 100m freestyle. Afterwards, he embarked on a worldwide swimming tour, which he unofficially used to introduce surfing to a waiting world. Surfing's foremost ambassador hit the waves in California and New Jersey (1912), Sydney (1914) and NZ (1915), sowing the seeds of today's global surf culture. New Zealand Maoris had been surfing canoes for centuries before Dutch explorers arrived, yet the same Calvinist missionaries that all but destroyed Hawaiian surf culture saw to it that surfing vanished, until the Duke hit the waves of Lyall Bay, Wellington. Following the Aussie curve, surf lifesaving clubs held sway until Americans introduced lightweight balsa and fibreglass boards, providing the catalyst for a national Boardriders Association (1963), NZ Surfing Championships (1963) and *New Zealand Surfer* magazine (1965). Tahitians were noted by Captain Cook riding paipo boards and surfing their canoes, a practice that slumbered until the 1950s and modern surf travellers arrived. Bruce Brown's *Endless Summer* crew only rode the gentle inside waves but by 1969, surf clubs and competitions were being organised by locals on the fearsome reef passes and Papeete local Arsene Harehoe dominated the scene for two decades. Tonga, Fiji and Samoa were slower to rediscover their surfing heritage until foreigners founded surf camps in Ha'atafu, Tonga (1979), the world famous Tavarua, Fiji (1982) and Samoa ('90s), although many spots had been discovered earlier and kept secret for years. The huge potential offered by the western archipelagos of New Caledonia, Vanuatu and the Solomon Islands, where a few dialled in ex-pats with boats have the reef passes to themselves, is only just coming to light this decade. The same can be said for the exposure of lonely Pacific specks like Majuro, Pohnpei, Tabuaeran, Rarotonga, Huahine, Raiatea and the vast Tuamotu where the travelling logistics keep the world at bay.

STÉPHANE ROBIN

Grommets carry locally sourced and shaped, solid wood boards in a refreshingly sustainable scene from a traditional island society at ease with the ocean. Malaita, Solomon Islands.

Opposite – **Tahiti's threatening reef-pass, Teahupoo has imprinted it's gaping maw on the mind of modern surf culture, challenging the limits of the world's best competition and tow-in surfers.**

Today

Hawai'i remains the centre of the world's surf culture by virtue of it's stunning wave resources that have allowed it to establish the planet's most prestigious surf competitions. The Duke, The Eddie and the Pipeline Masters have been fought over by the best, including local legends like Gerry Lopez, Reno Abillera, Larry Bertlemann, Dane Kealoha, Michael & Derek Ho, Johnny-Boy Gomes, Kalani Robb and Sunny Garcia to name a few. Specialist Hawaiian shapers have forged gleaming reputations for big-wave equipment and a crew of ocean toreadors have pushed the boundaries of tow surfing, led by the iconic talent of Laird Hamilton. Being so isolated, everything costs more to import, but the islands support four major surf labels and almost 100 surf shops. The rest of the Pacific Islands (except NZ) are the polar opposite, with little or no surf industry, save that attached to servicing the surf camps and resorts. Tahiti is another exception, cultivating some great local surfers and developing the contest scene on the back of the Teahupoo media frenzy, which became a pro tour stop in 1997. New Zealand's surf industry shows more Australian influence than Polynesian, yet retains a bucolic, laid-back attitude, especially on the South Island, away from the crowds of Raglan, where the legendary length of ride has encouraged local groups to enforce the line-up. Duke Kahanamoku championed the necessity for surfers to show each other some aloha spirit – the friendly, hospitable, welcoming vibe that Hawaiians are famous for. This spirit wasn't in evidence in the '40s when Gene "Tarzan" Smith and Tommy Zahn were beaten up on Oahu's North Shore, beginning a long history of intimidation from locals, annoyed by the burgeoning crowds, the end of wave sharing and a perceived lack of respect being shown, particularly by certain brash Aussie pros in the '70s. Violent clashes ensued, often

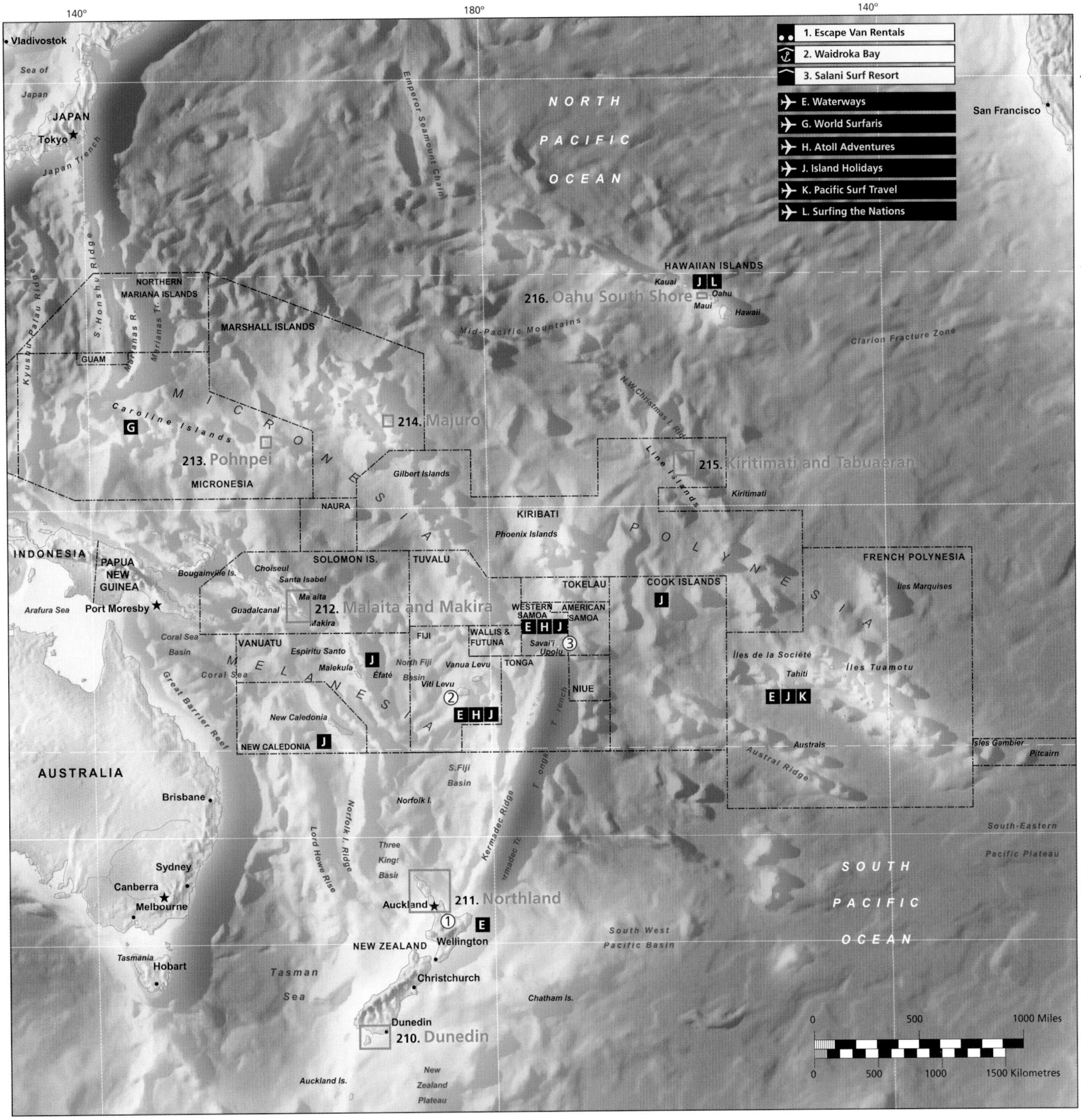

1. Escape Van Rentals
2. Waidroka Bay
3. Salani Surf Resort
E. Waterways
G. World Surfaris
H. Atoll Adventures
J. Island Holidays
K. Pacific Surf Travel
L. Surfing the Nations
NORTH PACIFIC OCEAN
SOUTH PACIFIC OCEAN
216. Oahu South Shore
215. Kiritimati and Tabuaeran
214. Majuro
213. Pohnpei
212. Malaita and Makira
211. Northland
210. Dunedin
HAWAIIAN ISLANDS
MICRONESIA
MELANESIA
POLYNESIA
JAPAN
Tokyo
Vladivostok
San Francisco
AUSTRALIA
NEW ZEALAND
FRENCH POLYNESIA
COOK ISLANDS
KIRIBATI
TUVALU
TOKELAU
FIJI
TONGA
NIUE
VANUATU
NEW CALEDONIA
SOLOMON IS.
PAPUA NEW GUINEA
INDONESIA
MARSHALL ISLANDS
NORTHERN MARIANA ISLANDS
GUAM
NAURA
WESTERN SAMOA
AMERICAN SAMOA
WALLIS & FUTUNA
Tropic of Cancer
Equator
Tropic of Capricorn
0 500 1000 Miles
0 500 1000 1500 Kilometres

instigated by the Hawaiian Black Shorts, a loose band of enforcers that provided a blueprint for similar intimidation to take place on other islands in the chain, before spreading to French Polynesia and NZ. Hawaiian surfers still police many line-ups with an iron fist, but extreme crowding has blurred the local/visitor lines a little. Ultra patience and serendipity play a big part in scoring at the famous breaks and respectful, shoulder-hopping deference is advisable at semi-secret spots. As surfing matures, the words from an aging Duke hold pertinence and much aloha; "There are so many waves....take your time – wave come. Let the other guys go; catch another one."

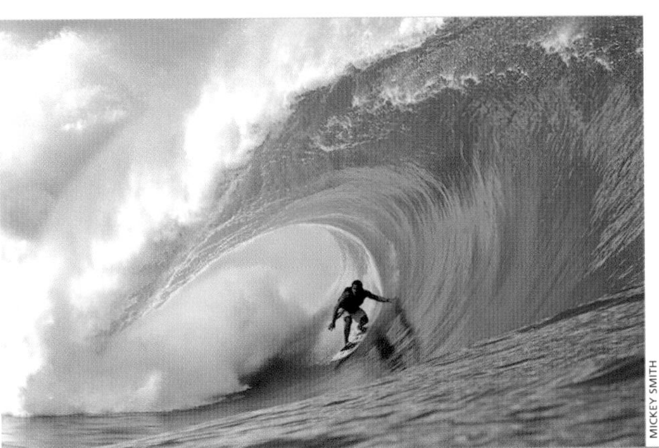

MICKEY SMITH

210. Dunedin

Long Point

Summary

+ Plenty of swell action
+ Loads of long pointbreaks
+ Among NZ's best beachbreaks
+ Uncrowded, full-on nature
+ Close to world-class snowfields

- Cold water, windy & wild
- Farmland access, long hikes
- Rare classic conditions on points
- Long haul flights

Otago and Southland offer some of the most challenging and rewarding surf breaks to be found anywhere in the country. Swells can get huge and it's no wonder that the Rex Von Huben memorial Big Wave contest is held here, usually in October and attracting a hard-core of the country's best to celebrate the life of a legendary Dunedin local. Over the decades, Dunedin surfers have gained recognition as chargers and Papatowai as the official tow-in break in New Zealand. North Otago spots are rare because good NE swells don't quite break often enough, but when they do, points like Murderers show their world-class colours.

Papatowai

Aramoana Spit

Hollow **Karitane** rivermouth bar rights awaken on E swells while further outside, The Point is a sucky, challenging right, breaking close to the rocks from

TRAVEL INFORMATION

Local Population: 120,000 Dunedin
Coastline: 6500km (4040mi) South Island
Time Zone: GMT+12h
Contests: South Island Surf Champs (April)
Other Resources:
www.surf.co.nz
www.surf2surf.com
www.hydrosurf.co.nz

Getting There – No visa for <30 days visit. Dunedin airport (DUD) is serviced by Air New Zealand and Qantas for within NZ and has direct flights from Australia (Coolangatta) with Freedom Air and Origin Pacific. Auckland (AUK) flight is 2.5h (1451km, $150 USD). 5h drive from Christchurch, 2.5h to Invercargill. Departure tax is $20.

Getting Around – The Southern Scenic Route around the Catlins in South Otago provides access to most surf breaks. Farming is the largest industry in Otago and Southland, finding livestock wandering on roads is not rare. Drive safely and on the left. Portobello Rd is the main route to the world famous Royal Albatross Colony at the entrance to Otago Harbour. Escape Campervans (office in Christchurch) are perfect for surfers.

WEATHER STATISTICS	J/F	M/A	M/J	J/A	S/O	N/D
total rainfall (mm)	73	70	75	68	65	69
consistency (days/mth)	11	12	12	11	12	12
min temp (°C)	10	7	4	3	5	7
max temp (°C)	19	17	12	11	15	18

Lodging and Food – Villa Rustica near Carey's Bay is a good place for surfers with Dr. Surf's Longboard Clinic and Otago Surf Tours: Rod Rust. Stafford Gables YHA is located in the student town of Dunedin and has dorm rooms at $12. Many backpackers at $10-30/day. Expect $12-25 for a meal. Great wines!

Weather – Dunedin has a temperate climate, however the city is recognised as having a large number of microclimates and weather conditions often vary. It is also greatly modified by its proximity to the ocean. This leads to semi-warm summers and cool winters that can be frosty but significant snowfall is uncommon. Spring can feature "four seasons in a day" weather, but from November to April it is generally settled and mild. Temps range from 3-12°C (37-54°F) in winter and from 7-19°C (45-66°F) in summer. Prevailing winds are from the S (cool, damp), and from the NW (hot and dry in summer, cold and dry in winter). Annual average rainfall is 800-900mm (31-35in) and a few millimetres of snow may cover the city briefly once a year. Use a 5/4mm fullsuit with boots and optional gloves and hood for winter but a 4/3 will do for summer.

Nature and Culture – The snow season lasts from June through to September. 24 ski areas and 12 heli-ski operators offer some of the best alpine experiences anywhere on the planet. Famous Queenstown (Coronet Peak, Remarkable) or Wanaka (Treble Cone, Wardrona), are 4.5h away, or go to Mt Hutt in Canterbury. Go rock fishing or paua (abalone) diving.

Hazards and Hassles – A shark net is put out in summer at St-Clair beach with a "shark bell" on the Esplanade, but the last attack was in 1971. Otago surfers are being driven out of the water by a growing population of sea lions. Weather patterns can be harsh and can close in quickly. Crossing private properties is a privilege not a right and respect must be given to the landowners wishes.

Handy Hints – Take a gun and full winter equipment with 5/4 if visiting after April. Surf supplies abound in Dunedin city, with Quarry Beach, Hydro Surf, R&R Sport and Board Base. South Coast Boardriders, established in 1966, is one of the country's strongest surfing clubs. Esplanade Surf School operates at St Clair.

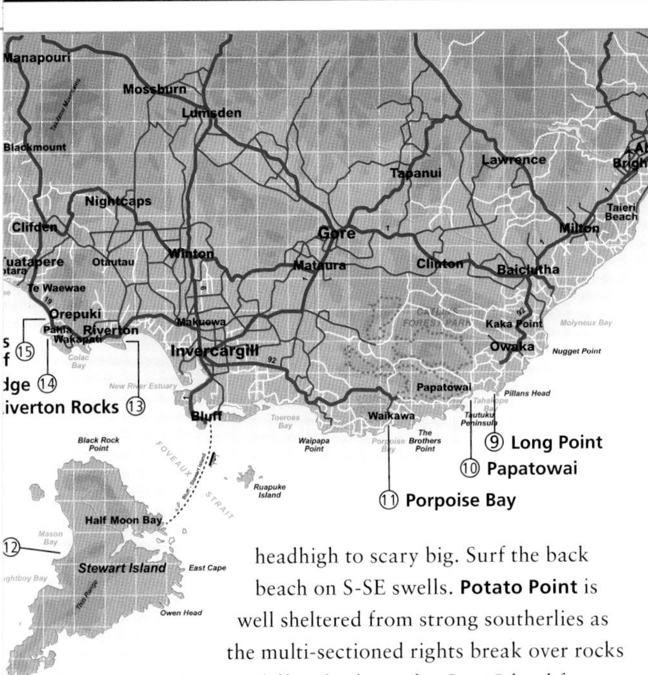

headhigh to scary big. Surf the back beach on S-SE swells. **Potato Point** is well sheltered from strong southerlies as the multi-sectioned rights break over rocks beneath steep cliffs. Check nearby Goat Island for more breaks. The epic rights at **Murderers** need rare NE swells, producing a fine mal wave when small, or a hollow racetrack at headhigh, with ample tube time when the sand is lined-up. Beware the rocks, sharks & steep slippery access road. Consistent **Aramoana Spit** can throw square barrels on NE swells, breaks on all tides and SW winds. The jetty provides easy entry for experts when big. Seals and sharks present. Dunedin's southern beaches shelter some of the best beachbreaks in the country. Flat days are rare but strong rips and heavy storms are a common occurrence. **Sandfly Bay** requires a long hike over sand hills down to an average beachie, best on small swell at low tide. It's also a Yellow Eye Penguin reserve and neighbouring Boulder Beach is now closed to surfing as there are penguins nesting there. Not far is **Smails Beach**, suited to small S swells with an established left in the east corner and lots of rips. **St-Clair** is the hub of Dunedin surfing, blessed with good quality beachbreak peaks and when there's a big S swell, the long right point near the Salt Water hot pools sections off over rock, sand and kelp. West of Blackhead's barrelling beachbreak is **Brighton**, where lines of S swell bend around a large rock island. Easy workable walls after a hollow take-off, but positioning and the paddle-out is tricky at size. The locals at Brighton Surf Club can advise on where to search in the unchartered waters of The Catlins area. Drive to **Long Point** on a medium S swell to catch some ledgy lefts. Take-offs can be hairy and walls are fast, but it's very rippable. Farmland access requires permission and respect. **Papatowai** holds some of New Zealand's biggest waves, where tow-in teams and experienced paddlers try to ride the long barrelling right or lethal, ledging left. Big boils and tendrils of kelp add to the stress of this hellmen only wave. There's also some beachbreak at Tahakopa Bay. Mere mortal surfers will probably enjoy **Porpoise Bay**, a rivermouth beachie with a selection of hollow and powerful peaks plus a bombie on big swells. Hectors Dolphins often play around here. There's lots of disorganized swell in the Foveaux Straight, but some breaks handle it and the good news is that the Trans-Tasman current brings warmer water. Stewart Island is still a frontier in New Zealand and the lack of roads means chartering a boat from Half Moon Bay to get to the promising southeast coast. **Mason Bay** is a very isolated west-facing beach, 1h boat ride from the mainland. There are more bird watchers than surfers on the island. West of Invercargill, **Riverton Rocks** hold really long, cruisey rights if a big S swell wraps in at low tide. Check nearby Colac Bay beach and Nick's Point if it's not big enough. Don't eat it at **Porridge**, where the grinding left pointbreak throws up heavy barrels over rocky reef in S swells and NE winds. Farmers permission required for here and Beatons quality lefts in the next bay south. Before hitting the huge area of virgin breaks in Fjordland, take a look at **Frentzes Reef**, a left reefbreak on large S swells. Park near Monkey Island and check the fun beachbreaks down Te Waewae Bay.

SURF STATISTICS			
Spot	Size	Btm	Type
①	8/2		
②	8/2		
③	10/2		
④	8/1		
⑤	6/1		
⑥	6/2		
⑦	10/2		
⑧	10/2		
⑨	10/3		
⑩	25/10		
⑪	8/2		
⑫	8/2		
⑬	8/3		
⑭	10/4		
⑮	6/3		

WARREN HAWKE

Murderers

WARREN HAWKE

Porpoise Bay

This region is wide open to big Southern Ocean swells ranging consistently from 1-3m (3-10ft), but 4-6m+ (12-20ft) waves are a regular occurrence throughout the year. There's a choice of over 40 breaks within a 1hr drive of Dunedin and conditions can be checked via the St Clair web cam. At these latitudes, SW-SE swells are dominant and cyclonic NE swells fairly rare. The east coast normally remains off or sideshore unless high pressure brings E winds. Atmospheric changes can be drastic and the beginning of the year is often calmer than the second half. Choose mid-seasons because summer might be a bit calm while winter will probably feel too icy and out-of-control. Semi-diurnal tides with 8ft (2.4m) maximum tidal range. Dunedin (E) tide is 1.5h earlier than Porridge (S).

SURF STATISTICS	J F	M A	M J	J A	S O	N D
dominant swell	NE-SW	NE-SW	E-SW	E-SW	E-SW	E-SW
swell size (ft)	3	4	5	5-6	5	3-4
consistency (%)	70	80	70	50	60	70
dominant wind	SW-W	SW-N	SW-N	SW-N	SW-NW	W-NE
average force	F5	F4-F5	F4-F5	F4-F5	F4-F5	F4-F5
consistency (%)	38	52	48	32	50	53
water temp.(°C)	12	11	9	8	9	10
wetsuit						

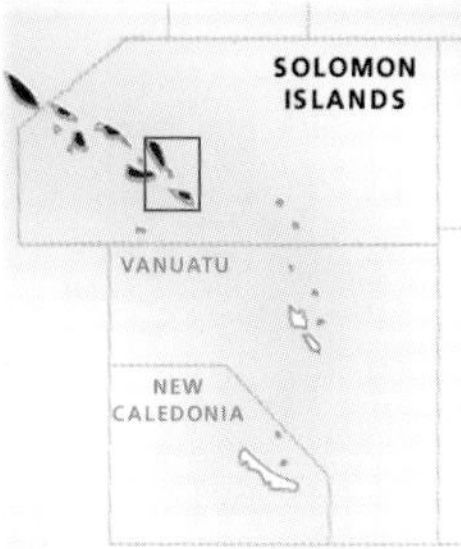

212. Malaita and Makira

Malaita
MICHAEL KEW

Summary
+ Hundreds of secret spots
+ Clean tropical perfection
+ NE & SE swells
+ Diving paradise
+ Truly breathtaking scenery

– Some swell inconsistency
– Lack of tourism infrastructure
– Extremely remote access
– High rainfall, malaria & disease
– Saltwater crocodiles & sharks

Covering an area of 80,000km² (30,888mi²) between 5° and 12° south of the equator and about 500km (312mi) east of Papua New Guinea, the Solomon Islands probably holds the largest unexplored quality surf territory in the South Pacific. The biggest island is Guadalcanal, next to Malaita and Makira, with other major islands being San Cristobal, Santa Isabel, Choiseul, Rennell, New Georgia and the Santa Cruz group. The topography varies from low-lying coral atolls to lofty volcanic peaks and the densely forested mountain ranges are intersected by precipitous, narrow valleys with fast flowing rivers, impassable except by canoe. Only 120,000 out of 485,000 live and work in an "urban" environment, leaving the bulk of the population within a subsistence economy, in one of the world's least developed

STEPHANE ROBIN

STEPHANE ROBIN

TRAVEL INFORMATION

Local Population:
Malaita 140,000,
Makira 22,500
Coastline:
Malaita 548km (340mi)
Time Zone: GMT +11
Contests: None
Other Resources:
surftheearth.com.au/STE%20Solomons.html
surf-forecast.com/breaks/SkullIsland.shtml
solomonairlines.com.au

Getting There – No visa; one of the most remote destinations with only a few connections to Honiara (HIR) from Brisbane (BNE, 3/wk, about $750) and Auckland, Port Moresby, Port Vila and Nadi. Fly into the country on Solomon Airlines for cheaper domestic flights. Henderson Field Airport, Airport Motel just 800m away, town is 8km (5mi) away. Dep tax: $6.

Getting Around – Solomon Airlines operates daily scheduled flights to Kirakira (Makira, $135 r/t, 11/wk) and Auki (Malaita, $80/r/t, 3/wk). Flights are cheap, but not reliable and boardbags may cause luggage problems on Twin Otters (6ft10" max) and Islander planes. Road system is light, take motorized canoes and boats (cheap).

Lodging and Food – Only a dozen int'l standard lodges and resorts, mainly for divers and mostly in Guadalcanal, Gizo, Munda and Marovo Lagoon. Try Maravagi on Florida islands, north of Honiara. In Makira and Malaita, dirt cheap rest houses will be the norm with no A/C, maybe fan & nets. Basic fish & chips, sweet potatoes ($3-4 a meal). Auki, the province's capital, has a population of 4,000 and boasts a variety of shops, hotels, and restaurants.

WEATHER STATISTICS	J/F	M/A	M/J	J/A	S/O	N/D
total rainfall (mm)	380	330	250	310	240	260
consistency (days/mth)	17	12	14	15	14	14
min temp (°C)	24	23	23	23	23	23
max temp (°C)	30	30	30	29	29	30

Weather – Lying within 12° latitude of the equator and more than 1500km (932mi) from the nearest continent, the Solomon's have a wet tropical climate, featuring high, uniform temps (mean diurnal variation is 7°C/12°F) and humidity, with abundant rainfall in all months. From December to March, NW equatorial winds bring hot weather and heavy rainfall that lessens during February when the equatorial trough is normally furthest south. From April to November, the islands are cooled by drier SE trade winds, resulting in places on the southern coasts of the larger islands receiving more rainfall between June and September. Damaging cyclones occasionally strike during the rainy season. The annual mean temperature is 27°C/80°F and annual rainfall averages 3,000mm/120in (up to 5,000mm/200in), and humidity is about 80%. Water temps are among the warmest on earth.

Nature and Culture – Islanders (Melanesians, Polynesians, Gilbertese, mostly) are unique and staunchly Christian. Towns are quiet, King Solomon Hotel operates Honiara's only nightclub. Makira: copra mill in Kira Kira, turtle beach and Natagera houses on Santa Ana Island. Malaita: Auki, relaxing provincial centre, shark calling, manufacture of shell money.

Hazards and Hassles – Ethnic tensions continue to trouble the island nation, but tourists are not specifically targeted. Travel advisory for Malaita and south end of Guadalcanal. Medical facilities are limited; the nearest reliable hospitals are in Australia. High-risk area for chloroquine resistant malaria. Immunizations; Hepatitis A, polio, tetanus, typhoid.

Handy Hints – Cyclones are usually early stage and therefore not life-threatening. Solomon's takes a lot of dedication and patience to score the best surf. Take everything you need, but not too much because of transport restrictions. One strong all-round board, leash, wax and good snorkelling stuff.

countries. Ethnologists and divers have paved the way, since the Marovo Lagoon is blessed with 30m (100ft) visibility, warm waters and countless WWII underwater relics. The northern shores were probably discovered in the late '80s and by 1996 a surf camp almost started up on Malaita, but things turned out ugly between the partners. The Crossing made a well timed appearance in 1999-2000, but only a few surf media wanderers like Surf The Earth's manager Nick Blanche, Stéphane Robin or Mike Kew have ventured along the northern sides of Malaita and Makira. Maybe it is because sharks were often worshipped and a few Malaita Islanders still believe spirits reside in them.

On the northern tip of Malaita island, **Malu'u** Lodge provides a decent base for exploring the righthander bending round the reef on NE swells as well as the lagoon entrance. Check the 2 sections of the reef pass at **Manu**, where rights shoulder into a deepwater channel. 61km (38mi) from Auki is **Fakanakafo Bay** with several spots nearby (Fouia & Atori), including a rivermouth peak and a long stretch of beachbreak that's quite a hike to reach. **Leli Island** is a scythe of reef, 20mins boat ride from the bay, where chunky, sectiony lefts will hug the curve of coral in big swells. Locals on strange home-made seko palm boards can sometimes be found at **Uruilangi** a fun, small swell, easy access reef and at **Sinalangu**, an inconsistent, low tide right, next to the harbour entrance. Ulawa Island has a coral sand beachbreak at **Su'ulausi Harbour** and one long consistent left reef at **Su'uholo**, near Eresi Point. On Makira island, two thirds of the 22,500 Melanesian people live on the northern coast leaving the steep southern shore sparsely populated. Makira has more swamps than other islands making land transport tricky, especially to the good southern spots. Boat out to the north tip of **Malaupaina**, one of the Three Sisters Islands, which holds a pretty beefy right in light winds and large swells. The shallow reef is intimidating, as are the large saltwater crocodiles in the area! **Kirakira** is the main town to rent a boat, get supplies and maybe catch a few average black sand beachbreaks near the rivermouth. **Tawarogha** has been exposed to the surfing world, thanks to it's long, hollow consistent rights, working with both SE and NE swells.

STÉPHANE ROBIN

STÉPHANE ROBIN

① Malu'u
② Manu
③ Fakanakafo Bay
④ Leli Island
⑤ Uruilangi
⑥ Sinalangu
⑦ Su'ulausi Harbour
⑧ Su'uholo

Sulione, Foula, Atae Cove, Manu, Auki, Alon, Fakanakafo Bay, Malaita Island, Fandindi Point, Olomburi, Malaita Province, Su'u, Su'u Bay, Anuta Paina Island, Indispensable Strait, Malaita Island, Maramasike Island, Hugnoll, Su'upeine Bay, Cape Zele'e, Hadja, Ulawa Island, Beagle Islands, Guadalcanal

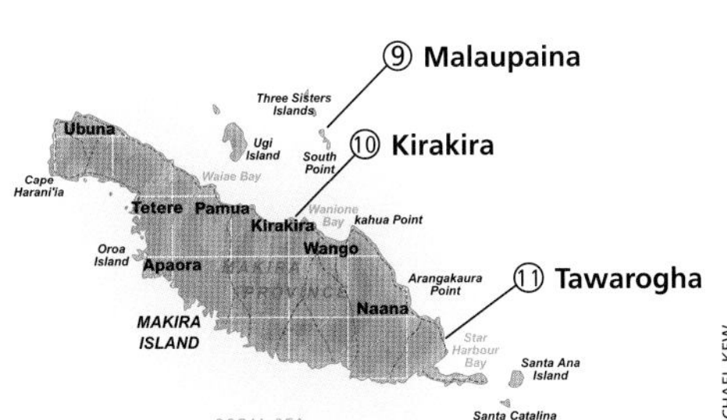

SURF STATISTICS			
Spot	Size	Btm	Type
①	6/2		
②	8/2		
③	6/2		
④	10/2		
⑤	8/2		
⑥	8/3		
⑦	6/2		
⑧	8/2		
⑨	8/2		
⑩	5/2		
⑪	8/2		

Lots of different swell patterns could potentially provide year-round surf, but the N-NE swells from Dec to April are the most reliable. Typically, it will be a mellow 2-5ft (0.6-1.5m), clean and often perfect with only occasional flat spells. The same time of year sees the most powerful waves arrive in the Coral Sea cyclone season, with 8ft (2.5m) SE swells possible on southern shores that are usually flat (no spots shown). Tasman lows send long-distance S swells in July-August, coinciding with ESE windswells, hitting east-facing shores like Ulawa island or Tawarogha. January to March sees a period of W- NW monsoonal winds. From May to October, the persistently strong SE trade winds blow, picking up plenty of moisture over the ocean and heavy rainfall is guaranteed, especially on the windward side. The transition months between the 2 seasons are marked by a greater frequency of calm winds. Most tides are small, but significant, with 3ft (1m) max tidal range and diurnal cycles (1 tide a day).

SURF STATISTICS	J F	M A	M J	J A	S O	N D
dominant swell	S-SW	S-SW	SE-S	SE-S	SE-S	S-SW
swell size (ft)	3-4	3	2	2-3	1-2	2-3
consistency (%)	60	50	40	50	20	40
dominant wind	SW-NW	W-N	E-SE	E-S	E-S	E-S
average force	F3	F2-F3	F2-F3	F3	F3-F4	F2-F3
consistency (%)	55	42	65	85	76	49
water temp.(°C)	29	29	29	28	28	29
wetsuit						

MICHAEL KEW

Malaita

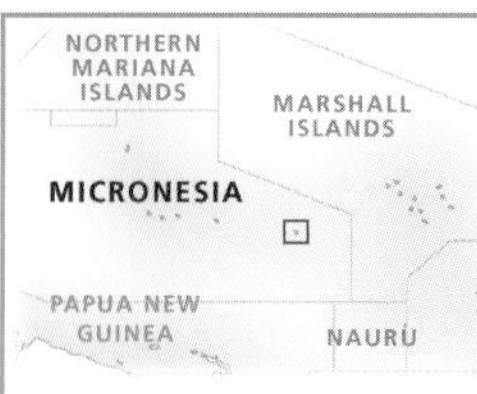

213. Pohnpei

Easy Pass

SIMON WILLIAMS

Summary

+ North Pacific & typhoon swells
+ Warm, crystal clear water
+ P-Pass perfection
+ Island sight-seeing
+ Safe, politically stable and clean

– Inconsistent N swells
– Not for beginners
– Occasional crowds & rips
– Extremely rainy
– Very expensive trip

Pohnpei is often confused with the ancient Italian city of Pompei, rather than a speck in the Pacific Ocean, forming part of the Federated States of Micronesia (FSM), lying more than 5000km (3,200 mi) southwest of Hawaii. Further confusion occurs because the FSM is one of 8 island nations inside the region of Micronesia including, Kiribati, Marshalls, Palau, Nauru, the Northern Marianas, Guam and Wake Island. The FSM is made up of more than 600 islands scattered across over 3.9 million square kilometres (1.5M sq/mi) of the Pacific, divided into the four states of Yap, Chuuk, Pohnpei, and Kosrae. Being mostly low coralline atolls, Pohnpei is different since it's the tip of a 5 million-year-old extinct shield volcano. The entire island is made up of black basalt rock, surrounded by a deep lagoon up to 8km (5mi) wide, circled by many linear, patch and pinnacle reefs. Referred to as the Garden Island of Micronesia, Pohnpei sits in the

MICHAEL KEW

Freddos

SIMON WILLIAMS

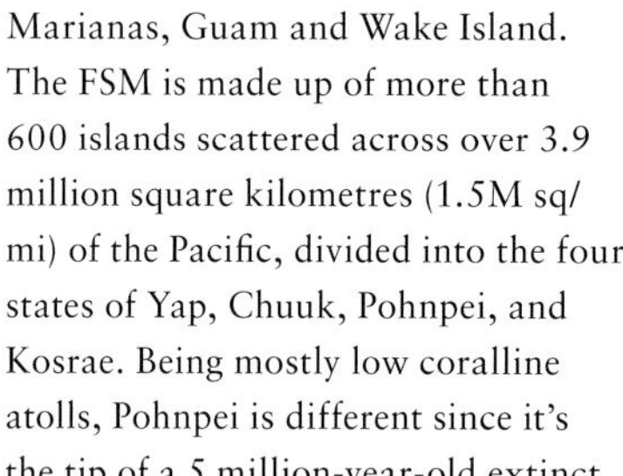

TRAVEL INFORMATION

Local Population: 37,492 (Palikir 11,600)
Coastline: 67km (43mi)
Time Zone: GMT +11
Contests: None
Other Resources:
pohnpeisurfclub.com
prh.noaa.gov/pohnpei/pohnpeiMarine.php
Video:
Rip Curl My Search
Inaugural Hobgood Challenge

Getting There – Visa, 30days. Getting affordable tickets to Pohnpei (PNI) can be tricky. Round-trip from LAX range from $1,100 to $2,000. Australians fly through Fiji which is the best route. Only Continental Airlines serves FSM. Island-hopper route from Honolulu to Guam: Majuro, Kosrae, Pohnpei, Chuuk. Less comfortable and often more expensive.

Getting Around – No paddle spots so use Pohnpei Surf Club boats at regular times. All the boats (Orange, Blue, Green, Yellow) are equipped with cell phones, radio, first aid kits, coolers for food and drinks, ice, shaded area, seat cushions, and fishing and diving equipment when needed. It's all included in the package.

Lodging and Food – PSC costs between $165-200/night (peak season is 11 Nov - 20 Mar). 9 double rooms with private bathroom, hot water, A/C, TV, telephone and wireless internet. PSC is limiting surfer numbers to a maximum of 18, or stay at the Village Hotel. All You Can Eat Rotary Sushi for $7. Eat until you drop! Expect from $15-20 for meals daily.

WEATHER STATISTICS	J/F	M/A	M/J	J/A	S/O	N/D
total rainfall (mm)	283	411	463	427	427	417
consistency (days/mth)	17	22	25	22	20	19
min temp (°C)	24	24	23	23	23	23
max temp (°C)	30	30	30	31	31	31

Weather – Pohnpei has a tropical, humid climate that keeps the fertile landscape lush and green year-round. Rain is a substantial part of the Pohnpei experience since it is one of the wettest places on earth with an average annual rainfall of 4860mm (191in). The largest part of the rainfall comes at night, when on-shore breezes are quickly cooled as they rise up the mountain slopes. Temps are constant, ranging from 23-30°C (74-86°F). Most of the year, there is a NE trade wind. A typical day in Pohnpei is cloudy with intermittent showers and the sun breaking through now and then. The mountains aren't quite high enough to act as a complete block, so the rainfall on the windward and leeward sides of the island does not differ greatly. Major wind storms and destructive typhoons are rare. Boardshorts only in the "Pool".

Nature and Culture – Explore beautiful waterfalls, hike to the ancient ruins of Nan Madol, or try world-class diving. Visit Outer Atolls like Ant and Pakin, only 16-50km (10-30mi) offshore. Deep sea fishing, snorkelling, bird watching, canoeing. Climb or visit Sokehs Ridge and the World War II historical sites. Check Rusty Anchor, the best bar on the Island.

Hazards and Hassles – Since boats are always in the channel, there is no reef walking when you paddle in and out. Most surfers do not use booties, but they can be very helpful at times. Above 5ft (1.5m), waves at P-Pass get dangerous for inexperienced surfers. Rips can get pretty intense at times.

Handy Hints – Mid-range surfboards (6'4' to 7'0') work best. No good hire boards available from PSC. Bring everything with you. Either fly direct for a short trip or use the opportunity of island hopper flights to surf Guam and Kosrae.

middle of the "Pool", the warmest ocean temperatures in the world, fed from the east by the Northern Equatorial Current. Secretly surfed by a lucky few until a Surf Report Issue in Feb 1998, the media have frenzied over some of photos depicting the smoking barrels of P-Pass.

Waves break out on the barrier reef or near a reef pass, so it's boat access only and it's always shallow on the inside. Up to 4ft (1.2m), the waves are user-friendly, but once the surf gets bigger, things get serious quickly. Late take-offs, fast down-the-line rides, and hollow barrels are what most surfed spots offer and the best of them is **P-Pass** (Palikir Pass). It takes any swell from W-NE, with straight N being the best direction. P-Pass works with no winds or with light NE-E trades, which blow dead offshore as the swell lines wrap around the reef. These rights can be surfed at any tide, but it does get very shallow on a full low tide. **Easy Pass** is only a 5min boat ride from the Pohnpei Surf Club, which are small outside rights rideable at high tide from 2-4ft, but there's nothing easy about the treacherous inside. **Main Pass** breaks under the same conditions as P-Pass, but it is always bigger, and has a super-shallow inside section. It's a challenging spot in big waves, with a west and a north take-off spot, a long wall and an incredible inside barrel section, inevitably drawing comparisons to Sunset Beach in Hawaii. Holds chunky swells and bigger is always better, because smaller days sees the reef go dry at any tide. The east side of Pohnpei has 3 different passes that work in totally different conditions from one another. A 20min boat ride to **Freddos** will reward with occasional lefts when the trade winds are low. It holds big swell and can offer fun walls, good hooks and quick barrels. Across the channel, **Sonden's** also works without tradewinds, plus any size swell from small to triple overhead. Reminiscent of Macaronis in Indo, **Spaghettis** fun lefts require a huge N swell or an E swell without the E winds. Sharp bottom. The next big reef pass is **Nahpali**, a long sectiony right, which always has waves, but is usually blown out. It's rippy, sharky and a 40min boat ride. On the other side of the famous ruins of **Nan Madol**, more wind exposed rights peel and section off into the bay. **Nahlap** has a fun right reefbreak ideal for beginners. The waves pick up in SE swells from July until October, with 3-4ft faces and light or no winds.

P-Pass

SIMON WILLIAMS

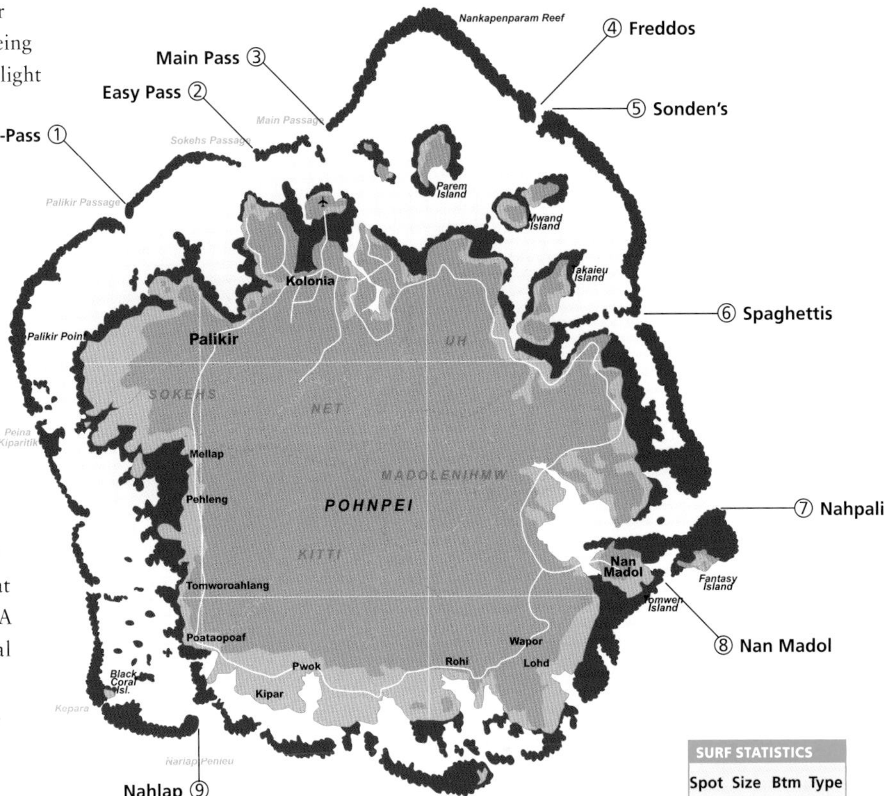

SURF STATISTICS			
Spot	Size	Btm	Type
①	10/2		
②	4/2		
③	15/4		
④	12/3		
⑤	18/2		
⑥	6/2		
⑦	6/2		
⑧	8/2		
⑨	8/2		

Most of the swells that reach Pohnpei are generated by typhoons in the western Pacific or North Pacific winter storms, although it doesn't necessarily receive the same swells as Hawaii. Pohnpei surf season runs from early October thru to early May. June is usually flat, and by late July the winds die out, shifting from absolutely no winds to variable. During the months of August and September, some breaks on the exposed windward side come alive with glassy or offshore conditions and E swells generated by trade winds east of Pohnpei. SW swells can arrive with the strong monsoonal winds that blow in from western Micronesia and the Philippines. These waves hit the east to southwest sides of Pohnpei with less power and size. The trades pick up from late December all the way to late May and blow strong. Semi-diurnal tides with diurnal inequality, hit a 3ft (1m) tidal range max.

SURF STATISTICS	J F	M A	M J	J A	S O	N D
dominant swell	NW-NE	NW-NE	NE-SE	NE-SE	NE-SE	NW-NE
swell size (ft)	3-4	3	3-4	4-5	2-3	3-4
consistency (%)	70	50	40	30	60	70
dominant wind	NE-E	NE-F	NE-E	NE-E	NE-E	NE-E
average force	F4	F4	F3-F4	F3	F3	F3-F4
consistency (%)	93	89	73	39	35	70
water temp.(°C)	28	28	29	29	29	29
wetsuit						

P-Pass

SIMON WILLIAMS

214. Majuro

Secret spot

ALL PHOTOS MICHAEL KEW

Summary
+ Mellow atoll ambiance
+ User-friendly waves
+ Clean water
+ No surf crowds

– Expensive flights
– Windy, inconsistent, small waves
– Overcrowding and pollution around D-U-D
– Lack of surf spots

The Marshall Islands, in the middle of the equatorial Pacific, are a Micronesian republic of 29 atolls plus five individual islands and all are open to swells from both hemispheres. Information about the Marshall Islands surf potential is scant, limited mainly to what expats surf seasonally on Majuro and Kwajalein atolls in the Ratak and Ralik Chain, which translates as sunrise and sunset chain. Fickle at best, the Marshalls are not one of the world's great surfing destinations, and while dreams of a Pacific version of the Maldives have crept through surfers' minds, it's far from the reality. There are a few decent waves in the Marshalls, but nothing world-class. Arno, the scenic atoll just east of Majuro, might have a wave or two if the conditions cooperate. The majority of Majuro's surfing is done around the D-U-D Municipality, which is comprised of Darrit, Uliga, and Delap, crowded villages connected by a paved road. It is a dirty place, with lots of litter, dust, ramshackle buildings, and cars. It's possible to drive along the narrow road from D-U-D all the way west to Laura, which is considerably cleaner and more typical of natural Marshallese beauty. Majuro has no honeymoon resorts,

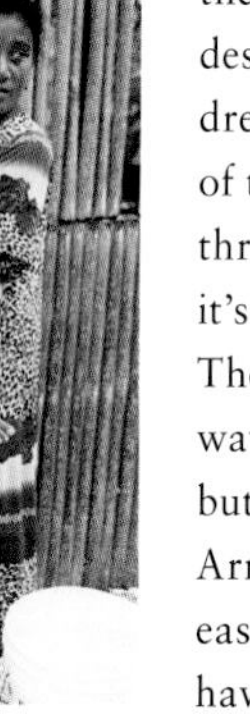

Bridge

TRAVEL INFORMATION

Local Population: 31,000
Coastline: 80km (50mi)
Time Zone: GMT +12
Contests: None
Other Resources:
visitmarshallislands.com
yokwe.net,
marshallislandsjournal.com
rreinc.com

Getting There – No visa is required. Amata Kabua International Airport (MAJ) is eight miles west of D-U-D, and the only way to reach the atoll by air is on Continental Airlines flights from Honolulu (HNL), which average about US$2,000 return. Some cruise lines also stop in Majuro.

Getting Around – A car is not entirely necessary, unless you're going out to Laura. You can get around D-U-D using a taxi; fares average about $0.50 cents each way, but the cars can't carry surfboards. Walking or riding a bike works in the small D-U-D zone.

WEATHER STATISTICS	J/F	M/A	M/J	J/A	S/O	N/D
total rainfall (mm)	185	235	289	312	334	313
consistency (days/mth)	13	16	20	21	20	19
min temp (°C)	25	25	25	25	25	25
max temp (°C)	29	30	30	30	30	30

Lodging and Food – D-U-D has a few decent accommodation options. Hotel Robert Reimers is friendly and clean, with a good restaurant downstairs (Tide Table). Flame Tree is a cool hostel/restaurant with cheap rates. The most upscale place is the Marshall Islands Resort, and its restaurant (Enra) offers great food, specializing in fish. Also check out the Long Island Hotel and the Uliga Inn.

Weather – Majuro's climate is pretty much the same all year: hot and humid, temps averaging 27°C (81°F). Rain is frequent. It can get very windy, especially during the winter. Ocean water temp is around 26°C (80°F).

Nature and Culture – Beyond D-U-D, it's all coconut palms, coral rubble, turquoise lagoon, and blue Pacific. It's all very flat, and the atoll is so narrow in some places that it is only a stone's throw from the ocean to the lagoon. Culturally the Marshallese are some of the world's friendliest people, quick to share a smile and a meal.

Hazards and Hassles – The shallow coral reefs are your biggest concern, especially at the Bridge. Also beware of the searing tropical sun. Crime is not an issue.

Handy Hints – Bring plenty of sun cream and all surf gear, because there are no surf shops. If the surf is flat, take a lagoon tour or deep-sea fishing charter.

Laura

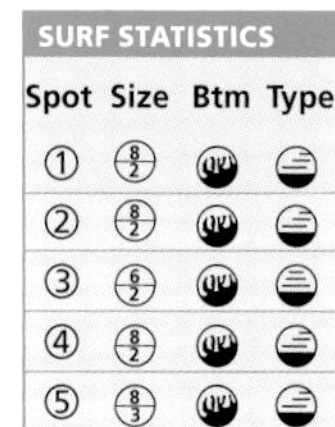

no extensive white sand beaches, and not much tourism infrastructure, yet it retains a peculiar charm in the smiles and ease of its people. Majuro atoll is the Marshalls nerve centre, home to the republic's primary government, most of its businesses, and about half of its entire population, making it one of the most densely populated atolls on Earth (31,000 people). International flights also go to Kwajalein Atoll, but it's strictly controlled by the US military, who have been testing ballistic missiles and nuclear detonations on surrounding islands, including the biggest ever explosion of a dry hydrogen bomb on Bikini Atoll in 1954.

Visiting surfers are rare. The handful living on Majuro are generally expat American teachers and Seventh Day Adventist church volunteers who frequent the sucky tubes at the Bridge, Majuro's marquee surf spot. Very shallow, hollow, and somewhat dangerous, the **Bridge** can provide quick, snappy rides if you're fast on your feet. The 12ft (4m) high bridge was built to span a narrow channel the Japanese blasted through the reef in 1983, to spare small boats the long trip up to Calalin Channel, to gain access to the lagoon anchorages. On Majuro's southeast corner is **Delap**, in front of the hospital, which offers a fun, sectiony righthander during S swells. This is Majuro's most popular wave because it handles the prevailing NE trade wind. Darrit holds an occasionally fun left and right on either side of **Rita Pass**, but it's very sensitive to both NE trade wind and lower tide. At **Calalin Pass** there is an equally fickle righthander that suffers from lots of strong currents as it is the main passage into the lagoon. It's almost always onshore when it breaks in the N swell season, plus it's a 35km (22mi) boat ride across the lagoon from the anchorage to access it. On the atoll's western tip, there is a rare S swell lefthander at **Laura** that is dead offshore with the trades. Just to the north is a quasi beachbreak (lots of coral heads) that can be fun and punchy during westerly windswells, but it is often blown-out or too small.

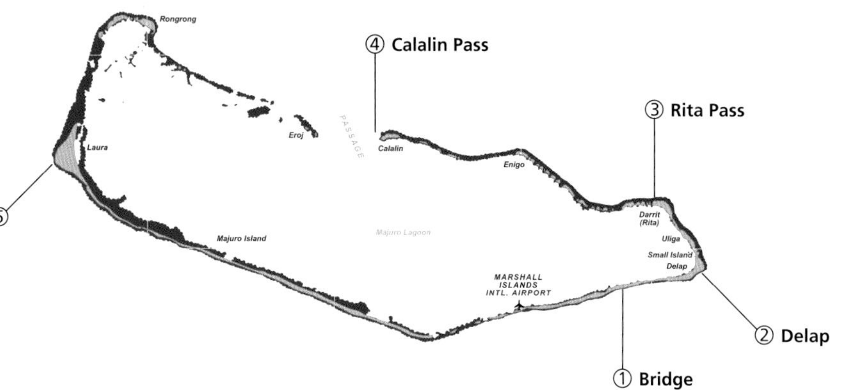

SURF STATISTICS	J F	M A	M J	J A	S O	N D
dominant swell	N-NE	N-NE	N-S	S	N-S	N-NE
swell size (ft)	6-8	4-6	3-5	2-3	2-4	4-6
consistency (%)	90	85	65	30	60	90
dominant wind	NE	NE	NE	NE	E	NE
average force	F6	F5	F3	F2	F3-F4	F5-F6
consistency (%)	98	85	50	30	60	95
water temp.(°C)	26	26	26	26	26	26
wetsuit						

The primary source of decent sized waves are wintertime (Dec-Mar) N groundswells from the North Pacific. Unfortunately, these coincide with the strong prevailing NE trade wind, and most of Majuro's surf spots work on S swells, arriving from June-Sept. These swells have a long way to travel and can be shadowed and dissipated by the archipelagos to the south (Fiji, Kiribati, Tuvalu), resulting in often weak and inconsistent surf. The upside is that Majuro's surf is usually offshore on the atoll's south coast, and places like the Bridge and Laura are normally quite clean. Tides do exceed 5ft (1.5m) and affect most waves. The water is as predictable as the air – boardshorts will do it plus a rashie for the wind and sun.

HAWAI'I
KIRIBATI
WESTERN SAMOA
AMERICAN SAMOA
FRENCH POLYNESIA

215. Tabuaeran and Kiritimati

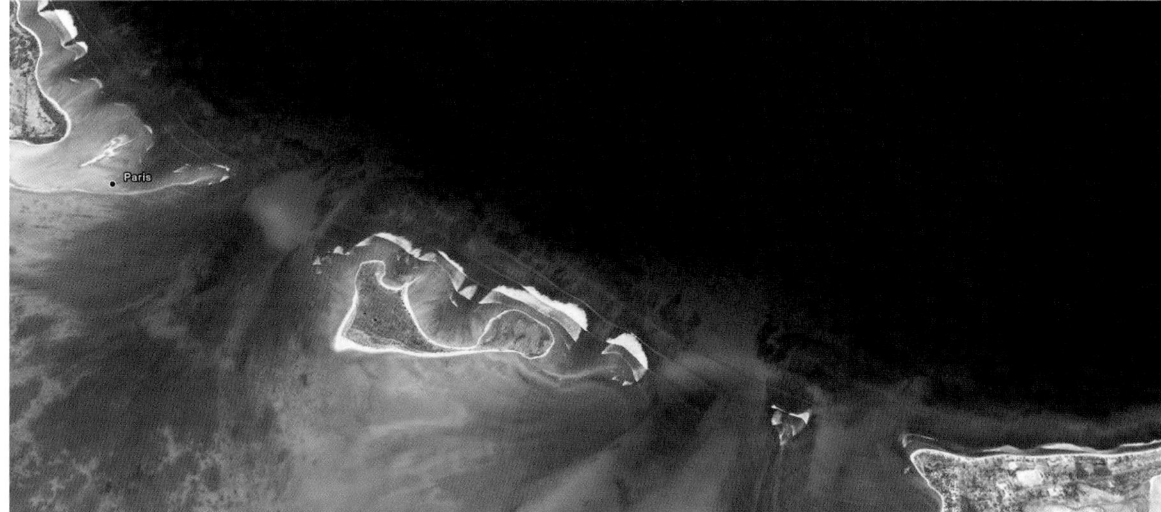

London and Paris passes, Kiritimati

GOOGLE EARTH 5114955

Summary
+ Clean N & S swells
+ Virgin, crystal clear line-ups
+ Various quality spots
+ Largest lagoon in the world
+ Great diving & fishing

– Difficult access to spots
– Inconsistent in summer
– Expensive, infrequent transport links
– Remoteness and high costs

Kiribati (pronounced kee-ree-bass), comprises of 32 low lying atolls plus 1 island, sprinkled across the Central Pacific, straddling both the equator and the International Date Line, until the government moved it in 1995. Stretching for 3220km (2000mi) from east to west and covering a vast 3.5M km/sq (1.35M mi/sq), Hawaii is the closest neighbour, a mere 1900km (1180mi) away. Most visitors arrive by cruise ship, stopping at Tarawa in the Gilbert's group and Kiritimati in the Line group mainly for diving, bone fishing and very occasionally for surfing. Kiritimati (formerly known as Christmas Island, but not be mixed up with the Indian Ocean one) is the biggest atoll in the world and comprises over 70% of the total land area of Republic of Kiribati. In 1957, British government detonated a series of hydrogen bombs nearby. The Kiribati name for Fanning Island is Tabuaeran meaning "heavenly footprint" as the island's shape suggests. Chuck Corbett, aka Pacific Charlie, left the North Shore in 1979 in search of emptier line-ups and after 12 years around Tarawa, moved to Fanning to surf English Harbor's freight trains.

JOE DUNN

London

MICHAEL KEW

TRAVEL INFORMATION

Local Population:
4500 Kiritimati
2500 Tabuaeran
Coastline:
Tabuaeran
1,143km (710mi)
Kiritimati
150km (93mi)
Time Zone: GMT +12
Contests: None
Other Resources:
fanning-island.com
tobaraoi.com

Getting There – No visa anymore, Kiribati Immigration charge $25USD to enter the country and $20AUD to leave. Kiritimati (CXI) is reached in 3.5hrs by weekly Air Pacific flight from Nadi, Fiji or Hawaii: $900 r/t. No flights to Tabuaeran. Fly Tarawa (TRW) with Air Nauru and get a WKK supply ferry cruising 4-5 times per year, costs $320 per cabin.

Getting Around – Tabuaeran is 165 nautical miles NW of Kiritimati or 36h sail and traffic is very low. Make appointment with Chuck Corbett at the end of winter so you can sail with him. Surfing on Kiritimati can be limited to a few spots if you can't afford a boat; quite a few boats are used by divers /fly fishers.

WEATHER STATISTICS	J/F	M/A	M/J	J/A	S/O	N/D
total rainfall (mm)	149	324	326	110	164	134
consistency (days/mth)	10	18	19	8	12	11
min temp (°C)	24	25	25	25	24	24
max temp (°C)	30	30	30	30	30	30

Lodging and Food – A handful of places in the $30-150 range. Captain Cook Hotel close to the airport charge $85 per room or Mini Hotel is $25/50 single/dble. Meals are on a fixed cost of $30 a day. Both catholic and protestant parishes have basic rooms $20 a night. Norwegian Cruise Line comes to Tabuaeran every week.

Weather – Kiribati enjoys a maritime equatorial climate tempered by prevailing easterly trade winds. Temps vary little between days and nights throughout most of the year, ranging from 25-32°C (77-90°F) with an annual mean of 27°C (80°F). Although the island lies outside the tropical hurricane belt, there are occasional gales and even tornadoes. The country does not experience tropical cyclones but does have strong winds and rain during the rainy season between December and April. Rainfall varies between 1020mm (41in) near the equator and 3050mm (122in) in the extreme north and south. It can be irregular and long periods of drought are not uncommon. Boardshorts only.

Nature and Culture – Internationally renowned for bone fishing and bird watchers are overwhelmed by thousands of migratory seabirds. Local dance is practised everywhere. Spectacular diving. Kiribati outrigger canoes, said to be the fastest in the Pacific are regularly raced in the lagoon. Second World War relics litter beaches in South Tarawa.

Hazards and Hassles – Besides reef dangers like cuts and sharks swimming around, pay attention to hepatitis A, B, and C. Stir in dengue fever, lice, ciguatera, staph and staph-spreading flies.

Handy Hints – Chuck's Island Trader is for rent: Expect $2000/wk for 4pax. Trips would be 1 week for Kiritimati and 2 weeks for Tabuaeran. There is a divers association on Kiritimati. Strong Australian influence on Kiritimati means pay in AUD$. Kiribati bends the dateline to keep all its islands on the same side and is a full 24hrs ahead of Hawaii.

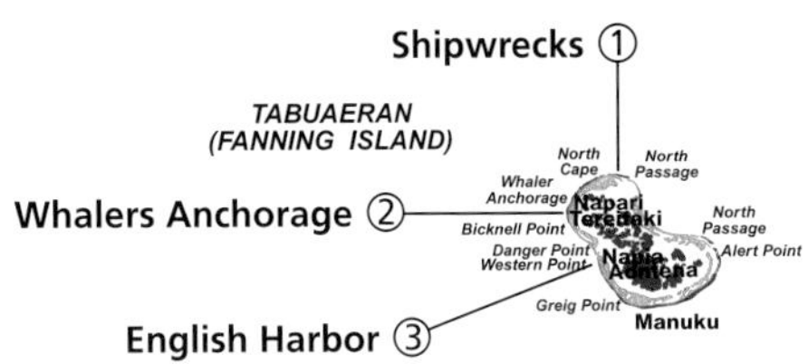

There are 4 main breaks which could be considered world-class and a number of good but lesser quality waves. At the northern tip of the atoll is **Shipwrecks**, a sandy bottom bay with lefts and rights breaking in winter N swells. **Whalers Anchorage** is a very consistent righthander during the winter as it receives the same swells as the north shore of Oahu, only smaller. Along the southern edge of the main reef pass at **English Harbor** is a long fast left that breaks consistently from April to September on SW to SE swells. Can be world-class on it's day, plus there are good rights across the channel on winter W-NW swells. Straight S swells for the left and due W for the right are very rare. Because of the consistent wave action at the pass and Whalers, the bottom is user friendly coral rubble strewn on flat reef, as opposed to jagged live coral common to so many other Pacific spots. Despite isolation, no local surfers, and poor inter-island flight service, Kiritimati has long been known to have good waves. The largest land area atoll in the world became part of Kiribati in 1979 and has a rapidly growing population of 7000 people. Being an avid fly fisher of the fabled "bone fish", Patagonia's founder Yvon Chouinard has been a Xmas addict since 1984, as well as North Shore photographer Bernie Baker. Chuck reckons there are 18 spots in a 8km/5mi radius from London to Poland Point. **Bridges Point** is the obvious spot with a fun right, holding double overhead walls, sometimes referred to as a mix between Maalaea (fast) and Trestles (fun). NNW swells will make long and fast walls while W swells will bump up good bowls off the point which can shoulder and roll 150m to the lagoon, perfect for a longboard. Trades can mess it up as there is a 40km (26mi) fetch blowing from the SE. Within paddling distance is **Cockrane's Reef**, a long, walled-up left that bends through almost 180° to join the rights, that are a good bet up to 4ft (1.2m). On the northern end of Cook Islet is **Coral Head**, another good left up to 5ft (1.5m), being well sheltered from the trades. The best left is called **Annie's**, one of several reef protected coves in the middle of Cook Islet. With 4 makeable sections, Outside Annie's is like an A frame West Peak at Sunset, very hollow and a guaranteed barrel for those with the balls. On bigger waves, there is a nice end section for projecting floaters. **Paris** is a stretch of 5 sheltered bays or cuts in the reefs, offering a swathe of fun spots which are trade wind protected, but close-out over 4-5ft (1.2-1.5m). It only takes 30 min by boat from London, but by land, it's 2h30. Try **Poland Point**, which gets occasional rights off the exposed reef on the western corner, which can handle some N in the winds.

London

MICHAEL KEW

Tabuaeran is blessed with year-round swell, but Kiritimati is way more consistent from November to March, when it receives the same winter swells as the north shore of Oahu: smaller size but even longer periods and constant offshores. There are breaks for all skill levels, from beginner to experts with gentle bathymetry on Kiritimati, which means close-outs when big, but fun when small. On Tabuaeran, surf is consistent, overhead and much larger at times from November through March. If Teahupoo or Sunset Beach get big, it will get there 18 to 24 hours later and about half the size. Winds are easterly trades that blow offshore year-round. Chuck Corbett shares his time between winters on Kiritimati and summers on Tabuaeran. Despite minimal tidal range, not more than 2.5ft (0.8m), waves are often better at high tides and at English Harbor, there is strong side-shore rip to the wave on incoming tides.

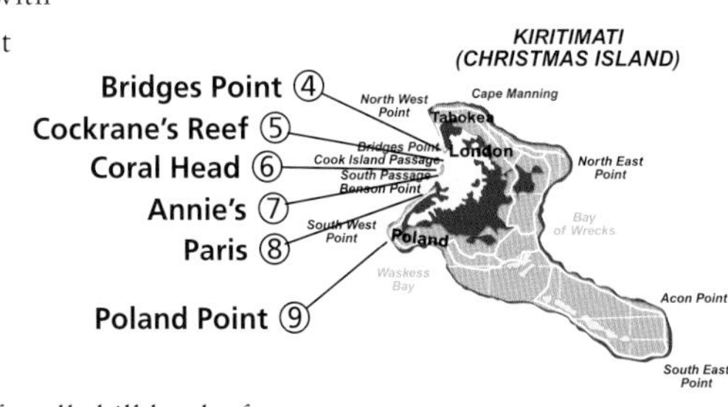

SURF STATISTICS			
Spot	Size	Btm	Type
①	8/2		
②	10/2		
③	10/2		
④	12/3		
⑤	8/2		
⑥	6/2		
⑦	5/2		
⑧	8/2		
⑨	10/2		

Paris

MICHAEL KEW

SURF STATISTICS	J F	M A	M J	J A	S O	N D
dominant swell	W-N	SW-NW	S-SW	S-SW	SW-NW	W-N
swell size (ft)	4	2-3	2	3	3-4	4
consistency (%)	80	60	40	50	60	80
dominant wind	W-NE	N-E	E-SE	E-SE	E-SE	NE-E
average force	F3-F4	F2-F3	F3	F3-F4	F3-F4	F3
consistency (%)	62	56	66	71	63	38
water temp.(°C)	29	29	29	29	29	29
wetsuit						

216. Oahu South Shore

Sandy Beach
LAURENT MASUREL

Summary
+ Consistent, all season swells
+ Rich surfing heritage
+ Beginner-friendly Waikiki reefs
+ Big city entertainment
+ Perfect weather, unique scenery

- Messy windswells
- Intense crowds & locals
- Some pollution & sharks
- Expensive US destination

Oahu is one of 8 Hawaiian islands located in the Pacific Ocean, about halfway between California and Japan. Although Oahu is only the third-largest island in the group, the vast majority of the state's population lives there. Oahu is thought of as paradise, with it's mix of spectacular, exotic scenery and fantastic weather.

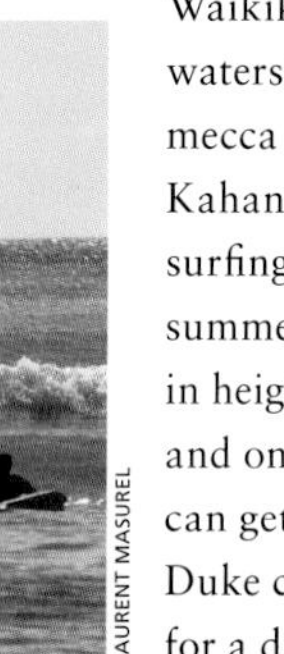
Queens
LAURENT MASUREL

Waikiki means "spouting waters", is the state's tourism mecca and the place where Duke Kahanamoku helped to relaunch surfing a century ago. During summer (June-Sept), swells vary in height from 2-8ft (0.6-2.5m) and on very rare occasions, can get huge like in 1917, when Duke caught a 35ft (11+m) wave for a distance of 1.25 miles (2 km). Stretching from Duke Beach near the Hilton Hawaiian Village to the Duke statue on Kuhio Beach, hundreds if not thousands of all kinds of waveriders are in the surf almost every day of the year, enjoying the fun, user-friendly conditions, unlike the wild and dangerous North Shore.

Ala Moana
JOHN CALLAHAN/TROPICALPIX

On the east side, **Kailua Bay** is better for kitesurfing, but will hold a reef peak at the north end, best on E swells.

TRAVEL INFORMATION

Local Population: Oahu 876,151
Coastline: 180km (112mi)
Time Zone: GMT -10
Contests: Makaha Classic, HSP series
Other Resources:
surfnewsnetwork.com
surfingoahu.com
wwwwaikikibeachboys surfcamp.com/
Video:
Hangloose
Out of Order
Free Ride

Getting There – It's better to have a biometric passport to get into the US. Honolulu (HNL) is the major Pacific hub with daily flights from North America West Coast, Sydney, Auckland, Manila and Japan. Most major airlines travelling to Oahu or any of the Hawaiian islands charge $80, often one way per surfboard! Choose your airline carefully, or rent your boards.

Getting Around – The Bus is Honolulu's public bus network. Oahu-Maui is the only inter-island route with Hawaii Superferry. Most car rental agencies require an age limit of 25. It costs $150-200 per week for an economy car. Gas is about 25% more expensive than the US mainland. Traffic can be intense on weekends.

WEATHER STATISTICS	J/F	M/A	M/J	J/A	S/O	N/D
total rainfall (mm)	104	86	43	43	65	108
consistency (days/mth)	10	9	8	8	9	11
min temp (°C)	19	19	21	23	22	20
max temp (°C)	25	27	29	29	30	28

Lodging and Food – Anything from historic hotels and condominiums, landscaped resorts and boutique hotels, familiar brands and trend-setting chic addresses. Prices vary with the view: Diamond Head, ocean or Ko'olau mountain views are at a premium. The Aloha Surf is a 3-star hotel: $85-100/nt. Surfcondos: April 16th - Sept 30th: $150/day for 4 pax.

Weather – Waikiki features a marine, tropical climate, being in the middle of the Pacific and on the equator. It is situated on a narrow plain between the ocean and the Ko'olau mountain range that serves to block trade wind moisture, resulting in a drier climate. The area enjoys warm, balmy weather year-round with temps ranging from 19-27°C (66-80°F) in winter and between 21-30°C (70-86°F) in summer. From October to April, the kona (SSW-SW) wind brings hot, sticky air and cooling NE-E trade winds blow the rest of the year. Average annual rainfall is 900mm (36in), mostly from November through March. Boardshorts, year-round.

Nature and Culture – Being a prime honeymoon trip, Waikiki provides big-city amenities, shopping, culture and entertainment. Honolulu was recently ranked first among America's largest cities for having the cleanest air and water, and the lowest crime rate. Visit the Bishop Museum.

Hazards and Hassles – Sharp coral reefs and unpredictable shorebreaks have caused many serious neck and spinal injuries to all kinds of surfers. Strong currents frequently accompany big surf. Car break-ins can be a problem. While Oahu's north and west sides are more notorious for localism, it also exists on the south shore. Tread carefully.

Handy Hints – Hawaii is influenced by pidgin, a kind of slang found on most Polynesian islands. World famous Waikiki Beach Boys offer daily surf lessons & outrigger canoe rides. Low rental rates; standard board = $50 for first 2 days then $10/day for rest of week. Surftech Performance rental = $75 for 2 days then $15/day.

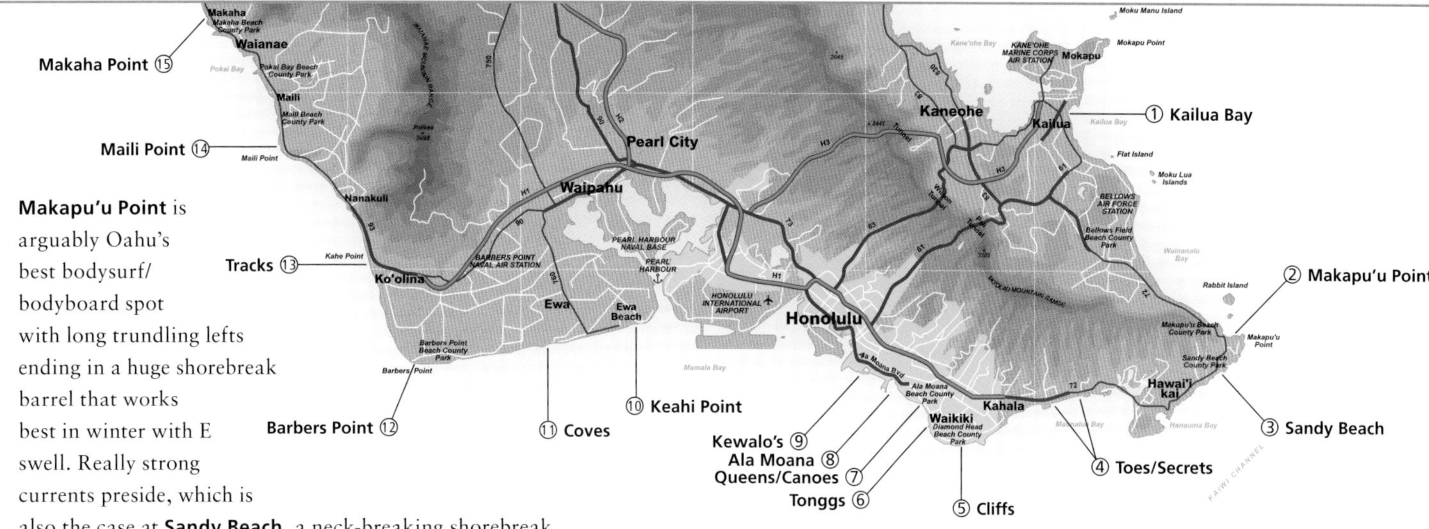

Makapu'u Point is arguably Oahu's best bodysurf/bodyboard spot with long trundling lefts ending in a huge shorebreak barrel that works best in winter with E swell. Really strong currents preside, which is also the case at **Sandy Beach**, a neck-breaking shorebreak for crazy, talented lids and fins on any E-S swell. Near Kawaiku'i Beach Park, check the uncrowded offshore reefs of **Secrets** long rights & good shortboard lefts on high tide and **Toes** longboard peak when winds are calm or N. Below the Diamond Head Rd lookouts, **Cliffs** is a brace of reefs and channels with consistently long walls that absorb the crowds of surfers and kites. Messy in trades, it can be classic on N or glassy days and is often the biggest south shore spot. The lefts at **Tonggs** are improver-friendly with the odd hollow section over the coral. Paddle out from the tiny beach off of Kalakaua. **Queens & Canoes** are fabled fun Waikiki reefs packed with all kinds of surf crafts. Queen's rights offer ripable walls up to 6ft (2m) over forgiving reef, while Canoes can handle bigger, mushier waves for longboarders and learners. Further outside check Popular's less crowded and less localised rights then more set-ups heading west including Three's, Four's, Kaiser's, Inbetweens and Rockpile. Confident and patient surfers with a low profile may just have a chance of snagging a wave at the infamous Bowl at **Ala Moana**. Long, shacking lefts peel down a shallow reef outside the Ala Wai Harbor. For less localised but equally sucky and pitching waves, **Kewalo's** speedy lefts are an option, but hazards include shut-downs on coral heads and sharks in the busy, rip-torn boat channel. Further away at Ewa Beach is **Keahi Point**, a large beach with several wind exposed reefs that only clean up on N winds. Shortboarders can often find a friendly peak along the sand and reef mix between Ewa and Nimitz Beach, including **Coves**, a consistent left with short punchy waves on S or W swells. In Kalaeloa near the industrial park, **Barbers Point** sees lengthy lefts on headhigh S swells or broken up peaks on wrapping 3-5ft (1-1.5m) N-NW swells. In Kahe Beach Park, **Tracks** long reef with sandy inside produces lefts on S-SW swells, while good punchy rights break on N-NW swells. It's always offshore and crowded. **Maili Point** gets screaming fast lefts over shallow coral on bigger SW-W swell with trades. Nearby are Green Lantern rights on NW swells. Last is **Makaha**, consisting of four distinct breaks: the Point, the Bowl, the Blowhole and the Inside Reef. Rideable at any size, these epic rights become a challenge over 10ft (3m). Visiting *haoles* need to be very respectful of the tight-knit Hawaiian families that live and play in Makaha. Featuring canoe, tandem, stand-up, bodysurfing and longboards over 10 feet, it brings together the entire community. 4th December of 1969, Greg Noll, took off on a 30ft (10m) Makaha monster, considered the largest swell in recorded history.

SURF STATISTICS			
Spot	Size	Btm	Type
①	6/2		
②	8/2		
③	6/2		
④	6/2		
⑤	8/2		
⑥	6/2		
⑦	8/2		
⑧	10/3		
⑨	8/3		
⑩	6/3		
⑪	6/2		
⑫	8/2		
⑬	8/2		
⑭	15/4		
⑮	25/3		

Oahu is ultra-consistent because surf can come from all over the Pacific. North Pacific swells deliver the highest waves (8-20ft/2.5-6m) with mid-to-long 10-18 second wave periods mostly from Oct - May. From April to Nov, NE tradewind swell ranges from 4-12ft (1.2-4m) with short 5-8 sec periods. Common between April and October, South Pacific swells travel great distances with very long 14-22 sec wave periods, but small wave heights (1-4 ft/0.3-1.2m). These S swells translate into very energetic waves when they hit south-facing coastlines. Waves from kona storms associated with fronts passing just north of Hawaii are very steep with moderate heights (10-15ft/3-5m) and short to medium 8-10 sec periods. Kona storm waves have the greatest impact on south and west-facing coasts. Waves from hurricanes and tropical storms (June-November) can reach extreme heights (10-35ft/3-8m) and occur mostly on east, south and west-facing shores. Tides are semi-diurnal with daily inequality and hardly ever reach 2ft (0.6m) on spring tides.

JOHN CALLAHAN/TROPICALPIX

Three's, Waikiki

SURF STATISTICS	J F	M A	M J	J A	S O	N D
dominant swell	W-NE	W-NE	E-SW	E-SW	E-SW	W-NE
swell size (ft)	5-6	4-5	2-3	4-5	5	5-6
consistency (%)	95	85	75	80	85	90
dominant wind	NE-E	NE-E	NE-E	NE-E	NE-E	NE-E
average force	F4	F4	F4	F4	F4	F4
consistency (%)	51	66	76	88	77	65
water temp.(°C)	24	24	25	26	27	25
wetsuit						

Jostling kelp crowds the channel, as a Vancouver Island wedge dishes out some pleasure and pain for the hardy, rubber-clad locals from Canada's first surf town, Tofino.

North America

TIM MUNN

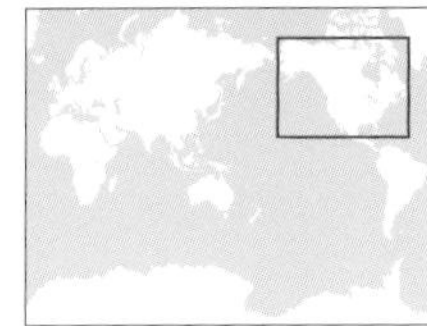

Surf Culture

In 1885, three young Hawaiian princes rode waves off the mouth of the San Lorenzo River in Santa Cruz using surfboards milled from local redwood. Jonah Kuhio Kalaniana`ole and his brothers David Kawananakoa and Edward Keli`iahonui were nephews of Queen Kapi'olani, wife to Hawaii's last king, David Kalakaua.

In the spring of 1907, 23-year-old Irish-Hawaiian beachboy George Freeth, demonstrated the sport of Hawaiian kings to the astonished throngs at Redondo Beach. Freeth stayed on in California to become the first official lifeguard on the Pacific coast, distinguishing himself in the winter of 1908, when he single-handedly rescued six Japanese fishermen. Duke Kahanamoku, en route to winning a gold medal and setting a world record in the 100m freestyle at the 1912 Olympics in Stockholm, stopped to give surfing demonstrations at Corona del Mar and Santa Monica, which captivated the large crowds in attendance. On his return from Stockholm, he introduced surfing to the East Coast at the steel pier in Atlantic City, New Jersey, but it would take 50 years to catch on, exacerbated by a 1939 ban on surfing in the state. Wisconsin born Tom Blake, who was inspired by the Duke and his aloha, arrived in Waikiki in 1924, immersing himself in Hawaiian surf culture and set about creating lighter replicas of ancient boards, resulting in the fabled Blake hollow paddleboards, which became popular around the world as lifesaving tools. Blake's many innovations (the first waterproof camera housing, the first surfboard fin, the first sailing surfboard) set the tone for the continued innovation and technological development of the surfboard which followed. The 1920s saw surfing grow in Southern California, helped along by some film roles for The Duke and also Tom Blake, who first surfed Florida while on a Miami film set. Blake, along with Sam Reid, discovered the beautiful peeling waves of Malibu in 1925. During

Tom Blake was a surf innovator extraordinaire, credited with designing and building the very first lightweight hollow surfboards, the surfboard fin, the waterproof camera housing, the sailboard, the collapsible surfboard and the first surfboard leash. He died in 1994, aged 92.

JEFF DIVINE

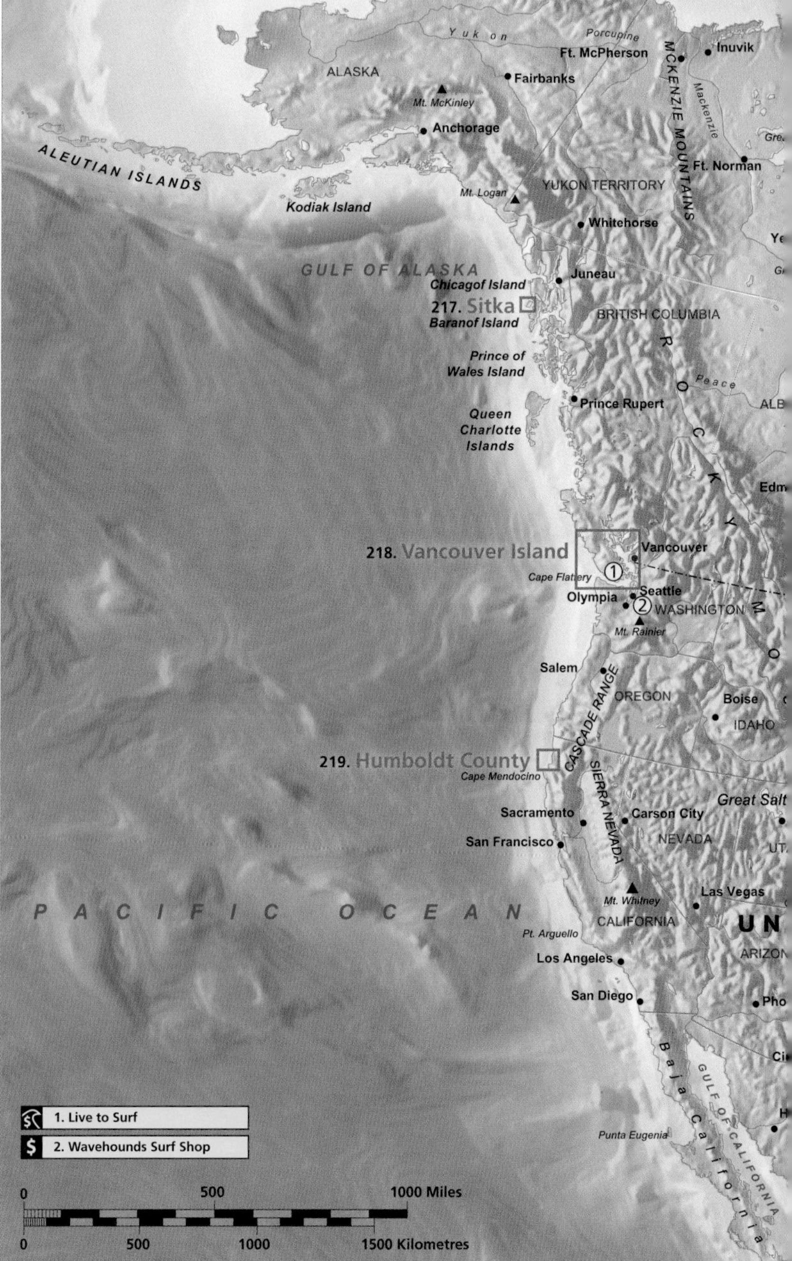

the 1930s, surf clubs sprang up around California's major surfing areas (San Diego, San Onofre, Corona Del Mar, Palos Verdes, Hermosa Beach, Santa Cruz, etc.), and the first Pacific Coast Surfriding Championships were held. Tom Blake's patented Hawaiian hollow surfboard went into production in 1932, a few years after the Pacific System Homes factory began output, including the famous Swastika models (1935). Blake's hollows replaced the scattering of solid planks that had found their way to the lifeguards of New York, Virginia Beach pioneers John Smith and Babe Braithwaite and Florida innovators, Bill and Dudley Whitman. World War II effectively put a stop to surfing in America, but the Malibu crew of Kit Horn, "Buzzy" Trent, and Peter, Lucky and Corny Cole remembered these as golden years of crowdless wave-riding.

DOC BALL

The pre-war Southern California surfers had the waves to themselves, yet still preferred to share rides and a camaraderie that got swallowed up by the crowds of the '60s. Long Beach flood control, 1939.

100° 80° 60° 40° Arctic Circle 60°
Baffin Island
Cape Dyer
Kap Fervel
Iqaluit
NORTHERN TERRITORIES
LABRADOR SEA
Cape Chidley
Rankin Inlet
Hudson Bay
QUEBEC
Labrador
Churchill
MANITOBA
Goose Bay
NEWFOUNDLAND
Cape Bauld
Belcher Is.
Newfoundland
40°
St. John's
Cape Race
Moosonee
PRINCE EDWARD IS.
40°
ONTARIO
NEW BRUNSWICK
NOVA SCOTIA
Winnipeg
Halifax
Thunder Bay
221. Great Lakes
L. Superior
MAINE
Augusta
Cape Sable
NORTH DAKOTA
MINNESOTA
Montreal
Ottawa
VERMONT
Montpelier
NEW HAMPSHIRE
Concord
Bismarck
L. Huron
MICHIGAN
Toronto
Boston
MASSACHUSETTS
Cape Cod
SOUTH DAKOTA
St. Paul
WISCONSIN
L. Michigan
NEW YORK
Albany
Hartford
Providence
RHODE ISLAND
CONNECTICUT
New York
Pierre
Missouri
Mississippi
Madison
Lansing
Detroit
PENNSYLVANIA
Trenton
NEW JERSEY
IOWA
OHIO
Harrisburg
NEBRASKA
Des Moines
Chicago
INDIANA
Columbus
WEST VIRGINIA
Annapolis
Dover
DELAWARE
220. New Jersey
WASHINGTON D.C.
MARYLAND
Lincoln
Springfield
ILLINOIS
Indianapolis
Charleston
Richmond
VIRGINIA
Topeka
KANSAS
Jefferson City
St. Louis
Frankfort
KENTUCKY
MISSOURI
NORTH CAROLINA
Raleigh
Cape Hatteras
BERMUDA
Nashville
TENNESSEE
OKLAHOMA
ARKANSAS
Cape Fear
Columbia
SOUTH CAROLINA
Oklahoma City
Little Rock
Atlanta
GEORGIA
TEXAS
Red
Alabama
Savannah
Tropic of Cancer
Jackson
Montgomery
ATLANTIC OCEAN
Dallas
LOUISIANA
ALABAMA
MISSISSIPPI
Tallahassee
Jacksonville
Austin
Colorado
Baton Rouge
New Orleans
Orlando
Houston
Mississippi Delta
Tampa
FLORIDA
20°
San Antonio
Rio Grande
Miami
GULF OF MEXICO
BAHAMAS
Monterrey
DOMINICAN REPUBLIC
Habana
MEXICO
UNITED STATES OF AMERICA
CANADA

LEROY GRANIS

Miki Dora, aka Da Cat, slinks along a Malibu wall in 1962. Tom Blake and Sam Reid hiked through the old Rindge Ranch in 1925 and discovered the wave that would lend it's name to a type of surfboard and become the incubator for modern beach culture.

JEFF DIVINE

Psychadelic spray jobs were a particularly '70s thing. David Nuuhiwa and the Brotherhood's John Gale, compare palettes in Laguna Beach, 1971.

Competitive surfing used to gauge success by how many people it could attract to the beach, but now it is all about live webcasts and a global audience that dwarfs even the mega crowds of the '80s OP pro in Huntington, CA.

Military material developments allowed the brilliant Bob Simmons to create the first balsa-foam-fibreglass "sandwich" surfboards in the late 1940s. Then, Joe Quigg built a lightweight balsa with rounded rails and a fibreglass fin that was ultra-manoeuvrable. The era of the Malibu surfboard was born. At the dawn of the 1950s, Dale Velzy opened the world's first real surfboard shop in Manhattan Beach, California, followed by Hap Jacobs, Jack O'Neill, Hobie Alter, Dave Sweet, Dewey Weber, and so on. Bud Browne's surf movies stoked surfers up and down the West Coast in the mid-'50s, and he was soon joined by the likes of John Severson, Bruce Brown, Greg Noll, and finally Hollywood with the milestone release of Gidget in 1959. Soon Hobie and Sweet were making surfboards out of polyurethane foam and fibreglass, while Jack O'Neill and Bev Morgan/Bobby Meistrell (Dive 'n Surf) started designing the first wetsuits for surfers. In 1959, Nancy and Walter Katin, Newport Beach makers of canvas boat covers, started making surf trunks. These, along with the Hawaiian (or Aloha) shirt, were the foundation of the modern surfwear industry. That same year, the first West Coast Surfing Championships were held at the pier in Huntington Beach. The 1960s dawned with the creation of *The Surfer* magazine by filmmaker John Severson, as surf culture grew into a significant fashion force, backed by the rhythms of California rock 'n' rollers Dick Dale and the sound of surf music. In 1961, the United States Surfing Association was founded by Hoppy Swarts, and a song titled "Surfin'" (written by Brian Wilson and Mike Love) became a SoCal hit. Hang Ten signed Phil Edwards as the first surfer to have a signature clothing line. Surfing's popularity was exploding on the East Coast and during the mid-'60s, more surfboards were sold in New Jersey, Virginia, and Florida than California, Oregon, and Washington. Bruce Brown's milestone film, *The Endless Summer*, hit the surf-film circuit in 1964, then went mainstream in 1966. On the flip side, Hollywood was spinning out surfploitation films like *Beach Blanket Bingo* and the first man-made-wavepool opened in Tempe, Arizona. Catalyzed by the short, neutral-buoyancy wave-riding vehicle of Santa Barbara kneeboarder George Greenough, surfers cut two feet from the fronts of their surfboards in 1967-68, kicking off the pivotal shortboard

JEFF DIVINE

revolution. The Eastern Surf Association was formed, becoming a breeding ground for future greats. This was also the decade that surfing took hold along the fringes of North America like on Vancouver Island, Washington and Oregon, New England and the Gulf of Mexico. The competition scene hiccupped in the late '60s hippy years, but by 1976 the International Professional Surfers had cobbled together a world tour, and have been chasing sponsors with increasing success ever since. Aussies dominated until 1985 when Santa Barbara surfer, Tom Curren was crowned world champ. American women captured the first 12 world titles, yet got virtually no respect in a male-dominated sport and media. By the 1980s, three-fin "thrusters" took over, allowing pioneering aerialists like Bud Llamas and Christian Fletcher to blaze the "new school" trail for future champs Kelly Slater and Lisa Andersen to follow. Andersen won four consecutive women's championships in the 1990s, fuelling the continuous growth of women's surfing. Nine-time world champ Slater is widely accepted as the greatest surfer ever. Tow-in surfing eventually found its mainland arena at a spot called Mavericks near Half Moon Bay, California, and its most suggestive potential at the Cortes Banks, a seamount some 100 miles off the coast of San Diego, where jetted-up teams ride 50ft+ waves in the middle of the ocean.

Today

Southern California is the nerve centre of the global surf industry with all the major players maintaining a presence in the heart of the largest surfing population on the planet. The birthplace of surf media has seen a flotilla of surf mags come and go since 1960, currently supporting the original, authoritative *Surfer*, perennial sparring partner and now stable mate *Surfing*, high-brow *The Surfers Journal*, high voltage *Transworld Surf* and highly specialist *Longboarder* or *Bodyboarding* to name just a few. Whether Huntington Beach or Santa Cruz represents the ultimate surf city is a moot point as almost every coastal county plus the landlocked Midwest states, has some kind of surf shop, eager to service the staggering number of active surfers and wannabes. The Surf Industry Manufacturers Association claim that there are in excess of 5046 surf outlets across the USA turning over more than $7.5 billion dollars a year. Trying to put a figure on numbers of US surfers is guesswork, but estimates range from 2.4m (2002; Boardtrac) to a current population of 4 times that. Southern California surfer figures are often touted at 1M and a similar number fight over the slim pickings in Florida, while the East Coast as a whole, has long supported more waveriders than the West. To put these figures into context, the USA makes up close to half of the global estimate of 17-23M surfers, defined as someone who has participated in the last 12 months. With some creative accounting, achieved by dividing the number of surf spots (100,000±) along the world's 400,000km coastline with the planets' 23M surfers, it appears there are 230 surfers per spot. Extrapolate to the USA (20,000km coast = 5% so 5000 spots shared by 9M surfers) and the crowd factor jumps to 1800 surfers per surf spot! These wildly contentious figures don't translate to daily reality, but do serve to illustrate the incredible growth surfing has experienced over the last 5 years and how the surfing resource has remained static, resulting in uber-crowds at many banner breaks along North American shores. This huge population has fed various national amateur organisations, all of which have been plagued by lack of unity and behind the scenes politics. However, the recently formed Surfing America has become the National Governing Body, (formerly the remit of the USSA then the USSF) and finally re-unified with the National Scholastic Surfing Association (NSSA), to select the US team to compete in the World Surfing Games. Surf associations have formed along the geographic lines of Western, Gulf and Eastern, whereby the ESA is the largest amateur surf association in the world with membership numbers exceeding 7000 and a regional structure to attract

CHRIS GIULIANO

Performance levels have literally sky-rocketed in recent years, whereby boosting air is becoming commonplace and is highly scored in pro contests, providing the rider lands it.

surfers at a local level. The grassroots are also well served by individual Surfrider Foundation chapters, promoting education and activism on local and national environmental issues. The first recorded incidence of localism was perpetrated by Hawaiian surfers on Californians Gene "Tarzan" Smith and Tom Zahn on Oahu during the '40s, but it was soon to feature on the mainland. Localism was rampant throughout the '70s as pockets of aggressive surfers used abuse, theft, and violence to protect their waves from outsiders, but has now contracted to isolated urban pockets and semi-secret breaks in far-flung corners of the continent, including Vancouver Island, Washington, Oregon, Northern Cal and a handful of the East Coast's better breaks. A couple of Los Angeles beaches have gained extra notoriety when local surfers have been convicted in high profile assault cases, while tyre slashing, windshield waxing, dropping in, snaking, stink eye and general abuse are all part of the local's arsenal and can surface anywhere from Alaska to Alabama. On the plus side, it is now so crowded at some breaks, it's impossible to discern the old from the new and a certain resignation among the locals, plus the threat of litigation, is reducing the instances of violent conflict.

217. Sitka

Shelikof's Island

KEVIN GRIFFIN

Summary
+ Variety of quality spots
+ Empty, wilderness line-ups
+ Reasonable water temps
+ Mt Edgecumbe backdrop
+ Great salmon & halibut fishing

– Cold, inconsistent surf
– Loads of rain
– Changeable winds
– Remote, difficult access
– Expensive

According to Charlie Skultka, the first surfboard landed in Sitka in the '80s, carried by a warm offshoot of the North Pacific Current and may have travelled all the way from Japan. Surfer Mag sent a team in 1993 and Dave Parmenter's cover story heralded Sitka as "The Land Duke Forgot". However, the largest surfing community in Alaska (about 30 surfers) is now located in the remote town of Yakutat (pop. 800), on the Gulf of Alaska midway between Anchorage and Juneau, regularly surfing good beachbreaks and a quality left on big swells. Eastern Kenai Peninsula near Seward and the islands of Montague and Hinchinbrook do have surf potential and protect the Prince William Sound, where, the Exxon Valdez spilled over 11 million gallons of oil, polluting over 1,500mi (2,415km) of coastline in 1989. Closer to Anchorage are some occasionally ridden waves in Homer, Nikiski and Anchor Point inside the Cook Inlet, which leads to the Turnagain Arm tidal bore in Girdwood. Kodiak Island has perhaps the widest selection of readily accessible surf breaks in Alaska, although most

Sandy Beach

KEVIN GRIFFIN

Kai's Place

KEVIN GRIFFIN

TRAVEL INFORMATION

Local Population: Sitka – 9,000
Coastline: Alaska 19,924km (12,380mi)
Time Zone: GMT-9
Contests: none
Other Resources:
coldsalt.com
grizzlysurf.com
alaskasurfing.com

Getting There – USA visa rules. Fly to Anchorage (ANC) with many flights from the lower 48 states. New York is 8h away while Japan is 6.5h. Daily flights by Alaska Airlines from Anchorage (ANC) to Sitka (SIT), from $410 (3h) or fly from Seattle. Sitka is a popular port for most cruise lines that sail the Inside Passage. Sitka to Juneau 8h45 (Fast Speed Ferry is 5-6h).

Getting Around – Bush planes, skiffs, fishing boats and ferries are the most realistic way of finding quality waves. Hire a taxi or rent a bike to get to Sandy Beach or get in the Cold Salt Surf Shop boat to surf Kruzof Island breaks: $55 for Sealion Cove or $40 for South Kruzof reefs (min 2 surfers).

Lodging and Food – Sitka has over 200 hotel rooms, many bed and breakfasts, lodges, vacation rentals, as well as campgrounds and RV facilities. Cascade Inn $85-140, Sitka Hotel $50-110, Biorka B&B $65-85. Youth Hostel just reopened. Expect $20 for a basic meal. Local restaurants are full of halibut and other fine seafood.

WEATHER STATISTICS	J/F	M/A	M/J	J/A	S/O	N/D
total rainfall (mm)	289	256	222	252	510	341
consistency (days/mth)	19	18	15	16	22	21
min temp (°C)	-7	-2	5	8	4	-3
max temp (°C)	-2	8	16	18	12	2

Weather – Thanks to the warmth brought by the Alaska Current, SE Alaska is an oceanic climate that supports a temperate rain forest, with the most rain falling in the south. Annual rainfall ranges from 3810mm (150in) in Ketchikan to 762mm (30in) in Skagway, leaving Sitka somewhere in the middle at 2413mm (54in). May and June are the driest months while July and August are a bit wetter but warmer as well. Normal temps run from 13°C (56°F) to 20°C (68°F) with temperatures dropping about 5°C at night. There can be up to 20h of daylight in early summer but as low as 6h in January. The weather does change with amazing frequency, be fully prepared. During summer, water temps are around 13°C/56°F, which is roughly the same as water temps in Northern California. A 4/3mm fullsuit with boots is sufficient. During the winter, a 6/5/4mm with hood included and 5-7mm gloves and booties are required to withstand 5-6°C (41-43°F).

Nature and Culture – World-class salmon and halibut fishing (May–Sept), sea kayaking, hike up Mt Edgecumbe (2700ft/823m), SE Alaska's only volcano. Ocean-going charters provide views to marine wildlife: humpback whales; sea lions; sea otters and seabird rookeries. Spare some cash for breathtaking flightseeing with floatplane charters.

Hazards and Hassles – Bearanoia is an issue when surfing any break outside Sitka. Camping in the wilderness requires special precautions to avoid trouble with bears - be careful! Water temperature is not as ball-shrinkingly cold as anticipated. Rips can be fast and lava reef bottom is nasty on shallow parts of the reef.

Handy Hints – Contact Cold Salt Surf Shop (907-738-1348, www.coldsalt.com) to join one of their daily trips to the surf breaks on Kruzof Island. Owner Kevin Griffin rents all the gear. Wetsuit + board rentals ($35/day). Surf lessons at $50. Ideally, you need a boat, airplane, all terrain vehicle, camping equipment, fuel, gun, chainsaw and whiskey!

BOB KEMP

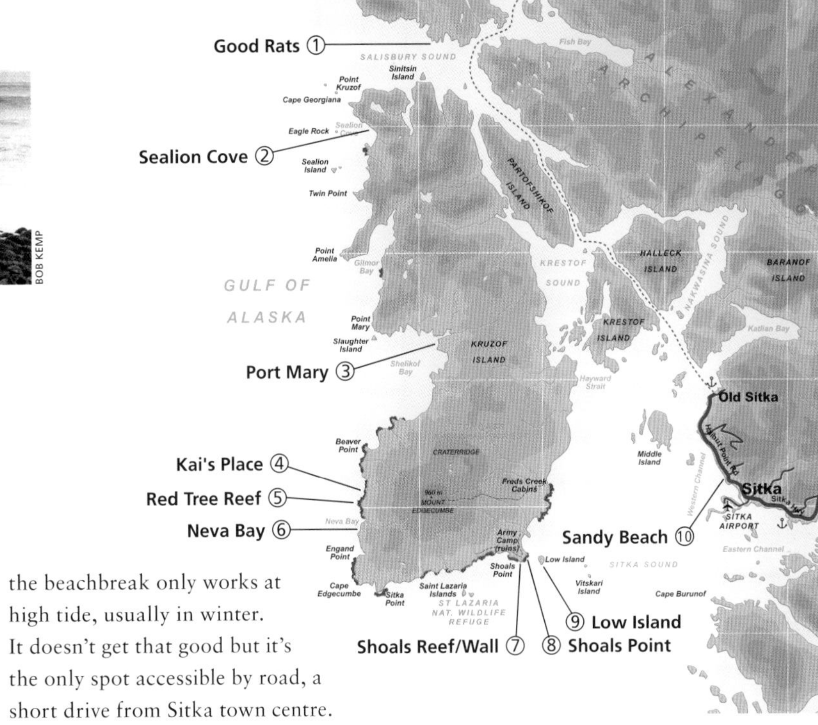

tend to be fairly inconsistent during non-winter months. Surf spots can be found north of Kodiak City and along the scenic coast road south to Cape Chiniak and on to the Pasagshak State Recreation area for some south-facing beachbreak. The huge potential out in the Aleutian Islands remains untapped, while the tundra coast of the Arctic Ocean is mainly flat or frozen. Glaciers have created much of Alaska's southern coastline of large bays, inlets, and prominent fjords, while the high altitude mountains of the Alaska Range skirt this part of the coastline, often plunging directly into the Pacific Ocean. Located about 95mi (150km) from Juneau on the seaward edge of Alaska's southeast panhandle, Sitka is one of Alaska's oldest and most historic towns, having been home to Native Alaskans, Russian fur traders, and a U.S. military garrison before becoming the capital of Alaska in the mid 19th century. Most of the surf is on offshore islands so local surf shop owner Kevin Griffin runs a taxi service in his 22ft C-Dory 110 Hp to surf the Kruzof Island breaks.

The most remote option is **Good Rats** rights on mid tides and E winds, but it is a long way from anywhere. On Kruzof Island, the same applies to the beginner-friendly sandy beachbreaks at **Sealion Cove** or Shelikof Bay aka **Port Mary**. Both favour rights and W swells with winds in the E quadrant. Further west-facing spots include **Kai's Place**, a rocky left, **Red Tree Reef**, a peak that needs big SW swell and **Neva Bay**, another righthand reef, under the shadow of Mt Edgecumbe, a snow covered extinct volcano. All three need any E wind, the right mix of swell size and tide height and are about a 1hr boat ride from Sitka. Most often, a boat trip to Kruzof Island is to surf the southern reefbreaks, and **Shoals Reef/Wall** is the premier wave, about 30min from town. Primarily rights, this offshore lava reef works best on S swells, although W will also break and it handles up to 15ft (5m) in any N wind. **Shoals Point** is fairly consistent, working on the same conditions, but it gets treacherous in bigger swells when the Wall will be better. Shoals Reef and Point break on grizzled lava rocks so expect some power and sketchy conditions if it gets overhead. Only experienced surfers should apply. Nearby **Low Island** has the same lava rocks and is offshore in NW-NE winds, but the 3 peaks line up best in medium SW swells. Sitka is situated on Baranof Island forming part of the barrier for Alaska's Inside Passage where the Alaska Marine Highway ferries provide a year-round service for passengers and vehicles. Although Yakutat and Kodiak feature better known surfing locations, Sitka boasts one of the most accessible places to paddle out when the surf is up. To surf **Sandy Beach**, you need a really big SW swell and the beachbreak only works at high tide, usually in winter. It doesn't get that good but it's the only spot accessible by road, a short drive from Sitka town centre.

The most dominant swell source is from mid-latitude depressions tracking across the North Pacific, typically born around Kamchatka or the Aleutian Islands and striking land in western Canada or northwest U.S.A, way south of Sitka. The swells from these lows come in from a S-SW direction, or sometimes W and are biggest in winter (October to March) but low daylight and freezing temps mean it's probably not the best time to visit. Quite long-period swells are possible, especially if the depressions deepen around Asia. The North Pacific is pretty seasonal, so local storms are needed produce some windswells to interrupt the summer flat spells. Be quick as conditions constantly change. Choose between seasons for the best surf, September being the ultimate month for scoring classic days. Conditions can be very inconsistent, don't expect surf every week. Buoy Station 46084 - Cape Edgecumbe Buoy AK is the one to watch. Expect 14ft (4.3m) tidal range on spring tides with irregular semi-diurnal variations, while the variations become more extreme further north.

SURF STATISTICS

Spot	Size	Btm	Type
①	8/2		
②	8/2		
③	6/1		
④	8/2		
⑤	8/2		
⑥	8/2		
⑦	15/3		
⑧	8/2		
⑨	8/2		
⑩	5/1		

SURF STATISTICS	J F	M A	M J	J A	S O	N D
dominant swell	S-W	S-W	S-W	S-W	S-W	S-W
swell size (ft)	6-7	5-6	4-5	3-4	6-7	7
consistency (%)	20	50	60	40	30	20
dominant wind	E-S	E-S	SE-SW	SW-NW	SE-SW	E-S
average force	F5	F5	F4	F3-F4	F4-F5	F5
consistency (%)	43	44	45	49	47	48
water temp.(°C)	6	6	9	13	12	8
wetsuit						

Shoal's Reef

KEVIN GRIFFIN

218. Vancouver Island

TIM NUNN

Summary
+ Consistent swells
+ Mix of beaches, reefs and points
+ Waves for all abilities
+ Wildlife
+ Luxury lodge options

– Messy stormy swells
– Beaches often onshore
– Expensive local costs
– Rare, localised pointbreaks
– Cold and super rainy

Canada has the world's longest coastline and with 52,455 islands, it should also host the largest number of surf spots. However, being located so far north between 45° to 80° latitude, frozen water is an issue, as well as a regular swell supply. So far, surfers have been exploring the southern corners of this vast country, finding Nova Scotia on the eastern seaboard and Vancouver Island to the west well endowed with some quality reefs, points and beaches. Literally hundreds of spots exist along the remote nooks and crannies of Vancouver Island, but access is challenging without a boat or seaplane, which is how the experts like Tatchu Surf Adventures manage to get surfers to the northern areas of the Brooks Peninsula, Nootka Island and the Hesquiat Peninsula. There is, however, 2 areas of easy

TIM NUNN

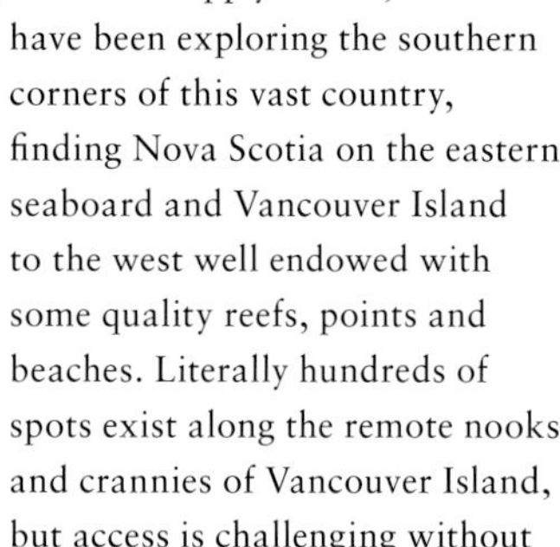

JEREMY KORESKI

TRAVEL INFORMATION

Local Population: BC 4.3M
Coastline: VI 2668km (1658mi)
Time Zone: GMT -8
Contests: Rip Curl Stew, Cox Bay, June '07
Other Resources:
surfingvancouverisland.com
bcsa.ca
cedarsurf.com
livetosurf.com
Video: 49° (2002)

Getting There – Straight 180 day visa for most nationalities. Best is to fly into Seattle (BFI) in the US or Vancouver (YVR). Air Canada now charges for boardbags over 6'6". There are also domestic flights to Victoria (YYJ) or Tofino (YAZ). Canada has the largest seaplane fleet. Tofino is 5h from Victoria and 3h from Nanaimo (200km/124mi). Get there by coach or from the BC ferry terminals at Nanaimo.

Getting Around – Many ways to travel around using public transport like The Tofino Bus, BC Ferries and Washington State Ferries. Jordan River in Juan de Fuca Provincial Park, along the West Coast Road (Highway 14) is 60km (37mi) from Victoria. From $165 per week for a rental car at GSA in Victoria. Motorhome/RV rental around $100/d. Take a scenic seaplane cruise (Tofino Air).

WEATHER STATISTICS	J/F	M/A	M/J	J/A	S/O	N/D
total rainfall (mm)	183	106	67	37	119	217
consistency (days/mth)	19	16	12	7	13	21
min temp (°C)	0	3	9	12	8	3
max temp (°C)	6	12	20	23	16	8

Lodging and Food – Many options for all budgets especially deluxe. Many B&Bs are located right on Tofino's beaches. Stay at Tofino Hostel ($80/dble or $29/dorm bed). Cox Bay has the private Pacific Sands Beach Resort: $$$. Camp near the surf at Greenpoint Campground with trail access to Long Beach. Try Dolphin Motel near Chesterman Beach.

Weather – In contrast to the relatively dry climate of the heavily-populated Straight of Georgia region, Vancouver Island receives the lions share of precipitation, however, it's remarkably mild by Canadian standards. Port Renfrew experiences about 12 days of snowfall and only 15 days of snow cover over the year. However, cool summers go with the mild winters and the weather is very changeable. Average daily temps range from 3°C (37°F) in January to 15°C (59°F) in July. The annual average rainfall can reach an impressive 6650mm (260in) in the mountains, dropping to a 10th of that in the rain shadowed capital, Victoria. July is the driest month and November the wettest. A 4/3mm with booties in summer and a 5/4 mm hooded suit with 3/5mm gloves and boots in winter.

Nature and Culture – Tofino is a mecca for outdoor adventure like hiking the boardwalk trails in the ancient, dripping rainforest, biking on the beach at low tide, kayaking, sport fishing and whale watching (Jamies Whaling Station). Between Nov-April, check the famous snow resort of Whistler (Olympics 2010), 2h from Vancouver or Mt Washington actually on Vancouver Island.

Hazards and Hassles – River Jordan locals resent kooks showing up at their inconsistent pointbreak from the nearby cities of Victoria (pop: 300,000) and Vancouver (pop: 2M), and have been enforcing tough localism. Cold water, rain, wild surf and fast weather changes are the things to worry about. Don't forget about the possibility of startling a bear on the trails or beaches at remote spots.

Handy Hints – Surf gets big, so take a longer board with extra float for the full neoprene kit. Inner Rhythm runs camps near Ucluelet, while Surf Sister specialize in female only surf camps. Many surf shops to rent gear like Live to Surf in Tofino, Long Beach Surf Shop, and Storm Surf Shop in Ucluelet. Read "The Cedar Surf" by Grant Shilling.

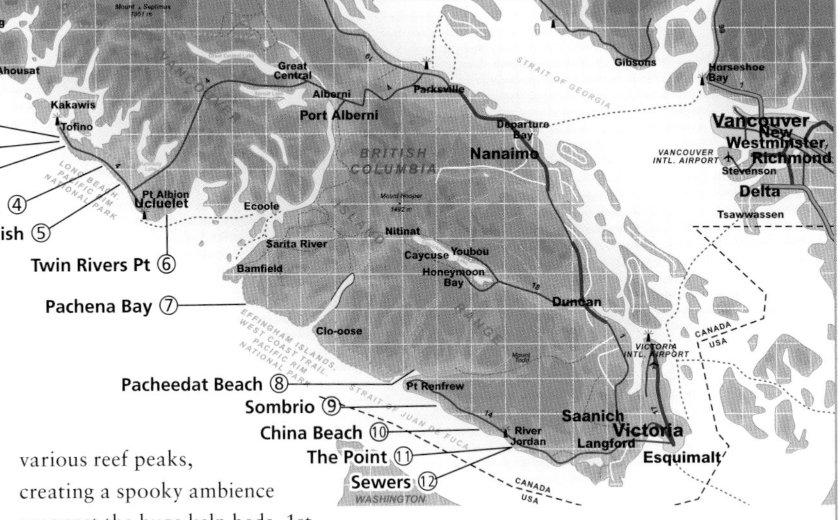

road access to the surf at Tofino and inside the Strait of Juan de Fuca. Blessed with some reliable beachbreaks, Tofino is the closest thing to a surf town on the west coast and is home to about 1,700 friendly residents who have embraced high-end ecotourism with luxurious amenities. Points and reefs are a feature of the stretch inside the Strait, coming to life with strong winter swells. Stunning, old-growth, temperate rainforests provide the backdrop to the breathtaking beaches. In recent years, locals like Peter Devries and the Bruhwiler brothers have proved that you can do all the warm water tricks in full winter kit, prompting more people each year to don some rubber and hit the waves in this spectacular natural environment.

Chesterman Beach needs a bit of size to break since it's sheltered and the southern part is good for learners, while there are bigger waves towards the north end. There is also the option of more beginner friendly beachbreak at MacKenzie Beach in the next bay north. Parking lots fill up quickly in summer. **Rosie's Bay** is a rocky little cove between Chesterman and Cox with punchy, sectiony peaks, favouring lefts at lower tides and is a haunt for local shortboarders. The main Tofino spot is **Cox Beach**, a crescent beach with tapering walls that line up best in the middle, while each end provides wind protection from the N and S respectively. It's the usual contest site, there's a webcam and plenty of accommodation nearby. **Long Beach** is actually a series of beaches stretching for over 10km (6mi), where usually mellow waves provide an endless choice for the many surf schools that operate on this stretch. Closes-out when the waves get overhead and there can be some currents, so lifeguards are on duty July & August. At the southern end of Long Beach, **Wickaninnish** is a popular spot with hotels, trails, viewpoints and the Wickaninnish Centre for the Pacific Rim National Park. Strewn with driftwood and protected from S winds, it's more friendly beachbreak for learners. Next bay south is the stunning Florencia Bay which is usually a bit more powerful. Ucluelet has a couple of unreliable beachbreaks at Big Beach and Little Beach, but a 30min drive to **Twin Rivers** on a good W swell should see the point at Mussel Beach working. It's a fast tubing wall when it lines up, but there are some sharp rocks (and locals!) to avoid. The 77km (48mi) West Coast Trail starts near Bamfield about 10min from **Pachena Bay** where very average straighthanders roll into a deep bay that faces SW. There's a great campground to use as a base for exploring the surrounding wilderness, but surfing is not permitted along the West Coast Trail. Pachena Point has been surfed since the '60s, but is off-limits without a boat. Once in Port Renfrew, cross the bridge to reach Port San Juan or **Pacheedat Beach**, aka Gordon Rivermouth, a quality beachbreak, best on NE wind and a strong W swell. Most Juan da Fuca Strait spots are winter breaks, that only work when good sized, long period swells arrive, usually accompanied by storms. The line-up at **Sombrio Beach** is not for the faint-hearted and often experiences a persistent mist, enshrouding the various reef peaks, creating a spooky ambience amongst the huge kelp beds. 1st Peak, Chickens and 2nd peak are some of the options for intermediate to experienced surfers, with the lefts usually more walled up and faster. It's a 20min walk from the trailhead. Further down the Strait is **China Beach**, a very average rocky beachbreak, next to Highway 14 and a quick walk from the parking lot. Mellow peaks and easy rides make it a good place for beginner/improvers, but it wont break much in summer. Historically a logging camp, River Jordan has become a surfing town thanks to long wrapping rights known as **The Point**, Sewers, and Rock Piles, but it has also developed a reputation for intolerant, aggressive locals. Despite being somewhat inconsistent, these waves crank when it's on, which is mid-winter, big W-NW swell and a NE wind. The Point at the rivermouth can have very long rides (and some lefts back into the river), down the line speed walls and bowly barrel sections over the sand boulder mix. **Sewers** named for a defunct sewage pipe, gets really hollow and fast, for experienced surfers only, since localism gets the worst there. Further inside the Strait, there are other spots on huge swells, but remember that SE winds blow out most breaks.

SURF STATISTICS			
Spot	Size	Btm	Type
①	6/1		
②	6/2		
③	8/1		
④	6/1		
⑤	6/1		
⑥	8/3		
⑦	6/1		
⑧	6/2		
⑨	8/2		
⑩	6/2		
⑪	10/2		
⑫	8/3		

Storms originating in the Gulf of Alaska generate most of the better swells that lash the coastline of British Columbia, from late September through March. Other SW-W swells come all the way across the Pacific from Japan, or are caused by more localized weather systems. In summer, the distant Southern Hemisphere swells have a lesser effect, particularly on southern Vancouver Island, which is blocked by Washington's Olympic Peninsula across the Strait of Juan de Fuca. Winter swells vary between 3-15ft (1-5m), lighting up the sheltered pointbreaks, while summer surf favours the beaches between Tofino and Long Beach. NW wind is dominant in summer while winter gets more W and SW. Spring tides are 10ft (3m) max, affecting some rivermouth cobblestone breaks. Check La Perouse Buoy Forecast.

SURF STATISTICS	J F	M A	M J	J A	S O	N D
dominant swell	SW-NW	SW-NW	SW-NW	SW-NW	SW-NW	SW-NW
swell size (ft)	7-8	6-7	4-5	3-4	6	7-8
consistency (%)	30	60	70	50	80	60
dominant wind	S-W	SW-NW	W-N	W-N	W-N	S-W
average force	F5	F4	F4	F3-F4	F4	F5
consistency (%)	47	50	60	68	49	49
water temp.(°C)	7	9	11	15	14	10
wetsuit						

219. Humboldt County

Summary
+ Big, consistent swells
+ Uncrowded Californian surf
+ Offshore winds during storms
+ Beautiful scenery
+ Huge redwood trees

– Onshore winds and fog
– Swells often too gnarly
– Harsh climate
– Cold water
– Great white sharks

North Humboldt is a beautiful and dramatic destination, home to giant redwood trees and no shortage of big, heavy surf. It is a rugged, cold-water zone that appeals to a certain type of surfer, and although not obviously a world-class surf trip, North Humboldt can produce excellent winter waves. The spots are all beachbreaks, with a few exceptions around Trinidad. The surf is very consistent, challenging, and rewarding for those who like to charge.

Heading south from Orick, **Freshwater Lagoon** is a commonly surfed spot in the Humboldt Lagoons State Park due to its proximity to Highway 101. Small, peaky swells are needed and the ever-changing sandbars make it a real lottery particularly further south at **Stone Lagoon** and **Dry Lagoon**. **Big Lagoon** is usually the least surfable, featuring nasty shoredump, apart from when the lagoon overflows into the sea, creating a decent sandbar. All of the beaches behind the lagoons are fickle, waiting for the

optimum conditions of clean, small swell, lower tide and E wind. All of these waves can suffer badly from strong currents and there's bound to be few sharks around. At the north end of Patrick's Point State Park, **Agate Beach** is a thick, righthand barrel that is fast and shallow. Hazards include crowds, scattered rocks and a gnarly shorebreak. Along the headland is **Patrick's Point** itself, a long, powerful left with several sections and an ability to handle huge

TRAVEL INFORMATION

Local Population: 58,000
Coastline: 89km (59mi)
Contests: Local
Other Resources:
surfrider.org/humboldt
stormriderguides.com

Getting There – US visa necessary for many nationalities. The nearest international airport is San Francisco (SFO). From there, fly directly to the Eureka-Arcata Airport, which is in McKinleyville. Take U.S. Highway 101 to Eureka if travelling by road. Greyhound services all towns in the area.

Getting Around – Rental cars are available at the airport and in Arcata and Eureka (an economy size costs approx. $35/d), and are essential to explore the region. Gas costs about $2.75/gallon. Since most of the surf spots are located along Highway 101, it's easy to find them. Get a local map before heading out.

Lodging and Food – Eureka has hotels and hostels catering for every budget. Arcata also offers a choice of accommodation, but hotels are cheaper in Eureka. Trinidad and the Patrick's Point area have a couple of expensive B&Bs. There is a campsite near to North Jetty at the Samoa Boat Ramp County Park. Further north are the campgrounds at Clam Beach, Patrick's Point, Big Lagoon, Freshwater Lagoon, Gold Bluffs, and Prairie Creek. Good food is available in all of the towns.

WEATHER STATISTICS	J/F	M/A	M/J	J/A	S/O	N/D
total rainfall (mm)	267	153	50	14	76	256
consistency (days/mth)	20	15	8	5	15	20
min temp (°C)	5	6	9	12	10	6
max temp (°C)	12	13	15	16	16	13

Weather – The weather in North Humboldt is never dull. Winter is very rainy and windy, with consistent big swell. Spring has stiff, cold northwest wind, sunnier days, and colder water due to upwelling. Summer is usually very foggy, with small to medium-sized and usually junky waves, plus the coldest water of the year. Autumn is the best chance to score good waves and weather simultaneously. A year-round fullsuit as well as booties, gloves, and hood are required.

Nature and Culture – Eureka is an unremarkable city, but heading north past Arcata, the renowned Redwood Coast scenery begins, featuring the biggest trees in the world. Arcata is an interesting, progressive college town with plenty to do, whilst Trinidad is a quaint old fishing village. North of Trinidad is some of California's prettiest landscape. The Plaza in Arcata has the best nightlife in the region.

Hazards and Hassles – The biggest hazards are the large, unpredictable waves and heavy currents. North Humboldt is also a haven for white sharks, and shark attacks are fairly common. Rocks can be a problem at spots like Trinidad and Patrick's Point. The area is not known for friendly locals.

Handy Hints – A bigger board and a thick wetsuit along with booties, gloves, and hood are necessary to surf Humboldt waves. This area is cold, sharky and powerful - all of these extremes should be planned for. Pleasant surprises await those who don't expect too much.

swells, but beware of sketchy boils and exposed boulders. Patrick's Point is best at high tide in a southeast wind, on a clean west-northwest swell, 8-20ft+ (2.5-6m+). When the swell is big, the inside beachbreak shuts down, making it hard to get in and out. On smaller days, a crowd is possible. **College Cove** is a sheltered bay, so it's good in big swells and protected from the prevailing NW wind, which also makes it a haven for nudists. **Trinidad State Beach** is generally an average, rocky beachbreak in scenic surroundings. It's very much the poor cousin of **Camel Rock** to the south. This popular beach can resemble a righthand point in good swells, holding 3-8ft (1-2.5m) depending on the banks. Next to the Camel Rock is a good paddling channel, one of the reasons this beach gets very crowded. **Moonstone Beach** also attracts the crowds to its wide, flat sands, often perfect for beginner's, although sometimes it fires on a peaky W swell with any E wind. There has been 4 documented non-fatal attacks on surfers and regular shark sightings here. Near Arcata airport, **Clam Beach** has an uneven bottom and usually closes out. For this reason, it is rarely surfed despite a clear view of the break from the Redwood Highway 101. Clam also has heavy currents and pulls a lot of swell. **Mad River Beach** is a sharky, dangerous break that is quite isolated. As with all the waves in this area, small, clean swells with a high tide and east winds are the ideal conditions. Along the north spit above Eureka, **Bunkers**, Bay Street, and Power Lines are all sandbars that can have good waves. Bunkers itself holds giant, perfect cloudbreak, resembling a cold Sunset Beach on the best days. The **North Jetty** of the Humboldt Bay entrance is justifiably famous. Intense, hollow rights and long lefts form off the jetty, with a river-like paddling channel against the wall. Generally, lower tide is better, but North Jetty can break on any tide. The peak can handle triple-overhead plus – a SE wind and 3-12ft (1-4m) northwest swell is perfect. The jetty is the hub of surfing in North Humboldt so it is often crowded. South of the jetty, an experts-only, black-diamond wave breaks. The Humboldt Bay **Harbor Entrance** is known amongst mariners as the most dangerous in the state. For surfers, a thick sand-bottom peak breaks right in the entrance. Access and exit is by jumping off and then clawing back onto the jetty. Serious lefts, and steep, dredging rights that barrel into the 45-foot-deep (15m) boat channel make this place strictly for the experienced. Handling 8-18'+ (2.5-5.4m+), the Harbor Entrance also has

Big Lagoon

treacherous currents. It should be surfed an hour before and up to an hour after low tide. An outgoing tide sucks hard out to sea, whilst on an incoming tide the rip pulls directly into the impact zone. The Harbor Entrance is the heaviest wave around, attracting many of the top surfers in the area.

SURF STATISTICS	J F	M A	M J	J A	S O	N D
dominant swell	NW	NW	NW	NW	NW	NW
swell size (ft)	12-20	10-15	6-10	4-8	6-15	12-20
consistency (%)	99	85	65	30	60	95
dominant wind	SE-NW	NW	NW	NW	NW	NW-SE
average force	F5	F4	F3	F3	F3-F4	F4-F5
consistency (%)	85	80	70	50	50	75
water temp.(°C)	9	10	10	10	10	10
wetsuit						

The major source of waves for North Humboldt is the Gulf of Alaska in autumn/winter (Oct-Mar), with powerful storms brewing swell ranging in size from 3-40ft (1-13m). Storms originating off Japan also produce long-range, organised groundswell. Late spring through summer (May-Sept), waves can originate from either big southerly groundswells or locally generated windswells, but it is usually the latter, accompanied by lots of sea-fog and frigid water. Dominant winds are NW, often blowing cold and hard during spring (Mar-June) and bringing fog during summer (June-Sept). A few spots like the Harbor Entrance and Camel Rock can handle NW wind. Storm SE winds can blow offshore at every other spot in the winter. Tides are a factor at all spots, particularly the beachbreaks. Full cold water rubber necessary.

SURF STATISTICS			
Spot	Size	Btm	Type
1	6/1		
2	6/1		
3	6/1		
4	6/1		
5	10/4		
6	25/5		
7	6/2		
8	6/1		
9	10/1		
10	6/1		
11	6/1		
12	6/1		
13	15/2		
14	20/6		
15	15/2		

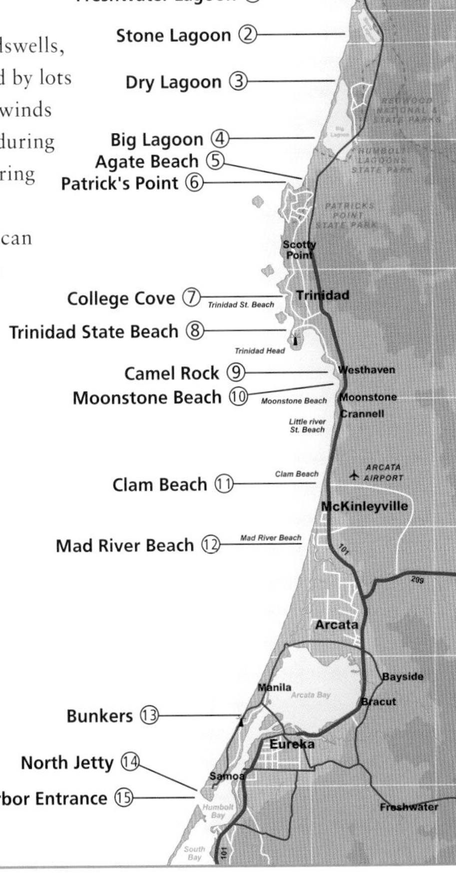

Camel Rock

220. New Jersey

Casino Pier

SMUGGLER

Summary
+ Good winter consistency
+ Winter morning offshores
+ Heaps of breaks
+ Some powerful waves
+ Proximity to NYC

– Beachbreak only
– Rippy when big
– Beach tags in summer
– Pollution
– "Bennies" summer invasion

New Jersey, the most densely populated state of the USA, got its name from the largest of the English Channel Islands, Jersey. Inhabited by Native Americans for more than 2,800 years, the first European settlements in the area were established by the Swedes and Dutch in the early 1600s. No one spotted the surf potential until 1912 and the visit of Duke Kahanamoku, which marks the debut of surfing on the East Coast. With 127 miles of coastline and a myriad of jetties, NJ boasts the most powerful, challenging beachbreaks on the East Coast. Long, straight barrier islands, punctuated by frequent inlets or jetties, are home to one of the largest East Coast surfing populations. While Jersey has plenty of wave potential, it is also home to 108 toxic waste dumps and it's one of the few states in the USA where you have to pay for the privilege of using the beach in the summer - about $6 a day!

Atlantic City

PAUL KENNEDY

Casino Pier

ANDREW DEMING

TRAVEL INFORMATION

Local Population: New Jersey 8.5M
Coastline: 130mi (210km)
Time Zone: GMT -5
Contests: 1983 OP Pro East
Other Resources:
njsurfingclub.com
nynjsurf.com
atlanticsurfsessions.com
stormriderguides.com

Getting There – No visa. Atlantic City lies 1hr from Philadelphia airport (PHL) and 2hrs from Newark (EWR). NJ Transit trains connect EWR to the northern spots (Allenhurst, Manasquan...) and also PHL to Atlantic City. NJ Transit bus line #319 goes from NYC to the southern spots (Atlantic City to Cape May). Boards allowed but avoid peak hours.

Getting Around – Public transport is not an easy option for the surfer. Unless you know someone in the area, book a rental car/van (from $230/wk - over 21), but get ready for nightmarish parking in summer. Gas is still pretty cheap. Access is easy unless private property faces the spot or beach tags season is on.

Lodging and Food – Large choice of accommodation (especially in Wildwood area), from basic motels ($50/dble) to luxury hotels. Prices usually double in summer, book in advance. Try Super 8 Motel in Atlantic City. Blueberry Campground (13mi from AC) has 4pax rental trailers for $540/wk. Huge portion, fast-food restaurants everywhere, but finding healthy food means searching and paying more.

WEATHER STATISTICS	J/F	M/A	M/J	J/A	S/O	N/D
total rainfall (mm)	84	92	77	102	73	86
consistency (days/mth)	11	11	9	10	8	11
min temp (°C)	-5	2	12	18	9	0
max temp (°C)	5	13	24	29	22	10

Weather – Atlantic City is separated from the mainland by a series of low-lying meadows and a narrow strait. The Atlantic Ocean helps moderate the continental climate and summers are humid and warm with an average temp of 75°F (24°C). Winters are cold with temps between 23-50°F (-5-10°C). Average rainfall is about 42in (1050mm) and evenly distributed, unless hurricanes bring heavy rainfall. Violent spring storms have damaged beachfront property over the years, and floods are not uncommon. Conditions in New Jersey change quickly: be prepared for 52°F (11°C) water in July and 75°F (24°C) air in January! Check the weather report. From November to April, use a 5/4mm fullsuit with boots, gloves and hood. A 3/2mm fullsuit or a springsuit are fine during summer.

Nature and Culture – Beach and gambling are the big attractions. Climb the 228-steps of Atlantic City's historic Absecon Lighthouse to check the sandbanks. Roller coasters all over the place. Seafood Festival each June in Belmar, where you can skydive too. Whale watching from Cape May peninsula, also visit the Cape May Point State Park. NYC is close.

Hazards and Hassles – The numerous jetties and piers are not kind to boards or bodies! Sharks are around, but attacks very rarely occur (last one in Surf City, June 2005). NJ beaches are among the worst places on the planet for biting greenhead flies, and jellyfish swarms occasionally blow in. Lock car well and don't leave valuables. Newark, NYC and other nearby city tourists ("Bennies") arrive in droves from early June to Labor Day, when beach tags are enforced by local councils.

Handy Hints – The Jersey shore is loaded with about 60 good surf shops. The perfect Jersey quiver would include a longboard for the small, busy summer waves, an all-round shortboard, plus a longer thruster for high performance in large surf. Many surf schools all along the coast.

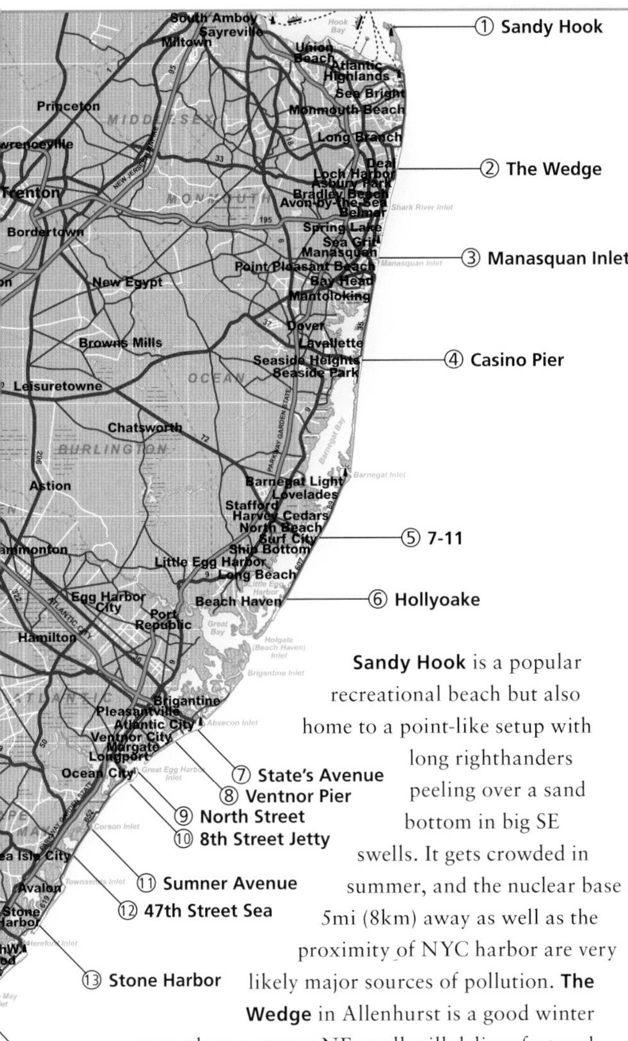

Sandy Hook is a popular recreational beach but also home to a point-like setup with long righthanders peeling over a sand bottom in big SE swells. It gets crowded in summer, and the nuclear base 5mi (8km) away as well as the proximity of NYC harbor are very likely major sources of pollution. **The Wedge** in Allenhurst is a good winter spot where a strong NE swell will deliver fast and bowling lefthanders near a crescent-shaped jetty.

The tight takeoff zone is often busy, and paddling out can be difficult with rocky surprises. **Manasquan Inlet** is generally regarded as the best wave in Jersey, and as a consequence it gets heavily crowded with some localism. On a S/SE swell and a low tide, you can surf long, fast, hollow barrelling rights that can hold serious size. Another focal point of Jersey surfing is the **Casino Pier** in Seaside Heights. It's a real crowd-puller to both the mad boardwalk scene as well as the wind-protected, left and right options up to double overhead, either side of the massive pier. You can explore the 10mi (16km) stretch of the wild Island Beach State Park that extends further south, but there's more chances of finding great waves in Surf City. The spot known as **7-11** works all-year-round, with all tides and swell directions and is perfect for beginners. **Hollyoake** in Beach Haven has a bay-like setup that produces long, punchy lefts on a NE swell with quite good NW wind protection. Atlantic City is a hectic place with luxurious casinos, non-stop gaming action, hot nightlife and heavy beach activity in summer. It's the world's longest boardwalk (6mi/9km) and home to several spots, like **States Avenue** (aka Gas Chambers), which accepts any swell, serving up long left walls off the wooden groin and the rights off the steel pier have a high barrel potential. No beach tags are needed, but it's almost impossible to park. Neighbouring **Ventnor Pier**

Asbury Park

SMUGGLER

is also a magnet for all swell directions and big summer crowds. Other side of the Great Egg Harbor Inlet lies Ocean City, where **North Street** jetty is the most consistent break around, always bigger in size and larger in crowds. **8th Street Jetty** is a famous contest site thanks to it's year-round consistency and ability to handle plenty of size, but then paddling out gets very tricky. A good beginner spot and longboard heaven is **Sumner Avenue** in Strathmere, which catches the smallest E-S swells and improves with the tide. Long lefthanders for all standards are on offer at Sea Isle's **47th Street** jetty on a NE swell, and preferably from low to mid tide. Facing a huge convent, **Stone Harbor** is another fun wave for everyone, from beginner to high intermediate. Cape May is the country's oldest seaside resort, with good S swell exposure and excellent NW to NE wind protection, attracting crowds to the best spots. Bigger swells create lefthanders off the jetty in **Stockton**, but the sandbars are ever-changing with erosion and replenishment activity. **Broadway** is the spot everyone hits when it's huge and NE, fighting over the jetty lefts and a few bowly rights down the beach.

SURF STATISTICS

Spot	Size	Btm	Type
①	12/2		
②	8/2		
③	15/2		
④	12/2		
⑤	8/2		
⑥	12/2		
⑦	15/2		
⑧	15/2		
⑨	10/2		
⑩	18/2		
⑪	8/2		
⑫	12/2		
⑬	10/2		
⑭	8/2		
⑮	8/2		

Low or high pressure systems and tropical disturbances are the main swell sources. Typical swells are S and NE windswells. The "nor'easters" (lows that intensify while moving up the Atlantic Coast) usually bring head-high to double overhead surf for 2 to 4 days. Depending on their position, high pressure systems can create NE windswells from fall to spring. In summer, Bermuda Highs can push S windswell to the NJ shores, but tropical storms and hurricanes in late summer and fall remain the best source for heavy groundswell, creating many days of classic, overhead surf as they approach from the S. Winds are lightest in summer with afternoon S seabreezes. The winds usually stay offshore more in fall and winter after storms and can get quite gusty from late fall to early spring. There is usually always wind at some point in the day, and Jersey has extremely variable swell, wind and weather. Expect a maximum tidal range of 5ft (1.5m) on springs.

ANDREW DEMING

Monmouth Beach

SURF STATISTICS	J F	M A	M J	J A	S O	N D
dominant swell	NE-S	NE-S	NE-S	NE-S	NE-S	NE-S
swell size (ft)	5-6	4-5	3-4	2-3	4-5	5-6
consistency (%)	70	60	50	40	60	70
dominant wind	W-N	SW-N	S-SW	S-SW	N-NE	W-N
average force	F5	F4-F5	F4	F4	F4	F4-F5
consistency (%)	59	49	39	45	35	57
water temp.(°C)	3	8	15	21	18	9
wetsuit						

221. Great Lakes

Steamers, Lake Michigan

SETH TYLER

Summary
+ Unique freshwater experience
+ Rare crowds
+ Quality surf possible
+ Inland surf culture
+ Great local camaraderie

– Inconsistent
– Long drives required
– Ice and thick rubber
– Pollution
– Private access to some breaks

Glaciers gouged out the 5 Great Lakes, creating the biggest lake system on the planet, containing 6 quadrillion gallons, or one fifth of the world's freshwater supplies. Their total shoreline, including islands and channels, extends for some 10,900 miles (17,549km), more than the US West and East coasts combined! The sheer size and concomitant fetch of these lakes explain the presence of surprisingly large, surfable waves with the right weather conditions. Because the system extends over 700mi (1120km) from W to E and 500mi (800km) from N to S, a surf experience on the NW shore of Lake Superior can be vastly different from a session on one of Erie's southeastern beaches. The first Great Lakes surfer was a GI returning from Hawaii with a longboard in 1945, but surfing really started to grow on the eastern shore of lake Michigan and north-eastern corner of Lake Erie from 1963/64. Despite

Inside Grand Haven channel

INGRID LINDFORS

SETH TYLER

TRAVEL INFORMATION

Local Population: Michigan 10M
Coastline: 10,900mi (17,549km incl. channels, mainland and islands)
Time Zone: GMT -4 to -5
Contests: Dairyland Surf Classic (for 20 years)
Log Jam Surf Club Invitational
Great Lakes Surf Luau
Other Resources:
thirdcoastsurfshop.com
greatlakesurfing.com
superiorsurfclub.com
great-lakes.net
greatlakes.org (env)
Video: Unsalted, 2005

Getting There – No visa. Coming from abroad, most int'l flights will land in Chicago (ORD) or Detroit (DTW). Toronto (YYZ) can be another option. It's easy to get cheap flights from all over the Americas or Europe.

Getting Around – Public transport exists, but it's not convenient with boards. Due to huge distances between spots, rent a car with unlimited mileage ($200/wk). Driving from Chicago to Sheboygan takes 2.5h, 4h to Detroit and 8h to Duluth or Toronto. Heavy traffic around major towns.

Lodging and Food – Basic motels ($70/dble) to luxury hotels. Lower rates out of summer. Try Fountain Park Motel (down to $40/dble) in Sheboygan. The cultural diversity means a huge variety of food in the Great Lakes region.

WEATHER STATISTICS	J/F	M/A	M/J	J/A	S/O	N/D
total rainfall (mm)	50	55	75	80	84	72
consistency (days/mth)	12	12	12	9	10	13
min temp (°C)	-13	-7	5	12	4	-8
max temp (°C)	-2	11	23	26	18	4

Weather – The Great Lakes have a continental temperate climate with 4 distinct seasons. Winters are generally long and cold with night temps below 32°F (0°C). The moisture picked up by the prevailing winds from the west can produce very heavy snowfall, especially along lakeshores to the east such as Michigan, Ohio, Pennsylvania, Ontario, and New York. Storms can bring combinations of rain, snow, freezing rain and sleet with annual average rainfall about 40in (1000mm). During summer, storms pass to the north and warm, humid weather with occasional thunderstorms is followed by days of mild, dry weather. The lakes moderate seasonal temperatures by absorbing heat and cooling the air in summer, then slowly radiating that heat in autumn. From November to April use a 6/5mm fullsuit with boots/gloves/hood, a 4/3 either side of summer, when a 3/2mm should do.

Nature and Culture – The lakes are exploited for their natural resources and mistreated for economic gain. Water quality across the lakes is variable. Sewage systems are designed to overflow into the lakes. Introduction of many non-native and invasive species like sea lampreys or zebra mussel are a real threat. Heaps of culture in major towns (Art Attack in Sheboygan, early May).

Hazards and Hassles – Cold shock and hypothermia are real dangers. Wave action can break up frozen sheets of shoreline ice sending big chunks into the line-up, creating heavy obstacles. Piers and jetties concentrate wave energy, but surfing close to them can be risky. The lakes are prone to sudden and severe storms, particularly in the autumn. Access to the coast can be a problem and surfing is currently banned in Chicago.

Handy Hints – From boardshorts in summer to hooded 6 mil wetsuit for late fall and winter, along with thick gloves & booties. Rental and lessons only available at the great Third Coast Surf Shop (New Buffalo, Michigan), Windward Sports in Chicago, Superior Surf System in Duluth, and TWC near Detroit. Use Vaseline on your face in winter.

poor consistency (about 10 surfable days per month in season) and often inhospitable conditions, there are more freshwater surfers joining the line-ups each year.

Lake Superior is the largest surface, deepest and coldest of the Great Lakes, and unsurprisingly, has the biggest surfable waves. Its western end hosts the best spots, with optimal conditions being a strong, long duration, NE wind, followed by offshore NW. Bordering the town of Duluth, **Lester River** (aka L-train) is a potentially excellent left point next to the rivermouth. **French River** is an easier spot with reef and shore breaks. Superior's best wave is **Stoney Point**, a steep, powerful, reef peak that gets big in NE blizzards. Long rides here and round the headland at Boulders. Other areas to check are the eastern end and southern fringe of Superior, plus the western base of the Keweenaw. With numerous cities and more than 70 potential spots, Lake Michigan is the most surfed lake. Sheboygan, Wisconsin, works in any N or rare SE windswells and **North Point** moulds hollow lefthanders with board-breaking power. **Elbow** is a soft, but long right, peeling off the bend in the breakwater. Racine breaks on all E wind/swell variations at the uncrowded breaks of **Wind Point**. The Chicago city beachbreaks are best with spring N/NE winds and all the Illinois breaks from Chicago up to Zion will work on a NW wind. Grand Haven is surf central in Michigan, and the **South Pier** handles the bigger SW to NW windchop, plus there's easy access from the end of the pier and more jetty breaks to the south. Indiana's short coast has some waves around Michigan City. Lake Huron is the least explored and it's history of numerous shipwrecks, hints at the size and power of the surf. Dominant winds flow more S to W, so the best waves hit the long, sandy beaches of Ontario. Peeling off the south side of the **Harbor Jetty** at Bayfield is a noted bigger wave right. With a NW or SW wind, **Sauble Beach** can offer mellow to juicy waves, popular with kiters. In the southern confines of Georgian Bay, there are a few reefbreaks that break with size in the rarer NW gales. Lake Erie is the smallest of the lakes and the only one to completely freeze in winter. Consistent SW winds means the biggest waves will hit the New York State coast beachbreaks from Buffalo down to Dunkirk and the pointbreak at **Wright Park Beach Point**. A man-made jetty/reef holds tricky, rocky rights at **Palmwood Point**, Crystal Beach in large SW to W windswells. **Pleasant Beach** shows more shape and power for shortboarders. Lake Ontario is far deeper than Erie, so longer duration windswells give the chance of a cleaner wave after the wind has died down. In summer, an E breeze is prevalent and sometimes strong enough to fuel some decent spots. The rocky, cobblestone shore at Grimsby leads into the long established surf spots around **The Bridge** and beaches of Hamilton. Toronto beachbreaks can pick up the SW windchop as it heads towards **Sandbanks**, which picks up all available swell along its 8km (5mi) of beach, reef, and pointbreaks. **Stony Point** receives the biggest Ontario lefts and rights over a dangerous rocky bottom.

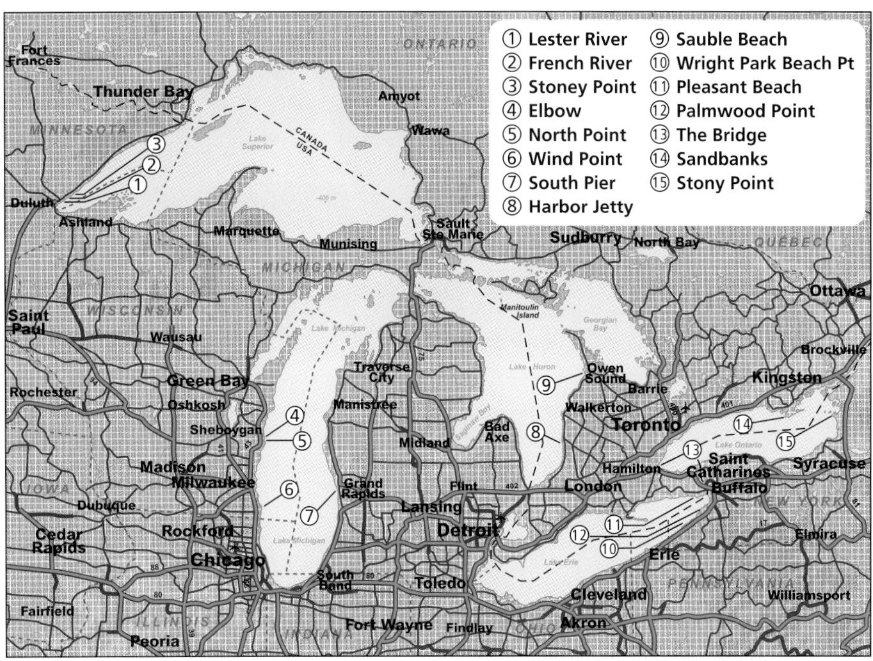

Fetch is the key element in Great Lakes wave formation. Several hours of wind blowing in excess of 20 knots over 50mi (80km) of water produces surfable waves. The largest waves on the lakes easily surpass 10ft (3m) faces, and waves more than 20ft (6m) are occasionally recorded, usually in spring and fall. In summer, wind speeds are at their lowest, so surfable days are few and far between. In fall, the clash of warm and cold air masses through the region produce strong winds. In winter, inhospitable conditions (shelf ice, snow) make surfing pretty difficult. Like autumn, spring is characterized by variable and sometimes volatile weather. SW winds resume their dominance as warmer air and increased sunshine begin to melt snow and ice, but the lakes are slow to warm (10-15°C by end of May).

SURF STATISTICS	J F	M A	M J	J A	S O	N D
dominant wind	W-N	N-S	N-S	S-SW	NW-S	NW-SW
average force	F5-F6	F5	F4-F5	F4	F4-F5	F5-F6
consistency (%)	52	36	38	42	50	53
water temp.(°C)	3	5	10	18	14	6
wetsuit						

SURF STATISTICS

Spot	Size	Btm	Type
①	8/2		
②	6/2		
③	10/3		
④	10/3		
⑤	8/3		
⑥	6/2		
⑦	8/3		
⑧	6/2		
⑨	6/2		
⑩	6/2		
⑪	8/3		
⑫	8/2		
⑬	6/2		
⑭	6/2		
⑮	8/2		

SETH TYLER

Stoney Point

NSP®

the most Fun in Surfing
NSPSURFBOARDS.COM

Surf explorers and even Hollywood producers were drawn to El Salvador's righthand points, until civil war broke out, effectively keeping the wild east and Punta Mango in the shade until the late '90s.

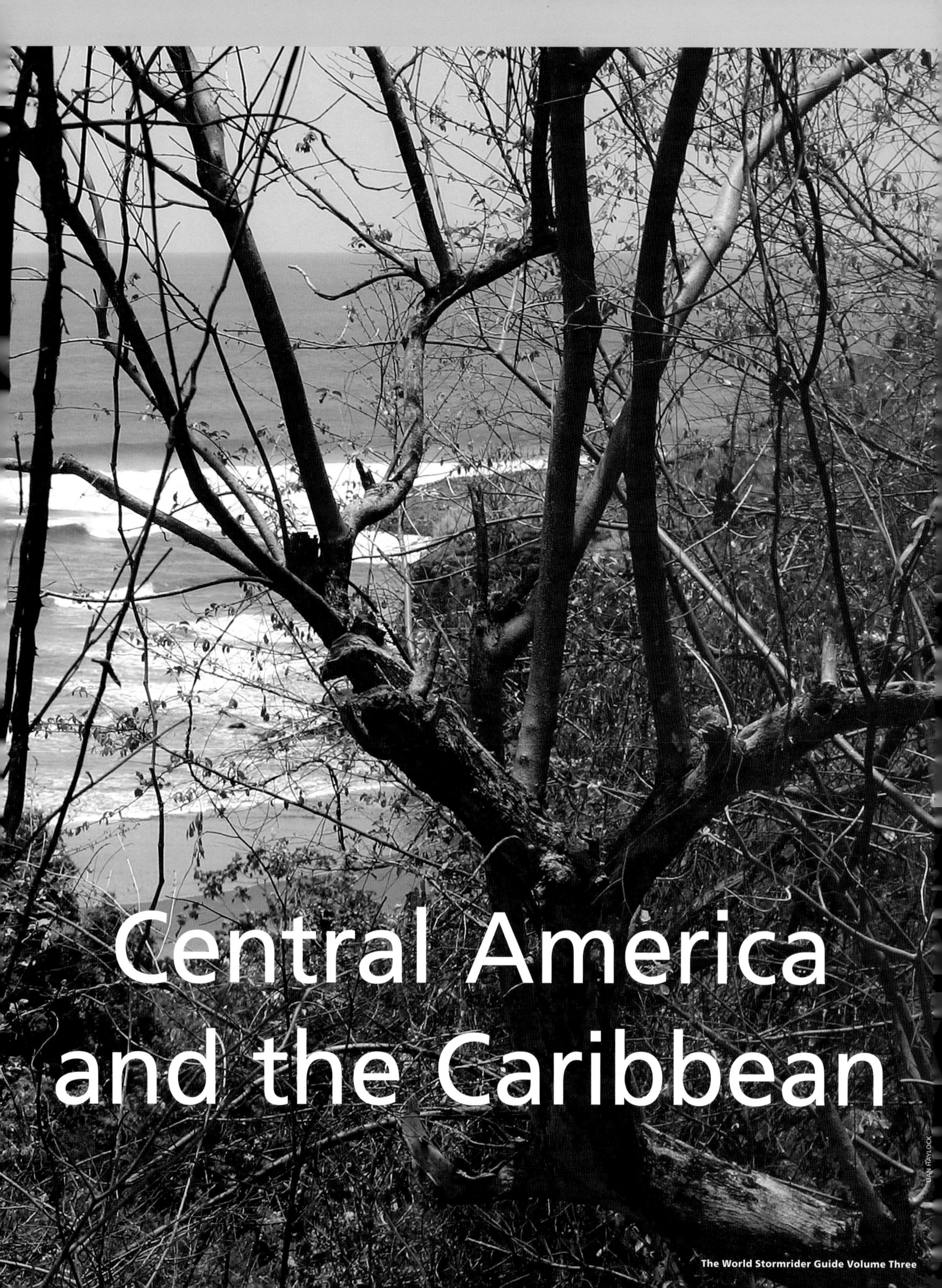

Central America and the Caribbean

DAN HAYLOCK

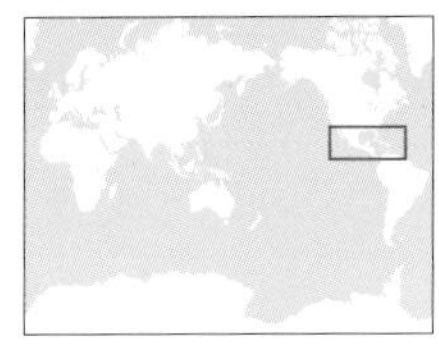

Surf Culture

The earliest forays south of the USA border were undertaken by San Diego surfers who didn't have far to go from the Tijuana Sloughs in the late '40s. Deeper drives into Mexico proper occurred once Bud Browne released *Surf Crazy* (1959) and Greg Noll's *Search For Surf* featured waves from their road trip to Acapulco and Mazatlan. Locals soon got their hands on boards and Baja duo Hernandez and Cota competed in the '66 World Champs. Meanwhile, Puerto Rican riders had tested the famous NW breaks by the start of the decade, before visitors like Butch Linden and Johnny Fain helped establish it's reputation for great winter waves, leading to Domes being the venue for the 1968 World Championships. Linden and Fain went on to pioneer breaks in Barbados in 1965, leaving boards behind for talented locals to quickly learn and field a team for Puerto Rico, three years later. Other Californian travellers brought boards to various Caribbean islands and by the late 60's, most of Jamaica's popular breaks were found by youngsters Cecil Ward, Pin Head, Apache, Gordon Cooper, Paul Blades or Ridgley, Jamaica's first black surfer. Back on the Pacific side, mid-60s trail blazers had wet their heads in Guatemala and El Salvador, avoided Nicaragua and chanced a few remote waves on both sides of Costa Rica, oblivious to it's future as one of the world's top surfing destinations. Panamanians had a head start from US surfers living in the Panama Canal Zone circa 1962, who would head west to escape the silted up Panama City breaks. A small team competed in the 1968 World's, but political upheaval kept surfing in obscurity for the '70s and '80s. Civil war did a similar job in El Salvador, despite the fact that surfing legends like Gerry Lopez and George Greenough spent a whole month there in 1977, shooting Hollywood surf flick *Big Wednesday.* Greenough was the first to sail down through Central America and stopped at both La Libertad and Panama's Santa Catalina, which was known as the "Island of the Moon". Multi-hull sailor/explorer Ted Vitally got chased from Nicaraguan waters in 1976, where harbours were full of soviet ships and entrances were mined. It was down to the wanderlust of 2 budding journalists, Kevin Naughton and Craig Peterson, to fully pique the surf world's interest in Central America when they took one of the greatest surf trips of all time, putting famous waves on the map like Petacalco and La Libertad, without ever naming them, in a series of *Surfer* articles starting in 1973. The '70s were a heyday for Puerto Rico, building on it's increased profile after the '68 World Champs and many a curious surfer looking to escape the growing crowds and find more consistency, struck out to neighbouring islands. The Bahamas had also been surfed right through the '60s, becoming a favourite with East Coasters and offering plenty of discovery potential for those with a sturdy boat to navigate the 100's of cays. Yacht's were the perfect tool for exploring the Windward Isles and sailors in the late '60s were the first to sample Carib juice on islands like Tortola in the British Virgin Islands. Patrick Abadie and Francois De Corlieu started surfing Guadeloupe mid '70s, and 10 years later the first club, Karukera, appeared. The '80s were the real discovery years for smaller islands like Antigua, Barbuda, Trinidad and Tobago, while Jamaica's more established scene had only just stumbled onto the country's best wave Zoo, which sadly got destroyed in the 2004 hurricane Ivan. Cuba's first surfers were Spanish and Quebec crews, but communism

DECKHAND ℅ BARRY CHURCH

***International Surfing Magazine* Caribbean exploratory on a windjammer in April 1969. From left to right. Joe Twombly, Dick Catri, Bill Saunter, Tim New, Barry Church (standing), Butch Van Artsdalen (hat), Chuck Dent, Bill Bolender and Paul Chapey. Yacht's were the perfect vehicle required to uncover the treasures of both the Windward and Leeward Isles. This crew pioneered many small island breaks including Martinique, where the local kids paddled out on logs.**

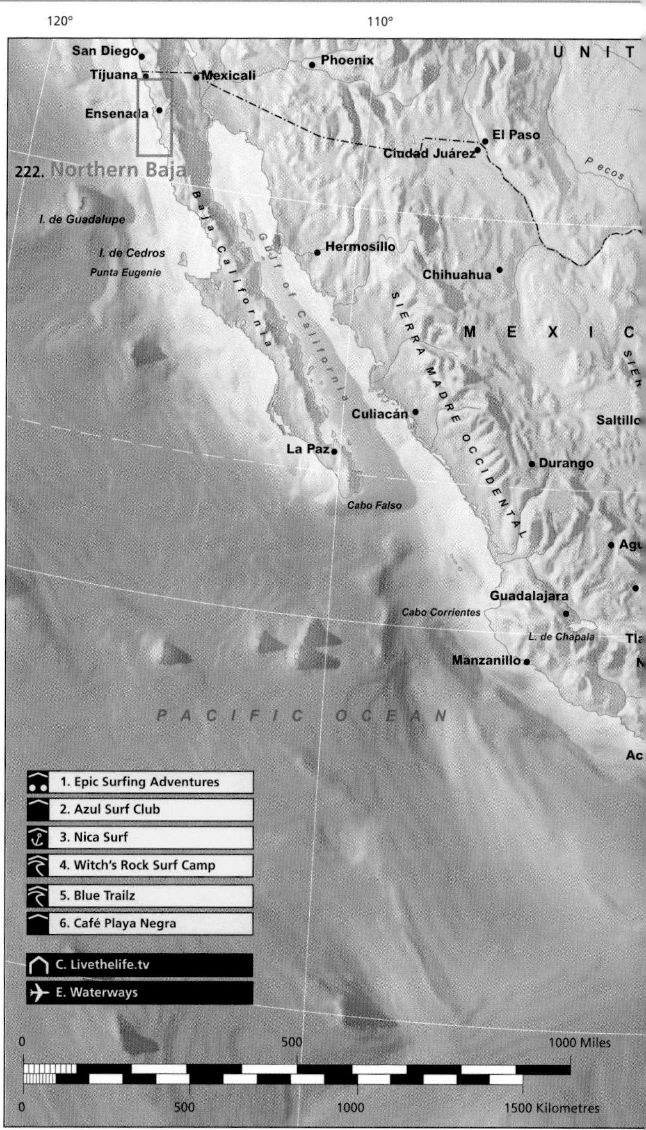

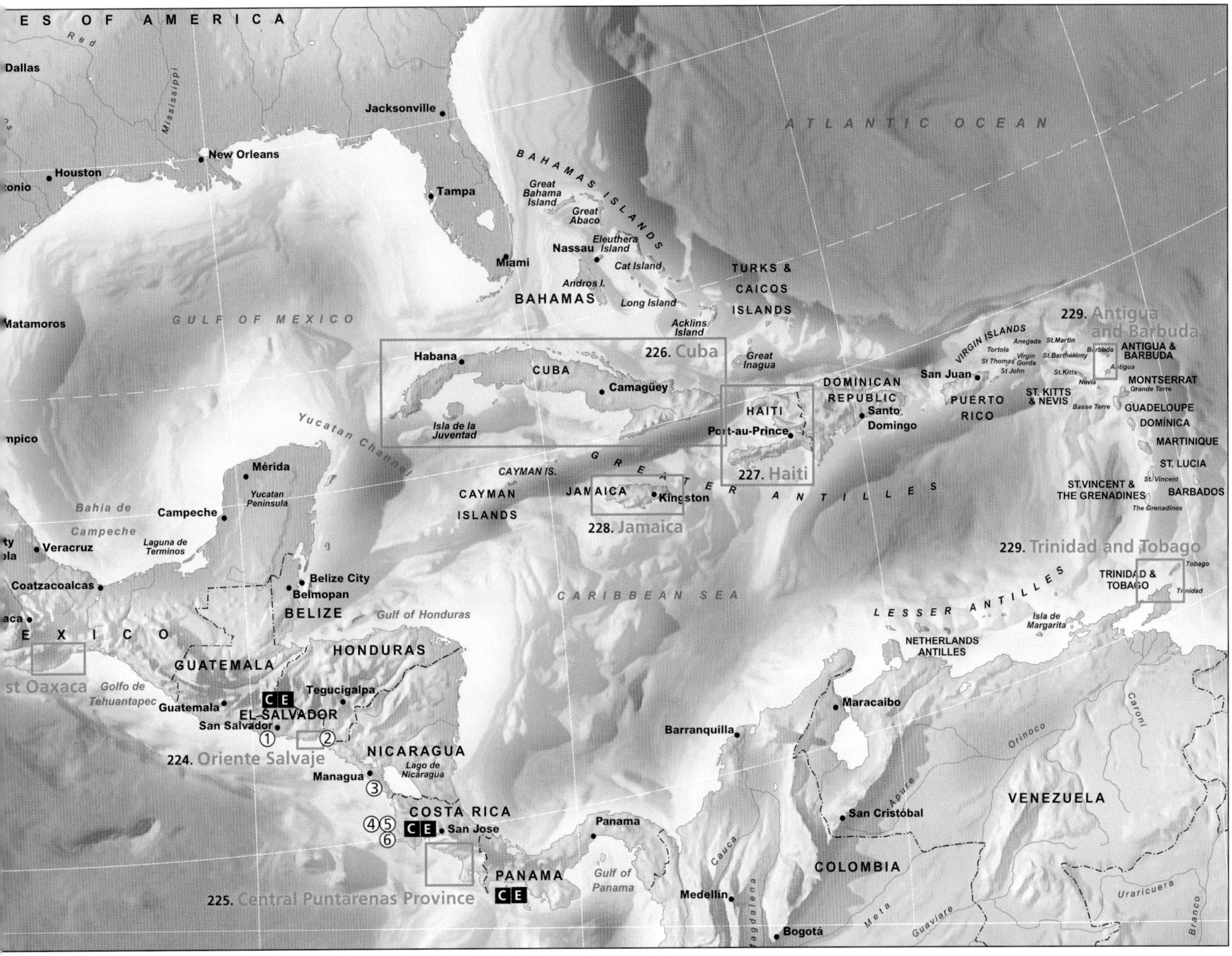

224. Oriente Salvaje
225. Central Puntarenas Province
226. Cuba
227. Haiti
228. Jamaica
229. Antigua and Barbuda
229. Trinidad and Tobago

kept line-ups empty until around 1993, when visiting pros left boards near Havana and the local kids Yoan, Tido and Felix started making their own boards from stringerless refrigeration foam and wooden fins.

Today

The biggest theme in Central America today is the phenomenon of gringo land ownership. From the new gated communities of Baja to the cutting up of virgin jungle in Panama, the big land grab has been going on for years. Costa Rica, seen as the most stable of CenAm governments has experienced the greatest impact with rocketing land prices forcing the estimated 1M tourists per annum to look at neighbouring Nicaragua and Panama for more affordable property. Many of Costa Rica's 100 or so surf shops and countless surf camps/accommodation/ transport outfits are run by foreigners/expats so the ±5000 local surfers have access to all equipment and services. Mexico has close to eight times this number of native surfers (and coastline), but far less shops and patchy surf tourist infrastructure. Caribbean surf scene is often split along a 30/70 local/visitor ratio, so tensions can arise quite easily, at both semi-secret spots and the big-name line-ups. Puerto Rico is fairly notorious for crowd factor and localism, while the small population islands like Barbados, Guadeloupe, Bahamas, Tortola and Tobago have some daunting crews dominating the best breaks. This also applies to Costa Rica at the busy Playas Negro, Grande and Jaco area where extra respect is demanded from the tourist hordes. Mexico and El Salvador can be dangerous places to travel, especially at night and surfers have recently become regular targets for armed robbers in Baja, while El Salvador has one of the world's highest murder rates, which increased 25% from 2004-07.

BARRY CHURCH

Fred Hemmings on one of his winning waves in the finals of the 1968 World Surfing Championships at Rincon, Puerto Rico.

222. Northern Baja

JAMIE BOTT

Summary
+ Quality right pointbreaks
+ Consistent winter swells
+ Year-round destination
+ Wind protected options
+ Cheap tacos, beer & tequila

– Lack of lefthanders
– Surprisingly cold water
– USA style crowds
– Basic accommodation
– Lots of potential dangers

US surfers have been crossing the clandestine-proof border into the Baja (Lower) California desert peninsula for decades. Baja constitutes the major getaway for Californian waveriders, who jump in the 4X4 and drive the Mex1 Highway as far south as possible, looking for countless, quality righthand pointbreaks, consistent beach and reefbreaks and cheaper, simpler living. For those seeking real adventure and remoteness, there is no need to drive too far, since Baja Norte has all the prerequisites to satisfy the intermediate to expert surfers. With the highway following the coast all the way down from the border to Ensenada, access to a varied range of breaks is simple.

San Miguel
GOOGLE EARTH ID 511 4955

JAMIE BOTT

On weaker S-NW swells, **Rosarito** has highly consistent beachbreak around the pier, plus reefs and rivermouths, where pollution and the nuclear power plant are concerns. This crowded party town offers waves year-round and for all levels, as well as good facilities. The right pointbreak at **Calafia** features disco music blaring from the cliff-side

TRAVEL INFORMATION

Local Population: 260,075
Coastline: 3,200km/1988mi Baja
Time Zone: GMT -6
Contests: No Fear Mexican Surf Fiesta, San Miguel
Other Resources:
clubmarenarentals.com
bajasurfadventures.com
bajaquest.com
Video:
Shack Therapy (2006)
Ten Toes Over (1994),
Siestas y Olas
Baja 3000

Getting There – $20 tourist card (included in plane fare) for stays up to 180 days. Passport required. Closest airport is Tijuana (TIJ). Aeroméxico and Mexicana are the largest Mexican airlines ($50 board fee), or land in San Diego/LA then cross the border. Mexican inter-city, low cost flights to TIJ with Aviacsa, Avolar or Volaris.

Getting Around – No San Diego rental companies allow their cars to be driven south of Ensenada, except Dollar, who require a Mexican insurance policy ($10/day). Tijuana prices are similar to SD. Most spots are reachable with a standard car, but a 4WD can be great to explore. Mex 1 Highway is the main axis as there are a lack of coastal roads between spots.

WEATHER STATISTICS	J/F	M/A	M/J	J/A	S/O	N/D
total rainfall (mm)	51	28	50	3	5	38
consistency (days/mth)	6	5	2	1	2	5
min temp (°C)	8	11	14	17	15	10
max temp (°C)	17	19	21	24	23	20

Lodging and Food – Several hotels for all prices (Colonial Motel in Rosarito $30/dle, Desert Inn Ensenada $70/dle). Club Marena at K38 rents houses, same at Las Gaviotas (fr $120/night). Baja Surf Adventures camp in Quatro Casas. Free-camping possible at places but campsites are safer and cheap (like at K38, around $15/vehicle). Great but spicy Mexican food!

Weather – There is a Mediterranean climate in San Miguel that can best be described as sunny, mild and dry. Fresh ocean breezes and strong sun mean temperatures average from 16°- 24°C (61-75°F) year-round, cooled by the California Current. The desert E Santa Anna wind drops temps during fall and winter. Winters are mild and windy, while a coastal fog occurs in early summer. Average annual rainfall is less than 100mm (4in) mostly from December to March. Bring a 2/2mm steamer or springy in the summer, and a 4/3 with optional booties in the winter. Mornings can be cool, with a strong offshore breeze hiking the chill factor. Cold currents also influence the summer months, so a thermal rash vest is useful.

Nature and Culture – Acres and acres of deserts and sand dunes! Ensenada is a fast-growing tourist destination. Good snorkelling and diving options; fishing is best during summer and fall. Whale watching at Ensenada from December through March. Strong winds offer great potential for kite/wind surf. Wine tasting and golf courses too.

Hazards and Hassles – Things can get nasty near the border so get past Ensenada to avoid hassles. Drugs, theft, drunk drivers, police, gun-crime, pot-holes, car breakdowns, summer flash-floods, scorpions, snakes, etc. Do not run out of gas, water or food in remote areas. Travelling US surfers have been robbed at gunpoint even in proper campsites.

Handy Hints – Most surf shops are in Tijuana, San Miguel & Ensenada. A 7-8'ft board is a good bet as many spots can handle large swells. Bring wax, extra leash, ding and first-aid kit. English is widely spoken, US dollar accepted everywhere.

San Miguel

IVAN MARTINEZ CORTEZ

bar, but is mushy without a strong S swell and gets rocky at low tide. **K38**, aka El Morro, is a famous but very crowded right, peeling fast and hollow over an urchin farm. Best on a S swell, or a stronger W to NW pulse at low to mid. Working on similar swells but higher tides, **K38.5** is another fast, walled-up right reef plus a left across the bay. Escape the thicker crowds by paddling to **K39**, an outside-breaking reef able to produce quality lefts and rights in any sizeable swell. Facing a guarded condo community, the semi-private reef off **Las Gaviotas** is more of a longboard wave for all levels. Sometimes sectiony and often crowded, it prefers a due S swell. **K55/Campo Lopez** is a very consistent setup similar to K38, where juicy barrels are common especially at the point on a NW swell. Urchins constitute the main crowd, except at the decent beachbreak just N of the rocks. Campo guards try to restrict access for non-guests. Busy **K58/La Fonda** is where the best-shaped beachbreak in the area delivers very consistent barrelling lefts and rights, especially near the rivermouth. At size, paddling out can be punishing. The crowded campsite offers a good party scene. **Salsipuedes**, the legendary right pointbreak, will soon be a retirement haven of 2,680 residences, and public road access is history since 2007. Having a boat is now the only way to enjoy the inconsistent, fast peeling rights at the point or the reef peak facing the ex-campground. Therefore, the epic right point of **San Miguel** will get over crowded when a W to NW swell fuels fast, powerful, tubing waves at the cobblestone rivermouth. It's more hollow, but more sectiony at low tide. Ensenada is the jumping-off point for Baja's most famous big-wave spot, **Killers**, 20km (12mi) offshore on the Islas Todos Santos. An underwater canyon maximizes long period W-NW swell energy down the point, creating huge, powerful and shifty deepwater waves. South of Ensenada, the highway leaves the coast and dirt trails lead to wind protected rights like **Santo Tomas**, a south-facing point plus some rocky beachbreak. There are accommodation options, unlike at **San Antonio del Mar**, where free-camping is the best way to enjoy the uncrowded and consistent beachbreaks. **Cabo Colonet** likes a solid S to W swell to kick-start the long but inconsistent rights hugging the cliff. Endangered by a project to build the third-largest port in the world. Construction would also threaten the fun but busy right pointbreak and reefs of **Quatro Casas**, best on a S swell and there's an excellent campsite on the bluffs that protect the break from NW wind. **Shipwrecks/Freighters** is best on a wrapping NW swell and holds some size. N Wind protection is good, but the beached ship right in the line-up can shorten the long, mellow rights. There are some excellent reef options around to escape the crowds generated by the surf camp. A similar but more consistent and quieter pointbreak is found at **Punta Camalú**, with reef and beachbreak options up and down the cove.

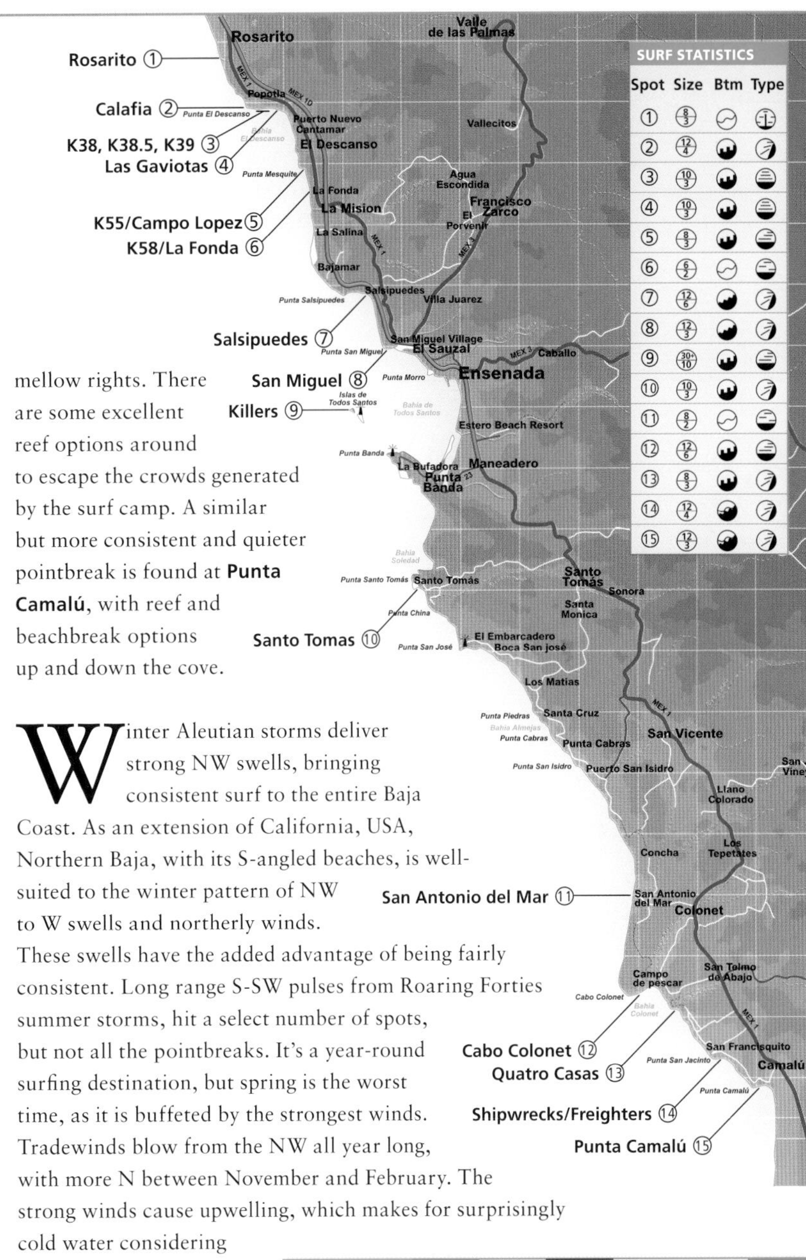

Winter Aleutian storms deliver strong NW swells, bringing consistent surf to the entire Baja Coast. As an extension of California, USA, Northern Baja, with its S-angled beaches, is well-suited to the winter pattern of NW to W swells and northerly winds. These swells have the added advantage of being fairly consistent. Long range S-SW pulses from Roaring Forties summer storms, hit a select number of spots, but not all the pointbreaks. It's a year-round surfing destination, but spring is the worst time, as it is buffeted by the strongest winds. Tradewinds blow from the NW all year long, with more N between November and February. The strong winds cause upwelling, which makes for surprisingly cold water considering the latitude. Mixed semi-diurnal tides are similar to So Cal, with variations up to 2m – get a tide chart.

SURF STATISTICS	J F	M A	M J	J A	S O	N D
dominant swell	W-N	SW-N	S-W	S-W	SW-N	W-N
swell size (ft)	4	3-4	2-3	3	4-5	5-6
consistency (%)	80	75	55	60	70	80
dominant wind	NW-N	NW	NW	NW	NW	NW
average force	F3-F4	F4	F3-F4	F3-F4	F3-F4	F3-F4
consistency (%)	47	60	64	56	61	61
water temp.(°C)	15	16	18	20	20	16
wetsuit						

JAMIE BOTT

223. East Oaxaca

Salina Cruz

WESLEY ALLISON

Summary
+ Consistent summer swells
+ Little or no crowds
+ Many classic breaks
+ No mass tourism
+ Sunny weather and warm water

– Strong trade winds
– Sketchy access to some breaks
– Mainly righthanders
– Limited air access
– Rainy surf season

The third largest country in Latin America still has plenty of surf potential to be uncovered and those looking for warm water, classic pointbreaks, powerful beachbreaks, offshore winds and no one else out, should seriously think about the eastern part of Oaxaca (pronounced "wah-hah-kah"). The state is one of the last frontiers in mainland Mexico, despite also being home to Mexico's famous, world-class surf and tourism-oriented area of Puerto Escondido. Huatulco to Salina Cruz, is almost untouched by development and characterized by verdant jungle slopes meshing with spectacular white sand beaches. Dredging beaches, rifling points and secret jetties are visited by powerful southern hemisphere swells from April to October. Only the lack of tourism infrastructure and sketchy access to the spots can explain the low crowd level.

MEZ/ESM

Salina Cruz

WESLEY ALLISON

Huatulco is the most recent tourist destination developed by the Mexican Government, who are keen to learn from

TRAVEL INFORMATION

Local Population: Salina Cruz - 76,219
Coastline: Oaxaca - 533km (331mi)
Time Zone: GMT -6
Contests: None
Other Resources:
wavehunters.com/salina/salina.asp
aboutoaxaca.com
oaxaca-travel.com

Getting There – Passport and $20 tourist card required for entry. Get to Huatulco (HUX) by plane connecting via Mexico City. Only Continental Airlines (through Houston) and some charters fly direct to Huatulco. Another option is to land in Oaxaca (OAX) or Puerto Escondido (PXM) then drive.

Getting Around – Car rentals available at HUX/OAX/PXM airports, but no 4WD available. Normal cars won't handle many of the sketchy access tracks to the breaks. Rainy season doesn't help. Salina Cruz Surf Tours can access the remote spots. Salina Cruz lies 134km (83mi) east of Huatulco (2-3h), on coastal Highway 200.

Lodging and Food – Salina Cruz Surf Camp at Punta Chivo (with restaurant, bar & pool). Also hotels and posadas in Salina Cruz ($20-60/dle). Wide variety of accommodations in Huatulco. Pepe's Cabana's ($6/nt) at Barra de la Cruz or luxury "Villa las Tortugas" at nearby Playa El Mojon (from $2000/wk). Tremendous diversity of regional cuisine, mainly based on fish and shellfish.

WEATHER STATISTICS	J/F	M/A	M/J	J/A	S/O	N/D
total rainfall (mm)	4	1	165	197	181	14
consistency (days/mth)	1	1	8	10	7	1
min temp (°C)	21	23	25	24	23	21
max temp (°C)	30	32	33	32	31	30

Weather – The coast of Oaxaca lies well within the tropics and its climate is often referred to as "eternal spring". The city enjoys sub-tropical weather, so temps vary between 21-30°C (70-86°F) in winter and between 25-32°C (77-90°F) in summer. A dry season occurs from December to May. The rainy season extends from June to November and September is generally the rainiest month with the highest levels of humidity. During the rainy season there are also hurricanes and the offshore ones can have a strong impact on the amount of rainfall. The seasons deeply influence the vegetation, that varies from brownish to lush green. Usually the rain lasts for just a few hours after which the sun comes out. Average annual rainfall is 1100mm (44in). Boardshorts only.

Nature and Culture – Mexico is a country with over 3,000 years of history and culture. Oaxaca, the State Capital, declared Humanity's Cultural Patrimony by Unesco. Festival Música por la Tierra in Huatulco every May. Good diving options at Santa Cruz, also gentle rafting on Copalita and Zimatan rivers. Sea turtles nestling site at Morro Ayuta.

Hazards and Hassles – Waves aren't like Puerto Escondido, but big days happen. Banditos are known to work the Highway 200 at night. Don't get stuck on tracks during rainy season. Drive defensively as locals will pass on curves. Mosquitoes are a constant nuisance. Sharks are around.

Handy Hints – No surf shop in Salina Cruz, so bring own equipment or get/rent a board in Puerto Escondido (Central Surf Shop). Ideally, a shortboard for hollow waves plus a longboard for the classic points. Avoid travelling at night or alone. Don't help thieves by leaving things lying around. Bring a mosquito repellent. Beware of Federales. Try El DexKite Litros Bar in Huatulco.

previous mistakes, so modern water and sewage systems will ensure no waste goes into it's 9 pristine, but wave-less bays. **La Bocana** is a fun beachbreak, great for beginners and the highly sandbank dependant rivermouth is worth a check too. Barra de la Cruz was re-named **La Jolla** for the controversial Rip Curl Pro Search WCT event in 2006. A "once-in-a-decade swell" offered amazing conditions to the top 44 surfers, with deep barrel rides up to 12 seconds, being webcast all around the world. The heavily localized, righthand pointbreak now gets crowded, despite its need for a big S or SE swell to even begin to show signs of life. Inconsistency aside, when it's on, it's worth the $2 access charge to the village and these long, epic rights in a beautiful setup. An out of service lighthouse marks **Morro Ayuta Point**, which is almost impossible to find without local knowledge or a surf guide. It's an excellent righthand sand pointbreak that is mainly surfed by a few locals. Barreling waves peel from the top of the headland, with very long rides when conditions are ideal (solid S swell, offshore NW winds). Also quite hard to find and access are the uncrowded, consistent beachbreak peaks of **San Diego**. There's a good right point at the mouth of the bahia; a boat would make exploring easier. Linked to the Highway 200 by a track beside quarries, **Concepción Bamba** has better protection from the wind and higher consistency than the pointbreaks around. A juicy, very hollow righthander peels off a small breakwall, offering short but intense rides if the tide is not too high (backwash). Another slightly longer breakwall delivers a heavy, thick barreling right. **Punta Chipehua** is a remote but quality right, peeling over rocks and sand when a solid S swell hits. Best from low to mid tide, they don't close-out when big, but have no tolerance to the regular 20-30 knot NE-E trade winds. **Punta Chivo** is easy to get to through a small fishing village then a walk out to the point. It's a fun, mushy wave great for longboarders and beginners and home to Salina Cruz Surf Tours, the only surf camp around. NE-E blows it out but any W wind and S swell is fine. Working under similar conditions **Punta Conejo** is the premier pointbreak and is sometimes able to deliver rides up to 500m with a strong S swell. Because the trades blow it out it is very inconsistent, but highly sought after. East of Salina Cruz, **La Ventosa** is a highly consistent beachbreak, best with a small to medium summer S/SW swell and a low tide. There are miles of A-frame peaks to the east, but the offshore trade winds are sometimes too strong to surf here!

WESLEY ALLISON

Barra de la Cruz

WESLEY ALLISON

La Jolla/ Barra de la Cruz

Summer (April to October) is the surf season, but also the wet season. The big southern hemisphere swells hit the Oaxaca coast with consistency and size, producing 3-10ft (1-3m) S to SW swells. They tend to be a little bit softer here than around Puerto Escondido. Chubascos, tropical cyclones off mainland Mexico, occasionally deliver 6-15ft (2-5m) waves (Aug-Nov). The narrowness of the Tehuantepec isthmus and the gap in the Sierra Madre generates trade winds known as the Tehuano, strengthened by the temperature contrast between the warm Gulf of Mexico and the colder Pacific Ocean. From October to April, the surf is often blown-out due to strong N-NE winds (25-30 knots), backing off to 10-20 knots during the surf season, when the direction is more variable, but mainly offshore. A rainy episode can turn off the fan, creating perfect glassy conditions. With variations up to 5ft, tidal range isn't too important on the points and beaches.

SURF STATISTICS	J F	M A	M J	J A	S O	N D
dominant swell	NW	S-SW	S-SW	S-W	S-W	NW
swell size (ft)	3	4-5	5-6	7-8	6-7	3-4
consistency (%)	70	85	90	90	90	70
dominant wind	NW-N	N-E	NE-E	NE-E	N-E	N-NE
average force	F4-F5	F3-F4	F3-F4	F3-F4	F4-F5	F4-F5
consistency (%)	45	37	48	55	40	47
water temp.(°C)	23	26	28	29	28	26
wetsuit						

HONDURAS
EL SALVADOR
NICARAGUA
COSTA RICA
PANAMA

224. Oriente Salvaje

Las Flores

DAN HAYLOCK

Summary
+ World-class right pointbreaks
+ Variety of breaks
+ Unspoiled beaches
+ Warm water & friendly winds
+ Cheap living

– S swells only
– Rain through best swell season
– Gets crowded during season
– Quiet nightlife
– Petty theft & high crime rate

Since the first surf explorers in the '60s discovered the great pointbreak potential of El Salvador the country has gone through a tumultuous time. A brutal army-led civil war killed nearly 100,000 people between 1979 and 1991, followed by economic devastation and violent social unrest. Things have improved dramatically, although many Salvadorans are armed, shootouts are common, and the homicide rate (one of the highest in the world) increased 25% from 2004 to 2007. Surfers are returning, often using the services and experience of a local surf operator, which seems the best way to enjoy the unreal density of quality pointbreaks and avoid many problems. The western La Libertad area has always been the focus of attention, but the newly discovered Oriente Salvaje (Savage East) now attracts more and more travellers to some epic right points with very few local surfers.

Punta Mango

SCOTT WINER

DAN HAYLOCK

TRAVEL INFORMATION

Local Population: 6,948,073
Coastline: 80km (50mi)
Time Zone: GMT -6
Contests: None
Other Resources:
azulsurfclub.com
wavehunters.com/lasfloressurfclub
epicsurfingadventures.com
elsalvador.travel
akwaterra.com
Video:
Latin Guns
The Far Shore

Getting There – Visa not required for most visitors, a US$32 departure tax must be paid. Comalapa International Airport (not far from La Libertad) serviced by major carriers including Taca (hub), United, American, Delta, Continental and Copa Airlines. El Cuco is a 2.5h drive from the capital, or a 40min helicopter flight.

Getting Around – Despite the war ending it's still an unstable country where violent crime persists. Favour surf camps and guided tour options (Akwaterra) instead of renting a car and travelling by yourself (expensive and risky). Excellent bus service (cheap and frequent), reliable taxis. Boating to some breaks is the way to go - talk to the fishermen at Las Flores.

Lodging and Food – Several levels of accommodation in El Cuco. Azul Surf Club has great rooms and services (wk package from $750-1500), they donate 10% of the proceeds to the local community. Epic Surfing Adventures (5d packages from $550-1300). Higher class Las Flores Surf Club has full board packages ($1750-2350). Akwaterra 5 day guided tours from $550. Try corn and rice flour pupusas, as well as the local Pilsner beer.

WEATHER STATISTICS	J/F	M/A	M/J	J/A	S/O	N/D
total rainfall (mm)	7	28	226	306	227	26
consistency (days/mth)	1	3	16	20	18	3
min temp (°C)	20	22	23	22	21	20
max temp (°C)	30	31	30	30	29	29

Weather – Oriente Salvaje has a tropical climate with warm to hot daytime temperatures and warm nights. The rainy season, known locally as invierno, or winter, extends from May to October; almost all the annual rainfall occurs during this time and usually falls in heavy afternoon thunderstorms. Verano is the summer dry season, running from November to April with light rainfall, NE trade winds and dry, hot, hazy air. Temps vary little between seasons and are most affected by altitude. Annual average rainfall is 1700mm (68in). Water temps vary between 26-28°C (79-82°F) so boardshorts only.

Nature and Culture – Central America's most ecologically damaged country introduced environmental laws only since 1998. Conchagua volcano is the highest point around the La Union Bay (1231m/4038ft). Visit the Laguna de Olomega. Parrots nest in the rocks at Punta Mango. Heaps of butterflies, often in the line-up. Volcanic landscape (extinct). Violent political history.

Hazards and Hassles – Theft is a major issue, watch any valuables and make use of the safes in hotels. Hepatitis A/B, tetanus, diphtheria, cholera and typhoid constitute significant threats. Also dengue fever, so use mosquito repellent and nets. Avoid public transportation, and hanging out alone, making yourself a target for armed robbers. No real shark threat, earthquake a possibility.

Handy Hints – Limited surf supplies, take ding repair & extra fins. Bring a 6' to 6'5 plus a 6'8 to 7'2 board, a longboard can be great too. Reef booties at low tide and strong sun protection required. Water quality much better during dry season. Avoid Semana Santa (week before Easter). Best to bring US$ and speak Spanish. Women should not venture out alone, especially at night.

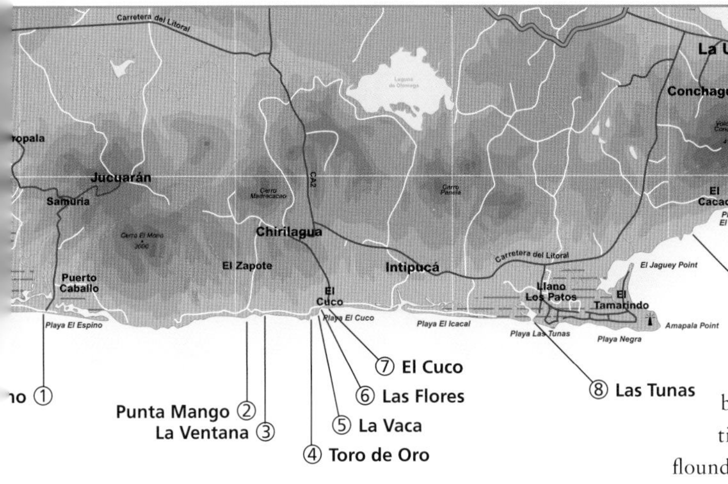

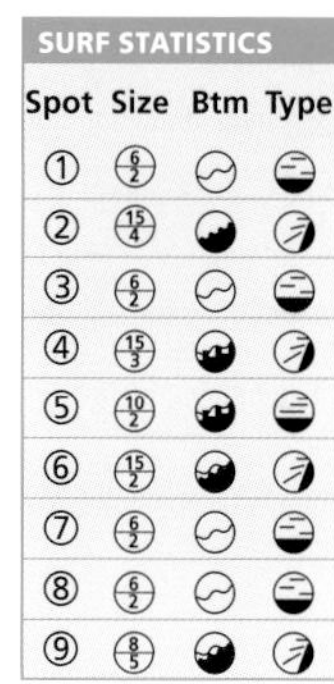

SURF STATISTICS			
Spot	Size	Btm	Type
①	6/2		
②	15/4		
③	6/2		
④	15/3		
⑤	10/2		
⑥	15/2		
⑦	6/2		
⑧	6/2		
⑨	8/5		

Easily accessed by road, the seaside resort of **El Espino** sits on a 12km (7mi) long beachbreak surrounded by mangroves, a rivermouth and the impressive Chaparastique volcano in the background. It is mainly a beginner spot, but the sand banks can line-up and offer tubes to the more experienced surfers. **Punta Mango** is the main attraction, an epic right pointbreak peeling over barnacle encrusted boulders. With a solid S-SW swell and an incoming tide, hollow racetrack walls deal out juicy barrels to the inevitable crowd of boaters, especially at its ideal size, from head-high to double overhead. It's possible to drive during the dry season, but the bad roads and thefts make the 30 minute boat ride from El Cuco or Flores advisable. **La Ventana** named after the hole in the cliff is a super-fun and very consistent beachbreak ideal for the smaller days. Best by boat and usually empty. Not for the faint-hearted, **Toro de Oro** is best accessed by boat due to the nasty, volcanic rock shoreline. Better with a bit of W in the swell to stop it sectioning off and swatting the unwary into a rock-strewn dead-end, it can look very appealing from the side, but only the best will negotiate the fast, long rides. Further inside in the next bay, **La Vaca** acts as a pressure valve for Las Flores, which gets a bit slow at high tide. The occasionally hollow rights are faster but shorter, and favour swells in the 2-6ft (0.6-2m) range. Intermediate to experienced surfers will focus on **Las Flores** (or Punta Silla), a Salvadorian dream set-up and one of the premier surfing locations in Central America. Compatible with the largest swells and always better at low tide, the waves first wrap around a rocky point full of palm trees, jack up over the take-off rocks, then reel off down a sandbar offering more speed and barrelling sections. Lengthy rides up to 300m are common, but the increasing crowds make it hard to get priority. Mellower shoulders at high tide but still fun. **El Cuco**, a tiny village abandoned during the civil war is now home to several surf camps and consistent beachbreak that is often slow and mushy, but great for beginners and especially good on high tide with a 4ft (1.2m) swell. Characterized by its floundering ranchos on the beach, the village of **Las Tunas** has lots of rocky beachbreaks as well as a rivermouth with potential quality sand banks. Also check the nearby Playa Torola and its similar setup. The majestic Gulf of Fonseca, bordered by Nicaragua and Honduras, offers a beautiful setting but inconsistent surf. The easternmost right pointbreak known as **Lucky Man's** needs a big S swell to wrap around and generate long, fun performance walls over a rock/sand bottom. There are other fickle beach and reef breaks to discover between Playitas and El Tamarindo, best by boat since it is a very wild area.

DAN HAYLOCK

Toro de Oro

DAN HAYLOCK

La Ventana

Most swells are generated by the southern hemisphere low pressure systems. The narrow swell window favours S-SW swells, SW being the best direction. A true W swell will rarely get in to Eastern Salvador unless it is huge. Highest consistency occurs during the wet season (May-Oct), with many 4-7ft (1.2-2.2m) waves and some 8-12ft (2.5-4m) days. During this period, winds are usually offshore in the mornings then shift to light to moderate SW onshores at mid-day. Nevertheless, some breaks near headlands and points remain well wind-protected. The dry season (or "summer", from Nov-Apr) offers consistent surf too, with numerous swells in the 3-5ft (1-1.5m) range. Sunny offshore conditions prevail, often for days. The lack of strong local offshores prevents the upwelling effect, unlike in neighbouring Nicaragua. The tidal range never goes over 6ft (1.8m), which only slightly affects most rocky pointbreaks.

SURF STATISTICS	J F	M A	M J	J A	S O	N D
dominant swell	S-SW	S-SW	S-SW	S-SW	S-SW	S-SW
swell size (ft)	2-3	4-5	6	6-7	5-6	3-4
consistency (%)	70	80	85	90	80	75
dominant wind	NE	NE	NE-SW	NE-SW	NE-SW	NE
average force	F4	F4	F3-F4	F4	F3-F4	F3-F4
consistency (%)	73	54	41	58	47	63
water temp.(°C)	26	27	28	28	28	27
wetsuit						

225. Central Puntarenas Province

Rio Sierpe Rivermouth

BLUETRAILZ.COM

Summary
- + High summer consistency
- + Low crowds
- + Osa National Park rainforest
- + Dominical surf town
- + Great exploration potential

- – No world-class waves
- – Heavy summer rains
- – Crocs at rivermouths
- – Expensive Osa accommodation
- – Tricky access to Drake/Corcovado breaks

BLUETRAILZ.COM

Ollie's Point, Witches Rock, Playa Grande, Tamarindo, Playa Negra, Mal Pais, Jaco, Hermosa, Matapalo, Pavones are the famous and familiar names on the Costa Rica surf map. Being the first Central American country to embrace US surfers, with the first surf tours beginning in 1985, many areas became a victim of their own success. There are still some amazing places lurking off the surfers beaten tracks and the area that extends south of Dominical to the Corcovado Park on Osa Peninsula still offers a lot to explore in lush tropical scenery. The wet season from May to November, is synonymous with consistent S-SW swells hitting a variety of quality rock and sand set-ups.

The rivermouth of **Boca Damas** delivers long, fast, sectiony and sometimes hollow lefts and

Playa Hermosa

BLUETRAILZ.COM

shorter rights. Usually bigger than nearby breaks, and best with incoming tide. The long walk from Quepos, the strong currents, crucial tide factor and local crocs should convince most to get a boat ride from Damas. The **Quepos Jetty** used to peel point-like into the rivermouth before the building of Pez Vela marina killed the wave. The only spot

TRAVEL INFORMATION

Local Population: Dominical 600
Coastline: 200km (124mi)
Time Zone: GMT -6
Contests: National Surf Contest in Dominical
Other Resources:
crsurf.com
surfingcr.net
surf-costarica.com
tourism-costarica.com
visitcostarica.com
Video: Lost in Costa Rica 1&2 (1998)

Getting There – Valid passport required, most visitors can stay up to 90 days (others 30). Int'l arrivals are in Juan Santamaria (SJO) in Alajuela, 10km from San José. National airline Lacsa charges for boards. Sansa offers daily flights from San José to Drake's Bay (DRK) for $182/rt, and to Quepos (XQP) for $106 (12kg max). Alternatives are rental cars and public buses.

Getting Around – A rental car offers the best flexibility. You must be 21 to rent a vehicle and have a major credit card in your name to secure the deposit. Expect $260-320/wk (Tricolor, Dollar). Check www.graylinecostarica.com for buses. For uncrowded surf in Osa peninsula, catch a boat in Sierpe or Drake's Bay (around $120/day + gas).

WEATHER STATISTICS	J/F	M/A	M/J	J/A	S/O	N/D
total rainfall (mm)	4	19	203	201	270	72
consistency (days/mth)	1	2	16	18	20	7
min temp (°C)	23	23	22	23	23	22
max temp (°C)	35	35	33	32	32	31

Lodging and Food – Quepos & Manuel Antonio have dozens of hotels. Large choice in Playa Matapalo too. In Dominical, try cabinas Pyramis or cheaper camping Antorchas ($8). Roca Verde Hotel in Punta Dominical. Drake Bay area is more expensive (Drake Bay hotel $50/dbl, Marenco Lodge $80/dbl, Rancho Corcovado $100/dbl, Wilderness Resort). A typical food bill would be $8-10.

Weather – Dominical has a mild sub-tropical climate all year-round. There are two seasons; the dry season is generally between late December and April and the green or wet season lasts from May to November, but still offers an average of about 5hrs of daily sunshine. September and October are the rainiest months including sudden tropical thunderstorms, lightning and heavy rains. Temps vary little between seasons, ranging from 29-32°C (84-90°F) during the day and 20-23°C (68-74°F) during the night. Water is boardshort warm.

Nature and Culture – Abundant wildlife. Manuel Antonio, Marino Ballena and Corcovado National Parks really deserve a visit. Canopy Safari in Manuel Antonio ($70). February month-long Festival del Mar in Quepos. Diving can be good when surf is flat. Great night life in Quepos, it's quieter in Dominical.

Hazards and Hassles – CR is the safest nation in Central America. The surf and theft are the main dangers, along with the crocodiles, bugs, spiders, scorpions. Dangerous roads at night, many potholes. A 4x4 is a plus during rainy season. Inspect rental cars at check-in for previous damage.

Handy Hints – English is widely spoken. Surf shops in Quepos (Tropical, Burro, Surfing Safari) and Dominical (El Tubo, South Wave, Salsa Bravo, Piña). Renting a board is easy, cheap (from $10/day) and often a good solution. Booties can be useful to walk on reef. It always pays to get up early. Take mosquito repellent and hiking boots.

BLUETRAILZ.COM

Playa Matapalo

in town is now the **Quepos Bombie**, a recently discovered slab that is located south of the jetty, breaking way out off the point, making it a rare tow-in option. The tourist magnet Manuel Antonio National Park has fun but semi-consistent beachbreak options along the 3km long Playa Espadilla but the northwest corner at **Playitas** holds the best waves from mid to high tide and there is also an outer reef righthander with a solid swell and a high tide. Locals are chill, waves for all standards, and it's a great place to hang out. It's 11km (7mi) from Roncador to **Playa El Rey** where an isolated long stretch of beach hides fair to good quality peaks, especially near Rio Naranjo rivermouth. Closes-out when big, but is always bigger than the nearby breaks. Camping possible, but bring all supplies. Another similar spot with endless peaks and no crowds is found at **Playa Matapalo**. Dominical is a laid-back surf city, less developed than Jaco and Tamarindo, with a highly consistent, strong barrelling beachbreak at **Playa Dominical**. It can hold serious size without closing-out, gets bigger near Rio Baru rivermouth, but broken boards and drownings are frequent here. The protected bay of **Dominicalito** is popular with beginners/improvers since it is a smaller, softer beachbreak, but watch out for some hidden rocks at low. Another great wave for beginners when small is the left at **Punta Dominical**, but when it's fuelled by a serious swell, it holds up to triple overhead with long, hollow rides. Go at higher tides and don't get caught inside! The incredibly scenic **Playa Hermosa** benefits from well-shaped waves that usually break half the size of Dominical, perfect for beginners, intermediates and longboarders. **Punta Uvita** is the gateway to Marino Ballena, the only marine park in CR. The whale tail shaped point creates good shelter for the soft beachbreaks when the area is maxed and onshore NW is blowing. **Playa Ballena** is one of the best beginners waves in the area thanks to gently peeling, long rides. Also check the uncrowded beaches of Piñuela, Ventanas, Tortuga

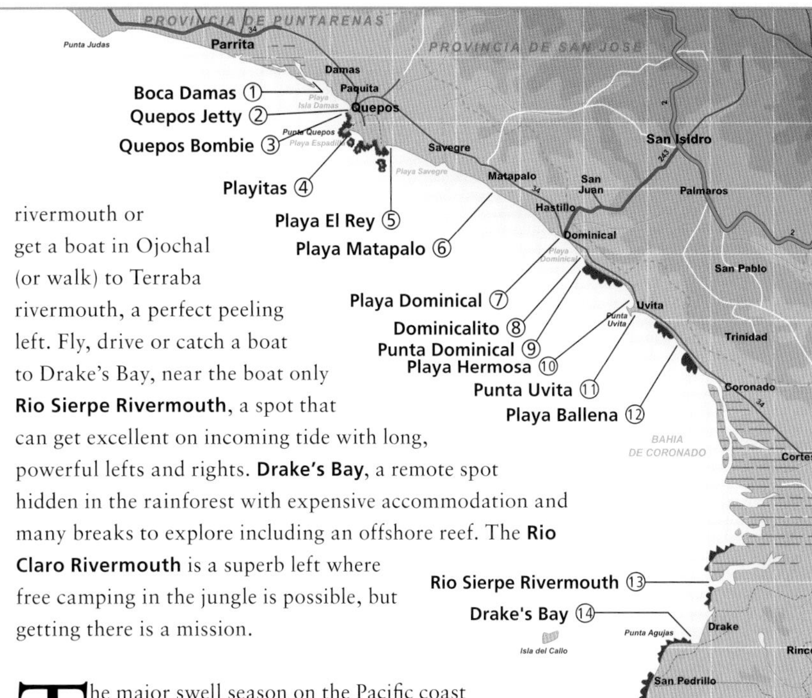

rivermouth or get a boat in Ojochal (or walk) to Terraba rivermouth, a perfect peeling left. Fly, drive or catch a boat to Drake's Bay, near the boat only **Rio Sierpe Rivermouth**, a spot that can get excellent on incoming tide with long, powerful lefts and rights. **Drake's Bay**, a remote spot hidden in the rainforest with expensive accommodation and many breaks to explore including an offshore reef. The **Rio Claro Rivermouth** is a superb left where free camping in the jungle is possible, but getting there is a mission.

The major swell season on the Pacific coast runs from May to November, with a S-SW predominance ranging from 3-12ft (1-4m) swells. The summer (Dec-April) WNW artic swells that can provide clean 3-4ft (1-1.2m) waves for Guanacaste hardly reach this stretch of coast, except a few west-facing breaks around Drake's Bay. There is a gentle SW-W monsoon-like period from May to December (wet season), with light and variable winds. Typically, mornings are offshore before a seabreeze picks up, so it always pays to get up early. The tidal factor is very significant with variations up to 10ft (3m) that seriously influence all breaks. Get a chart in a surf shop or on www.crsurf.com.

SURF STATISTICS	J F	M A	M J	J A	S O	N D
dominant swell	S-SW	S-SW	S-SW	S-SW	S-SW	S-SW
swell size (ft)	2	3	4-5	5	4-5	2
consistency (%)	60	70	80	80	75	60
dominant wind	W-NE	W-NE	SW-W	SW-W	SW-W	SW-W
average force	F2-F3	F2-F3	F3	F3	F3	F3
consistency (%)	52	40	50	57	65	56
water temp.(°C)	28	28	28	28	28	27
wetsuit						

SURF STATISTICS			
Spot	Size	Btm	Type
①	8/2		
②	8/3		
③	15/6		
④	10/3		
⑤	6/2		
⑥	6/2		
⑦	12/3		
⑧	6/2		
⑨	15/3		
⑩	6/2		
⑪	6/2		
⑫	6/2		
⑬	8/2		
⑭	8/2		
⑮	8/2		

GUILLAUME LARRE

Punta Dominical

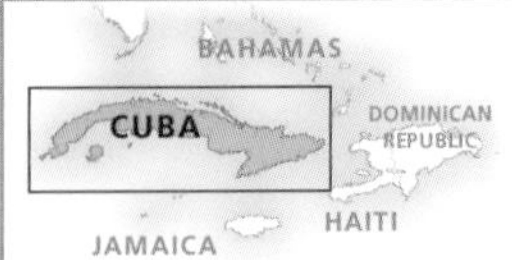

226. Cuba

La Setenta
OLIVIER SERVAIRE

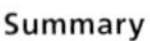

Summary
+ Uncrowded outside Habana
+ Exploration possibilities
+ Boca de Yumuri pointbreak
+ Perfect winter climate
+ Cultural interest

– Short, inconsistent swell season
– Onshore winds
– Low quality Habana spots
– Difficult travel logistics
– Expensive accommodation & food

Beyond the postcard clichés of Mojitos, salsa dancing and cigars, Cuba has consistent surf along the Habana seaside promenade. The country also hides decent waves in warm, tropical and largely empty water. Blocked from the bulk of Atlantic wave activity by the fringe of the Bahamas, Cuban surfing is a winter-only affair with the northeastern coast gathering up only the biggest swells as they filter between gaps in the Bahamas. This stretch lacks consistency but when the waves arrive they hit all manner of beaches, bays and rocky headlands. Fortunately, northern Cuba also has another source of surf, the big storms that reliably churn out of the Gulf of Mexico and send stormy swell marching towards the north western corner of the island, around Havana. A third and much rarer swell generator comes from lows passing below the island, normally in the form of hurricanes, which can produce massive waves for the south coast of Cuba.

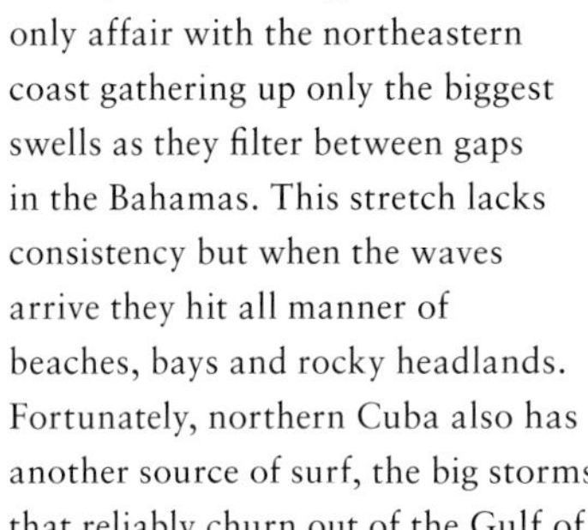

OLIVIER SERVAIRE

DUSTIN HUMPHREY

TRAVEL INFORMATION

Local Population: Habana 2.2M
Coastline: 3,735km (2,320mi)
Time Zone: GMT-5
Contests: Local
Other Resources:
Video: Sipping Jetstreams
havanasurf-cuba.com
cubanbeaches.com

Getting There – A tourist card is required in advance through a Cuban embassy or with a travel agent. Most of the big carriers fly into Habana (HAV) or Holguin (HOG). US citizens will have no problems with the Cuban authorities but they will experience major problems with their own government. Package deals are often cheaper but provide no mobility. $25 departure tax.

Getting Around – Around Habana, it's cheaper and easier to rent a taxi when required. To explore further, an expensive hire car is necessary (from $80 per day). Cuba boasts Latin America's most extensive system of roads. Domestic Cubana flights can be pricey: Habana to Guantanamo is approximately $150 o/w. Private buses are better value and ok with boards.

Lodging and Food – Cuba is one of the cheaper Caribbean countries but that doesn't mean good value. Accommodation in Havana and the resorts is expensive, and unsuspecting tourists pay top prices for dirty, noisy lodgings with terrible service. The food situation isn't much better; thanks to the US embargo there is very little actually available and food is expensive.

WEATHER STATISTICS	J/F	M/A	M/J	J/A	S/O	N/D
total rainfall (mm)	58	52	142	130	161	68
consistency (days/mth)	5	4	9	10	11	6
min temp (°C)	18	20	22	24	23	20
max temp (°C)	26	28	31	32	31	27

Weather – The Cuban climate is mild subtropical, the orientation from west to east means refreshing trade winds and marine breezes. During the short winter occasional cold air masses come from the north, but they are short duration. The average temperatures throughout the year oscillate between 20 and 35°C (68-95°F). The Eastern region enjoys warmer weather. From August to October, the main hurricane season can affect the island, with winds that reach 200km/h (124mph) and heavy storms. This occurs at the same time as the rainy season (May-Oct), before the dry season (Nov- April). Average rainfall is from 860mm (34in) in the east, to 1730mm (68in) in Habana and it falls mostly in summer and autumn, but there can be torrential rain at any time of year. Average water temps don't drop below 25°C (77°F) – a light vest in the winter will meet all needs.

Nature and Culture – Old Havana is easily the highlight of a visit to Cuba. It's an open air art gallery that is fully deserving of UNESCO World Heritage Status. The town of Baracoa and the countryside surrounding it are a perfect place to relax under a palm tree and soak up the atmosphere. The diving throughout Cuba is superb.

Hazards and Hassles – Escape the tourist resort bubble. Shallow reefs like Setenta can be ridiculously sharp. Cuba is a very safe and friendly country. Although touts in the tourist areas can be tiring, bear in mind that they are just trying to get by.

Handy Hints – Take all surfing equipment and maybe some spares for the local surf community. The US embargo means that no surf equipment is available anywhere in the country. More importantly, there are also no medicines, imported foodstuffs, educational materials and all the other items most people take for granted.

Starting on the beaches around Havana, **La Setenta** is the pick of the spots. It's located to the west of the old centre, just in front of the distinctive Russian Embassy in the Miramar district. A shallow table of flat, dead but painfully sharp coral produces messy peaks that often close out. In fact, were it not for the slab of concrete sticking out into the ocean here that provides a marginally easier entry and exit point, this spot hardly differs from any other part of the reef that lines the Havana coastline. It can get very busy and, unfortunately, surf etiquette doesn't appear to have caught on in a big way in Cuba. Much quieter than La Setenta are the long sandy beaches of the **Playas del Este**. Generally gathering less swell, they are worth checking out when La Setenta is too big or stormy. There are a number of individual beaches here, but the overriding feature is strong currents. Due to the nature of the sandbar waves, their exact form varies from day to day. Heading east from Havana to Varadero, **Sun Beach** is the number one tourist spot in Cuba. There is an average beachbreak with exposure to the NW, but beware, lifeguards sometimes shut the beach when the surf is up. A 27km (17mi) long causeway links **Cayo Coco** to the mainland, a good option for package tour surfers staying at one of the many resorts like the El Senador. There's a mixture of sandy beach, rocks and coral reef but shallow waters and the Bahamas shadow make Cayo Coco very inconsistent. Between here and the tourist town of Holguin there are definitely other waves. The pretty port of **Gibara** has waves at Playa Caletones on NE swells. Rarely ridden, the pick of the spots is a fast and hollow left breaking on a shallow rock shelf just to the west of Gibara. The wave is short and intense, with a tube section, but it does need a good swell to get going. Even further east, the best wave in Cuba, **Boca de Yumuri**, is found near Baracoa. A classic cobblestone right point, it reels into a stunning bay for several hundred metres. Boca de Yumuri breaks from 3-8ft (1-2.5m) and gathers any sign of a NE swell through a gap between the Bahamas and the Turks and Caicos. It also handles any tide, and is offshore in an E wind. It's a very long drive from Habana (two days minimum), and as a consequence is rarely surfed. The south coast of Cuba has plenty of potential but it only really breaks on rare hurricane swells, which occur most frequently in September and October. It can go from flat to massive very quickly. The best known south coast spot, is a ledgy and unpredictable righthand reefbreak called **Windmills**, but it is found inside the forbidden Guantanamo Bay military base. The south coast is packed with potential, and due to its fickle nature remains entirely uncrowded.

STUART BUTLER

Boca de Yumuri

As already mentioned Cuba is a winter-only surf destination. The best wave-generator is Atlantic groundswell coming from the NE. Unfortunately, the Bahamas act as an effective barrier and only the biggest swells manage to seep in through gaps in the islands and onto Cuban shores. These swells suffer from a reduction in size and power but 6-8ft (2-2.5m) waves are not unheard of. The dominant wind is from the NE so early mornings or sheltered bays are the way to go. The coastline around Habana receives swells from the NW, which are generated by intense storms in the Gulf of Mexico. Between November and March these occur around once a week, but the quality is usually poor and onshore winds and rain are a frequent accompaniment. Rare hurricane swells can strike from the north or the south and produce big waves. These are highly unpredictable but September and October are the most likely periods. Tidal variation is small, not exceeding 2ft (0.6m).

SURF STATISTICS	J F	M A	M J	J A	S O	N D
dominant swell	NW-NE	NW-NE	NW-NE	SE-S	SE-S	NW-NE
swell size (ft)	2-3	2	1-2	1	1-2	2-3
consistency (%)	40	30	20	10	20	40
dominant wind	NE-E	NE-SE	NE-SE	E-SE	NE-SE	NE-E
average force	F4	F4	F3-F4	F4	F4	F4
consistency (%)	55	69	80	73	70	65
water temp.(°C)	25	26	28	29	29	27
wetsuit						

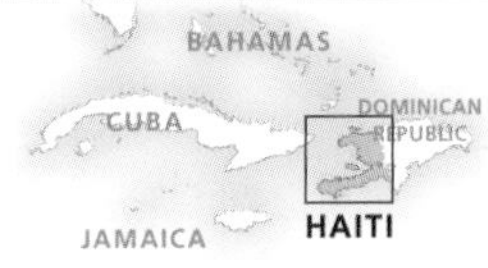

227. Haiti

Secret spot, Cap Haitien

ALL PHOTOS JOHN CALLAHAN/TROPICALPIX

Summary
+ North & south coast season
+ Morning offshores
+ Totally empty spots
+ Unspoiled tropical paradise
+ Artistic cultural background

– Small & inconsistent
– Wrecked country
– Shallow & treacherous
– Dangerous Port-au-Prince
– Transport hassles

Being neighbours with the surf-rich Dominican Republic ensures there is no doubt that Haiti gets surf and on both coasts of the western extremity of the second largest Caribbean island, Hispaniola. It's probably easier to fly to the Dominican Rep. and connect overland to Haiti's north coast where shallow reefs greet the winter NE swells. It takes real determination to check Haiti's empty surf since economically, the country has become the poorest nation in the northern hemisphere. Being the first and only successful slave revolt leading to free nationhood, Haiti has a tradition of collectivism, activism and military coups. Recent history has been marked by the repressive dictatorship of Francois Duvalier, "Papa Doc.", who ruled for 14yrs until his death in 1971, backed by the dreadful 'Tonton Macoutes' paramilitary group. Former liberation theology priest Jean-Bertrand Aristide was overwhelmingly elected president in 1990, in the first democratic elections in Haitian history. Aristide

Ginsu

TRAVEL INFORMATION

Local Population: 8,528,000 (Cap Haitien 200,000)
Coastline: 1,771km (1,100mi)
Time Zone: GMT -5
Contests: None

Getting There – American Airlines (New York, Miami), Air France and Air Canada offer regular, direct flights to Port-au-Prince (PAP). No visa required, small departure tax to be paid. Overland Crossing in the north is convenient between Santiago and Cap-Haïtien, while the Malpasse/Jimaní crossing in the south links Santo Domingo to Port-au-Prince. There is a direct 5h bus called Ayido from Santo Domingo to Cap Haitien.

Getting Around – Avoid sketchy driving around PAP, flying domestic (Tortug'Air, Caribintair) to Cap Haitien (CAP) to save 8h drive or Jacmel (JAK) about 4h drive but boardbags may cause delays. Hotel can arrange pick-ups then organise local transport (4WD, taxi-boat). Road network is truly disastrous. Rental cars start at $60/d but not recommended.

WEATHER STATISTICS	J/F	M/A	M/J	J/A	S/O	N/D
total rainfall (mm)	43	123	161	108	168	60
consistency (days/mth)	4	9	10	9	12	6
min temp (°C)	22	23	24	24	24	23
max temp (°C)	31	31	32	33	32	31

Lodging and Food – Only the main tourist beaches have good places to stay like Cormier Plage near Cap Haitien, Kayanol Village in Labadee or Hotel Jacmelienne in Jacmel. Expect to pay $30-50, but there are local rooms for $10 and meals can be anything from dirt cheap ($1-2) to $25 for international standard cuisines. If arriving on the north coast through Dominican Republic, stay at Hotel El Bistro in Montecristi.

Weather – Haiti has a warm and humid tropical climate. Temps range from 15-25°C (59-77°F) during winter and from 25-35°C (77-95°F) through summer. Most rainfall occurs between April and November with a peak during June and July. Because the rain is brought by NE trade winds, heavy rainfall occurs in the northern plains and the southern peninsula. Average rainfall is about 1370mm (55in). There are often severe storms during the hurricane season (Jun-Oct) when there is a risk of floods. The southern peninsula is more vulnerable to hurricanes and suffered heavy damage from hurricanes Allen, Gilbert and Georges (1980-1998). Water remains warm year-round - take booties for the shallow reefs.

Nature and Culture – Haiti is mountainous and wild. Don't miss the Bassin Blue waterfalls near Jacmel. Visit Citadelle Laférière from Cap Haitien. Artisan's Market, located near the beach has rich art and crafts. Coffee is among the best while The Rhum Barbancourt is a fine cognac. Play soccer or dominos with locals.

Hazards and Hassles – Haiti is top of the list on the travel warnings because of frequent riots and kidnappings in Port-Au-Prince, mostly on wealthy Haitian or exposed expats. 80% of the population live below the poverty line, so expect a bit of chaos. Hardly anyone out in the surf, but beware of the staghorn coral, urchins and really shallow spots. Local transport can be tough.

Handy Hints – No need for a gun but a longboard can be useful. Speaking French helps resolve any problems with locals. Tropical storm Noel was the deadliest Caribbean storm since Jeanne hit Haiti in 2004, killing 1,500 people and triggering flooding and mud slides that left 900 people reported missing, presumed dead.

Ginsu

was quickly overthrown by a coup, but the military junta backed down in the face of imminent U.S. military intervention; some 20,000 U.S. troops landed in September 1994, allowing Aristide's return to power. Since the U.S.-led Multi National Forces withdrew in 1995, there have been 5 UN peacekeeping missions to Haiti and the turmoil mainly affects the capital city, Port-Au-Prince. Security improves in the coastal towns and there is plenty to explore for the curious trailblazers who fancy some empty Caribbean juice.

In January 2007, a mixed group of surfers led by John Callahan went to check the North Coast around Cap Haitien. **Caracol** has lefts and rights over coral on both sides of the reef pass, but access is via a taxi boat and it is inconsistent. The main attraction for tourists is Labadee Beach, operated by Royal Caribbean Cruise Lines, who anchor huge ships in the deepwater bay, while most of the 2,000 passengers have no clue that they're in Haiti. There is a small fishing village called "Habitation Labadie", a mix of traditional Haitian dwellings and prosperous hill-perched villas or stay at Cormier Plage and check **Ginsu**, the main spot on the north coast. These quality rights are not easily accessible from the road and the reef is so shallow and urchin-covered that it is best to paddle out from the next cove round from the break. Ginsu is fast, but very ripable, once past the dry reef section at the start and it can throw out some nice tubes sometimes. Supposedly, there is also a good left near Dragon's Bay. Further west, stop at **Le Borgne**, and find a right reefbreak/rivermouth, close to Pointe Barre Boeuf, that can peel down the line for a long way and give some E wind protection. There are way more spots to discover before NE swells get sheltered by the fabled pirate's hide-out "Turtle Island". The north coast is a long way from the capital city for weekend expats, but the south coast can be reached within 3-4h to cover the short 86km/54mi distance to Jacmel. The main wave is called **Pistons**, because it breaks off an 80-year-old shipwrecked engine, located deep in the Bay of Jacmel. Good lefts will appear when ESE winds create enough fetch to reach 4-6ft (1.2-2m) seas with 5-7 sec periods. Morning offshores dive off the steep mountains in the background plus the wave is shaped by the rivermouth, piling sand up on the reef. Locals Vadim and Russel are usually the only surfers there. Jacmel is renowned for its distinctive artistic traditions and is one of the major production centres for indigenous arts and crafts. Way out on the peninsula tip are lots of potential SE-S swell rides on the **Tiburon Reefs** just south of city. There's a decent coastal road that skirts the reefs, so it's just a matter of timing a visit with a summer swell.

The main surf season is winter (Nov-March) when NE trade-winds and Atlantic lows produce almost constant swells. True NW-N groundswells find it hard to reach Haiti's north coast which is shadowed by the Bahamas and the Turks & Caicos islands. Occasional long distance NE swells will sneak in but most of the surf is generated by cold fronts or stiff trade winds. Typically, the surf will be 2-5ft (0.6-1.5m) with possible 6-8ft (2-2.5m) days. The south coasts of the Greater Antilles (Puerto Rico, Hispaniola, Jamaica) really score some decent E-SE windswell between July and September. Expect 2-4ft (0.6-1.2m) surf, unless a hurricane swell hits from Sept-Oct jacking up 10-12ft (3-4m) waves. Tides are irregular semi-diurnal types and rarely exceed 3ft (1m). Check Buoyweather virtual buoys.

SURF STATISTICS

Spot	Size	Btm	Type
①	5/2		
②	5/1		
③	5/1		
④	6/1		
⑤	6/1		

SURF STATISTICS	J F	M A	M J	J A	S O	N D
dominant swell	N-NE	N-NE	S-SE	S-SE	N-NE	N-NE
swell size (ft)	3	2	0-1	2-3	1-2	3
consistency (%)	60	40	10	50	30	60
dominant wind	NE-E	NE-E	NE-E	NE-E	NE-E	NE-E
average force	F4	F4	F4	F4	F4	F4
consistency (%)	78	76	74	80	70	79
water temp.(°C)	26	26	28	28	29	28
wetsuit						

Ginsu

228. Jamaica

Copa

RONAN GLADU

Summary

+ Decent winter consistency
+ Warm water, friendly waves
+ Various left pointbreaks
+ Low crowd factor
+ Rastafari culture and music

– Frequent onshore conditions
– Poor roads on eastern side
– Sometimes small & gutless
– Kingston insecurity
– Difficult access, some private coast

Being the third largest island in the Caribbean, Jamaica stands out on the map, but it is relatively obscure in terms of Caribbean surf destinations. Famous for Bob Marley, reggae music and Rastafarian culture, its natural bounty includes 120 rivers, 150mi (240km) of beaches and 6 mountain ranges, where the tallest peak reaches 7,402ft (2256m) in the Blue Mountains. Despite its size, only the eastern tip receives a decent amount of windswell worth exploring, with options for both north and south coasts. The north coast boasts some bigger NE swells, white-sand beaches and quality rivermouths favouring rights, but it is often onshore. The south shores enjoy better consistency and some good lefts, often brushed by NE offshores, along grey sand beaches with not a soul in sight!

STEVE FITZPATRICK

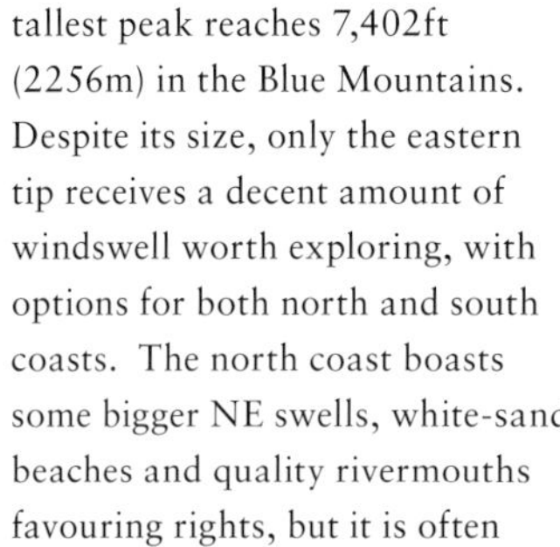

Outside Zoo

BRIAN NEJEDLEY

Approaching Kingston Airport, Plump Point **Lighthouse** is clearly visible below, one of the south coast's most

TRAVEL INFORMATION

Local Population: 600,000 Kingston
Coastline: 1022km (635mi)
Time Zone: GMT-5h
Contests: Nationals
Other Resources:
theliquidaddiction.com
quashi.com
geocities.com/jamnesiasurfclub
Video:
Broken Down Melody
Drive Thru Caribbean

Getting There – US and UK citizens get 6 months, most other western countries 30 days. Jamaica is easy to get to from both US (Miami, New York) and Europe (London, Germany). Beware, most visitors land at Montego Bay (MBJ), but Kingston (KIN) is much better. Regular port of call for cruise ships. $27 dep tax. JUTA: Jamaica Union for Travellers Association. Equipped with a fleet of well-maintained, air-conditioned cars, buses, coaches and luxury vehicles

Getting Around – Buses are unreliable but driving solo can be a bit sketchy sometimes; avoid areas like the Jamrocks and some roads require local knowledge for remote spots. Renting a small car costs $41/day. Guided tours with full board at Jamnesia cost $200/day and $185 with Jahmekya ($150 for triple).

WEATHER STATISTICS	J/F	M/A	M/J	J/A	S/O	N/D
total rainfall (mm)	19	33	97	85	143	60
consistency	3	3	4	6	8	5
min temp (°C)	19	20	22	23	23	21
max temp (°C)	30	31	32	33	32	31

Lodging and Food – Expect $50 for a room and $7 a meal. Jahmekya hotel (12 rooms), within walking distance of 3 spots has cable TV. Pay $80 for double with full board. Jamnesia Camp in Bull Bay offers camping from $10 and simple rooms from $35/night. Morgan's Harbour Hotel in Port Royal start at $111/dble. Try Boston Style Chicken and Ital (rasta veggie cooking).

Weather – Two types of climate are found on Jamaica: an upland tropical climate prevails on the windward (N-E) side of the mountains whereas a semi-arid climate predominates on the leeward (S-W) side. Jamaica's climate is tropical with constant temps all year-round 25-30°C (77-86°F). Warm trade winds bring rainfall throughout the year, with peaks in May and October. The island receives refreshing onshore breezes during the day and cooling offshores at night. The average annual rainfall is 1960mm (78in). Showers are usually intense but brief and can be a welcome cool-off. Jamaica lies at the edge of hurricane alley and sometimes scores direct hits. Boardshorts only.

Nature and Culture – Kingston is close for bars & nightlife: Livity, Weekendz, Village Café, Passa Passa nightclub. Lots of natural sights like Reach Falls or the Bath Fountain hot mineral spring and the Blue Mountains (best coffee in the world?). The Rasta Brethren's mission at Zion Hill is to educate others to the true words of Haile Selassie. Check the Bob Marley Museum.

Hazards and Hassles – Kingston has some really rough neighbourhoods like Trenchtown. Police often harass Rastas for weed possession, don't smoke anywhere with anyone. Sharks can be a factor but last fatality was 1922. Mind the sea urchins, fire coral, jelly fish, sea lice and sunburn. Crowd pressure is minimal; local surf operators will take clients to semi-secret gems.

Handy Hints – Jamnesia Surf Club, at Bull Bay was established by the Wilmots to help the development of surfing through surf events. There is board repair & rental facilities while Patrick Mitchell makes Quashi boards. No surfshop. Many words and phrases are unique to Jamaica: you 'nyam' (eat) your 'bickle' (food) and 'labrish' (gossip) with friends!

consistent spots, and a real treat for those fresh off the plane. It looks like a long and soft left pointbreak from the air, but more often than not, it's the short barrelling rights that the regular crowds covet. Also located along the Palisadoes peninsula, a cargo ship ran aground, forming a perfect 200 yard long, mechanically peeling, lefthander. The Wreck was the prime south coast surf spot, however, wave action has spun the ship and reduced it to a semi-submerged heap of rusting metal. In the '80s, **Zoo** was the discovery of the decade, a great barrelling, left reefbreak, which was surf central until Sept 2004 Hurricane Ivan's 12-15ft (4-5m) waves blew the reef away, highlighting how fragile surf spot ecosystems can be! Bull Bay, (also called 9 Miles, because of its distance from downtown Kingston) is one of the largest settlements of Rastas on the island and home of the Wilmot family, a real Jamaican surfing dynasty. Facing their Jamnesia guest-house is **Copa**, possibly the best rights on the South Coast when strong SE swells hit. **Makka's** is the main option for fun ripable lefts, providing very long rides when it connects on any SE swell. Often a contest site, Makka's can accommodate hurricane swells and draws a crowd with some localism. Jahmekya surf lodge is located between Morant Bay and Port Morant, where guests can visit lots of uncrowded waves like the long left point/rivermouth at **Rozelle Beach** as well as many semi-secret spots like Jelly's, Little's, Canon Cave, Graveyard or Winterfed. Holland Bay also hides some waves, but like many spots on the northeast coast, access can become a problem. **Hector's River** is a typical example where fun lefts & rights over sandy reef are visible from the scenic look-out, but walking down the 100ft (30m) cliff is not an easy task. Each district is usually referred to by it's parish name like St-Andrew (Kingston), St-Thomas (Yallahs) or Portland (NE tip). **The Ranch** is one of those secluded breaks in North Portland with restricted access and no less than four reefbreaks that enjoy some consistency. One of the reefs holds some size; look for the white fence on the shoreline. **Long Bay** picks up all the NE wind swell onto summer sandbars plus a left off a coral bulkhead in winter. **Boston Bay** is Jamaica's first recognized surf spot, offering white sand beach, crystal clear water and its notorious spicy Jerk chicken or pork, which always draws a small crowd of locals, expats and tourists. Lefts wedge off the outside rock or there's a fat right on the other side of the tight, wind protected bay.

Sharks Cove

RONAN GLADU

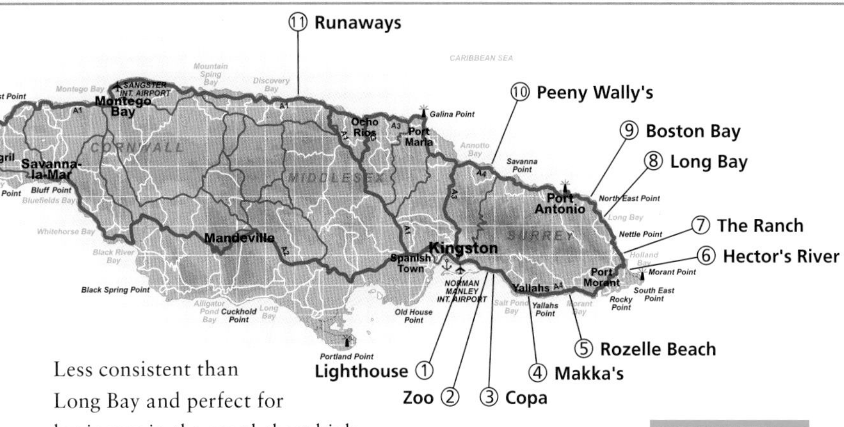

Less consistent than Long Bay and perfect for beginners in the usual chest-high soft breakers. **Peeny Wally's** is the best right point around, breaking on most conditions, making it a regular contest site. Performance walls perfect for gouging manoeuvres, it's easier to walk back after a long one. Not far is the Shark's Cove private property; ask the Jamnesia guys to take you there. The whole north coast up to Montego Bay has waves but quality is a problem with constant onshore NE trades often wrecking the surf. Try **Runaways** for a small wave on bigger NE windswells and hopefully offshore SE winds.

SURF STATISTICS			
Spot	Size	Btm	Type
①	8/2		
②	8/6		
③	10/4		
④	8/2		
⑤	6/2		
⑥	6/2		
⑦	10/2		
⑧	8/2		
⑨	8/1		
⑩	8/2		
⑪	4/1		

Located in the northwestern Caribbean Sea, Jamaica seems an unlikely place for swells to develop. Cut off from the large NE swells of the North Atlantic by Cuba and Haiti/ Dominican Republic, Jamaica seems trapped in the middle of the tranquil Caribbean Sea, except when a hurricane passes by, which could provide a good S-SE swell or else slam into the island and wreak havoc! Winter (Dec-March) is the best time to expect NE-SE windswells, typically 2-6ft (0.6-2m) at 5-7 second period, producing fun, mellow waves that are a bit slow on the left points (except on the biggest swells up to 8ft), but strong enough on reefbreaks. Summer (June-Sept) also produces S-SE swells with plenty of small, playful waves on the south coast. Jamaica is blessed with an 8 month surf year and the 4 calm months are broken up into scattered 1-2 week flat spells. 3ft is the biggest semi-diurnal tide.

SURF STATISTICS	J F	M A	M J	J A	S O	N D
dominant swell	NE-E	NE-E	E-SE	E-SE	NE-SE	NE-E
swell size (ft)	3-4	2	0-1	2-3	2	2
consistency (%)	60	40	10	50	40	60
dominant wind	NE-E	NE-E	E-SE	E-SE	NE-SE	NE-E
average force	F4	F4	F4	F4	F3-F4	F4
consistency (%)	73	71	73	77	81	77
water temp.(°C)	27	27	28	29	29	28
wetsuit						

Zoo

STEVE FITZPATRICK

229. Antigua and Barbuda

Galley Bay

ALL PHOTOS YEP

Summary
+ Perfect Palmetto Point
+ Uncrowded conditions
+ Sailors paradise
+ Deluxe tourism services

– Very inconsistent
– Shallow, uneven coral reefs
– Lack of land access spots
– Uber expensive, no budget options

Antigua and Barbuda are located on the Leeward side of the Eastern Caribbean, ideally positioned in the NE corner of the island range. Mostly low-lying, these islands lack the central range of mountains common to much of the Caribbean. The highest point, Boggy Peak, is just 402m (1,319ft). The rocky coastline of the two islands has numerous bays and inlets, some of which have been turned into harbours. The water offshore is shallow, reducing the impact of the swell and cutting the number of surfable spots down to around ten. Tourism in Antigua and Barbuda is strictly luxury only. Most hotels are self-contained, all-inclusive resorts, the majority of which are owned by Americans.

Palmetto Point

Barbuda sits 40km (25mi) north of Antigua and has a coastline of long pink and white sand beaches protected by barrier reefs. On the west coast **Palmetto Point** (aka Fuckallya), can be an epic, righthand, sandbar barrel.

TRAVEL INFORMATION

Local Population: Antigua 68,000; Barbuda 1,500
Coastline: Antigua 103km (64mi); Barbuda 50km (31mi)
Time Zone: GMT -4
Contests: None

Getting There – 6 months visa automatic. Fairly cheap flights and special package deals to VC Bird Airport (ANU) with Virgin, BA, US Air, AA, Continental, Delta, BWIA and Air Canada. LIAT is the major inter-island carrier. Very small 8 person planes fly to Barbuda (BBQ). Peak season is also the swell season (mid-December to mid-April). $20 dep. tax.

Getting Around – Renting a car is crucial in Antigua, it costs about $50 per day. Visitors need a special permit to drive in Antigua that costs $12 and is valid for six months. Driving is on the left-hand side of the road. The Barbuda Express ferry takes 90 min and costs $50 return. Rental cars in Barbuda are expensive ($80) and hard to get. Stay in the Palmetto Hotel or walk.

Lodging and Food – Staying in Antigua is not cheap but rooms are available for $50 at the Capuccino Lounge in St-Johns. Most all-inclusive resorts like Galley Bay start at $575 night. Any beach hotel under $100 will be hard to find. Barbuda has high-end tourism, K Club (from $750), Coco Point (from $545), and Palmetto Hotel ($150). The Codrington can have basic rooms for $50.

WEATHER STATISTICS	J/F	M/A	M/J	J/A	S/O	N/D
total rainfall (mm)	64	64	101	126	150	125
consistency (days/mth)	9	8	9	12	12	13
min temp (°C)	23	24	25	26	25	24
max temp (°C)	28	29	30	31	30	29

Weather – Although drier than most other Caribbean Islands, Antigua and Barbuda have a tropical climate tempered by sea breezes and trade winds. They have a pleasant year-round climate. Average daily temperature drops a few degrees in winter (December to March) from the usual high of around 30°C (86°F). A&B are fairly dry throughout the year except during the rainy season (mid September to November) when daily showers can be expected. Hurricane season runs from June to September and visitors are advised to keep an eye on the weather forecast during this period. Annual average rainfall is about 1000mm (40in) and days of constant rain are very rare. Boardshorts only.

Nature and Culture – Sailing is huge, and centred around the English and Falmouth Harbours, which become lively from December to the end of April when the Antigua Sailing Week starts, an annual world-class regatta since 1967. Calypso and Soca music are big or check out De Jam Festival (DJs from around the world). The 2007 Cricket World Cup took place in A&B. Barbuda is home to an abundance of birdlife.

Hazards and Hassles – Reefs are shallow and dangerous with staghorn coral. Be careful when it's small. Backpackers may not feel at ease staying in St. John's - most visitors are super wealthy tourists. Many remote breaks can only be accessed by boat. Barbuda is dry and barren, and winds can be very strong.

Handy Hints – Surf shops sell clothes and accessories, and bodyboards for children. No board rentals are available. Surfing in A&B is suitable for those on a work posting, sailors, or the very rich. There is no need for a gun at all, only a strong board for small reef waves or fast beachbreaks.

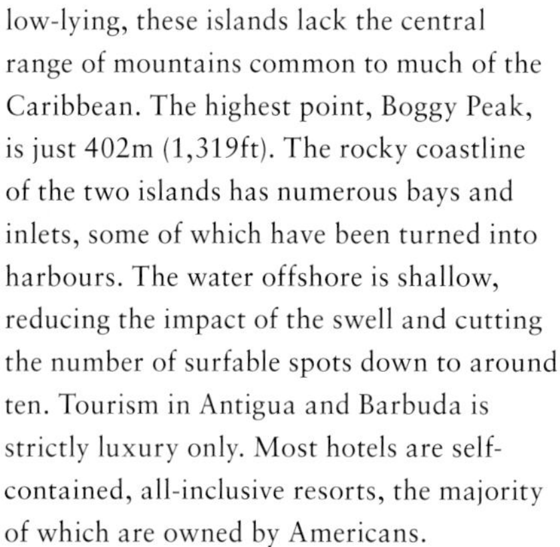

Named by a crew of French surfers in October 2001, this shorebreak right can produce serious tubes in almost dry water, really suitable for experts only. On SE swells, lefts are a possibility, and the pink sand beach is stunningly beautiful. **Spanish Point**, on the southwest tip of the island, is a barrier reef with sectioning lefts that need calm wind to break. There are beachbreaks on the eastern shore, but they are usually rough and out-of-control.

Antigua has a greater density of spots. Just south of the beach resorts at Dickenson Bay and Runaway Bay is **Sand Haven** (also called Lashings). With a N-NE swell running, a semi-consistent left and right reefbreak breaks near to the St. James Club. The beaches most convenient to St. John's are Fort James, a popular public beach, and Deep Bay but neither hold much shape or size. Also in the vicinity is **Fort Barrington**, a semi-secret left pointbreak near a resort and Salt Pond mouth. Visible in the distance is **Galley Bay**, the most consistent north side spot. Although they may look tempting, the outside lefts are stupidly shallow and break over staghorn coral. The series of four crescent beaches at **Hawksbill** are also highly regarded as beach sites but as far as the surf goes, it's pretty disorganized. Several reefs from Landing Bay to Hawksbill have decent waves but some are exclusive to the hotels, and therefore private. Offshore, Sandy Island can get all-time conditions but requires the fickle combination of good N swell and no wind, not to mention a boat to access the spot. On the road that winds along the less developed south coast is **Fisher's Hill**, where rare lefts spin over shallow reef. Land access through pineapple fields is almost impossible, so boating in is a better option. **Rendez-Vous Bay** is quite a popular beach and there is an offshore reef with waves, best accessed by boat. SE trades create sloppy waves on the beach. Without doubt, the best wave on the south coast is **Turtle Bay** near Proctor's Point, a scenic set up with a quality left reefbreak on S-SE swell. Again, it can be ridiculously shallow. On the East Coast, the main beach is **Half Moon Bay**, now a National Park and a good choice for a family outing. This wave is fairly consistent with SE trades but generally messy. Smith Island located offshore definitely hides secrets.

Because of a large underwater plateau between the two islands, most of the Antigua spots exposed to the north are plagued by the shadowing effect from Barbuda and the swells lose a lot of energy and size before getting to the coast. The true groundswell, producing 3-6ft (1-2m) waves, corresponds to the bad winter storms and cold fronts. Most of the time the surf is made up of windswell, rarely getting above 2-4ft (0.6-1.2m). This also means that most of the consistent spots are onshore, breaking small on razor-sharp coral. The winds are NE almost all year but during summer SE trades blow. Good windswells are quite rare, the surf quality is often a choice between onshore mush over sand with a bit of size, and smaller side-shore walls over sketchy reef bottoms. Hurricane season (summer) can have epic days but sailing becomes more dangerous. Tide changes are almost nil with 1ft (0.3m) range max.

Hawksbill Bay

Galley Bay

Goat Point
Billy Point
Goat Island
Rabbit Isl.
Kid Isl.
Cedar Tree Point
Hog Point
The Caves
Two feet Bay
ATLANTIC OCEAN
Low Bay
Codrington
The Highlands
Pigeon Cliff
CARIBBEAN SEA
The River Landing
BARBUDA
Cattle Bay
Welsh Point
Palmetto Point
Pelican Bay
Pelican Point
Spanish Point
Coco Point
Gravenor Bay
Palmetto Point ①
② Spanish Point

SURF STATISTICS	J F	M A	M J	J A	S O	N D
dominant swell	NW-NE	NW-NE	S-SE	S-SE	NW-NE	NW-NE
swell size (ft)	3-4	3	2	2-3	3-4	4
consistency (%)	60	50	40	50	60	70
dominant wind	NE-E	NE-E	E-SE	NE-E	E-SE	NE-E
average force	F4	F4	F4	F4	F3-F4	F4
consistency (%)	80	77	85	85	73	76
water temp.(°C)	25	26	28	30	28	26
wetsuit						

Spot	Size	Btm	Type
①	6/1		
②	6/3		
③	4/2		
④	6/2		
⑤	6/2		
⑥	6/3		
⑦	6/3		
⑧	6/2		
⑨	6/2		
⑩	4/1		

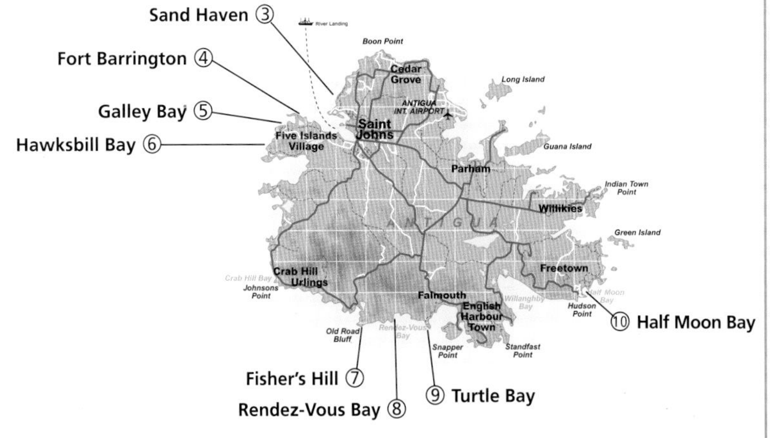

230. Trinidad and Tobago

Summary
+ Magic Mount Irvine
+ Spot density on Tobago
+ Cheap, excellent food
+ Craziest Carnival
+ Good flight links

– Inconsistent larger swells
– Strong localism
– Long drives to Trinidad surf
– Old Oak Rum hangovers
– Thievery and police roadblocks

Mount Irvine

BABY MARMOTTE

Located at the very southern end of the Windward Island chain and only 7 km from Venezuela on the South American continent, Trinidad and Tobago were populated by indigenous Amerindian tribes (the Arawaks and the Caribs) long before the arrival of Columbus in 1498. While Trinidad remained in the hands of the Spanish from the 15th Century until it became a British colony in 1802, Tobago was squabbled over by European powers. Just north of the Orinoco river delta in Venezuela, Trinidad is largely flat or undulating, ascending to a height of 940m (3084ft) in the Northern Range. Trinidad possesses sizable oil, gas and asphalt reserves, and its prosperity is linked directly to the production of petroleum and petrochemicals. The main surfing areas are situated in the north and north-east of the island near Toco, which is too far for a day-trip from Port-Of-Spain, but there is still a huge amount of coast line unexplored by surfers. Two thirds of Tobago is volcanic and mountainous, rising sharply in the east under a dense cloak of tropical

SIMON MCCOMB

Matelot

BABY MARMOTTE

TRAVEL INFORMATION

Local Population: 1.3M
Coastline: Trinidad 362km (224mi): Tobago 115km (71mi)
Time Zone: GMT -4
Contests: National – Sans Soucis
Other Resources:
Video: Souljahs I,II,III
surfingtt.org
geocities.com/surftt

Getting There – No visa. Direct flights daily from London to Trinidad (POS) on BWIA (national airline) : 800 -1000 USD. BWIA charges extra for surfboards. Weekly flights from Paris to Trinidad on AF. From North America, Air Canada, AA and BWIA fly to Trinidad daily. Tobago is 2h away from Port-of-Spain by fast ferry, or 15 minutes by air.

Getting Around – Rent a car (Autocenter) because the main surf area is a 2 1/2h drive from Port of Spain and taxi rides can turn out to be quite expensive. Costs are about 40 USD per day and fuel is cheap. Public transport is possible but not with surfboards. In Tobago you can walk to surf spots.

WEATHER STATISTICS	J/F	M/A	M/J	J/A	S/O	N/D
total rainfall (mm)	55	50	147	232	181	154
consistency (days/mth)	12	9	15	22	18	17
min temp (°C)	20	20	22	22	22	21
max temp (°C)	31	32	32	31	32	32

Lodging and Food – Guest houses in Toco (Patrice Bravo), space is limited but not in great demand. Staying in hotels entails very long drives. Most hotels in Tobago are scattered around Mt Irvine and Pigeon Point. Inexpensive tasty food like curry and rotis. Shark n' Bakes is a local delicacy.

Weather – The climate of both islands is warm and humid, with the dry season running from November to April, and the wet season from May until October. The wet season, also coincides with the June to October hurricane season, with storms most likely to hit in the August and September months. Hurricanes generally track to the north of Trinidad, but usually close enough to generate a significant increase in swell. The dry season is also the windy season, where Tobago in particular can see 20 knots averages for weeks on end. Fortunately, the best breaks in Tobago are on the west coast, and the trade winds are easterly.

Nature and Culture – World famous for flora & fauna. Bird or turtle watching and diving (Speyside) are popular. Mountain biking (Slow Leak Bike Tours) around the islands is excellent. Birth place of Soca music and a surf trip in February will coincide with the famous Trinidad Carnival, 2nd only to Rio's in size, where the focus is on dancing, partying and drinking.

Hazards and Hassles – Fights in the water are common, with violence directed to those who don't respect the locals or who try to paddle straight to the peak at breaks like Mount Irvine. Banditos are a concern: car jacking and theft of personal possessions isa possibility. Be watchful for poisonous snakes and giant centipedes.

Handy Hints – Don't forget mosquito repellent. Take a long-sleeve rash vest and a light-weight springsuit for dawn patrols. There are four surf shops in Trinidad, most famous is "Beach Break" located in the West Mall of Port of Spain. Alan Davis fixes dings and is the only shaper. Rent boards from the locals like Cool Runnings at Mount Irvine beach.

rainforest, while the flatter, drier western side offers the nicest beaches. This southwest coast is where all the surf spots are located with the exception of Crazy's. The Buccoo Reef National Park is the main coastal feature, offering not only great surf but also fantastic snorkelling and diving.

The crescent bay of **Las Cuevas** holds hollow, fast beachbreak peaks in N to E swells up to 6ft (2m). Always better at mid to high tide and bigger at the western end, a good walk from the fishing village and car park. Fairly consistent in winter, but flat in the summer months, unless there is a hurricane swell. **Blanchisseuse** is a nice sandy beach with some rocks on its eastern side and the best peaks usually at the western end, but there can be some very strong rips requiring strength and endurance. The protected bay and rivermouth of **Grande Rivière** is the place to head in huge swells when the rest of the north coast is maxed-out. Breaks over rocks on the eastern side by the cement jetty, in 2m+ (6ft+) NE to E swells, but mostly breaks during the hurricane season. **Sans Souci** is 15 minutes down the road from the Toco fishing depot where a big rock in the middle of the bay dominates the beautiful scenery. The sandbars develop on either side of the rock depending on the currents and when the left is working, it is usually the best. Takes N round to E swells at 0.5m-5m (2-15ft) and is excellent during hurricane season when it gets huge, clean and hollow. To the right of the main jetty in front of the fishing depot, **Toco** is a super hollow right that breaks only in a N swell. It's very inconsistent and the locals are all over it when it does break – surf elsewhere. **Salibya** is the only real barrier reefbreak on the island a short walk from the Toco lighthouse. It's a short paddle to the outer reef where hollow, sectioning lefts and rights break best at low to mid tide on N–NE swells in the winter months. Down the beach from **Balandra** fishing depot is an exposed, powerful, all tides beachbreak. Handles N–NE–E swells ranging from 2-10ft (0.5-3m) and is ultra consistent. On Tobago, **Mount Irvine** is generally considered one of the best waves in the Caribbean region. It's a hollow, high-performance right with a lot of barrelling sections over the dead coral reef in N–NE swells up to 12ft (4m). The heavy local crew jump of the rocks but it's safer to paddle out from the middle of the bay. It never breaks in summer, but is fairly consistent during the winter months. Walk about a mile up the beach from Store Bay to access **Sunset Left**, a reef that's a short paddle off the private Pigeon Point area. It gets nice and hollow, and works well with a N–NE swell, from 3-6ft (1–2m). It is a good alternative when Mount Irvine is packed and breaks in similar conditions. Half way along the beach towards Sunset Left is **Sunset Rights**, a very shallow, hollow righthander, especially at low tide. It rarely get above headhigh and only work when Mount Irvine and Sunset Left are breaking huge. Very inconsistent, but very good. Predictably located right at the end of the runway, **Airport's** is a hollow, punchy righthander. It works during wintertime, from 4–6ft (1.5 –2m) and is best at low tide. Big swell spot that's not as rare as Sunset Right, but not as consistent as Mount Irvine. **Crazy's** is the only break on the east coast of the island, located north of Scarborough, in Goldsborough Bay. Very poor quality, desperation wave working in junky E windswells only. Never reaches headhigh and is consistently bad.

SIMON MCCOMB
Conrado Beach Resort

In the dry/windy season months from Dec to April, E trades drive windswell in the 4–8ft (1.2-2.5m) range. During this time, cold fronts pushing off South Carolina and sometimes Florida will set up long period (12–15sec), 4 to 6ft (1.2m–2m) N–NW groundswells. These N swells wrap around the west coast of Tobago where perfect offshore conditions are generally the rule. The wet/hurricane season relies on trade wind NE–SE swells from June to October, is more fickle and generally smaller. However, westerly tracking tropical storms and hurricanes can not only create very light and variable wind conditions but also large, long period swells, sometimes as much as 30ft (10m). The more common hurricane swell is in the region of 12ft (4m) with a 15sec period, creating the best surfing conditions of the year. Winds are generally easterly, especially in the dry and windy season, ranging from 15 to 25 knots. Winds in the wet season are often lighter, with more variable directions, sometimes even W. The tidal range is 1–4ft (0.3-1.2m) and a rising tide can increase the size of the surf at some spots.

SURF STATISTICS	J F	M A	M J	J A	S O	N D
dominant swell	N-NE	N-NE	N-E	N-E	N-E	N-NE
swell size (ft)	3-4	2-3	1	1-2	3	3-4
consistency (%)	60	50	30	30	50	60
dominant wind	NE-E	NE-E	NE-SE	NE-SE	NE-SE	NE-E
average force	F4	F4	F4	F3-F4	F3-F4	F3-F4
consistency (%)	88	86	95	91	89	83
water temp.(°C)	26	26	27	28	28	27
wetsuit						

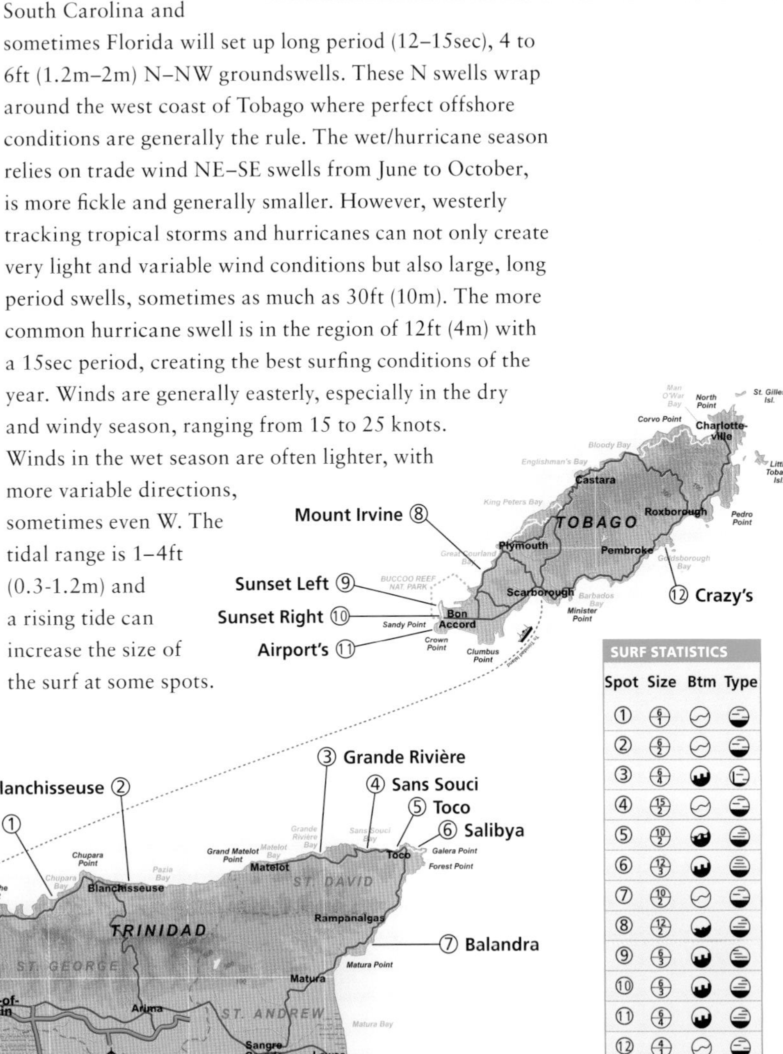

SURF STATISTICS			
Spot	Size	Btm	Type
①	6/1		
②	6/2		
③	6/4		
④	15/2		
⑤	10/2		
⑥	12/3		
⑦	10/2		
⑧	12/2		
⑨	6/3		
⑩	6/3		
⑪	6/4		
⑫	4/1		

Large, long and left sums up the western coast of this vast continent, where the Humboldt Current hoovers up the huge swells from the Roaring Forties latitude. Gleaming Ilo glasshouse.

South America

GONZALO BARANDIARAN

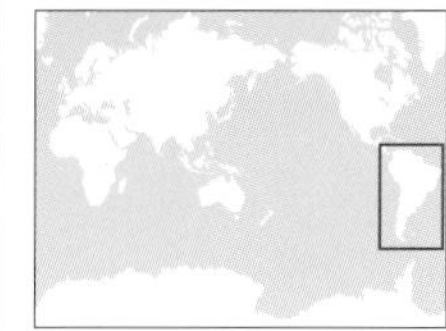

Surf Culture

Long before the Polynesians migrated across the Pacific, Peruvian fisherman had built a type of watercraft well-suited to utilise the power of the incredibly long lefts that dot the coastline. Built from totora reeds, these caballitos ("little horses") have been in use for around 4400 years, giving the pre-Inca civilisation the jump on Polynesians as the first surfing culture. In modern terms, Peru has been a leader in introducing surfing to South America, after sugar magnate Charles Dogny returned from Waikiki with some lessons under his belt and a Duke board under his arm. That was 1939, but recently, some 1920's style solid wood replicas were found in an old sugar warehouse at Chicama, where Hawaiian advisors had helped the emerging sugar industry between the wars. However it is Brazil that boasts the biggest influence since an unidentified American hit famous Copacabana Beach in Rio on a redwood log in 1928, followed by home-boy Paulo Preguica on a paddleboard a few years later. Plenty of boards (later called madeirites) were made from the Popular Mechanics plans, utilising US plywood (Brazilian ply was yet to appear), between 1939 and 1960, when the first foam and fibreglass boards hit Brazilian shores. Under the tutelage of Peter Troy, local shapers went on to start the first board factory in 1965. Ecuador has long been the biggest producer of balsa (the Incas built large balsa rafts to transport their armies), but the surf industry never got involved with the export or the trees themselves, severing the ritual importance that the ancient Hawaiians attached to their tree harvesting. First surfers had appeared in Uruguay (late '50s), Argentina and Ecuador ('63), Venezuela ('65), Chile ('69) and probably soon after for countries like Colombia. Competition has always been high on the agenda and in 1942, Dogny set up the well-off Club Waikiki, which went on to host a series of highly-rated, international surfing contests, culminating in the 1962 Peru Championships being the first truly worldwide contest, attracting teams from California, Hawaii, Australia, France and Peru. Further status was earned when Eduardo Arena formed the International Surfing Federation in Lima, a year before the city hosted the 1965 World Championships, won by Peruvian Felipe Pomar. The Carioca Surfing Federation founded in 1965, held the first Brazilian Surfing Championships under the watchful eyes of MacGillivray and Freeman's cameras in '66. The following year saw affluent Venezuelans join the national association and contest waves near Caracas, while Punta del Este was the first venue for a Uruguayan contest in 1969. Everyone else was a decade behind for various reasons and it wasn't until 1978 that Argentinean brothers Fernando and Santiago Aguerre formed the NSAA, partly in response to the military government's 1977 ban on surfing in Mar del Plata. They campaigned through the pages of the Argentina Surf and Skate Magazine and opened the first shop before the two year ban was lifted and they went on to build the global surfwear giant Reef Brazil when they relocated to California. Surfing exploded in Brazil during the '70s, with national and international competitions taking place, Rio local Pepe Lopez making the Pipeline Masters final and *Brasil Surf* hit the news-stands in 1975, followed by TV surf show *Realce* in '82. Pro tour stalwarts Flavio Padaratz and Fabio Gouveia where followed by Victor Ribas, Peterson Rosa and Flavio's little brother Neco through the '90s and '00s, leading the way for the current crop of rippers like World Junior and WQS Champ ('05/'06) Adriano De Souza.

INTERNATIONAL SURFING ASSOCIATION

While Polynesia is generally accepted as the cradle of surfing, very few cultures approached the surf in craft that required the rider to stand up. Totora reed horse and rider. Demonstration at the ISA World Masters Surfing Championship 2008, Punta Rocas, Peru.

Today

Brazil has emerged as a surfing super-power, supporting a huge population of over a million talented surfers, who absolutely blitz the generally small waves, with lithe style and a progressive attitude, resulting in an increasing number busting into the pro ranks in recent years. Brazil still hosts a mens and womens WCT leg at Santa Catarina and Rio, while no less than 7 mens and 4 womens WQS events are held all over the country. Most South American countries have hosted a pro contest at one time or another, including Argentina and Uruguay (1996), Chile was chosen for the Rip Curl Search (2007) and Peru currently hosts the womens WCT at Mancora. Ecuador has remained low key until the World Surfing Games were held at Salinas in 2004 and interest has increased in surfing the Galapagos Islands. South America has long had it's own surfwear brands, with labels like Hang Loose, Mormaii (manufacturing wetsuits since 1975) and an army of board shapers, catering to a huge local audience and aided by the government tradition of import protectionism. Media-wise, Brazil boasts a slew of constantly evolving surf mags including *Fluir*, *Inside*, *Hardcore* and *Almasurf*, plus a handful of TV shows dedicated to surfing. Urban areas support the bulk of the numerous surf shops estimated to exceed 1000. Peru's main mag Tablista, is still going since launch in 1985, while Chile has Marejada and Demolicion selling from the country's 40 or so surf outlets. A competitive edge is often apparent out in the line-up where the Latino machismo is allowed to flourish. Brazilian surfers often display a dog-eat-dog attitude when it comes to dropping in and have developed a bad reputation around the world for not showing any patience and aggressively burning other surfers, disregarding etiquette. Lima's breaks can get quite crowded, but considering the huge potential along the west coast, hassles in the water are totally avoidable.

CARIBBEAN SEA
NETHERLANDS ANTILLES
232. Caribbean Colombia
231. Caracas
TRINIDAD & TOBAGO
San José
Barranquilla
Maracaibo
Caracas
Cumana
Panama City
PANAMA
Gulf of Panama
233. Pacific Colombia
Medellín
Bogota
Cali
Huila
COLOMBIA
VENEZUELA
Georgetown
GUYANA
Paramaribo
SURINAM
FRENCH GUIANA
Cayenne
ATLANTIC OCEAN
240. Amapa, Para and Maranhão
Esmeraldas
Quito
ECUADOR
Chimborazo
Manta
Guayaquil
Machala
Piura
Trujillo
234. Ancash
Nevado Huascerán
Lima
PERU
Macapa
I. de Marajo
Belém
São Luis
Fortaleza
Natal
I. Fernando de Noronha
Recife
Maceio
Aracaju
Salvador
Ilhéus
Manaus
BRAZIL
Brasilia
Lake Titicaca
La Paz
Arequipa
BOLIVIA
235. Southern Peru
PACIFIC OCEAN
Arica
Iquique
Antofagasta
CHILE
PARAGUAY
Asuncion
Rio de Janeiro
São Paulo
Santos
Vitoria
Florianopolis
Porto Alegre
239. Rio Grande do Sul
236. Atacama and Coquimbo
La Serena
ARGENTINA
URUGUAY
Montevideo
238. Uruguay
Buenos Aires
La Plata
Valparaiso
Santiago
Concepcion
237. Biobio
Mar del Plata
Bahia Blanca
Viedma
Valdivia
Trelew
Comodoro Rivadavia
ATLANTIC OCEAN
FALKLAND/MALVINAS ISLANDS
Punta Arenas
Tierra del Fuego
Cape Horn
SCOTIA SEA
South Georgia
1. Peñascal Surf Hotel
2. Peruecosurf.com
C. Livethelife.tv
E. Waterways
0 500 1000 Miles
0 500 1000 1500 Kilometres

231. Caracas

Punta Care

YEP

Summary
+ Constant NE windswells
+ Lots of right pointbreaks
+ Epic hurricane swells
+ Relatively uncrowded
+ Impressive mountain backdrop

– Small, short period swells
– Onshore and turbid water
– Bad roads, expensive rentals
– Car thieves
– High mudslide risk

Venezuela is underexposed as a surf destination and although some surfers may have heard of Isla Margarita, the mainland remains a mystery. Talented Venezuelan surfers like Justin Mujica (2004 European Champion) or Magnum Martinez (South American las Latin Tour 2004 title) prove that there must be some good surf there. It's like Brazil or Florida, where surfers get year-round, warm-water, small waves to practice getting speed and making big moves. Between 2004 and 2007, the main highway bridge was cut and the 6 million people of Caracas were forced to drive 3 to 4 hours on very steep mountain roads to get to the coast only 20km (12mi) away. On the 18th December, 1999, catastrophe struck after days of unyielding rains caused mudslides that buried whole towns, killing 30,000 people and leaving 200,000 homeless. Since then, the coast has remained a bit of a wreck because governing bodies have decided to develop tourism in other parts of the country like Margarita or Los Roques. However, the Vargas State

YEP

Fido Point

YEP

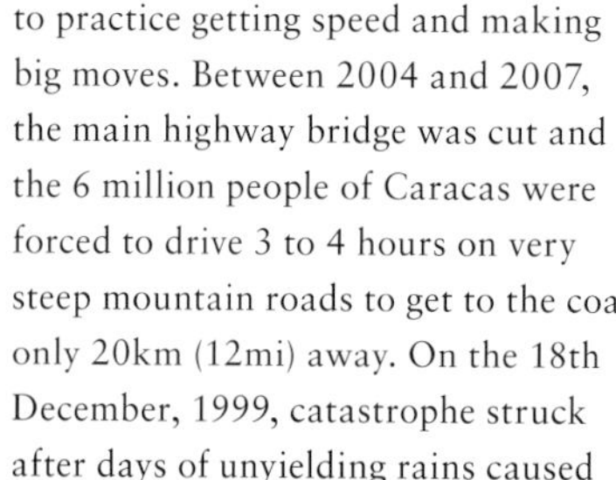

TRAVEL INFORMATION

Local Population: Caracas 6m
Coastline: Vargas 170km (106mi)
Time Zone: GMT -4
Contests: Nationals
Other Resources:
Video: Latin Guns
surfreportvenezuela.com
wavereport.com.ve

Getting There – 90 day automatic entry visa issued on arrival. Caracas (CCS) is well connected to the Americas and Europe. Simon Bolivar airport in Maiquetia is quite far from Caracas, but near the surf. When the main bridge was in repair, some people were flying domestic from Maiquetia to Caracas. Weekly boats arrive from Trinidad. $35 departure tax.

Getting Around – It's the cheapest petroleum in the world ($0.05 per litre), but the most expensive rental cars! Expect $80 per day for a small car. Car thievery and road damage is high so insurance is also expensive. Most people drive big beat-up cars for protection against big rocks that get washed across the coastal roads. Best idea is to get driven around by Juan "Cortado" Figueroa from surfreportvenezuela.com.

WEATHER STATISTICS	J/F	M/A	M/J	J/A	S/O	N/D
total rainfall (mm)	27	19	41	55	52	55
consistency (days/mth)	4	3	8	12	10	10
min temp (°C)	21	21	23	23	24	22
max temp (°C)	30	30	32	32	33	32

Lodging and Food – There are many high-rise hotels (Ole Caribe) in Naiguata or La Guaira, expect around $50-80/day. In Playa Anare, Villa Anare is $40 /dble, away from the coastal slums. In Cuyagua, posadas are $25/dble like Doña Meche or Cuyagua Mar. Juan Cortado rents flats near Fido Point. Meals cost around $3-5 in small places.

Weather – Caracas has a subtropical climate tempered by its proximity to the sea. It lies in a series of valleys 1000m (3280ft) above sea level and surrounded by majestic tree-clad mountains. Annual average temps oscillate between 25-27°C (77-81°F) and vary little year-round. The coldest month is January and the warmest one is May. The dry season runs from December to April and the rainy season from May to November. Average annual rainfall is over 1000mm (40in). Heavy showers are common but usually last an hour at most. A lack of cloud cover brings high daily sunshine hours. Boardies only.

Nature and Culture – Music and cars on the beach, are just part of the crazy beach party scene. Breathtaking mountain scenery plunges into the ocean. Caracas is close and worth a visit for colonial buildings and Las Mercedes nightspots, before taking the Cable Car back to the coast. Ambiance in Cuyagua is unreal, while Carnival is perfect for heavy party animals.

Hazards and Hassles – After 1999 mudslides, many coastal districts were destroyed; thievery and muggings have been on the rise since. Don't park or walk around Naiguata La Guaira and Maiquetia at night. Best is to go with someone who knows the region or stay out in the quiet areas from Punta Care to Los Caracas. Roads can be really bad. Beware of boulders.

Handy Hints – Fish and shortboards are ideal. There are lots of good shapers like Bachaco, Prisma and Kannibal charging $350 for a good shortboard, but they're not easy to find and there are no large surfshops. Check the peaceful Los Roques. Carnival time (February), Christmas and Easter week can be very busy with flights & pensions booked up.

coastline, overlooked by 2000m (6560ft) high peaks of El Avila Park, provides an incredibly verdant backdrop for surfing this quiet corner of the Caribbean.

New breakwaters and seawalls have destroyed a few good surfspots like Punta Piedras, but a few have also been created. Take Fido Point for example, where the 2005 Hurricane Emily swell destroyed the jetty, but a short barrelling right now breaks over the ruins. There is a high number of little boulder and rock right points, like Los Caracas, a popular beach about 2hrs drive east from Caracas, where the waves can be excellent near the **El Rio** rivermouth. **Anare** may not be an epic beachbreak, but it's consistent and the small town in front of the beach is really safe and friendly with a good hotel, plus a board shaper called Prisma. **Punta Care** is a long, right pointbreak, which gets really good over 4ft (1.2m) but it can get crowded. **Fido Point** offers short punchy rights off a broken jetty where the locals may be a little less welcoming. The whole beach is guarded on Sundays like **Playa Pantaleta**, a consistent beachbreak, which is best in cold fronts and can handle large swells. Pelua reef lefts work on rare occasions, but on a big swell, **Otro Pais**, (aka Camuri Grande Club or Paraiso) is the place to be. It's a fast, powerful, right pointbreak, where barrels are possible, but strong rips and restricted access require lots of paddling. **Carmen D'Uria**'s great rights are clearly visible from the coastal highway, but hardly anyone surfs there because it's dangerous to park near the *favellas* (slums). **Puerto Azul** is another right pointbreak, which is not so crowded, but again, the area can be a bit sketchy. **Los Cocos** is the most popular, consistent break with super fun lefts near the jetty, but expect crowds and pollution, or try Los Coquitos next door. **Tanaguarena** (aka La Playita or Boca del Rio) sports rocky rights that are shallow, dangerous and really powerful but unfortunately, all too rare. Another **Playita**, just north of the airport is also a fickle right pointbreak, with good jetty options just to the east. **Mamo** rights can be very long, breaking next to the Officer's Club that has restricted access, so park outside and paddle wide. The pretty colonial village of Choroni shelters legitimate reefbreak rights at **El Malecon**, and a decent shorebreak at Playa Grande. One of Venezuela's best beachbreaks is **Cuyagua**, where the hollow waves near the rivermouth hold some size and it's quite uncrowded during the week. Good camping and party scene. On the way to Cuyagua, check **El Playon** and the wedgy lefts and rights at La Punta, the beach furthest west. It's only a short 30min flight north by prop-plane to the beautiful archipelago of Los Roques. Famous for excellent kitesurfing, there is one consistent small-wave surf spot along with various options for world-class diving.

NASSER

Cuyagua

The venturi effect adds some strength to the Caribbean ENE trade winds when they hit the steep, mountainous coast and bring a constant supply of 2-6ft (0.6-2m) short-period windswell from November to March. During summer, wind direction turn more E and wave size decreases to more like 1-4ft (0.3-1.2). Late summer can bring straight N hurricane swells when the storm tracks into the Caribbean Sea, producing epic conditions, because the trades usually stop blowing and waves can reach 8-10ft (2.5-3m). Venezuela is more quantity than quality, with the majority of waves being punchy onshore shorebreaks or fun pointbreaks ruffled by the sideshores. Winds are usually calmer in the morning, but the waves are smaller as well, since the windswells often build during the day. Sometimes, mountain canyons create localized offshore winds. Tide cycles are semi-diurnal odd, so there is one big tide and one small tide twice a day.

SURF STATISTICS	J F	M A	M J	J A	S O	N D
dominant swell	NE-E	NE-E	NE-E	NE-E	NE-E	NE-E
swell size (ft)	3-4	3	2-3	2	3	3-4
consistency (%)	90	80	60	50	70	90
dominant wind	NE-E	NE-E	E-SE	NE-E	E-SE	NE-E
average force	F4	F4	F4	F4	F4	F4
consistency (%)	89	89	86	86	82	85
water temp.(°C)	26	26	27	28	29	29
wetsuit						

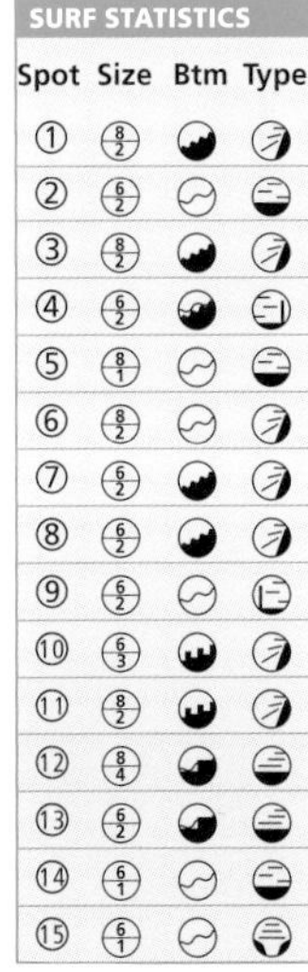

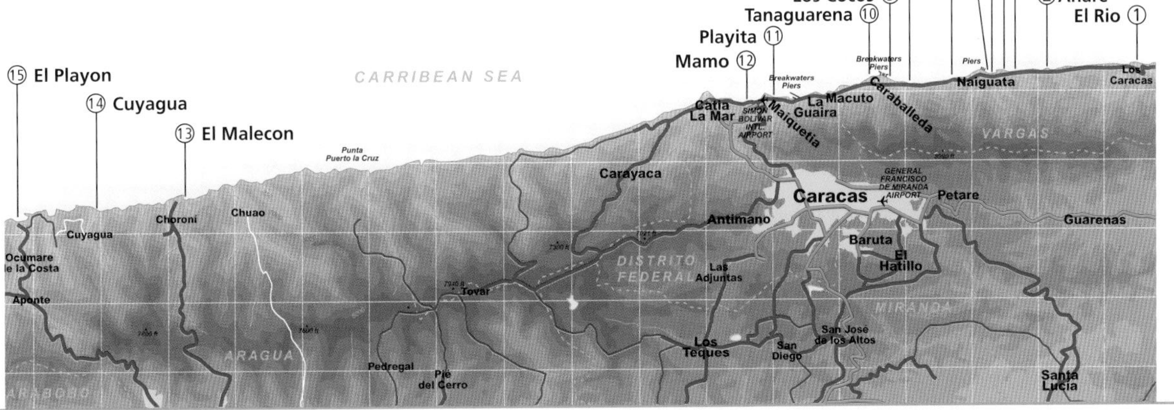

232. Caribbean Colombia

Los Naranjos

ALL PHOTOS STEPHANE ROBIN

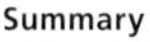

Summary
+ Very consistent
+ Warm water
+ Uncrowded
+ Dry surf season
+ Exploration possibilities
+ Coastal mountain scenery

– Poor quality waves
– Frequent onshores
– Street crime
– Heavy drug trade
– Civil war

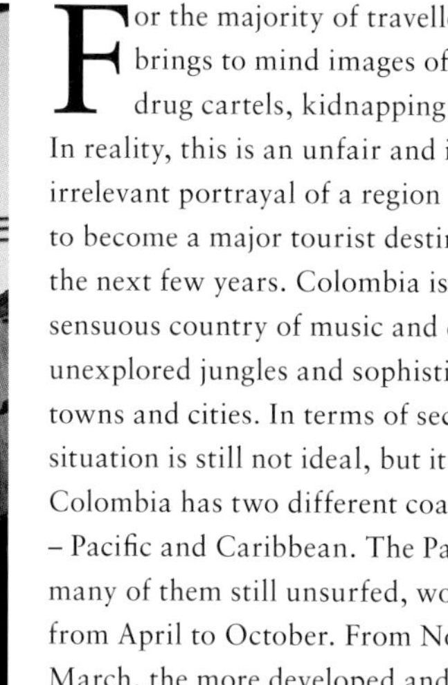

For the majority of travellers, Colombia brings to mind images of guerrillas, drug cartels, kidnapping and cocaine. In reality, this is an unfair and increasingly irrelevant portrayal of a region that is tipped to become a major tourist destination in the next few years. Colombia is a beautiful, sensuous country of music and dance, unexplored jungles and sophisticated towns and cities. In terms of security, the situation is still not ideal, but it is improving. Colombia has two different coastlines – Pacific and Caribbean. The Pacific breaks, many of them still unsurfed, work best from April to October. From November to March, the more developed and easier-going Caribbean coastline is the focus.

Los Naranjos

The vanilla yellow city of Cartagena de Indias has a strip of sheltered and average beachbreak, broken up by a line of short jetties. It's hard to pick any of these beaches above another, but the westernmost are the most exposed,

TRAVEL INFORMATION

Local Population: Cartagena 1M, Barranquilla 1.4M
Coastline: 3,208km (1,994mi): 1,760km (1,093) Atlantic
Time Zone: GMT -5
Contests: Nationals
Other Resources:
iguanamar.com
surfingcolombia.com

Getting There – Plenty of airlines serve Bogotá, from where connections are possible to Cartagena (CTG), Barranquilla (BAQ) or Santa Marta (SMR). National Airlines Avianca is reliable and cheap. Most Central American travellers fly through San Andres, which also has good surf. Departure Tax of $30. Travelling overland from any of Colombia's neighbours is not recommended.

Getting Around – Colombia is one of the few countries where travelling by public transport is safer than a privately hired car. The reasons for this are nothing to do with access to the surf, but rather security. Large 4x4's and rental cars are targeted by guerrillas and bandits more often than buses and taxis. AeroRebública domestic flights are cheap.

WEATHER STATISTICS	J/F	M/A	M/J	J/A	S/O	N/D
total rainfall (mm)	2	13	110	117	185	82
consistency (days/mth)	0	2	11	12	15	7
min temp (°C)	23	24	25	25	25	24
max temp (°C)	30	31	31	31	31	30

Lodging and Food – Every town has at least one basic hotel and all the coastal tourist cities have dozens of options suiting all price ranges. Colombia is cheap, with clean double rooms available for as little as $10. Colombian food can be monotonous, with greasy meals, fried chicken and plantains the usual fare.

Weather – The weather is hot all year-round in Caribbean Colombia, with the average temperature varying between 25-30°C (77-86°F). The most pleasant season extends from December to April, not only because it is the driest, but also the evenings are freshened by a light breeze, making the heat more tolerable. From May through to August, regular light showers make the hot climate heavier, and the temperature can reach 45°C (113°F). The months of September, October and November are the least appealing. Brief, torrential downpours occur every day, flooding certain areas. October receives about 235mm (9in) of rainfall. The water is warm enough for shorts and a rash vest year-round.

Nature and Culture – Cartagena is a World Heritage Site renowned for its beauty and extraordinary street life. The Parque Nacional Tayrona has good jungle trekking and the remains of a lost city called Pueblito. The twin peaks of the Sierra Nevada de Santa Marta are the world's highest coastal mountains at 5775m (18947ft). Ciudad Perdida is a Colombian highlight.

Hazards and Hassles – After decades of guerrilla insurgency, paramilitary death squads, massively powerful drug cartels, the highest kidnap rate in the world and, at times, virtual open warfare on city streets, not to mention a daunting petty crime rate, Colombia is finally becoming more secure. Stick to tourist areas, listen to local advice and avoid displays of wealth (i.e. a hire car).

Handy Hints – Surf spares are available from a few surf shops in Barranquilla. Embark fully versed on the local security situation and don't do anything stupid. Colombia can be very dangerous in places, but don't be paranoid most people leave with nothing but good memories.

Los Naranjos

particularly in front of the **Las Velas** hotel. These waves break on localised wind-swell and are usually weak, messy and a muddy brown colour. Things improve only marginally along the strip of coastline between here and the next city, Barranquilla, which has a better range of waves, including Caribbean Colombia's only known reef breaks. **Pradomar** is well-known for its soft rights off the jetty and lefts further down the beach, but the more consistent option is the slow, fat rights of **El Bolsillo** the next jetty north. It picks up all the NE swell, but maxes out in overhead conditions and the rips get really strong. **Punta Roca** is probably the best wave on the Caribbean coast, a heavy, ledgy A-frame reef that can get hollow. It's fairly inconsistent and will be busy with Barranquilla's friendly surf community, breaking best at higher tides and holding up to 6ft (2m). A good respite from the hustle of the cities is the Parque Nacional Tayrona - the jungle-cloaked bays and inlets house numerous perfect beaches. Of these, **Arrecifes** is by far the best. It's a highly consistent wave and unlike the Barranquilla and Cartagena areas is not battered by constant wind. The right breaking off the huge granite boulders at the eastern end of the beach is the best wave, though it does close-out a lot. With accommodation or camping possible right on the beach this is a truly idyllic spot to hang out for a few days and the waves are almost always empty. It's an hour-long walk through the jungle to reach the beach and visitors must pay a fee to enter the park. Not far to the east of Arrecifes, and possibly even more beautiful, is **Los Naranjos**. A small stream emerges here and creates a reliable low tide sandbar in front of the dramatic rock pillars. It gets hollow and is generally a cleaner wave than Arrecifes. It will hold up to 6ft (2m) and sharing the line-up is rare. To the east are plenty of other rarely surfed breaks. **Casa Grande** is a 3min drive, or 10min walk from the Hotel Mendihuaca. The wave will either tube or close out depending on the state of the bank. Further east still, **Buritaca** has two right pointbreaks and hollow waves in the rivermouth breaking in a beautiful, natural setting. **Viento Fresco** also has a quality righthand point, consistently breaking on all swells. Opposite Club **Las Gaviotas** is another rivermouth. There are further right points in the Finca de los Rivera area, with numerous exploration possibilities.

The waves that hit this stretch of the Caribbean are all locally produced windswells with very short wave periods resulting in messy and confused surf. On the plus side, it's consistent, with rarely a flat day between December and March. Catching the glassy morning conditions means being up early. The Barranquilla to Cartagena stretch is always windy during this period, but winds are often lighter in the morning. The hurricane season between August and November can sometimes produce a decent clean groundswell for Caribbean Colombia but this is much rarer than in the northern part of the Caribbean. Don't expect to come here and score epic, powerful waves. Most swells are in the 3-4ft (1-1.2m) range, but it can get to double this. The swell often builds through the day and then drops off again as the wind dies overnight. Tidal variation rarely exceeds 1ft (0.3m).

SURF STATISTICS

Spot	Size	Btm	Type
1	4/1		
2	6/1		
3	4/1		
4	6/2		
5	6/1		
6	6/1		
7	6/2		
8	6/2		
9	8/2		
10	6/2		

SURF STATISTICS	J F	M A	M J	J A	S O	N D
dominant swell	NE	NE	NE	NE	NE	NE
swell size (ft)	3	3	2	2-3	1-2	2-3
consistency (%)	90	90	70	80	60	80
dominant wind	NE-E	NE-E	NE-E	NE-E	NE-E	NE-E
average force	F5	F4-F5	F4-F5	F4-F5	F4	F4
consistency (%)	96	95	92	94	83	91
water temp.(°C)	26	26	27	27	28	27
wetsuit						

Punta Sur, San Andres Island

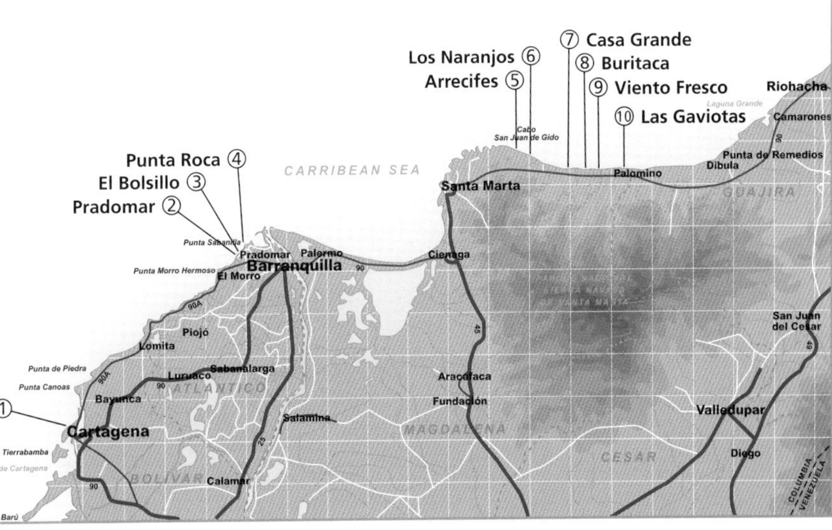

233. Pacific Colombia

Secret Right

ALL PHOTOS STEPHANE ROBIN

Summary
+ N & S groundswells
+ Variety of good lefts & rights
+ Amazing jungle waterways
+ Good services at El Cantil
+ Cheap, colourful, exotic Colombia

– Boat access only
– Rarely bigger than 6ft
– Extremely wet
– Air access – no longboards
– FARC kidnapping factor

The Pacific shores of Colombia have remained an obscure surf destination largely because of the dangerous security situation. Intense guerrilla activity, high street-crime statistics, and a heavy drug trade have served to keep Colombia off the radar for most surfers. Beyond these discouraging factors, most of the breaks are difficult to access. Pacific Colombia is one of the wettest shores in the world, receiving 5m (200in) of rain per year, meaning much of Choco Province has no roads. Getting there entails flying in, and getting around requires navigating the myriad of waterways. The Nuqui area receives long-distance swell from all over the Pacific, the direction of which dictates the best break on the day. Most visitors fly into Bogotá and Medellin, then take a small plane to Nuqui. There are breaks within walking distance from El Cantil Ecolodge, generally regarded as the best base for a surf mission.

Pico El Oro

TRAVEL INFORMATION

Local Population: 6.7M Bogota
Coastline: 3208km (1993mi); 1448km (900mi) Pacific
Time Zone: GMT -5
Contests: Local
Other Resources: iguanamar.com surfingcolombia.com www.elcantil.com

Getting There – Most flights get to Bogota (BOG), then Medellin (MDE), with 3 flights a week to Nuqui (NQU) with surfer-friendly Ada airline. Rival Satena won't take boardbags: no boards over 6'9. Medellin (EOH, domestic) to Nuqui is $150 return. Boats leave from Buenaventura (or Quibdo, 120 km away) but it's risky & expensive. $30 departure tax.

Getting Around – "Lanchas" (small passenger motorboats) take 35min to go to El Cantil. There is not much walking access around Nuqui or El Cantil, instead use lanchas or powerboats. For the Cabo Corriente spots, El Cantil hotel organises the powerboat (2 available). Based on 4 people, the cost is $45 per day each, so either come in a group or make sure other surfers will be there. The cost of slower Lanchas is $80 per day.

WEATHER STATISTICS	J/F	M/A	M/J	J/A	S/O	N/D
total rainfall (mm)	590	597	649	623	609	532
consistency (days/mth)	23	24	25	26	26	27
min temp (°C)	24	24	23	23	23	23
max temp (°C)	32	32	32	32	32	31

Lodging and Food – Basic accommodation around Nuqui is available. A week's stay in El Cantial Ecolodge costs about $500 with fullboard, transfers and netted beds in double rooms. High Season can be more expensive. Food is good but not always varied, and a small store sells basic stuff.

Weather – In Western Colombia the slopes of the Andes face the Pacific Ocean across a 100km coastal plain. This is one of the rainiest areas on the planet. The average rainfall in Nuqui is 5250mm (207in)! Rainfall has more variation throughout the hours of the day than the months of the year. In some places, rain falls on more than 300 days per year. The good news is that the coastal and offshore rain begins after midnight, then propagates westward over the ocean during the morning and sometimes afternoon hours. The sun does come out every day for a few hours; just don't expect to see much of the moon. The water is always boardshorts warm.

Nature and Culture – Great outdoor activities like fishing (Jan-June best), humpback whale watching (June-Oct), diving (big fish, some coral) and the honeymoon walking trip to the Del Amor Cascades (Love Waterfalls). Nature is everywhere and the wild forest houses native people and endemic species.

Hazards and Hassles – This area of Colombia is much safer now than 5 years ago. North of Nuqui there is no military presence on shore, although it is worth avoiding big rivermouths around Cali, where boats with illicit cargo might transit. Nuqui to Cabo Corriente is pretty safe. Bull sharks around rivermouths and rips can be a concern but the main hazard is rain and the threat posed by chloroquine resistant malaria below 800m (2620ft). There is one hospital for minor emergencies.

Handy Hints – Regarding safety, always ask in Medellin before departure. Locals can be a great help and beginners can even take surfing lessons at the El Cantil Ecolodge. Staff at the lodge can also fix boards, and it is possible to rent a longer board. The region plays host to amazing jungle life, so take binoculars.

Left near Nuqui

El Valle ①
Derecha Secreta ②
Jurubidá ③
Tribugá ④
Nuquí ⑤
El Cantil ⑥
Terco ⑦
Termales ⑧
El Mystic ⑨
Pico El Oro ⑩
Pela Pela ⑪
Juan Tornillo ⑫
Secret Right ⑬

Bahía Solano
El Valle
Puerto Utría
Punta Diego
Ensenada de Utría
Punta Jurubidá
Jurubidá
Tribugá
Golfo Tribugá
Nuquí
Panguí
Ensenada Coquí
Punta Arusí
Arusí
El Cantil
Coquí
Cabo Corrientes
Cuevita
Bahía Cuevita
Virudó
Pavasita
Pavasa
Donatera
Ensenada Catripe

The beaches local to the lodge are average, however, and the best way of accessing many of the better waves in the region is by powerboat. To make it economical, a group of four is ideal to hire a boat and explore.

El Valle is the northern limit of this region, a powerful beachbreak that is best suited to shortboards. At this break, local kids rent, sell and repair boards. In this region, **Derecha Secreta** is a heavy right that is very shallow. At **Jurubidá**, which requires a solid S-W swell, a decent righthand sand-bottom point can be found. Fun to surf, this low tide wave is best in morning offshores before the wind switches to light NW. The **Tribugá** rivermouth has both rights and lefts, but the longer lefts are better. At high tide it breaks close to shore and has good shape. Hazards at this spot include strong rips and occasional sharks. **Nuquí** itself has a fickle rivermouth left, which is a long, mellow ride when it works, although it needs a big SW swell. **El Cantil**, where most surfers stay, has a beachbreak that works in NW or big SW swell. The waves here are average, with shifting peaks best in early morning glassy conditions. Within easy reach are the lefts at **Terco**, which again requires NW swell or a big W/SW to get going. Just 10 minutes in a boat from El Cantil (or 1/2hr walk) is the **Termales** rivermouth, where the sandbanks dictate whether the left or right is better on NW or big SW swells. If the swell is big and from the SW, check **El Mystic**, a sectiony left reef, way out off the end of the bay. Most surfers bypass all of these breaks and take the 45 minute powerboat trip to **Pico El Oro** and **Pela Pela**. Both of these great lefthanders are better in SW swells. Pico El Oro breaks on big rocks and is regarded as the best wave in Nuqui. Mid-tide is the optimum time to hit it. Inside of Pico El Oro is Pela Pela, another left with barrel sections and a sharp, shallow inside over rocks. Just 5km (3mi) north of Cabo Corientes, **Juan Tornillo** is a good option in N-NE winds and SW swell. Round the cape is **Secret Right**, a big, open barrel on SW or big NW swells. This wave works best at low tide and can run for 100 metres or more. There are other spots in the area and further south.

Like the neighbouring country of Ecuador and the Galapagos islands, swell hits Colombia from all over the Pacific. In winter (Dec-Feb), it is more common to get very clean long-distance NW swells with offshores and slightly less rain, but consistency might be at stake. Winter visitors might be better off surfing the consistent Caribbean coast, or visiting one of many Colombian tourist hotspots, staying on standby for a flight to Nuqui when the forecast is good. Surf in this season is typically 2-4ft (0.6-1.2m) and very clean. During the more generous SW swell season, low pressures originating from New Zealand rather than Chile will deliver surf in the 3-6ft (1-2m) range with possible 8ft (2.5m) days, along with a light onshore seabreeze and heavier rainfall. Transition months are November and May, neither of which are ideal. Tidal variation can be as much as 15ft (5m). Tide charts are rare, so locals or a tide program can be of use.

SURF STATISTICS	J F	M A	M J	J A	S O	N D
dominant swell	NW	SW-NW	SW	SW	SW	NW
swell size (ft)	4	3	2-3	4	2	2-3
consistency (%)	70	50	60	70	50	70
dominant wind	NW-NE	NW-NE	NW-NE	SW-NE	S-W	NW-NE
average force	F4	F3-F4	F3	F3	F3	F3-F4
consistency (%)	89	92	44	45	58	62
water temp.(°C)	26	26	28	28	28	27
wetsuit						

SURF STATISTICS			
Spot	Size	Btm	Type
①	6/1		
②	6/2		
③	6/2		
④	6/2		
⑤	6/2		
⑥	6/1		
⑦	6/2		
⑧	6/2		
⑨	6/2		
⑩	8/2		
⑪	6/1		
⑫	12/2		
⑬	6/2		

Pico El Oro

234. Ancash

Secret spot

ALL PHOTOS GONZALO BARANDIARAN

Summary
+ Quality pointbreaks
+ No crowds
+ Great swell exposure
+ Close to Lima
+ Landscapes & Andes

– Lack of beachbreaks
– Distance between breaks
– Foggy days
– Petty theft
– Cool water temps

Ancash is a Quechua word meaning blue and this region is where the first Peruvian civilization, known as Chavín, originated and flourished in 600BC. It is a land of contrasts, with the 6,768m (22,204ft) white summit of the Andes mountains lying only 100km (62mi) from the deep blue Pacific coast. From Chimbote to Lima, much of the coast is a monotonous and inhospitable stretch of vast sand deserts, except along the green river valleys, cultivated with sugarcane, rice and cotton. Despite being blessed by highly consistent swells and a bunch of quality spots, this area is usually missed by travelling surfers who focus on the incredible waves further north, or the easily accessible breaks of Lima and Punta Hermosa. As crowd levels increase everywhere, this rich, empty surf region is definitely one worth checking out.

Puerto Huarmey

La Antenna

TRAVEL INFORMATION

Local Population: 1,139,083
Coastline: 350 km (218mi)
Time Zone: GMT -5
Contests: None
Other Resources:
surfvantrips-peru.com
localperu.com/localtours
peru.info
perucontact.com
Video: Peel, The Peru Project (2006)

Getting There – Most travellers don't need a visa for up to 90 days. Jorge Chavez International Airport (LIM) in Lima has plenty of international flights, but Peru has no international airline. Airport is 30min from Lima's historic centre by taxi – go for a regular cab company. $30 dep tax.

Getting Around – For a guided tour, check the Norte Chico tour from Surfvantrips or Local Tours. If travelling alone on a longer trip, go for the bus (safe and reliable), or rent a car for a shorter trip. Rentals at airport from $250/wk (Budget, Hertz). Pan American Highway runs along the coast, providing easy access to most spots.

Lodging and Food – Owned by US surfer Tato Debernardis, Fundo Centinela has spacious bungalows up to 5pax (approx $40/night) or tent site ($5), plus onsite restaurant and bar. Cheap accommodation in Barranca (Hotel Chavin $30/dble, hotel Continental $15/dble). In Huacho, try hotel Centenario ($25/dble). Try the ceviche del pato, picante de cuy, jaca-casqui, pecan-caldo and humitas de chochoca.

WEATHER STATISTICS	J/F	M/A	M/J	J/A	S/O	N/D
total rainfall (mm)	0.5	0	0.7	2	2	0.3
consistency (days/mth)	1	0	1	2	1	1
min temp (°C)	13	15	12	12	12	12
max temp (°C)	26	26	23	20	21	24

Weather – The region is affected by the cold Humboldt Current, the El Nino Southern Oscillation, tropical latitude, and the Andes mountain range. It has a spring-like climate all year-round. Foggy and sunny days intermingle around the humid sand dunes most of the year. Summers (Jan - April) have warm temps around 30°C (86°F), while winters (Jun - Oct) are very humid and range around 18°C (64°F). The spring and autumn average temps hover around 24°C (75°F). Days alternate between overcast skies with occasional fog during winter and sunny skies get hazy in summer. The only rainfall is a light drizzle locally known as garua. Many use a 4/3mm fullsuit with boots between June and November and a 3/2mm fullsuit the rest of the year.

Nature and Culture – Huascarán National Park counts 663 glaciers and the snow-covered summit of Huascarán, highest peak in Peru and second of the Americas (6,768m/22,205ft). Lots of ancient archaeological sites of Chavin de Huantar & Caral cultures, plus Paramonga pyramids. Check the Rataquenua view-point and Ancash Regional Museum in Huaraz.

Hazards and Hassles – Hidden rocks, currents, sea urchins and the shallow reef at Playa Grande constitute the main dangers while surfing. Avoid driving at night, heavy traffic and thefts in Lima, don't get lost near Paraiso. The 1970 Ancash earthquake was one of the deadliest natural disasters in Peru, killing more than 50,000 people and damaging 186,000 houses.

Handy Hints – No surf shops in Ancash region, boards & gear must be rented or bought in Lima (Klimax, Wayo Whilar, Sofia Mulanovich surf shop). Bring a 6'6" to 7'4" thick board for heavy waves. Booties & helmet are a plus (few hospitals). Due to petty theft even from taxis, leave a copy of your passport or ID card with your consulate in Lima. Free camping possible but not recommended.

Paraiso

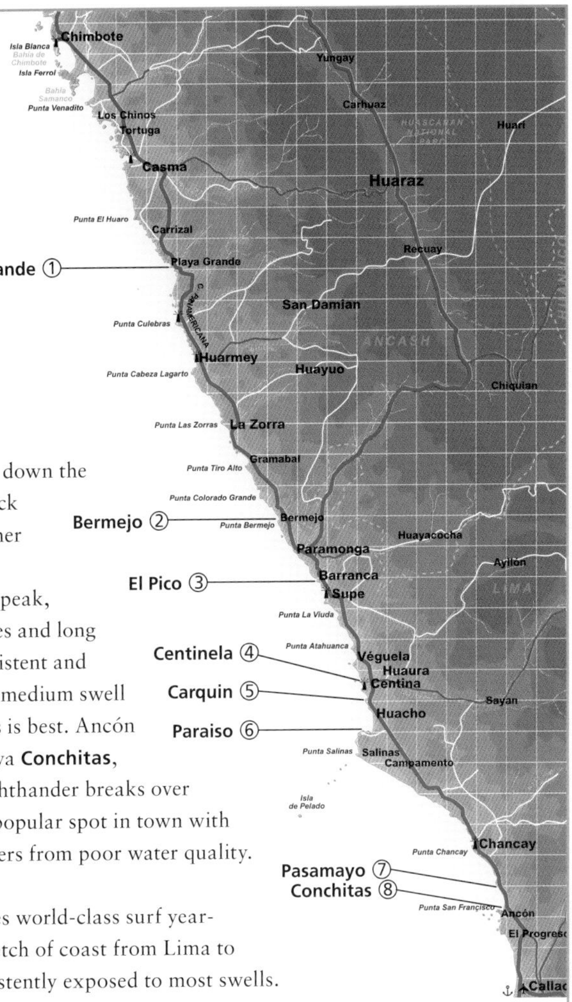

Visible from the Panamericana Highway near Km 336, **Playa Grande** is home to good beachbreaks and an excellent lefthand reefbreak that fires with S-SW swells. Extremely shallow even at high tide, the hungry reef delivers a very fast, tubular, but short wave that never closes out or gets busy. The vert take-off is followed by a slabby, square barrel that is one of the most dangerous waves in Peru! Experts only. **Bermejo** hosts an uncrowded, perfect, lefthand pointbreak where the trade winds blow offshore. The first section is fast and hollow in places, peeling over a stony bottom and best at low tide with a S swell. The second sandy section is a fun, easy wall, ideal for improvers. The town of Barranca has several lodging options and restaurants, but there is little to see and only mediocre beachbreak on the city beaches. If a solid SW swell hits, then the fickle righthand reef known as **El Pico** can deliver some excellent, powerful righthand tubes from mid to high tide. From Huaura, a labyrinth of dirt tracks makes it hard to find **Centinela**, one of the country's best left pointbreaks, with up to four consistent sections that attract weekend crowds. Best with a W swell and definitely better at low tide, the outside sections (4-10ft) are for experienced riders only, as they are very rocky with frequent rips. The sandy inside sections (2-7ft) wall up very nicely on a W swell and suit all standards. On S swells, only the powerful first section breaks. A shorter, smaller and much less consistent lefthander hugs the hilly headland at **Carquin**, 3km further south. The rare summer N swells won't suit many breaks in the area except the inconsistent, high tide lefthander at **Paraiso**. Nearby spots include El Rebote, La Antena, and Punta Salinas; take water and food to this remote spot. **Pasamayo** is located 35km (22mi) north of Lima, nestled at the base of massive sand dunes with the Pan American Highway truck lanes precariously perched above. Either park at toll and hitch a ride with a bus or truck, or get a boat from Ancon. Walking down the dunes is fun but coming back up after a long surf is another story! The reward is a very powerful, well-shaped reef peak, throwing out plenty of tubes and long ripable walls. It's very consistent and often too big, so a small to medium swell on windless early mornings is best. Ancón has a N swell option at Playa **Conchitas**, where a semi consistent righthander breaks over flat rocks and sand. It is a popular spot in town with nearby facilities, but it suffers from poor water quality.

Playa Grande

Central Peru receives world-class surf year-round and the stretch of coast from Lima to Chimbote is consistently exposed to most swells.

Near Paraiso

Regular S-SW swells can occur anytime from March through November, while the NW swell season (November to March) will turn on a few spots, but is definitely not the best time to surf here. Prevailing winds are from the SE-S and blow all through the year, offering a lot of sideshore conditions and offshores for a few points. Usually, SE morning winds turn more S after noon, so wake up early. The strongest winds occur in the winter months from May-October, while the summer months from November-April have considerably lighter winds. Tidal ranges are up to 6ft (1.8m) with most spots breaking better at low tide. Get a tide table in Lima's surf shops.

SURF STATISTICS

Spot	Size	Btm	Type
①	10/5		
②	8/2		
③	6/2		
④	8/3		
⑤	8/4		
⑥	10/5		
⑦	10/4		
⑧	8/2		

SURF STATISTICS	J F	M A	M J	J A	S O	N D
dominant swell	NW	S-SW	S-SW	S-SW	S-SW	NW
swell size (ft)	4	3	4	4-5	4	3-4
consistency (%)	70	70	80	80	70	60
dominant wind	SE-S	SE-S	SE-S	SE-S	SE-S	SE-S
average force	F3	F3	F3-F4	F3-F4	F3-F4	F3
consistency (%)	82	88	84	86	88	85
water temp.(°C)	21	20	18	17	16	18
wetsuit						

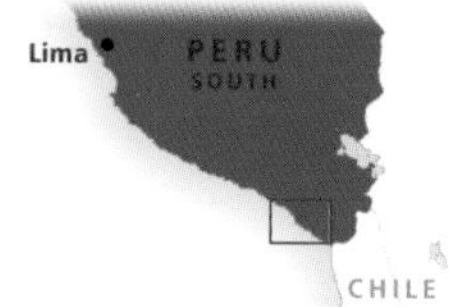

235. Southern Peru

Piedras Negras

JAVIER FERNANDEZ

Summary
+ Good consistency
+ Variety of breaks
+ No crowds
+ Very friendly people
+ No rain all year

– Cold water
– Remote area (few services)
– 4WD required
– Bad winter weather
– Pollution from Ilo copper smelter

Peru, South America's third largest country, is one of the great surf countries in the world. Curiously, its lengthy, 2400km (1500mi) coastline has only been explored in patches, and many waves still go unridden. Most surfers focus on the endless left points of Chicama or Pacasmayo in the La Libertad area, or else the high density of spots around Lima and Punta Hermosa. Those seeking consistency and big waves should seriously consider heading south to Arequipa, Moquegua and Tacna, the country's southernmost regions, where all that is needed is a spirit of adventure, a good wetsuit and ideally a 4WD. It's a varied, dusty terrain, where the rocky desert is gouged by torrential coastal rivers into valleys, gorges and canyons. With the Pan Am Highway veering away from the sea, access to the breaks requires patience, but this southernmost part of Peru is super-consistent during winter S swells from Antarctic lows.

WWW.DUIOPS.NET

Morro Sama

JAVIER FERNANDEZ

TRAVEL INFORMATION

Local Population: 170,000
Coastline: 250km (155mi)
Time Zone: GMT -5
Contests: None
Other Resources:
peru.info
ceticosilo.com/hoteles.php
Video: "Billabong Odyssey" (2003)

Getting There – Most travellers do not need visas. Jorge Chavez International Airport (LIM) in Lima has plenty of international flights. Arequipa (Peru's second largest city) is served by Rodríguez Ballón International Airport (AQP). LAN Peru has domestic flights from Lima to Tacna (1h30, $220/rt) or to Arequipa ($190). $30 dep tax.

Getting Around – Pan American Highway wanders too far inland, so public transport is not very suitable to explore the coast. No surf tours/camp to drive you around. To negotiate the trails, rent a 4x4 in Arequipa (www.gygrentacar.com) or Tacna. Arica is ultra-close.

Lodging and Food – Ilo has different levels of hotels, facilities, and is strategically situated near all the surrounding waves. Cheap hotels are Arequipa, Porteno, El Eden, Romicor, San Martin, Paraiso. For more comfort try Gran Hotel ($30/dble). Hospedaje El Tigre en Boca del Rio. Incredible seafood, excellent wines and piscos produced near Tacna.

WEATHER STATISTICS	J/F	M/A	M/J	J/A	S/O	N/D
total rainfall (mm)	0.5	0.4	2	5	6	0.5
consistency (days/mth)	1	1	1	2	3	1
min temp (°C)	18	15	11	9	11	14
max temp (°C)	28	26	22	20	21	25

Weather – Ilo has a sub-tropical, desert climate characterized by dryness, warmth and sunny days all year-round. During summer, temps range from 15-28°C (59-82°F) and skies are clear. Winter temps vary between 14-22°C (58-72°F), with occasional fog and persistent drizzles that peak in August and September. Annual rainfall averages 40mm (1.6in), officially making this area a desert. The weather conditions are created by two major offshore ocean currents: the cold Humboldt Current coming up from Chile and the Antarctic, which meets the warm, tropical El Nino current coming down from the Pacific along the Ecuadorian coast. Although average winter water temps shouldn't require more than a 3/2mm, from May to December, many use a 4/3mm fullsuit with boots and a 3/2mm fullsuit the other months.

Nature and Culture – On a flat day visit the Algarrobal museum (archaeology & agriculture) near Ilo or the Naval Museum in town. Sandboarding in Boca del Rio. Miculla is an extensive petroglyph site east of Tacna, estimated to be 1,500 years old.

Hazards and Hassles – No sharks cruise the area. Massive winter waves, rocky bottoms and strong currents constitute the main risks, along with earthquakes, tsunamis and volcanic eruptions (2001 southern Peru earthquake was a magnitude 8.4, the most devastating since 1970). Theft is a minor problem in southern Peru.

Handy Hints – Bring a medium size board plus a gun for some breaks! Peruvian boards are good and inexpensive (surf shops in Arequipa and Lima). Bring ding repair and extra leash. During austral winter, fog named 'garua' is quite depressing and water is cold so bring a 4/3mm wetsuit and booties. Winter camping is not recommended (too cold). Basic Spanish essential if you're unguided.

The popular resort of **Mollendo** has some highly-consistent, but often mushy beachbreaks that easily close-out above head-high. A short drive to Mejía will reveal strong, sometimes hollow shorebreaks at **Tiro Alto** that need a small to medium summer swell. Overlooked by a huge statue of Christ, **Punta de Bombón** offers a similar setup except that the Rio Tambo rivermouth can create better sand banks at this mainly summer break that tends to max-out in winter. A 60km (37mi) dusty drive on the coastal track leads to southwest-facing **Playa Platanales**. Depending on conditions, the place can either spit out quality, sizeable barrels or mushy beginners waves in small swells. In front of the Hacienda Pocoma, inconsistent **El Olon** is the second biggest wave in Peru after Pico Alto. The long lefts get tubular at the right stage of tide, hold up to 20ft (6m) of S or SW swell, and should be left to experienced big-wave surfers only. **Piedras Negras** is another high quality, lefthand reefbreak with a powerful, barreling take-off section from mid to high tide and is only surfed by a friendly local crew. Ilo is a bustling industrial port with one of the largest copper smelters in the country, as well as a copper refinery, only 2km from Piedras Negras, belching out large amounts of air and water pollution. The reef peak **El Colegio** faces the school's stadium and is user-friendly in offshore conditions. **Pozo de Lizas** is Ilo's designated summer beach attracting crowds of tourists and any small S swells onto good banks for learners. Check **Caleta Sama** in moderate S-SW swells, where a semi-consistent left pointbreak generates short, powerful lefthanders. The take-off is usually steep, and the spot has the capacity to hold a solid 10ft (3m). Close to Tacna, **Boca del Rio** is a small "recreation town", offering some nightlife and a collection of beaches with well-formed peaks. There is a large choice of waves, from beach to reefbreaks, but generally short rides. From here starts a long and almost linear stretch of coast that extends to Arica, Chile, where the 2007 Rip Curl Pro WCT was held.

Ilo

PAPITA SIERRA

S-SW swells from Antarctic lows are super-consistent and send plenty of large swells for at least 9 months solid (March to November). The biggest winter storms send oversized waves and huge close-outs, with breaking waves varying between 3-15ft (1-5m) and bigger at El Olon. There is still a fair amount of S-SW in the summer, complimented by the occasional summer NW swells between November and March. S-SE winds dominate, blowing for 65% of the year, with more SE, except between Oct-Nov. Glassy conditions occur for 10-12% of the year as mornings are typically windless, then around noon a gentle S sea-breeze creates a little chop on the wave face. Some spots are really wind sensitive and are only surfed in the morning, but the spots around Ilo benefit from better S wind protection. Tide range never exceeds 2m (6ft), but are important at the shallow reefs.

SURF STATISTICS			
Spot	Size	Btm	Type
①	5/2		
②	6/2		
③	6/2		
④	8/2		
⑤	20/6		
⑥	10/4		
⑦	6/3		
⑧	5/2		
⑨	10/4		
⑩	8/2		

SURF STATISTICS	J F	M A	M J	J A	S O	N D
dominant swell	S-SW	S-SW	S-SW	S-SW	S-SW	S-SW
swell size (ft)	3-4	4	5-6	6-7	5-6	4
consistency (%)	60	70	80	90	80	60
dominant wind	SE-S	SE-S	SE-S	SE-S	SE-S	SE-S
average force	F2-F3	F2-F3	F2-F3	F2-F3	F2-F3	F2-F3
consistency (%)	66	65	60	63	67	65
water temp.(°C)	21	19	17	15	16	19
wetsuit						

El Olon

JAVIER FERNANDEZ

236. Atacama and Coquimbo

El Muro and Derecharcha

ALL PHOTOS WILLY URIBE

Summary
+ Very consistent swells
+ Clean turquoise waters
+ Quality left & right points
+ Atacama desert beauty
+ Cultural & happening La Serena

– Heavy waves
– Cold water year-round
– Some tricky spot access
– Exposed to winds,
– Rocks and boulders

Since the Rip Curl Search WCT was held in Arica in 2007, the surf world has started to pay attention to Chile's 6435km (4020mi) long coastline, hunting for more consistent left pointbreaks and gnarly reefbreaks. Distances are so vast, Chile has a numerical naming system and this 'Norte Chico' zone straddles the regions of Atacama (Region 3) and Coquimbo (Region 4), relatively close to Chile's capital, Santiago. The stark, virtually rainless Atacama desert is divided by fertile river valleys and known for clear skies most of the year. Beyond Huasco to the north are some classic lefts at Porto Fino near Chañaral, or regular footers might fancy heading south of Totoralillo to Teniente, near Los Vilos, where some Superbank style rights can be ridden without the super-crowd.

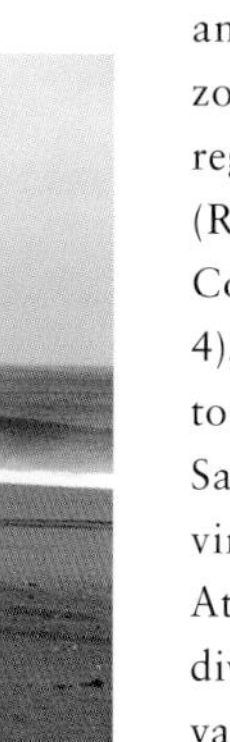

TRAVEL INFORMATION

Local Population: 254,336
Coastline: 250km (155mi)
Time Zone: GMT -4
Contests: Punta Teatinos Campeonato de Surf 2007 Eco Classic.
Other Resources:
surftotoralillo.cl
surfserena.cl
chilesafari.com
chilesurf.cl
surf.cl
Video: Perro En Bote - surfestival.blogspot.com

WEATHER STATISTICS	J/F	M/A	M/J	J/A	S/O	N/D
total rainfall (mm)	0	1	21	22	6	0
consistency (days/mth)	0	0	2	5	1	0
min temp (°C)	14	11	7	7	9	11
max temp (°C)	25	25	18	16	19	23

Getting There – No visa required. Santiago (SCL) is well connected with North America, Europe and Australasia. National airline is LAN Chile. From Peru, Bolivia or Argentina, it's much cheaper to get there by bus. From Santiago, there are buses departing twice an hour, sometimes every 15 minutes to La Serena, 6h away.

Getting Around – Car hire is ideal (base model $50/d; United). Be ready for long Pan American Highway drives. Real exploration requires a 4WD. Double cab pickups will cost $80/d while a minibus for 8 people will be $135/d. Public transport with long distance bus and local taxis can work fine for individuals.

Lodging and Food – Try Hotel Nomade in Barrio Inglés at Coquimbo for $32/dble. Luxury Jardim del Mar in La Serena is $91-160/dble. In Totoralillo, Polynesian style Tiki Tano has 10 cabins ($15-25/room) and a Thai food restaurant (often fully booked and expensive). Expect $3-5 for a basic meal; lots of cheap seafood. Plenty of people free-camp Tres Playitas.

Weather – Coquimbo enjoys a transitional climate between the arid northern desert of the Atacama and the pleasant Mediterranean climate of the central coast. In summer (Dec-Feb), daytime temps range between 11-25°C (52-77°F) whereas during winter (Jun-Aug), it drops by 4°C to average at 7-22°C (45-72°F) with lows reaching -5°C at night. There is a lack of precipitation with annual average rainfall under 100mm (4in). The "rainy" season runs from May through October, a time of the year known as the "Bolivian winter". Use a 4/3mm fullsuit with optional boots from May to December and a 3/2mm between January and April.

Nature and Culture – Chile's second-oldest city, La Serena is blessed with beautiful stone architecture, 29 churches, shady avenues and pretty plazas. Check the astronomical observatories of La Silla, European Southern Observatory and El Tololo. Visit Elqui Valley or the villages of Pisco Elqui and Vicuña, the birthplaces of pisco and the poet Gabriela Mistral respectively.

Hazards and Hassles – Water gets cold and mornings can be gloomy; pack booties and maybe a hood too. Don't get caught inside, some boulders and rocks are nasty plus there's urchins. Most of the spots are very uncrowded, more seals than surfers. Surf can get big, be prepared. Chile is generally safe but keep a low profile and valuables locked away.

Handy Hints – There are surf shops in La Serena but better bring everything, including a gun and a second wetsuit so you can always put on a dry one. Chile Safari is based in La Serena; two night package with lessons staying at Tiki Tano cabin and 4WD jeep transport is $280. Lots of killer videos on youtube.com

La Vedette faces NW, bending solid S-SW swells into standout barrelling lefts along a rocky point. Beware of rocks on the inside and check the long beach north if the swell is too small. Most contests happen at the popular, consistent summer beaches of **Tres Playitas**, where the wave size increases as you go north. From Huasco, cross the phenomenal desert full of purple flowers to remote, exposed **Playa Brava**, which offers a wild shorebreak, providing the SW swell is small and the S winds aren't blowing. The long, slow roads into Pinguino de Humboldt National Reserve, lead to **Agua Dulce**, a large, southwest-facing beach that works with the smallest swells over shallow sandbars. Breathtaking scenery and more pocket beaches nearby like Playa Palocillo. It's a 2h boat cruise from Punta Choros to get to **Isla Damas**, which gets some nice surf, including a sweet right reef, facing the SW swell and some pristine water beachbreaks at Playa Las Tijeras. Feels like the Galapagos with so much wildlife around including sea-lions and penguins. **Punta Teatinos** is a semi-right pointbreak capping a long beachbreak lined with good resorts, a golf course and a lagoon that attracts many bird species. La Serena threatens Viña del Mar's supremacy as Chile's premier beach resort, so it gets really busy and more pricey in January and February. The long Avenida del Mar joins 12 beaches, but it's **El Faro** that is the most consistent of these below average beachbreaks with lots of close-outs. The surf village of Totoralillo has a small circular peninsula of rocks and sand, holding 3 pointbreaks plus a sandbar in the shorebreak. The left is called **Pipe**, since it produces the most radical wave, a lightning fast barrel that's far from easy to thread, making it a popular bodyboard spot. On the south side of the peninsula, the long righthand point of **El Muro** is broken into three sections, with bigger, faster walls outside at Cabañas, through the shallow El Muro mid section and into the easier inside of Rocas, that will handle N winds. One thing they all have in common is some shallow rocks. In summer, the beach gets a bit crowded and dirty, with hotels right on the point. Beginners will do better down the beach at **Derecharcha** for fun summer rights. **Las Tacas** is a northwest-facing beachbreak that stays clean in S winds, but mostly closes-out in front of the Med style 5 star hotel circling the sands. Just before Tongoy Bay, check at **Playa Blanca**, which is sheltered from S-W swells by Punta Lengua de Vaca.

Cabañas, El Muro

Winter wave heights sometimes reach 20ft (6m) with 12-14 second period but late summer is the best time for very clean surf. The waves have juice all year and foreign surfers have been impressed by the raw power of the surf and the vast potential for discovery. There are rideable waves almost every day of the year, courtesy of the Humboldt current, which pushes constant swell along Chilean shores. Deep winter can feel chilly (sic!) so mid-seasons are best for swell, winds and weather. Summer is fine especially on the WSW-facing beachbreaks with potential for very long distance (20sec +) NW swells from the North Pacific, but it can be crowded and prices are higher. In the northern half of Chile, atmospheric circulation is largely controlled by the South Pacific High, resulting in winds blowing parallel to the coast north of 31°S. Further south, the winds take a more onshore westerly direction. Tides are semi-diurnal and can reach 5ft (1.5m) on extreme phases.

SURF STATISTICS	J F	M A	M J	J A	S O	N D
dominant swell	S-W	S-W	S-W	S-W	S-W	S-W
swell size (ft)	4	4-5	5	6-7	5-6	3-4
consistency (%)	75	75	85	75	85	55
dominant wind	S-SW	SE-SW	SE-S	SE-S	S-SW	S-SW
average force	F3	F3	F3-F4	F4	F3-F4	F3-F4
consistency (%)	72	82	58	62	69	73
water temp.(°C)	19	18	15	14	14	16
wetsuit						

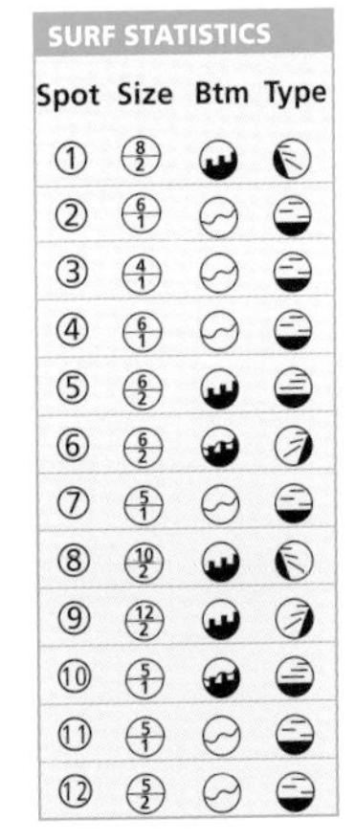

SURF STATISTICS

Spot	Size	Btm	Type
①	8/2		
②	6/1		
③	4/1		
④	6/1		
⑤	6/2		
⑥	6/2		
⑦	5/1		
⑧	10/2		
⑨	12/2		
⑩	5/1		
⑪	5/1		
⑫	5/2		

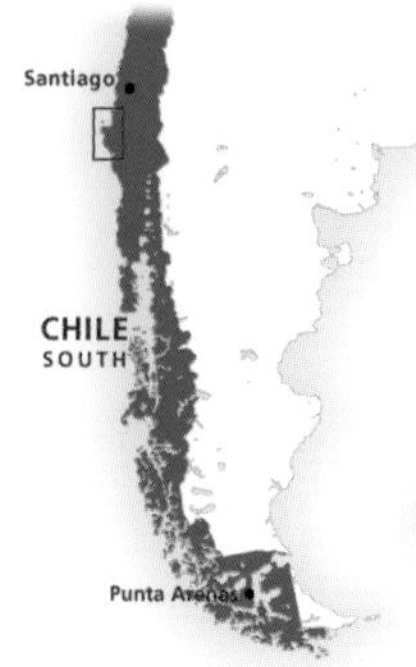

237. Biobio

Secret spot

SCOTT WALLS

Summary
+ Handful of world-class lefts
+ Beautiful region
+ Very consistent swells
+ Cheap, friendly

– Really cold water
– Sandbank dependent
– Exposed to winds & rains
– Some pollution problems
– Not easy to reach

Until recently, the southernmost limits of the surf in Chile was Pichilemu, in Region 6. Knowing that it's long narrow coastline contains 12 regions, that pretty much meant that half of the country remained unexplored. Chilean surfers started to tap the immense potential of virgin pointbreak and rivermouth lefts in the mid '90s, but word only got out 10 years later, when environmental issues emerged. Proposed pulp mills and coal-fired power stations like Los Robles in the Loanco area are threatening to poison some quality breaks with arsenic and lead, which convinced the locals it was a better plan to publicise the surfing resources than to keep it secret and see the waves disappear. These sleepy agricultural regions still plough using oxen and there are few accommodation options for budget travellers, as camping is the way to go. All the points/rivermouths in the area are heavily sandbar dependent, so either side of winter is best.

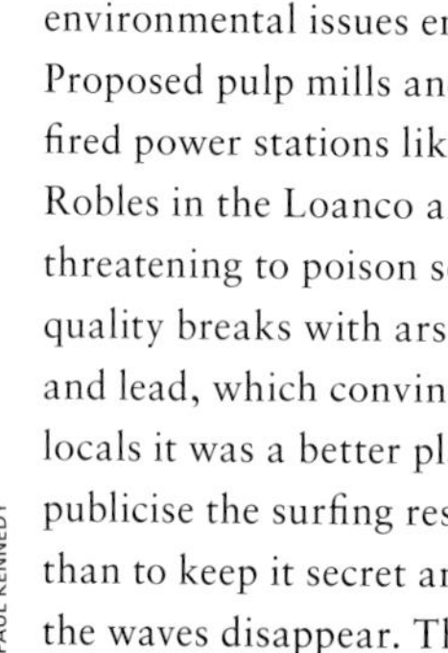
PAUL KENNEDY

Secret spot

PAUL KENNEDY

TRAVEL INFORMATION

Local Population: 353,315
Coastline: 360km (223mi)
Time Zone: GMT -4
Contests: Curanipe XIII OPEN Surf
Other Resources: surfingchile.com chilesurf.cl fechsurf.cl shoa.cl/ (tide) http://surfotos.cl
Video: Out There (2008) El Mar, Mi Alma – (The Ocean, My Soul)

Getting There – See Atacama, Zone 236. From Santiago, it takes 6h on the Pan American H'way to Concepcion. LAN Chile flies 4x daily Santiago to Concepcion from $80 o/w.

Getting Around – Expect 8h with Buses Tur from Santiago to Lebu ($14-20). Buses are cheap, very comfortable and carry boardbags. A 4WD double cab pickup will cost $80/d, while 8 seat minibus is $135/d. Basic car hire costs $50/d at United.

Lodging and Food – Expect $15-25 for a cheap room and $3-5 for a basic meal. Lots of cheap seafood. Stay in Suhaila Resort south of Curanipe ($60/dble) or Cabañas Mirador Alto Las Brisas or Hostal Refugio del Mar in Curanipe, well used by surfers. Look for Cabañas Rucamar, Miramar or Costamar in Cobquecura. Contact Curanipetur for bookings.

WEATHER STATISTICS	J/F	M/A	M/J	J/A	S/O	N/D
total rainfall (mm)	19	57	216	202	75	31
consistency (days/mth)	1	5	12	14	5	3
min temp (°C)	8	6	5	3	4	6
max temp (°C)	24	22	15	13	17	22

Weather – Talcahuano has a temperate Mediterranean climate influenced by the Pacific Ocean and the Andes Mountains. Winter months, from May to September, are cool and rainy with temps ranging from 3-17°C (37-63°F). The summer months, from December through February, are mild with temps between 6-24°C (43-75°F). The period of January and February is generally the driest time of the year. Average annual rainfall is 1200mm (48in), with a high between May and August. The weather is also influenced by the cold Humboldt Current that runs the length of Chile during summer and reacts with the hot air currents that come off the land. Use a 4/3 mm fullsuit with boots and 5/4mm with gloves and hood in winter gales.

Nature and Culture – Biobio river has world-class white water rafting, Impressive rock formation like Iglesia de Piedra near Buchupureo. Temuco City south is the gateway to the lakes and volcanoes like Pucon. Near Cobquecura is La Loberia, where 3000 seals live on 4 big rocks. In Concepcion Naval base, take a tour on the battleship Huascar.

Hazards and Hassles – Cold waters and windchill can cut down water time. Avoid winter if you're not that hardcore. Lefts break mostly on sand, but some large rocks stick out. Pollution at some of the rivers is becoming an issue. A soupy fog can cling to the coast for days with huge dark pelicans gliding in packs and very curious seals. Some localism likely.

Handy Hints – Take a gun along for 8-10ft days. Some gear is available in Santiago, but there's no surf shop in Concepcion. Learn some Spanish. Educated people, gorgeous mountains, snow resorts, quality wines: Chile is very addictive, stay as long as you can.

Secret spot

SCOTT WALLS

En route for **Curanipe** is Santos del Mar, Chile's latest tow-in outer reef where 30ft (10m) lefts have been ridden, but the lefthand rivermouth at the coastal resort is much friendlier and often used as a contest site. The first section known as La Cruz breaks further up off the rocks (Curanipe means black rock) but the long barrelling lefts called Tres Peñas break down by the black sand rivermouth. It's offshore with S-SW winds and fires at low tide. **Tregualemu** holds lefts in swells up to 15ft (5m), peeling over rock and sand with fast walls in front of a rivermouth. It's a private track to the beach, so ask for permission or walk down beach, 1km from the north. Easier access is **Pullay**, a sandy left point that's fun for learner/improvers and a great fishing spot for sea bass and sole. There are more fickle river-fed, sandbar pointbreaks in the area that, like all breaks dependent on the storms and currents to deposit the right amount of sand in the right spot, can have some awesome barrel sections, but only sometimes. **Rinconada** is a typical Chilean pointbreak set-up, but it doesn't get very hollow with long, rumbling walls and tapered cutback shoulders attracting crowds of learners in summer. Colourful fishing pangas sell great seafood on the black sand beach to the tourists and locals. In small swells, have a look at **Playa Monte del Zorro** for dumpy beachbreak and a protected left in the southern corner. **Praia Mela** is yet another nice rivermouth set-up that depends on the sand for speed of ride. A pulp mill is under construction on the nearby Rio Itata. Concepción is the capital of Region 8 and the second largest city in Chile, sitting alongside the Bio Bio river, which enters the sea at **Desembocadura**. Scattered rocks lurk in the beachbreak that picks up plenty of swell for the local bodyboarders. **Playa Sector El Piure** is one of 6 SW-facing beachbreaks, best in summer peaky swells, set in a wildly beautiful landscape that includes the crazy Skeletor Rocks nearby. Lebu is the capital city of Arauco Province, part of the 8th Bío Bío region. On small swells, **Cueva del Toro** may have some shape or walk north through the tunnel to get to Playa Millaneco. The main spot for experts and bodyboarders is **El Faro**, where explosive lefts hit the reef off the cape plus there are 2 jetties and a protected rivermouth sandbank for all abilities. **Punta Quidico** is another 120km (75mi) south, where the long rivermouth lefts below the small lighthouse can be leg-achingly long, tubular and comparable to the best points up north. **Tirua** is a less perfect set-up, with strong currents from the large river messing with the line-up, but it's offshore in a S wind and empty.

SURF STATISTICS			
Spot	Size	Btm	Type
1	8/2		
2	12/4		
3	8/3		
4	10/3		
5	5/2		
6	8/3		
7	6/1		
8	5/1		
9	6/1		
10	8/2		
11	10/2		
12	8/2		

SURF STATISTICS	J F	M A	M J	J A	S O	N D
dominant swell	S-W	S-W	S-W	S-W	S-W	S-W
swell size (ft)	5	5-6	6-7	7	6-7	4-5
consistency (%)	70	70	80	70	80	60
dominant wind	S-SW	S-SW	S-N	S-N	S-SW	S-SW
average force	F4	F3-F4	F3-F4	F4	F3-F4	F4
consistency (%)	69	54	44	40	21	67
water temp.(°C)	14	14	13	11	12	14
wetsuit						

Winter wave heights can reach 20' (6m) with 12 second period but summer is the best time for clean surf. Since there are so many rivermouths, the first swells of autumn should hit well sculpted sandbanks and spring flow rates can also build up the bars. Summer beachbreaks may pick up super-long distance NW swells but the points/rivermouths need wrapping S-SW. With more onshore W in the wind, it's important to find the protected southern corners. Tides are semi-diurnal and can reach 5ft on extreme phases, affecting most of the rivermouths.

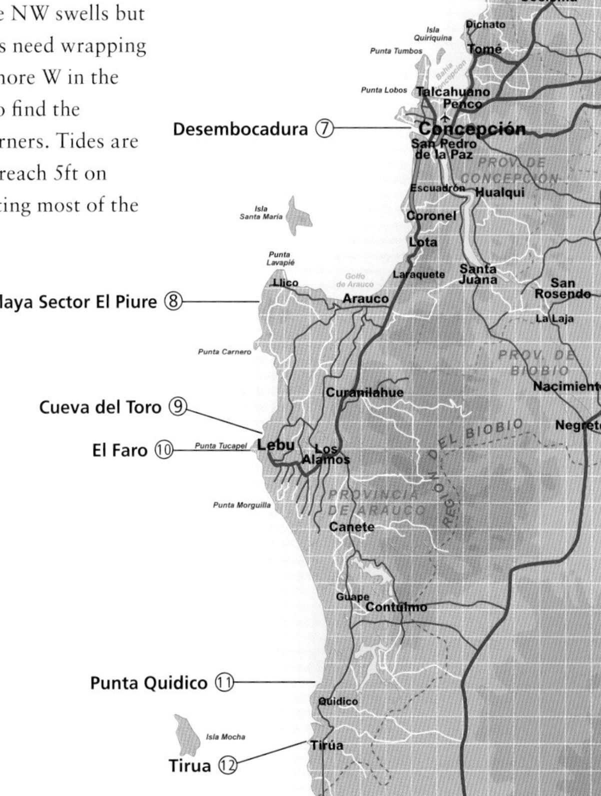

Secret spot

PAUL KENNEDY

238. Uruguay

Punta del Este

ALL PHOTOS MARROKE

Summary
+ Quantity of uncrowded spots
+ Semi-consistent pointbreaks
+ Cheap and safe
+ Relaxed line-ups
+ Punta del Este tourist hotspot

– Lack of powerful spots
– Small and average in summer
– Brownish, muddy water
– Unspectacular scenery
– Cold winter temps

Uruguay is a fairly unknown surfing destination, despite being neighbours with Brazil and having local riders paddling out as early as the late '50s. Omar "Vispo" Rossi began standing up on a homemade board, not even knowing he was "surfing", in Praia de Pocitos, one of the most exposed beaches in Montevideo. There are more than 80 breaks scattered along just 200kms (124mi) of Atlantic coast, with a very small number of surfers compared to the giant surfing nation to the north. There's everything from left or right pointbreaks to beachbreaks, not to mention the rivermouths and even outer reefs with big waves. Some of the best spots are not easy to get to and that is why they are seldom crowded. Knowing where to look can yield fun, mellow waves in the middle of the summer, with only the seagulls for company.

La Barra de Maldonado

Rio de la Plata is the widest river in the world and separates Argentina from Uruguay. It is almost 200km (120mi) wide at the point where it joins the Atlantic in Punta del Este. The capital city Montevideo gets some waves and big stormy swells can produce fun pointbreaks at places like **Solis Grande** or **San Francisco**, a pointbreak out by Punta Colorada in Piriapolis. Only a little more than an hour from the airport, Punta del Este is technically a

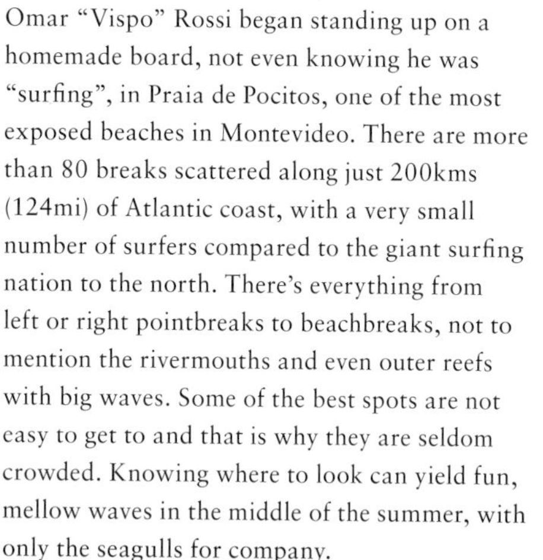

TRAVEL INFORMATION

Local Population: Montevideo 1.3M
Coastline: Atlantic exposed 220km (136mi)
Time Zone: GMT-3
Contests: National – Punta del Este, La Paloma
Other Resources: sunvalleysurf.com olasyvientos.com

Getting There – No visa. Most flights to Montevideo (MVD) go through Brazil (Pluna) or Buenos Aires (EZE). Direct flights from Spain (Iberia). High-speed ferries connect the 2 capitals in 2.5h ($60 o/w), Colonia being an even shorter ride. Because Uruguay is small, there's no need for domestic flights. Small departure tax.

Getting Around – The well maintained Interbalnearia highway connects most seaside resorts on the Atlantic coast. Compact cars are $40/day or $200/week. Beware of sandy, swampy access roads to the beach.

Lodging and Food – Unless you get a cheap package in Punta del Este, hotels will cost $100/day. Stay in La Paloma (1949 Hostel, $20/pax) or Santa Teresa (Hotel Oceanico, $55). Lively nightlife. Expect lots of BBQ's serving sausages, blood sausages and 1l bottles of stout beer or first-class red wines. Pay around $10 for a full meal.

WEATHER STATISTICS	J/F	M/A	M/J	J/A	S/O	N/D
total rainfall (mm)	80	82	86	92	89	76
consistency (days/mth)	8	9	10	10	9	8
min temp (°C)	18	16	11	9	11	15
max temp (°C)	25	23	17	15	17	22

Weather – As in most temperate climates, rainfall results from the passage of cold fronts in winter, falling in overcast, drizzly spells. Summer thunderstorms are frequent when high humidity and fog are common. The absence of mountains makes the coast vulnerable to rapid changes in weather. Seasons are fairly well defined, spring is usually damp, cool, and windy, summers are warm, autumns are mild and winters are chilly and uncomfortably damp. Average highs & lows in summer (January) in Montevideo are 28°C (82°F) and 17°C (63°F), while winter (July) averages 14°C (58°F) and 6°C (43°F). Rainfall is fairly evenly distributed throughout the year (950mm/38in annually). A winter warm spell can be abruptly broken by a strong "Pampero", a chilly and sometimes violent SW wind blowing in from the Argentina pampas.

Nature and Culture – Take a sunset stroll along Gorlero Avenue, Punta del Este's main place to see and be seen. In a few blocks there's restaurants, bars, shops, cinemas and the Feria Artesanal. Isla de Lobos, 8km (5mi) offshore, is one of the world's largest sea-lion colonies. Whales may be seen October-November. Easter is Semana Criolla when people from all around hit the capital to party.

Hazards and Hassles – Aside from rocks & some jellyfish in summer, things are pretty safe. No aggressive crowds, very little thievery, not much urban pressure (not Brazil). Avoid Punta del Este tourist traps in summer. Wind changes are fast and without warning so surf when you see good waves.

Handy Hints – There are surf shops, shapers and board repairs in the main beach towns. Equipment is cheap and decent quality. Use a thicker, longer board for the mellow waves. Surf Lessons with all equipment is $100 per 6 classes. Surfboards rental $20/day, wetsuit $10/day.

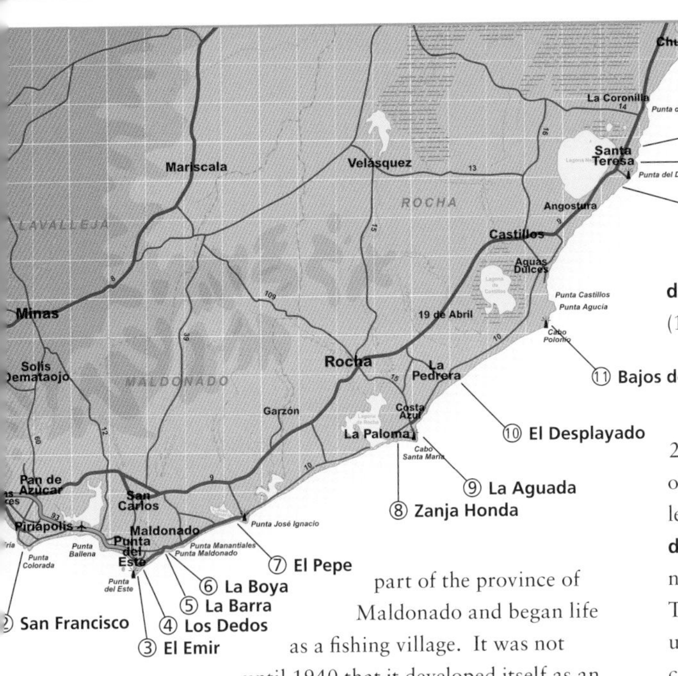

⑮ Barra del Chuy
⑭ La Moza
⑬ Playa Del Barco
⑫ La Viuda
⑪ Bajos del Polonio
⑩ El Desplayado
⑨ La Aguada
⑧ Zanja Honda
⑦ El Pepe
⑥ La Boya
⑤ La Barra
④ Los Dedos
③ El Emir
② San Francisco

part of the province of Maldonado and began life as a fishing village. It was not until 1940 that it developed itself as an exclusive vacation resort of international fame, and today boasts over 100 hotels ranging from quaint, colonial guest houses to the large Conrad Hilton, complete with casino. Its beautiful harbour, on the mansa (tame) side, attracts yachts from all over the world, while on the brava (wild) side, there's a dozen beaches with reefs, starting at **El Emir**, near famous Gorlero Avenue. Hundreds of hotels and buildings face the waves so expect some crowds at this decent beachbreak and at the nearby La Virgen lefts, a real quality reef. Not far is **Los Dedos**, with no real punch in the line-up, but a huge sculpture of giant fingers half-buried in the sand. Locals use other beaches, notably La Barra del Maldonado, a beautiful inlet that helps shape the waves. **La Barra** can be pretty powerful by Uruguay standards, and the rocks can be a hazard jumping in so it's generally an experienced surfer's spot. Out on the point is **La Boya**, possibly the best left in the country, with fast, hollow lefts over flat rocks and a crowd guaranteed. **El Pepe** is a long curve of sand with a rivermouth that can sculpt good banks and is sometimes called La Boca de la Laguna. Further east, the waves get stronger and bigger; if Punta del Este is 4ft (1.2m), then La Paloma and other Rocha spots will be 6ft (2m). With 6 beachbreaks, 5 pointbreaks and a local shaper, La Paloma is the place to wait for the right swell. **Zanja Honda** is the best spot with longer lefts and hollower rights over rock and sand, just west of La Botes, a spinning left point. It's also called Playa Solari and is one of the few places where a little localism exists. The main beachbreak is **La Aguada**, which faces due east, picks up plenty of swell and handles some size, so it is where most contests are held. **El Desplayado** at La Pedrera, has some really fun rights that wall up off a small reef at the southern end of the beach.

Spitting beachbreaks close-out on the sandbars of **Bajos del Polonio**, unless the swell is from NE-E. It's 230km (143mi) from Montevideo and is home to the second largest colony of seals in the country. Santa Teresa and Punta Del Diablo form the other main surf hub in Uruguay, sporting 15 major spots within a 25km (15mi) drive. **La Viuda** faces SE and picks up plenty of swell onto shifting sandbanks that often form up a nice left in the northern corner, but it can get crowded. **Playa del Barco** is a quality curve of open beachbreak with the northern access through Chero Chato and Las Achiras. There is plenty of potential for quality rights along this undeveloped coastline that has few hotels, but lots of campsites. **La Moza** is the best righthand point around, attracting weekend crowds to ride long, tubular walls with sections off the rocks at the southern end of a long beach. **Barra del Chuy**, is the most consistent wave in the country blessed with shorebreak power, but plagued by onshore winds. Just over the river frontier is Brazil, the surfing giant!

SURF STATISTICS

Spot	Size	Btm	Type
①	5/2		
②	5/2		
③	6/1		
④	6/2		
⑤	10/2		
⑥	8/2		
⑦	8/2		
⑧	8/2		
⑨	10/2		
⑩	10/3		
⑪	8/2		
⑫	8/2		
⑬	6/2		
⑭	8/2		
⑮	8/2		

Zanja Honda

In winter, the South Atlantic can be pretty consistent with lows forming between the Falklands and Argentina, veering on a NNE path towards Africa. Swells are quite regular, reaching 12ft+ (4m+) and 4-10ft (1.2-3m) is the mean range for winters. Autumn is the best season with slightly less consistency and intensity but cleaner conditions. Summers are really small, often going flat and anything under 3ft swell will not do much. The best time to surf in Uruguay is from April to November, even though in July, August and September the water sometimes drops to 10°C (50°F) and the air can get close to 0°C (32°F). In winter a 4/3 mm with boots, in autumn and spring a 3/2mm without boots and a short john or boardshorts in summer. Onshore winds are frequent after mid-morning and the best winds are S-SW for rights and NE-NW for lefts.

SURF STATISTICS	J F	M A	M J	J A	S O	N D
dominant swell	SE-S	E-S	E-S	E-S	E-S	SE-S
swell size (ft)	2-3	3	4	4-5	4	2-3
consistency (%)	50	60	70	75	70	60
dominant wind	NE-SE	NE-SE	NE-SW	NE-SW	NE-SW	NE-SE
average force	F4	F4	F4	F4	F4	F4
consistency (%)	61	49	34	37	81	57
water temp.(°C)	22	21	17	13	14	19
wetsuit						

La Barra de Maldonado

239. Rio Grande do Sul

Summary
+ Big wave option in Torres
+ Not polluted
+ Beach & party vibe
+ Friendly Gaúcho hospitality

– Average quality beachbreaks
– Not too consistent
– Almost no wind protection
– Regular strong rips

Praia dos Molhes

THIAGO MARQUES

The "Great River of the South" is the southernmost State of Brazil, bordered to the north by Santa Catarina, to the west by Argentina, to the south by Uruguay and to the east by the Atlantic Ocean. The region was originally settled by Amerindian peoples (mostly Guarani and Kaingangs), while European settlement started in 1627 with Spanish Jesuits. Despite being mainly rural for much of its early history, Rio Grande do Sul has been the scene of bloody wars: the dispute between Portugal and Spain for the Sacramento Colony, and the Guarani Missions War. Large communities of German, Italian and Polish settlers entered the state from the end of the 19th century, making it racially and culturally very different from most of the other Brazilian states. Gaucho is the common denomination of the inhabitants of Rio

Tramandai

MAURICIO DRUNN

Atlantida Pier

BOOZETENTACLE

TRAVEL INFORMATION

Local Population: 40,000
Coastline: 500km (310mi)
Time Zone: GMT -3
Contests: Rio Grande do Sul Pro in Torres
Other Resources:
fgsurf.com.br
disksurf.com.br

Getting There – Visa necessary for most visitors, check with embassy before travelling. International flights to Rio (GIG) or São Paulo (GRU/CGH). Portuguese airline TAP is often the best buy. Connecting flight to Porto Alegre International Airport (POA), from $250r/t, with Voegol, Oceanair, Varig or Webjet and make sure they take boardbags. $38 dep tax.

Getting Around – A rental car is useful but not necessary (from $320/wk, www.easyterra.com). Torres is located 200km (124mi) from Porto Alegre and 1000km (621mi) from Sao Paulo. Regional transport hub in Pelotas, with regular buses to Porto Alegre and Rio Grande every 30min. Highway BR-101 runs along Brazil's coast and connects 12 capitals.

Lodging and Food – Large choice of accommodation from pousadas to luxury hotels. In Torres, try Samambaia, A Furninha ($70/dble) or Guarita Park Hotel ($100/dble). The chimarrão is a local version of the local tea drunk in neighbouring Uruguay and Argentina. The barbecue locally known as churrasco is one of the most important elements of everyday life.

WEATHER STATISTICS	J/F	M/A	M/J	J/A	S/O	N/D
total rainfall (mm)	128	119	94	120	130	104
consistency (days/mth)	8	8	9	10	10	7
min temp (°C)	20	17	13	9	12	18
max temp (°C)	26	25	20	19	19	24

Weather – Rio Grande Do Sul lies within the south temperate zone and has a mild, temperate climate, however the coastal zone has more of a humid subtropical climate with 4 seasons. The dominance of the warm and moist maritime air creates summers similar to the humid tropics with temps between 25-35°C (77-95°F). Winter reveals mild average temps, but it's changeable and sudden windy, rainy weather characterizes this season. Winter temps range from 2-15°C (35-59°F). Autumns tend to be as changeable as winters but warmer. Spring is slightly drier than the other seasons. Average rainfall is about 1300mm (52in) and regular throughout the year. Use a 3/2 wetsuit from June to December, with optional 4/3 and boots in colder winter spots like Chui. A springsuit is sufficient for the rest of the year.

Nature and Culture – The state of Rio Grande do Sul is renowned as one of the most culturally rich states of Brazil. Ecotourism is well developed, as well as historical-cultural tourism whose main attraction are the Jesuit Missions. Torres is home of the Guarita Park biosphere reserve and a hot air balloon festival. Yearly book fair in Porto Alegre.

Hazards and Hassles – Never leave valuables and don't be flashy (cameras, watches, rings...), Brazilian thieves are experts and know every trick! Local water is usually not safe to drink; go for mineral water, beer or guarana. When driving, go with the flow. Localism is not a problem if you respect the rules. Watch out for the dangerous fishing nets.

Handy Hints – Plenty of surf shops where quality equipment is pretty cheap. Bring any board that works in small to medium beachbreaks. Be prepared for both warm and cool weather, and wake up early for offshore conditions. Try sandboarding in Itapeva or Cidreira. Rio Grande do Sul is the largest provider of top models and beauty queens in Brazil!

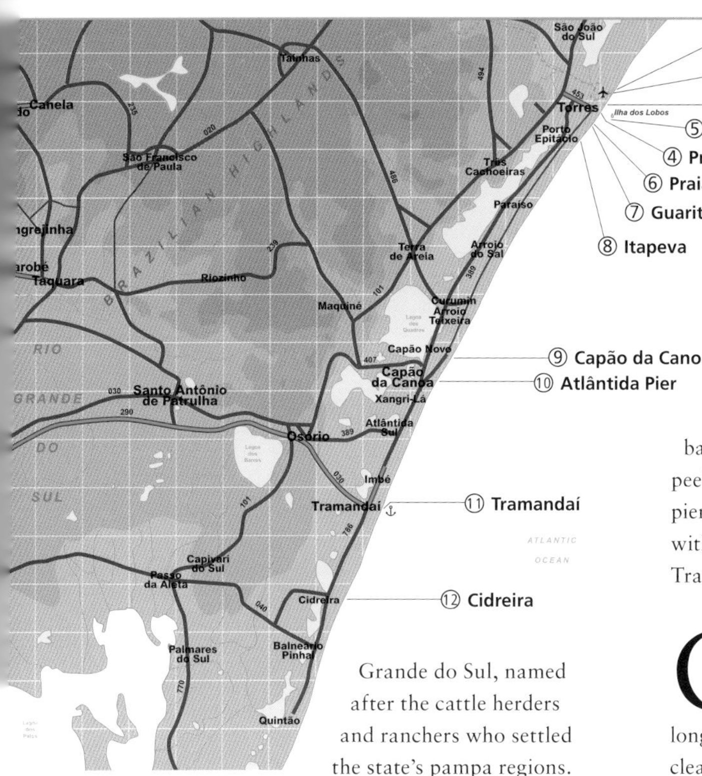

Grande do Sul, named after the cattle herders and ranchers who settled the state's pampa regions. Nowadays, the state benefits from an economy mainly based on leather, cloth goods, wine, cereals and wood and is highly regarded for it's hospitality and excellent quality of life. The coast is one straight sandy beach stretching 500km (310mi), broken only by 3 rivermouths (Rio Mampituba in Torres, Rio Tramandai and Arroio do Chui that straddles the border with Uruguay). The construction of jetties is the only other help for creating sandbanks, so don't expect more than average beachbreaks plus a few good surprises.

With pristine beaches and famous basalt rock formations that gave the city its name, Torres is the exception to the state's uninviting coastline. **Barra do Mampituba** is the north jetty that lines up good righthanders, best in a S swell. The canal between the jetties has smaller, hollower waves, but watch out for the dangerous boat traffic and nets. **Praia dos Molhes** starts from the S jetty, offering a decent left wall and protection from the N wind. When the sandbanks are well-shaped and an E swell hits, this popular contest site becomes very busy. Various peaks can be found along the 2km **Praia Grande** beach, but locals usually prefer its southern end for the rock & sand bottom. **Prainha** is another punchy beachbreak in a picturesque location, protected from SW winds. Its consistency and occasional barrels make it the local grommet wave. It's a 2km boat ride to **Ilha dos Lobos**, a rocky offshore islet, home to sea lions and the "Brazilian Teahupoo"! This rare but ledgy, thick, barrelling lefthander turns into a crazy tow-in spot at 10ft+ and should be left to the kamikaze only. **Praia da Cal** is another classic break located just south of the lighthouse hill. A S swell will deliver good but busy righthanders, and the tall cliffs offer decent S wind shelter. If it blows from the N/NE, **Guarita** will have protected peaks, peeling over a rocky bottom just outside of the tiny bay. It's inside the Guarita State Park, so expect summer and weekend crowds.

Quieter breaks are found along the wide open beach of **Itapeva** that will be better in the mornings on smaller peaky swells. There's a similar but more urbanized setup in **Capão da Canoa** and its 18km (11mi) of open beachbreak, but hope for a windless day. The t-shaped pier in **Atlântida**, a famous summer resort town, helps to hold the sand banks for longer rides, mostly rights in a S swell. Being the closest beach to Porto Alegre, **Tramandaí** has very busy peaks both sides of the pier and there will be some barrels on a W wind day. Another option can be the fickle peelers at the Barra de Imbe rivermouth. The southernmost pier in Brazil is in **Cidreira**, a less developed resort town with waves breaking under the same conditions as in Tramandaí/Atlântida.

SURF STATISTICS			
Spot	Size	Btm	Type
①	6/2		
②	6/2		
③	6/3		
④	6/2		
⑤	15/4		
⑥	8/2		
⑦	8/3		
⑧	6/2		
⑨	6/3		
⑩	8/3		
⑪	8/3		
⑫	8/3		

Cold fronts moving in a NE direction, arrive from the Antarctic or Argentine regions, and constitute the main source of swell. Due S swells have a longer fetch, offer a better period and also tend to be cleaner than the E swells that are generated closer to the shore. April and May usually see better shaped waves over summer sculpted sandbars, while June, July and August are the best months in terms of size. Flat periods mainly occur in summer (November to April), but can be interrupted by locally generated windswell or an occasional weak cold front. Expect heavy currents running parallel to the coast when a strong swell is around. Winds are usually calm to light offshore on early mornings, then they pick up at mid-morning to 10-15 knots SE (onshore). When a storm passes, the SE winds get stronger (15-25 knots). The mean tidal range is small 0.5-1m (1.6-3ft), and doesn't really influence the surf conditions.

Atlantida Pier

BOOZETENTACLE

SURF STATISTICS	J F	M A	M J	J A	S O	N D
dominant swell	SE-S	E-S	E-S	E-S	E-S	SE-S
swell size (ft)	2	2-3	3-4	4	3-4	2
consistency (%)	50	60	70	70	70	50
dominant wind	NE-E	NE-S	SW-NE	SW-NE	NE-S	NE-E
average force	F4	F4	F4	F4	F4	F4
consistency (%)	46	50	48	37	52	44
water temp.(°C)	22	21	16	13	15	19
wetsuit						

240. Amapa, Para and Maranhão

Rio Araguari

RED BULL 2003

Summary
- \+ Longest rideable waves
- \+ Virgin, mellow waves
- \+ Reliable and predictable
- \+ Uncrowded coastal waves
- \+ Amazing Amazon environment

- – Only 1 set of waves per day
- – Mainly boat expeditions
- – Jungle dangers and hassles
- – Onshore coastal slop
- – Costly trip

According to the Tidal Bore Research Society, this rare phenomenon is only found on 55 waterways. It is a wonder that has never been truly understood, even though predicting a bore wave's arrival and size is fairly easy. Unlike ocean waves, the bore has two currents: one at the top pushing ahead and another one below from the downstream river flow. At times, the mighty bore has wreaked great havoc on riverside infrastructure and last century several majestic bores were stripped of their power by human intervention. The word pororoca comes from "poroc poroc", which means "destroyer, big-bang", in the regional aboriginal dialect and the phenomenon was first shown on Brazilian TV after Jacques Cousteau aboard the Calypso first shot the phenomenon on the 28th March, 1982. It was breaking 15km (9mi) out to sea, outside the Araguari rivermouth, at about 10ft (3m) high and going 45 km/h (30mp/h), before they followed the bore 25km (15mi) upstream. In 1997, a country known for small waves became the Hawaii of the bore-riders with pioneers like Noelio Sobrinho, Guga Arruda and Eraldo Gueiros taking on the pororocas. The huge Amazon basin fed by a dozen rivers proves to hold the longest rideable waves on earth and in April, 2003, an unofficial world record was set. Picuruta Salazar managed to ride the bore for 37 minutes and travel 12.5km (7.8mi) before Serginho Laus, on 24th June 2005, and in the presence of an official Guinness adjudicator set the new distance surfing world record with a 33 minute ride

YEP

TRAVEL INFORMATION

Local Population: 5,651,475 Maranhao
Coastline: 1,800km (1,118mi) Amapa, Para & Maranhao
Time Zone: GMT -3
Contests: Arari, Sao Domingo (April)
Other Resources:
Video – Pororoca 2003
www.adrenalimitz.com.br
surfandonaselva.com.br/inicio.php

Getting There – No visa for Brazil for most, but Yellow Fever injection still necessary. Fly to São Luis (SLZ) for Mearim river; Macapa (MCP) for Araguari river or Belem (BEL) for Capim river. Manaus is way inside the Amazon. Main airport in the NE is Fortaleza (FOR), and return transfer to SLZ costs $150 (1h10). Int'l departure tax is $35 in Fortaleza.

Getting Around – Renting a car is unnecessary – travel by bus or air. Boat terminals ("hidroviaria") are crucial hubs for local transport to cross the myriad waterways and estuaries. By road, Cutias is 4.5h from Macapa, São Domingo is 3h from Belem and Arari is 3h from São Luis. Sao Luis by road is 7h (639km) from Belem.

Lodging and Food – If you go with Surfando Na Selva, everything will be included. Staying in aircon pensão cost $20-40 per person based on double occupancy. Average meal called "Prato do Dia" cost around $7 for a plate with drink. Try rice-of-Cuxá, fried fish or crab pie. An extra cold Brahma or Pilsen beer is a delicacy in these hot regions.

WEATHER STATISTICS	J/F	M/A	M/J	J/A	S/O	N/D
total rainfall (mm)	338	339	214	131	87	11
consistency (days/mth)	26	27	23	17	15	16
min temp (°C)	22	23	22	22	22	22
max temp (°C)	31	31	31	31	32	33

Weather – The Amazon Basin is among the wettest regions in the world, but the eastern Maranhao State gets a bit less rain. Typically, in centrally located Belem, the climate is hot, and the year is divided into a very wet season from Dec to May and a somewhat drier season from June to Nov. The rainy season peaks from January to April, but most months it rains a lot, although only in concentrated, refreshing showers for most of the year. At the mouth of the river Amazon, along the coast of Pará and in the western section of the area, the total annual pluviometric index exceeds 3,000mm (118in). Heat can be oppressive but on the coast, the NE-SE trade winds help and the climate is generally considered healthy. Water temps remain around 26-27°C (79-81°F) but much warmer in the estuary and rivers.

Nature and Culture – Except during Bumba-meu-boi and Carnival, Sao Luis is quieter than most Brazilian cities of its size. Go to Fortaleza or Belem for action and history. Ilha do Marajo is an unique environment, with remote ranches, water buffalos. Enjoy the Brazilian rainforest, travel in hammocks (rede) in Amazon boats: remember, rivers are roads!

Hazards and Hassles – Don't get too paranoid with jungle fauna: Jacaré (crocs) hunt river preys at high tide, sharks swim upstream. Freshwater means piranhas - just don't bleed! Lots of floating debris (trees, ship waste, snakes). Avoid candiru, a small parasitic fish that can swim up your urethra and dig in its spines. Not many mosquitoes in Arari but the Amazon basin is a high-risk, chloroquine resistant malaria zone.

Handy Hints – Although some locals surf shortboards, longboards or thick, bouyant boards are better for riding longer. Falling off a bore wave can mean being left over on the riverbank for some time waiting for the boat to return. Engine & propeller problems are part of the deal. Serginho Laus (pictured opposite) runs "Surfando Na Selva" expeditions: March - Sept: 5 days, 4 pax, from $2000 to $3,250 per person.

of 10.1km (6.3mi). Since 1999, an annual championship has been held in São Domingos do Capim and there is now frequent events on Rio Araguari or Rio Mearim.

Going from west to east there are several rivers that produce the pororoca, including the Cassipore, Araguari, Macapa Canal do Norte, Guajara, Moju, Marajo island, Guama/Capim and Pindaré/Mearim. **The Rio Araguari** is the biggest and longest bore wave in the Amazon, on the largest river of Amapa state, its source being high in the western Tumucumaque mountain range about 350km away. Araguari is the only river in the world to start breaking out at sea and this is where the Red Bull expedition took place in April, 2003 and on May18, 2007, 12ft (4m) sections were ridden. Cutias is the remote village where most expeditions start, and there are no "normal" ocean waves in the region. **Rio Capim** passes near Belem, in the State of Para and Sao Domingo do Capim provides easy access from land for those who can't afford the expense of hiring a boat. Locals wait for the bore on the mud flats and ride all sorts of surfcraft including pirogues (canoes/small boats). This 600km (370mi) tributary of Rio Guama, has lots of rideable bore sections for those armed with a boat and local knowledge. Before or after bore days, check the beaches for high tide, onshore windswells at **Crispim** or **Vila do Algodoal**. The coast is a bewildering jumble of creeks, estuaries, mangrove swamps and small islands, interspersed with some of the most remote beaches in Brazil! **Atalaia** is the centre of the Salinas scene with long stretches of mushy beachbreak best on N/NE swells up to 6ft (2m). Check the ivory strands at **Marieta**, a half hour boat ride from Salinas in summer NE swells. Access to **Chavascal** is by boat or a walk at low tide, but it is generally pretty small in winter despite facing NE. Nearby Praia de Ajuruteua is long and shapeless. French influenced Sao Luis, the capital of Maranhao, is not the best wave zone and beaches like **Itatinga** are more famous for shell collecting than surf. **São Marcos** has little to recommend it - the water is murky, unnaturally hot, heaps of tankers pass by to enter the rivermouth and there is a shark attack once every 10 years. There are more beaches to the east along Avenida Litoranea but the best bet is **Aracaji**, where the peaks break with more power and shape. Arari (the capital of watermelon!) is a 3h drive away and offers the cleanest bore conditions thanks to better weather and a narrower river. The **Rio Mearim** breaks in as many as 12 sections in a 1h30min journey from the rivermouth mudbank known as Cement Mix to the Arari village. The wave can range in size from a 8ft (2.5m) wall of whitewater to a tiny but superclean 1 to 2ft right. *Auera Auara.*

Rio Mearim

YEP

The tidal bore comes approximately every 12h50min so there's only one chance to ride per day and there's a shift of 40mins every day. Usually, there are rideable waves up to 3 days before and after full and new moon and these spring tides have a range of 6-7m (20-23ft) max. In Mearim, that translates to a period of 5 days surfing to be had early morning from between 5-8am to 7-10am. Unlike other bores, the wetter the season, the better because droughts mean more mud & sand banks will be exposed in the estuary and dissipate the bore energy. Bores travel at 15-25 km/h. River contours and depth are constantly changing and sets of waves can have 2 to 3 rideable waves but N°1 is often the best option. Sometimes, wave n°2 can have more power, break further away from the bank or be cleaner if there's some windchop. Most sections break either right or left with plenty of space for several surfers to ride at a time. Ocean waves usually range from 2-5ft (0.6-1.5m) on a coast plagued by countless shallow sandbanks. Best season for Maranhão is winter (Dec-April) when NE groundswells are running, while Para gets more waves in summer (July-Nov) with constant E-SE tradewinds. Extreme tidal ranges mean surf is mostly high tide.

SURF STATISTICS

Spot	Size	Btm	Type
①	12/2		
②	8/2		
③	4/2		
④	6/2		
⑤	6/2		
⑥	6/2		
⑦	4/2		
⑧	4/2		
⑨	4/2		
⑩	6/2		
⑪	8/2		

SURF STATISTICS	J F	M A	M J	J A	S O	N D
dominant swell	N-E	N-E	E-SE	E-SE	N-E	N-E
swell size (ft)	4	3	2-3	3	3-4	4
consistency (%)	–	–	–	–	–	–
dominant wind	NE-E	NE-E	E-SE	E-SE	E-SE	NE-E
average force	F4	F3-F4	F4	F4	F4	F4
consistency (%)	82	74	85	88	87	86
water temp.(°C)	27	27	27	27	27	27
wetsuit						

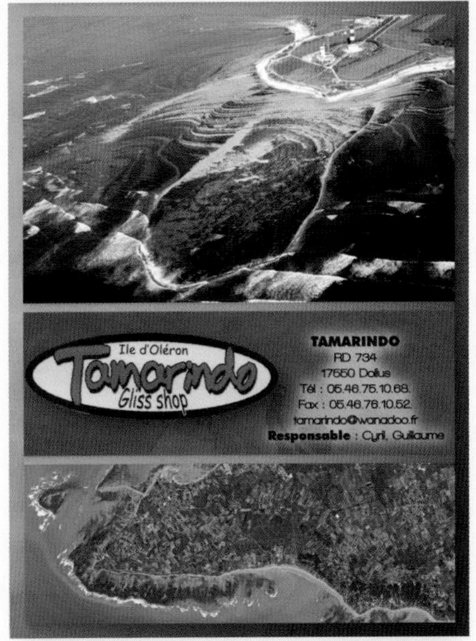
Ile d'Oléron
Tamarindo
Gliss shop
TAMARINDO
RD 734
17550 Dolus
Tél : 05.46.75.10.68.
Fax : 05.46.76.10.52.
tamarindo@wanadoo.fr
Responsable : Cyril, Guillaume

HCL
THE BODYBOARD HOUSE
ECOLE + CLUB 100% bodyboard
INITIATION / PERFECTIONNEMENT / ENTRAINEMENT
Cédric Greze
BREVET D'ETAT BODYBOARD
CHAMPION DE FRANCE
+33 5 56 26 31 82
+33 6 87 57 95 28
WWW.BODYBOARDHOUSE.COM

WAVE TROTTER'S
GUEST HOUSE
Accomodation for surfers in Lacanau, France
MATA HARI
SURF SHOP
FACING THE MAIN BEACH
Surf & Bodyboard - Repair / Rental / Lessons
2 rue Jules Ferry - 33680 LACANAU OCEAN - FRANCE
Ph : +33 (0)5 56 03 13 01 / +33 (0)6 63 04 06 01
Email : mataharisurfshop@cegetel.net

Since 1978
SURF CITY
surf/ bodyboard/ wetsuits
rental
6 bvd de la plage, 33680 lacanau-océan
+(33).5.56.03.12.56
surf-city.fr

KEVIN OLSEN
Surf House
Hossegor
coaching
learn to surf
surfcamp
SURFING IN FRANCE..
"WE DO IT IN ENGLISH"
Ave. du golf, 1888, Hossegor, 40150, France,
landline :+33 558 479 104, Mobile :+33 0626 328 759,
skype : kosurfcamps
Kevin Olsen Surf School, c/o Cream Café, Les bourdaines, Seignosse
www.kevinolsensurfhouse.com

BILLABONG
wetsuits
element
BILLABONG
KUSTOM
RIP CURL
SURF SHOP
mundaka
www.mundakasurfshop.com
Txorrokopunta, 10
48360 Mundaka.Bizkaia
Tel.: 94 6876721
Fax. 94 6876721

ESCUELA
CANTABRA
DE SURF
SINCE 1991
ESCUELA CANTABRA DE SURF
PLAYA DE SOMO
SURF SCHOOL, SURF HOUSE
SURF CAMP & SURF SHOP
Somo Beach, Cantabria, SPAIN
Contact: David & Nacho García
ecsurf@escuelacantabradesurf.com
Phone : (+34) 609482823 / 942510615
www.escuelacantabradesurf.com

BuenasOlas.com
The
Right spot
at the
Right Time
All the surfing info about
the Spanish North shore
www.buenasolas.com

surf-atlantico.com
SPAIN SURF ADVENTURES
Discover Spain's North Shore
Surfaris Weekends Self-catering
Groups Surf&Ski Stag&Hen Dos
www.surf-atlantico.com
"a point break from the routine"

Surf camps
austria portugal spain
MissionToSurf.com
[surfing] [kitesurfing] [windsurfing]
www.missiontosurf.com

www.oceanviewapartments.net
oceanview apartments
clean - comfortable - homely
Self Catering Apartments
overlooking Carrapateira beach
West Algarve, Portugal
Tel: +351 916 290 796

SURF PLANET
SAGRES
SINCE 1995
SALES
RENTALS
REPAIRS
SURF REPORT
Estrada Nacional nº268, 8650-355 SAGRES PORTUGAL
Tel/Fax. +351 282 624 815 | surfplanet@mail.telepac.pt

SURFCAMP
SURFIVOR
SURFIVOR
SURF CAMP
Cortegaça, Portugal ◆ Oporto Surf Region
Surf Camp for beginners and intermediates
Surf lessons, rentals, trips and guiding
NO CROWDS - endless beaches and empty surf spots
Beach, beers & BBQ
Low cost flights to Oporto airport
Right on the beach
INFOATSURFIVORCAMP.COM ◆ TEL: +351 939 336 434 ◆ WWW.SURFIVORCAMP.COM

WWW.
PENICHE
SURFCAMP
.COM
Accommodation
Surf school
Surf rental
Bikes
BBQ
Party
PORTUGAL

Surf School
Guided Tour
Rental

www.ineika.com
+34 928 53 57 44

Morocco's
leading surf
travel company

surf camp
self catering
luxury
yoga surf retreats
coaching
girls weeks

e: contact@surfmaroc.co.uk
t: +44 (0) 1794 322709
w: www.surfmaroc.co.uk

JEFFREYS BAY
UBUNTU SURF LODGE
WWW.JAYBAY.CO.ZA
+27 (0) 42 296 0376
LAID-BACK ACCOMMODATION
OVERLOOKING THE SURF
WALK TO SURFSPOTS
FREE BREAKFAST & INTERNET
GUIDED SURFARI'S
CAPE TOWN - GARDEN ROUTE - JBAY - WILD COAST

COFFEE SHACK
Coffee Shack offers a variety of accommodation, festive bar, meals, exciting 'day trips' & adventures
World class waves to yourself, local tips and expert advice from an ex pro surfer, lessons & learn to surf programs
tel +27-(0)47-5752048
www.coffeeshack.co.za

Africa Wild Surf Tours
:: Ultimate South African Surf Safari
Durban - Cape Town
:: Mozambican Trail
Durban - Mozambique
:: Wild Coast Expedition
Durban - Wild Coast - Jeffreys Bay
:: Learn to Surf Adventure
Durban - Jeffreys Bay road trip
AWS
Africa Wild Surf Tours
ZULU KINGDOM
www.awstours.co.za

E
AFRICAN SURFARIS
Welcome to the Adventure
www.africansurfaris.com
WaterWays
SURF ADVENTURES
www.waterwaystravel.com
South Coast
Mozambique
South Coast
Umfolozi River
South Coast
Mozambique
Explore Hidden Uncrowded Points, Reefs and Beach Breaks along the North and South Coasts of Durban South Africa and Mozambique. Sub-Tropical Climate, Warm Water and Sun All Year Round!
justin@africansurfaris.com
South Africa +27 82 901 6826
sean@waterwaystravel.com
USA +1 310 584 9900
USA (Toll Free) 888 669 SURF

C
LTL
LIVETHELIFE.TV
SURF RENTALS & REAL ESTATE
nicaragua / costa rica / france / portugal / spain / morocco / south africa / réunion / mauritius / maldives / bali / mentawai / australia / new zealand / fiji / hawaii / california
www.livethelife.tv

D
Indian Ocean Specialists:
MADAGASCAR
MOZAMBIQUE
REUNION ISLAND
MAURITIUS
SOUTH AFRICA
Also: Maldives & Indonesia
ADVENTURE TRUE BLUE SURF TRAVEL
Since 1998
We offer:
Charters & Resorts;
Tours & Hotels;
Info & Guides
True Blue has been there, surfed there & will get you there - GUARANTEED!
True Blue has offices in Cape Town & Durban, South Africa
info@truebluetravel.co.za +27 21 426 0881
www.truebluetravel.co.za

budgetsurfingmaldives.com
LOCAL ISLAND BASED PACKAGES
IN NORTH & SOUTH MALE' AND SOUTHERN ATOLLS

F
Can you keep a secret?
It's the surfer's ultimate dream to find and ride the perfect wave with nobody out. Tropicsurf sets the standard in luxury surfing adventures and sharing them with friends is our passion.
Telephone +61 (03) 8506 0153 Email info@tropicsurf.net www.tropicsurf.net
TROPICSURF
explore, dream, discover

G
The Worlds Finest Surfing Charters
Ocean Dancer Maldives
• Limited space available for surf season: May to October
• 7 night scheduled charters (Mon to Mon)
• 7 double staterooms: maximum 14 guests
WORLD SURFARIS
unique surf adventures
phone tollfree: 1800 611 163
info@worldsurfaris.com
enquire now www.worldsurfaris.com
Travel Agents Licence No. TAG1549 ACN 079 608 816

H
Maldives
Atoll Adventures
Pasta Point
@ Chaaya Island Dhonveli
USA: Waterways Surf Adventures
888 669 SURF (7873)
www.waterwaystravel.com
AUST: Atoll Travel
1800 622 310
www.atolltravel.com

Come to Heaven...
An eco-resort for surfers, couples and families
Ekas Bay, Lombok
www.heavenontheplanet.co.nz

I
Surfcamps and Boatcharter all over Indonesia
EAT - SLEEP - SURF
KIMA SURFARIS
KIMASURF.COM
kimasurf.com

EAST ASIA

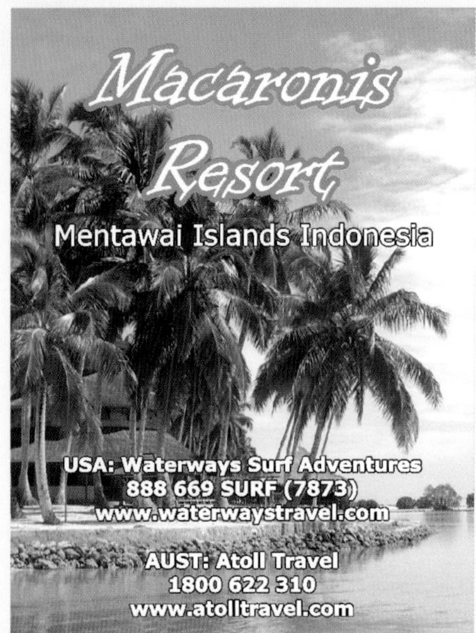

Macaronis Resort
Mentawai Islands Indonesia
USA: Waterways Surf Adventures
888 669 SURF (7873)
www.waterwaystravel.com
AUST: Atoll Travel
1800 622 310
www.atolltravel.com

Nemberala Beach Resort
Rote Indonesia
USA: Waterways Surf Adventures
888 669 SURF (7873)
www.waterwaystravel.com
AUST: Atoll Travel
1800 622 310
www.atolltravel.com

J
islandholidays
getting you the perfect break is our business
PLANNING A SURF TRIP?
Check out our new website with new diary page, movie clips, new destinations and latest specials
www.islandholidays.co.nz
Tel: +64800 336660 or +649 4861625
Email: pete@islandholidays.co.nz

ESCAPE
As seen on Lonely Planet BBC and C4 TV
The freedom to sleep around
Camper rentals New Zealand
Late model Campervans
Fully equipped for 3 travellers.
Over 150 flavours to choose from
No minimum age
Depots; Auckland, Christchurch, Wellin
24 hour free-phone helpline
Free unlimited Kms
Travels for the Car rate on the ferry.
Discount book and Local knowledge to help you Escape the beaten track.
NO HIDDEN COSTS !!
www.escaperentals.co.nz
Ph Intl: +64 21 2888 372 Free Ph within NZ 0800 21 61 71

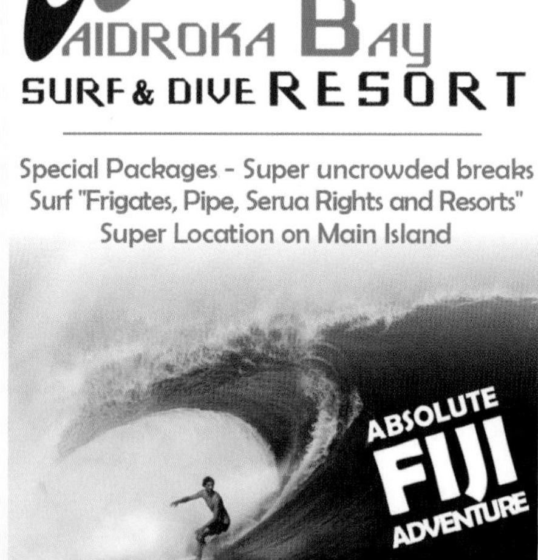

WAIDROKA BAY
SURF & DIVE RESORT
Special Packages - Super uncrowded breaks
Surf "Frigates, Pipe, Serua Rights and Resorts"
Super Location on Main Island
ABSOLUTE FIJI ADVENTURE
www.waidroka.com

Samoa
Salani Surf Resort
Savaii Surfaris
USA: Waterways Surf Adventures
888 669 SURF (7873)
www.waterwaystravel.com
AUST: Atoll Travel
1800 622 310
www.atolltravel.com

K
pacific surf travel
DESIGN YOUR VERY OWN SURF TRIP USING OUR GLOBAL TRIP PLANNER.
DIRECT BOOKING WITH PROVIDERS.
NO FEES REQUIRED.
WWW.PACIFICSURFTRAVEL.COM
flexibility.
customization.
best deals ever.

NORTH AMERICA

CENTRAL AMERICA

SOUTH AMERICA

LIVE TO SURF
The ORIGINAL TOFINO SURF SHOP

U Have to Get DOWN to get UP
Todo Azul Surf
Southern Swells
Spring! Summer! Fall!
El Salvador
Las Flores
Punta Mango
all inclusive packages
It's for the ki
lissette@azulsurfclub.com
001 (626) 487-4863
888-9-GoAzul
www.azulsurfclub.com
Azul
surf club

Spot Index with Zone Numbers